LOVE OF FREEDOM

LOVE OF FREEDOM

Black Women in Colonial and
Revolutionary New England

Catherine Adams and Elizabeth H. Pleck

OXFORD
UNIVERSITY PRESS
2010

Oxford University Press, Inc., publishes works that further
Oxford University's objective of excellence
in research, scholarship, and education.

Oxford New York
Auckland Cape Town Dar es Salaam Hong Kong Karachi
Kuala Lumpur Madrid Melbourne Mexico City Nairobi
New Delhi Shanghai Taipei Toronto

With offices in
Argentina Austria Brazil Chile Czech Republic France Greece
Guatemala Hungary Italy Japan Poland Portugal Singapore
South Korea Switzerland Thailand Turkey Ukraine Vietnam

Published by Oxford University Press, Inc.
198 Madison Avenue, New York, New York 10016

www.oup.com

Oxford is a registered trademark of Oxford University Press

Library of Congress Cataloging-in-Publication Data
Adams, Catherine.
Love of freedom : black women in colonial and revolutionary New England /
Catherine Adams and Elizabeth H. Pleck.
   p. cm.
Includes bibliographical references and index.
ISBN 978-0-19-538909-8; 978-0-19-538908-1 (pbk.)
1. Women slaves—New England—History.   2. African American women—New England—History.
3. African American women—New England—Social conditions.   4. African American women—
New England—Economic conditions.   5. Slavery—New England—History.   I. Pleck, Elizabeth Hafkin.
II. Title.
E443.A33 2010
306.3'62082—dc22   2009011638

9 8 7 6 5 4 3 2 1
Printed in the United States of America
on acid-free paper

In loving memory and tribute
James Curtis Johnson, 1936–1985
Naomi Ernestine Edwards, 1918–2002
Berhanu Abebe, 1937–2003

ACKNOWLEDGMENTS

What were the origins of antebellum black women's activism, literary output, and intellectual striving? Many black women in the nineteenth century, from the orator Maria Stewart to the reformer Charlotte Forten, identified a single role model, the revolutionary era poet Phillis Wheatley. Cathy Adams wanted to know if there were other individuals even prior to Wheatley who served as major sources of inspiration as well as to determine whether there were some unique patterns in New England slavery that encouraged black female achievement. Having written a book about black migration to late nineteenth-century Boston, Liz Pleck was eager to push back in time her research. Both of us sensed that what we knew about the nineteenth century had much deeper roots. Cathy Adams was especially drawn to African American women's literature and Liz Pleck was interested in family and legal history; in writing this book we have tried to combine our interests and skills. We determined the order of authorship of this book based on alphabetical order.

Cathy Adams began this research with a fellowship from the Museum of Afro-American History in Boston in 1995. Over the years we have accumulated many intellectual debts to scholars, researchers, and archivists in New England. Thanks for additional research leads to Ann Arcani, Kathyrn Grover, Ralph Luker, Bruce Mann, June Namias, Ellen Marlatt, Marla Miller, Sheryl Kujawa, Chernoh M. Sesay, Jr., Michael Terranova, and Emilie S. Piper. Melinde Lutz Sanborn generously shared her materials on blacks in New England prior to 1680. Paul C. Garman provided great help in answering our questions about the grave markers at the Common Burial Ground in Newport. Peter Benes allowed us to read advance versions of the articles in his edited collection about slavery in New England. Paul Rochelau, the Stratford Historical Society, the Massachusetts Historical Society, the Museum of Fine

Arts in Boston, and the Isaac Royall House supplied us with illustrations and photographs. Librarians and archivists at the American Antiquarian Society and the Connecticut State Library helped us in reading eighteenth-century script. We also thank Karen Eberhart at the Rhode Island Historical Society and the staffs of the Phillips Library of the Essex Institute, the Connecticut State Library and Archives, the Imaging Department of Harvard University library, the Newberry Library, the Massachusetts Historical Society, the Massachusetts Archives, the Andover-Harvard Theological Library, and the Interlibrary Loan Department of the University of Illinois, Urbana/Champaign. Max Edelson, Mark Leff, Sundiata Cha-Jua, Jean Allman, and Vernon Burton at the University of Illinois made valuable comments and suggestions. Graham Russell Gao Hodges and Gary Nash helped us understand the similarities between freedom suits in New England and the mid-Atlantic colonies. Emily Blanck kindly sent us a copy of her master's thesis about freedom suits in Massachusetts. Anthony Gerzina answered our queries about Lucy Terry Prince. Cathy Adams appreciates the opportunity she had to present part of this work at the Georgia Historical Association Conference in 2002 and thanks Leathorea Williams for her comments. Liz Pleck had the good fortune to talk about this work at the Early American History Conference in Tianjin, China, in June of 2007. Daniel C. Littlefield, Darlene Clark Hine, Alice Deck, and Estelle Freedman have lent support, moral and otherwise, and expertise over the years. Stanley Engerman gave us the benefit of a careful reading of the manuscript and suggestions for changes. Anonymous readers for Oxford University Press shared their research with us and saved us from innumerable errors. Colleagues at Armstrong Atlantic State University provided support and assistance. Cornelia Hughes Dayton generously allowed us to read and cite her unpublished research about Lucy and Scipio Pernam. Joseph Pleck lent his wise counsel as always and helped decipher colonial legal documents. Our work has been greatly improved because of the valuable editorial assistance of Susan Ferber at Oxford University Press and Nancy J. Hafkin. Nevin Johnson provided encouragement for this project. Bradley Curtis Adams, Bram Morgan Adams, and Daniel Pleck were the focus for the truly important things in life.

CONTENTS

ILLUSTRATIONS

LOVE OF FREEDOM

INTRODUCTION

Hagar Blackmore's Journey from Angola to New England

Several generations of black women in New England were willing to lay down their lives for the cause of freedom. For some a life in bondage was no life at all; in word, deed, and in the memory of their neighbors they testified to their love of liberty. Enslaved women in colonial and revolutionary New England sought their freedom through legal manumission, profession of their Christian faith, property ownership, and reunification of their families. Their story begins in the 1630s with the appearance of the first African women in Massachusetts Bay colony and ends with the emergence of a new ideal for educated free women, that of the African lady in the 1790s. Their long history of struggle injects new meaning into such key terms of American history as freedom, family, faith, entrepreneurship as well as womanhood. Rarely acting alone, black women often achieved their freedom alongside black men and black children. Yet amidst unity, common purpose, shared identity, and the bonds of family was a general belief in the subordination of women to men. This book chronicles the assumptions about family, masculinity, and femininity embedded in the love of freedom, the meaning of freedom for both black women and men, and the significance of gender to the development of the free black community right after emancipation from slavery.

Slavery and marriage based on patriarchal principles were both fundamental institutions of American life. Both of these institutions limited the nature of freedom black women could enjoy. Among slaves and free blacks physical force, ritual, law, religious beliefs, naming practices, women's educational disadvantages, and the gendered division of labor reinforced male dominance of women. While emancipation was equally meaningful to black women and black men, the moment of winning freedom actually brought to the fore longstanding conflicts between black women and men. Only subsequent to emancipation did race and gender consciousness become joined, often inseparably from the goal of education for black children as well as for adult black women.

New England slavery was human bondage in a particular legal and household form. The emphasis on southern plantations in the history of slavery has distorted understanding the overall significance of race and gender in slavery and emancipation, with its many regional variations. Everywhere slaves understood their condition as dispossession, being robbed of their families, their protectors, and their home place; everywhere they were threatened by sale or feared sale would come. All slaves were objects of trade, exchange, and value, commodities listed in an estate inventory next to the horses and cattle. In bearing children the enslaved woman produced human property, adding value to her worth as an unpaid laborer. Yet in New England's port cities the ability of a black woman to reproduce was more often a liability than an asset for her owner. In New England, the enslaved were both persons before the law and property; being defined as persons before the law provided more opportunities for enslaved women as well as men to become free through the courts than anywhere else in the British North American colonies. Moreover, in New England there was a more flexible definition of race than in the South that afforded a few individuals additional chances for legal freedom.

New England is usually thought of as the birthplace of abolitionism, not a site of slavery; in point of fact, it was both. The city of Boston was founded in 1630 and the first recorded evidence of the shipboard arrival of Africans in New England dates to six years later. The Massachusetts Puritans, having defeated the local Pequot Indians, captured and deported them on the *Desire* to the West Indies in 1638. The *Desire* stopped at Providence Island, the obscure Puritan colony off the coast of Nicaragua; the ship's captain, a personal friend of the Massachusetts Bay founder, John Winthrop, carried with him on his return voyage salt, cotton, tobacco and possibly three Africans, two women and a man. The purchaser of these three was an Anglican landowner on a large island in Boston harbor who had seen the value of African labor on his visits to the West Indies and Virginia. This crucial moment in the appearance of African laborers in New England comes a little later than in the British outposts of the West Indies or Virginia. The legal recognition of slavery appeared after the first Africans were put to work, with no British blueprint as to the rules. In such an undefined world, Massachusetts Bay colony became the first British colony to enact a law permitting slavery in 1641.

The association of Massachusetts with abolitionism is not undeserved so long as it is acknowledged that the first abolitionists were the slaves themselves. Slave manumissions, although few in number, date from the earliest wills on record in Boston. Individual whites were moved to manumit their slaves by conscience, knowledge of the plight of individual black people, fear of excessive reliance on slave labor, and the increasing presence of Africans in what was otherwise a homogeneous English population. The Boston merchant and judge Samuel Sewall was probably animated by all of these feelings when he published *The Selling of Joseph*, in 1705, the first pamphlet published in North America to condemn the slave trade and slavery. The pamphlet's impact seems to have been negligible at the time of publication. The fact that in his later years he advertised slaves for sale, available to be seen at his house, suggests that the charge of hypocrisy among Christians of conscience was not an idle one. For that reason, in matters of principle, Quakers, who first began opposing slave ownership among their members in 1716, deserve pride of place.[1]

With the possible exception of Narragansett, Rhode Island, New England did in fact have a tiny slave minority throughout the century and a half that slavery existed there. Most slaves' lives were closely intertwined with those of their white owners, white indentured servants, and often with local Indians as well. Slave populations were more concentrated than dispersed, as they were found more often in the seaport towns than in the countryside. There were few large plantations with slave labor housed in their own quarters in New England; rather, most New England masters owned only one or two slaves who lived in spaces such as the attics of their master's home. In 1700 the black population of New England numbered about a thousand, roughly half of whom lived in Massachusetts.

The New England region derived economic benefit not simply from Africans who labored in kitchens and fields but also from commerce with the West Indies and with the African slave trade. New England's relationship to slavery always looked to the sea. The first known slave voyage to the West African coast to bring back human cargo dates to 1645. Ships owned by New England merchants departed Boston, Bristol, Portsmouth, and Newport harbors for the ports of the West Indies but also sailed directly to the mouth of the Gambia River, where they traded rum for captives. The return trip was generally from the West African coast to the West Indies where the bulk of the Africans were sold.[2] Most of the slaves in New England came via ship from the West Indies rather than directly from the African coast. As more Africans were brought to New England and became a more visible presence, New England colonies passed many more laws to restrict and control slaves, free blacks, and Indians, who were seen as sinful, disorderly, possibly criminal, and likely to conspire against their owners.

The Stamp Act Crisis coincided with a real upsurge in antislavery sentiment among New England whites and encouraged more blacks to demand their freedom in the courts. By the 1760s white New England colonists perceived a connection between their own sense of "enslavement" by the British and the denial of liberty to Africans they had forcibly brought to their shores. The connection was not merely political but religious, since white and black Christians alike claimed that it was hypocritical to declare oneself a Christian while continuing to own slaves. The American Revolution initiated a rather drawn-out end to human bondage in New England. Vermont was first, emancipating slaves who had reached the age of maturity in its constitution drafted during the war (1777); five years later the Massachusetts Supreme Judicial Court ruled that slavery was unconstitutional in that state. In New Hampshire there was no similar state court decision, but law and practice tended to follow that of nearby Massachusetts. Beginning in 1784 Rhode Island and Connecticut took the statutory route to eliminating slavery, passing laws that provided for the gradual demise of the institution over a course of many years. The abolition of the slave trade, in which these colonies had participated and greatly benefited, came separately to an end from these efforts at emancipation. As a result of these changes, both black women and men became citizens of these states; black men enjoyed many formal legal rights but by no means all, and their rights were constantly threatened and always in need of defense. Free black women, like enslaved women before them, enjoyed the right to petition and the right to bring a case to court but did not possess the legal rights men held.

Hagar Blackmore, who arrived in Massachusetts Bay from Angola about thirty years after the first Africans appeared in New England, was the first African woman in the new world to explain how she understood slavery and freedom. Six months pregnant, Blackmore testified in Middlesex County Court in April of 1669 in a fornication case in which she had been convicted. She faced a punishment of a fine, a whipping, or both; her master's son, John, was held liable for support of the child she was carrying. The Puritans were intent on punishing "fornication" among Africans as well as their own people in order to enforce God's rule that sex should occur only within marriage.[3] Before the birth of her child Blackmore told the court that "she was stolen away from her husband and the infant that nursed on her breast." For her, slavery was a form of theft in which she had been robbed of her husband and baby and transformed into a form of property, an item for purchase. The word "stolen" also resonated with the Puritan concept of slavery as man-stealing, in their view a capital offense and a sin.[4] Their laws punished man-stealing as a crime because they used the Bible as their guide to the criminal law. For example, Exodus 21:16 considered man-stealing as a hanging offense: "He who kidnaps a man, whether he sells him or he is found in his possession, shall surely be put to death." However, Puritans also thought it was not a crime for third parties to purchase African captives taken (by others) in what they claimed were "just wars."

At least among the slaves initially brought to New England, it was common for masters to assign their property new names—in this case, Hagar Blackmore, which meant slave woman of African descent.⁵ A name was the link to one's past, to a lineage; providing this woman with a new name was part of the dehumanization of slavery, erasing her previous identity and substituting one chosen by an owner. The surname Blackmore was probably more neutral than the choice of the first name Hagar. Black Moor was a synonym for the word Negro, which meant person of dark skin from sub-Saharan rather than North Africa. In the Bible Hagar was the Egyptian "bondswoman," the concubine of Abraham who bore him a son because his own wife Sarah was unable to conceive. Abraham fathered Hagar's son, Ishmael, but in jealousy Sarah forced Hagar and Ishmael "to be forsaken" (a literal meaning of the Biblical word Hagar). Still, the English thought Sarah had dealt "hardly" with Hagar and felt some sympathy toward her.⁶

Hagar Blackmore was one of about 120 to 200 enslaved Africans living in the colony of Massachusetts Bay by 1660. Most were defeated and displaced people from what she referred to as Angola, the present-day Democratic Republic of the Congo, Angola, and the Congo.⁷ European traders, not allowed in the interior, purchased slaves, mainly war captives or fugitive slaves, from chiefs or African traders in the ports of the coast. Most of the slaves brought to New England, indeed, most of the Africans brought to North America prior to 1675, were from these areas.⁸ English ships were docking in the ports of Angola by the mid-1640s but their presence is not well documented; by 1659 we know that English sea captains were purchasing captured Angolans, usually at the northern ports of Cabinda or Soyo at the mouth of the Zaire River or to the south at Luanda, a port city established by the Portuguese in 1575, which became a center for their slave trade with North America.

Blackmore indicated that she remembered Angola and her family, but there was no opportunity in the courtroom for her to describe her experience on board the English ship that brought her to Barbados. What we know is that women captives on these voyages across the Atlantic were naked or wore ragged cloths that covered their genitals. Women sometimes broke into song in unison, expressing their longing for home. Dysentery, yellow fever, smallpox, malaria, and typhus spread quickly; when the crew found dead bodies, they often dumped them into the sea, where they would be devoured as food by the sharks trailing the ships. On these voyages women and children were not chained but confined separately from the men, as they were not considered threatening. Sailors perceived women, almost naked and free to move about on the deck of the ship, as sexual prey or as potential nurses to care for them when they came down with fever.⁹

Four to six weeks after leaving Angola English ships usually docked at Bridgetown, the major port in Barbados.[10] It was the first English landfall from Africa, an English-controlled island about one thousand miles to the east of the rest of the Caribbean. Barbados became the transfer point for shipments to other West Indian islands as well as for the coastal trade to the North American continent. The first English ship arrived at the island in 1625; Englishmen with excellent social connections looking for good investments received huge grants of land on Barbados where they carved out tobacco and sugar plantations. Hagar Blackmore was probably trans-ferred within a few days to a ship destined for a New England port. As she explained in court, she "was brought away to the Barbados from whence she was in short time shipped for New England."[11]

Some slaves were auctioned at the wharves and docks of New England ports; others had been purchased in advance by their owners and conveyed to them. Hagar Blackmore's owner William Manning, a wealthy Cambridge merchant, could use an African woman slave to clean, serve customers, and wash tankards since he kept a tavern in his home, which was often fre-quented by loud, drunken students from nearby Harvard College. Impor-tant in Cambridge politics, Manning had been elected constable and town selectman several times. Often away on business he gave his sons free rein of the house. One son was arrested as part of a group of inebriated young men found late at night shooting off their pistols. Another son, John, Hagar Blackmore claimed, was the father of the child she was carrying; she said that she had had "fellowship" with him several times. She also admitted to a one-night sexual encounter with Daniel Warro, an enslaved man who lived in Cambridge with his owner. Warro was brought to Cambridge from Vir-ginia, but was probably originally from Angola, as were most Africans in Virginia at this time, and thus might have been able to converse with Hagar Blackmore in her native language.[12]

Several months after her appearance in court Hagar Blackmore went into labor, attended, as most slave women were, by white female neighbors of her mistress. As was the custom of the time, a midwife interrogated her as to the identity of her child's father; it was believed that during the pains of labor, a woman would not lie about the paternity of her child. Blackmore told the midwife that the father of her baby was Daniel Warro, which relieved the Manning son of liability for paternity costs. The women found additional proof in her statement because her infant seemed to have "had the coun-tenance & colour of a Negro." There is no evidence that John Manning was required to appear in court again and thus the suit for child support against him appears to have been dropped.[13] Thereafter, Hagar Blackmore disap-pears from the historical record, one of the many slave women whose subse-quent history cannot be traced.

On the one hand, Hagar Blackmore was the quintessential sexual victim of North American slavery, pregnant, robbed of her name, her husband and child, brought to court without any kin to defend or protect her. On the other hand, she was also a survivor, engaged in a sexual relationship with an African man in Cambridge. Nor had her memory been erased despite the trauma of her passage from Africa; she recalled the time when she had been an Angolan wife and mother. She did not understand freedom as an abstract concept inherited from the Greeks, the Romans, or the English, but as something that made sense in terms of the world of Angola she had been forced to leave behind. People only enslaved members of another group; slavery meant being torn from one's lineage, to be a nonperson who had lost ties to the living and to one's ancestors.[14]

Africans transported to New England fought back against slavery, including collective rebellion on the slave ship. Both African women as well as men engaged in such rebellions before their ships sailed for the New World. More is known about the uprisings on slave ships in the 1700s than in the 1600s, when the vast majority of revolts broke out near the West African coast, were initiated by men, and failed; upon occasion the captives struck back against the captain and the crew as the ship neared the West Indies, and in one case men rebelled in Boston harbor. Such uprisings, although unsuccessful, reminded New England merchants how risky the African trade was, and discouraged a few from undertaking it for financial rather than moral reasons. There was one organized conspiracy for which rebels were banished but more often whites worried that slaves were secretly planning to kill them or set fire to their homes. For the most part, slaves resisted New England slavery not through collective revolt but rather by acts of disobedience or noncooperation as well as by asserting alternative prior identities or cultural practices such as maintaining a distinctive dialect, a way of dancing, a spiritual practice, or forming a community of friends.[15]

Resistance was not always life-affirming, however, since suicide was also a form of noncooperation. In forfeiting living rather than insisting on survival some slaves believed they were able to release their spirit to unite with those of the ancestors hovering over the African homeland. For that reason, slaves on board ships sometimes threw themselves overboard or starved themselves to death. Some Africans also committed suicide in New England—in a mutual suicide pact or a mother drowning her children.[16] Other slaves engaged in resistance by taking specific actions against the master—from trying to kill him to attempting to damage his reputation among his kin or neighbors. Others resisted by spreading rumors, burning down a master's house, lying, stealing, working slowly, breaking tools, or having sexual relations with someone the owner disliked. Enslaved women resorted to distinctly female means of resistance, such as feigning pregnancy, abortion, infanticide, or poisoning the master's food.

Many slave men and women not only wanted to resist their dehumanization while remaining the property of owners but also become free of their owners. Although there may have been many slaves who engaged in both kinds of action, we focus here specifically on those who wanted freedom from their owners and what it meant to them. Desiring and trying to obtain freedom, it turns out, was quite different from seeking equality between the sexes. Africans in New England did not understand freedom as equality between men and women but instead as precisely the opposite, the subordination of women to men. Many black men—and women as well—regarded achieving patriarchy in the household and in larger collective black life as the embodiment of freedom.[17] Gerda Lerner has defined patriarchy as "the manifestation and institutionalization of male dominance over women and children in the family and the extension of male dominance over women in society in general."[18] For black men equality meant leveling the distinctions between white and black men, while maintaining those between men and women by strengthening the authority of black men as masters of their own households. A recently emancipated black man wanted a deferential wife, whose very subordination proved precisely that her husband was the equal of a white man since he, too, was in charge of the governance of his home. There were advantages as well as disadvantages for black women in this definition of freedom. This principle of patriarchy appealed to many black women as well as black men in the positive meaning of respectability and in the security that monogamy in marriage offered, in the protection of inheritance rights for their children through legitimacy, and in various legal principles of coverture that upon occasion might be used to their advantage.[19] Among the greatest disadvantages was that black women faced invisible barriers that limited their desired independence of action and full participation in free black communities.

In the larger white culture of New England patriarchy was a principle embedded in the law, religion, domestic ideals, and sexual relations. The man was the head of a "little commonwealth," a form of family which served as a model for town and colonial government; women were expected to defer to and obey their men. It was a system of many parallel but unequal relationships, that of husband and wife, parent and child, master and apprentice, owner and slave. Patriarchy was also inseparable from a multitude of virtues, such as order, stability, hierarchy, and most of all independence. Propertied men were given the right to vote in town meetings because it was believed that only men not beholden to others had the necessary independence to make disinterested decisions on behalf of the community. Town patriarchs oversaw the rule of individual patriarchs, stepping in when needed to supervise households, making sure that a husband and father executed faithfully his responsibilities toward his dependents.

The legal cornerstone of patriarchy was coverture, a framework of the English common law in which the woman at marriage took her husband's surname as her own and had her legal identity subsumed under that of her husband. Under coverture, a married woman had no right to her own wages, could not make a contract, could not write a will, and could not acquire property on her own. One Boston lawyer explained the consequence of coverture for women was that "a little brook loses its name and distinct being after its confluence with a mighty river." Coverture transformed a woman into a wife, with more limited legal rights than that of a single woman or widow, and transformed a man into a husband, with expanded rights and obligations to his wife and other legal dependents.[20] It laid out not only a husband's marital rights but also his marital obligations, including that of supporting his wife and paying the debts she accumulated during the marriage. As a system of male rule justified in law, coverture also provided the rationale for the political exclusion of women since the interests of a wife were seen as being represented by the male head of household.

Women's historians have often assumed that coverture restricted white women but was irrelevant to black women because the basis of patriarchy was the orderly transmission of property from fathers to sons and most blacks did not own property. In fact, there were some black property owners who were indeed governed by the rules of coverture. More significantly, the rules of coverture affected considerably more than property ownership. They were used to deny an enslaved married woman the right to sue for her freedom. Only a single enslaved woman, a spinster, was allowed to do so; a black enslaved married woman, a femme covert, was deprived of this fundamental right. Much to the advantage of an enslaved husband seeking his freedom, his wife was not allowed to testify against him in court. Moreover, a slave had the right to make a will, even though doing so was uncommon; only single women and widows could make wills. Free black married women were even more subject to the rules of coverture. Some were affected adversely by support obligations, property provisions, and child custody rules; more suffered from their inability to bring a lawsuit on their own or from the rules of town residence, which denied a married woman her own right of domicile. Thus, both enslaved and free black men enjoyed a legal status superior to that of black women, slave or free.[21]

Although the free black woman was a legal dependent of her husband, she was quite a bit more independent when it came to making her own living. Because a free black husband suffered racial discrimination in the wages he earned and was often employed in seasonal, sporadic day labor or was at sea, his wife's steady income, even at very low wages, represented a substantial share of the money coming into the family. Yet detailed exami-nation of the marital power of three black working women in chapter 3 will show that their independence was largely a myth. Men's control over women was not constrained because of the economic power possessed by a black working wife. Even if his wife earned money, the free black husband was still expected to be the main (although not sole) provider for his family and their protector. Moreover, black patriarchy was also backed up by a general belief among neighbors that a husband could discipline his wife with moderate correction—despite the fact that New England law explicitly rejected such a principle.

It was not that black women in New England wanted patriarchy or free-dom; instead they wanted freedom, with patriarchal assumptions embed-ded within the definition of freedom. To be more accurate, black women had four major definitions of freedom, beginning with the most obvious one, that freedom meant legal self-ownership. Freedom did not arise simply because a white person granted it to a black person but because an indi-vidual enslaved man or woman won it in a court fight. There was a logical connection between the dehumanization of slavery and the emphasis on legal ownership of the self. If slavery was theft, then masters had purchased stolen goods, and these goods had to be restored to their rightful owners, individuals who owned themselves just as individuals also owned pieces of property. Black women who upheld this legal definition of self-ownership did not envision the individual standing alone or apart from her family or community—nor did Samuel Adams or John Hancock for that matter, but they did regard themselves as "individuals" whose right to freedom could be upheld in a court of law and who were deserving of the same kind of legal protections others enjoyed. Thus, New England legal culture and its defini-tion of individual liberties structured this definition of freedom.

Enslaved men and women also defined freedom as the ownership of property other than the self, the economic freedom that came with owning a house or a family farm. In Central or West Africa land was owned col-lectively, by a lineage, rather than by individuals. In this respect it can be said that blacks wanted what whites in New England already had, since land ownership was widespread in the region. Yet economic independence always had a racial meaning because a place of one's own meant independence from whites. In urban areas free blacks hoped to own their own home or their own shop (usually with living quarters in the back). The time to defend a right is when it is threatened, and black women went to court to hold onto their land when facing eviction or harassment by white neighbors.

Black women of New England also defined freedom as professing their faith in Christ. More than a few of the Africans from Angola had been bap-tized and converted to Catholicism but becoming a believing Protestant was

clearly a New England innovation. Some enslaved women sought to capital-
ize on the prevailing New England opinion that a fellow Christian should
not enslave another believer. Although there was some early ambiguity on
the question, by the early eighteenth century New England Puritans specified clearly that baptized slaves did not have to be freed.[22] Christian conversion was never merely a strategy for gaining manumission; it was thought of
more broadly as a faith that promised not simply freedom from suffering but
also the equality of all Christian souls.

A Christian woman was also expected to live according to the sexual
and moral code of her religion, which valued monogamy, piety, industry,
sobriety, honesty, and frugality in women as well as men.[23] God may have
granted freedom to humankind but God also expected conformity to the
Ten Commandments. In becoming professing Christians blacks in New
England were among other things seeking to refute the racist stereotypes of
them as hypersexual, lazy, dishonest, criminally minded, and animalistic—
and the occasional view that it was possible to tell a Jew, an Indian, or an
African by their smell. In petitions for freedom to legislative assemblies at
the time of the American Revolution enslaved men acknowledged that the
entire race was harshly judged because of the behavior of a few black criminals. By adopting proper speech, demeanor, and dress, and seeking education for their children, black people sought to prove they were "respectable"
and dispel these racial stereotypes; thus, what can be termed "the ideal of
respectability" was both black adoption of a personal code of conduct, based
on religious values, and a collective strategy of free blacks to enhance their
overall standing and secure their rights.

This ideal of respectability applied to the conduct of both men and women
and spelled out distinct gender roles for each sex. Black men were supposed
to show courage in war, keep their eyes open for sharp land deals, negotiate
effectively and engage in alliances with well-meaning whites; more broadly,
they were called upon to be good providers for their families and protectors of women and children. Women were never thought to be able to drive
a hard bargain. As exemplars of feminine respectability free black women
were instead expected to be dutiful wives, mothers, and daughters. While
men, too, were supposed to be sexually virtuous, women could be judged
more harshly for their sexual sins. As was the case for whites, sex prior to
marriage was not a grievous failing so long as a couple married soon after
the woman became pregnant, but cohabitation, adultery, and premarital sex
that did not lead to marriage was decidedly so.

A fourth definition of freedom for black women was freedom for the
family, a family living in its own place of habitation. Freedom for the family
meant more than adopting an identity as a wife, mother, or daughter, since
many enslaved women, including Hagar Blackmore, had insisted upon the

importance of those identities, even as they remained slaves. Nor did free-dom for the family mean returning to Africa to find one's kin since almost all women of African descent in New England had abandoned such efforts. Instead, it meant reunification of family members living in New England in their own place, where they might escape the constant demands, sexual overtures, condescending remarks, and preying eyes of white owners.

One form of freedom was rarely sought without pursuing the others; these four definitions of freedom easily flowed into each other. Black women and their families understood they might have to go to court to hold onto their own land. Conversion to Christianity ushered in new ideas of spiritual freedom as well as new ideals about family, marriage, and sexuality. It was only a small step for many women to move from this concept of equality of souls to the belief that rights (sometimes called "natural rights") such as that of ownership of the self given by God. It made sense to believe that if God had granted these rights, then an owner was doing an evil deed in taking them away. Freedom for the family meant not only reuniting separated fam-ily members but also achieving the goal of economic security or acquiring property. After a woman converted to Christianity she often legally mar-ried her partner, became a church member, sought baptism for her children, and hoped that her master might emancipate her and her family. There was also a reciprocal relationship between freedom and identity, since visions of freedom shaped a woman's sense of self and brought into focus certain ideal types of womanhood—the yeoman farm wife, the pious Christian mother, or the respectable African lady.

Black women's quest for freedom during their lifetimes was different than that of black men because men had more opportunities to gain skills, even during slavery, more personal mobility, and possessed the knowledge that even though whites considered them heathens or inferiors, they were also the superior sex. This is not to say that the white perception of black men was uniquely favorable. At times black men were seen by whites as less masculine but at other times as hyper-masculine, that is, as potential rapists of white women who were deserving of punishment by hanging or upon occasion by castration.[24] Black men also retained their African sense that they were the physically stronger, more honor-bound superior sex; in fact, it was precisely because they retained this sense of manhood that they felt so aggrieved. To be sure, broad generalizations about African traditional gender beliefs are foolhardy because Africans in New England came from diverse cultures, experiencing enormous change due to the disruptions caused by European invasion, warfare, large-scale migration, and new patterns of trade. Still, at the most basic level it can be said that in West and Central Africa's chang-ing cultures, age trumped youth, male trumped female, and men drew on their physical strength to defend their honor as men. These basic attitudes persisted, although many specific customs and rituals disappeared or were transformed in New England.[25] In sum, patriarchy, albeit without the legal concept of coverture, was significant in Central and West Africa, not just in New England.

At the same time, New England also offered special privileges to men that reinforced the distinction between slave men and women. Enslaved men in New England enjoyed access to skilled jobs, opportunities to learn to read or write, ceremonial leadership positions among fellow blacks, and freedom to visit and travel denied to black women—even making money as a fiddler was something only a man could do. In courtship and marriage expectations of male initiative prevailed; a black man called on the enslaved woman at her place of residence and asked her owner for her hand in marriage. Enslaved husbands often lived separately from their wives, and usually visited women at their quarters rather than the reverse, although an occasional master might give a wife permission to spend time at her husband's place in the evening if he lived nearby. Enslaved men also had more opportunities to hire themselves out and pocketed part of their earnings to be able to purchase their freedom.[26]

In both war and peace black men in New England had more personal liberty and opportunities to move about than women, despite the many formal restrictions on all blacks evident in "black codes" enacted early in the eighteenth century. In such laws black men were prohibited from owning guns and joining militias and all blacks were subjected to special curfews; yet in times of war black men were recruited for the militia and the navy, many black men did own guns, which they used to hunt, and blacks often found a way to evade evening curfews. On a routine basis, both enslaved women as well as men ran errands, but the man accompanied his master on horseback, or drove a wagon or cart loaded for the market, whereas it is impossible to find an enslaved woman who was given a horse to ride.[27] The enslaved man could be absent from his master's home overnight; he could manage his owner's farm for months in his absence. He tended the sheep or looked after cattle sent to graze on pasture land separate from town.[28] Black women were rarely entrusted with such responsibilities. Enslaved and free black mariners were also the cosmopolitans of their age, developing their own communication network, spreading news, gossip, carrying letters, linking otherwise isolated and separate black seaport communities. Black women remained on shore, denied the opportunities for mobility black men enjoyed. They may have had a memory of their African families and the ships that brought them to New England but they did not have new geographic knowledge formed by sailing to distant ports or travelling in the countryside.

Most of the slaves who were taught to write were male, as were the slaves who knew how to add. Masters who might have been willing to teach a slave how to read a few passages in the Bible were more reluctant for them to acquire the skill of writing. Some owners did overcome their unease since they saw the benefit in owning a slave who could take notes or even handle the master's correspondence. The male advantage in the skill of writing can be discerned from looking at town documents that required an individual to sign his or her name or make a mark next to it. Rhode Island town officials in fourteen towns between 1750 and 1800 examined transients seeking poor relief to determine if they were legal residents and therefore eligible for town support. The transient was then required to sign or make a mark next to a record of his or her testimony: 21 percent of black and Indian men could sign their names but only 6 percent of Indian and black women could do so. Thus, while it is true that most enslaved black men as well as women were illiterate, black men were three times more likely to be literate than black women.[29]

New England was a more multicultural environment for black men than black women; not only did they have more frequent social interaction with Indians than black women but they were also were able to gain more from them. Marriage between Indian women and black men was not uncommon; couples met at taverns in town or as servants living in the same household.[30] A black man who married an Indian woman gained tacit control over her land even though he did not hold legal title to it. An occasional Indian man took an African woman as his wife—or got her pregnant, without marrying her—but the couple invariably lived together in a town, not in an Indian enclave, where they appear to have been unwelcome. Racial categories and interactions grew more complex when these intermarried couples had children; biracial children from these unions might be designated a "mustee," or black or white, and as adults seemed to have intermarried with Indians, blacks, or whites.[31] Many of the biracial had dual identities, or simply opted for one of the two, although by the middle of the nineteenth century, more of the mustee had decided to define themselves as black.

Even during slavery, black men were the chosen leaders of their people who enjoyed certain male privileges. Special colony-wide elections occurred in the spring in the eighteenth century; towns allowed blacks to hold their own versions of these events, and masters living in the countryside brought their slaves with them to town to attend. On these Election Days whites sanctioned gambling, drinking, athletic contests, and parades among their slaves, which they thought a harmless way to boost slave morale for a couple of days as the winter cold was ending. During these celebrations black candidates campaigned for office and gave speeches, providing the first examples of black men speaking in public and soliciting votes. Black men lined up behind the candidate of their choice and some of them recorded the votes; black women were not allowed to raise their hands.[32]

Election Days were also times for the ceremonial performance of highly stylized gender roles in which black male "royalty" headed a procession on the town's streets accompanied by a female consort. The wife of the "Negro king" held his bridle, put his feet in the stirrup, and bowed to the ground before him to indicate her obeisance to him. Then she was lifted up to his horse, decked out in fancy clothes lent her by her mistress; her gender role was that of a servant, consort, or object of display.[33] In some towns the governor or king also presided over a slave court that punished minor infractions of the law by fellow slaves with flogging; sometimes the local white magistrate sent a black thief to the slave court for a whipping. The men who were elected were often African in origin and of "immense size and herculean strength," because of the persistence of West African respect for great male physical prowess; it was also believed that such men were best able to administer physical punishment to their black subjects—delivering powerful floggings at the town pump by using large wooden paddles or supervising their aides who did so.[34]

Historians have found in these festivals evidence of a black community otherwise invisible; carnivals that offered a day of release from the control of owners; the means by which the West African tradition of a procession led by a king was preserved; parodies of the white institutions of voting and governance; and critiques of black exclusion from politics.[35] Festivals were also training grounds for black male political leaders since in a few towns the royal court at Election Day festivals also drafted collective petitions for freedom. There was thus at least some connection between the leadership roles of black men in slavery and in freedom, as there was in the absence of black women from certain roles, rituals, and activities. For example, only black men drafted petitions on behalf of the entire black community in the last days of slavery or the early decades of emancipation, sent a letter to a newspaper, gave a speech in public, marched in a public procession or an informal black militia company, or served as a spokesman for black people; black women did none of these things. Political freedom went hand in hand with the belief that men were the rightful heads of their families, and public advocates for their communities, who could voice demands to the government for political inclusion and civil rights for their people.

A few black women held competing definitions of freedom, but on the whole, most shared a belief in the ideal of the free propertied Christian family governed by patriarchal principles—they did not recognize any contradiction between freedom and patriarchy. A few free single women and widows prospered without any man to take care of them, assisted by female relatives and neighbors, but many more were poor, sick, disabled, or blind, and had no real options other than to work as domestic servants or laundresses; widows often had to place their children in an indenture, a contract

A Poem on the Death of Charles Eliot, aged 12 Months.

Thro' airy realms, he wings his instant flight,
To purer regions of celestial light;
Unmov'd he sees unnumber'd systems roll
Beneath his feet, the universal whole
In just succession run their destin'd round,
And circling wonders spread the dread profound:
Th'etherial now, and now the starry skies,
With glowing splendors, strike his wond'ring eyes.

    The heav'nly legions, view, with joy unknown,
Press his soft hand, and seat him on the throne,
And smiling, thus; "To this divine abode,
"The seat of Saints, of Angels, and of **GOD**:
"Thrice welcome thou." —— The raptur'd babe replies,
"Thanks to my God, who snatch'd me to the skies,
"Ere vice triumphant had possess'd my heart;
"Ere yet the tempter claim'd my better part:
"Ere yet on sin's most deadly actions bent;
"Ere yet I knew temptation's dread intent;
"Ere yet the rod for horrid crimes I knew,
"Not rais'd with vanity, or press'd with wo;
"But soon arriv'd to heav'n's bright port assign'd,
"New glories rush on my expanding mind;
"A noble ardor now, my bosom fires,
"To utter what the heav'nly muse inspires!"

    Joyful he spoke — exulting cherubs round
Clap loud their pinions, and the plains resound.
Say, parents! why this unavailing moan?
Why heave your bosoms with the rising groan?
To **Charles**, the happy subject of my song,
A happier world, and nobler strains belong.
Say, would you tear him from the realms above,
Or make less happy, frantic in your love?
Doth his beatitude increase your pain,
Or could you welcome to this earth again
The son of bliss? — No, with superior air,
Methinks he answers with a smile severe,
"Thrones and dominions cannot tempt me there!"

But

But still you cry: "O Charles! thy manly mind,
"Enwrap our souls, and all thy actions bind;
"Our only hope, more dear than vital breath,
"Twelve moons revolv'd, and sunk in shades of death!
"Engaging infant! Nightly visions give
"Thee to our arms, and we with joy recieve;
"We fain would clasp the phantom to our breast,
"The phantom flies, and leaves the soul unblest!"
Prepare to meet your dearest infant friend
Where joys are pure, and glorys without end.

Boston, Sept.ʳ 1.ˢᵗ 1772.   Phillis Wheatley.

I.1. Phillis Wheatley's handwriting, 1773. Mary Wheatley taught her parent's slave Phillis how to write. Phillis Wheatley's capital D's and P's were a work of art, a sign of how much she had practiced forming her letters. She printed out, capitalized, for a child's residence in a family as unpaid labor in exchange for room, board, and perhaps some vocational training until the child reached the age of majority. Or these women were compelled to find a family that would house and care for their child while they supported themselves as live-in domestic servants.

Despite much recent interest in slavery in New England the black female experience is invisible and marginal in the story of slavery and freedom in New England. In part, the reason black women are absent is because there is simply much more information in the documentary record about black men. In sheer numbers, men made up more than half of the population of blacks in New England. Yet there are additional reasons why women so often recede into the background in the chronicle of black history. "The slave," as a generalized being, is often thought of as a male and the enslaved woman is instead considered the exception—a supplement or an aside to the main story, which is about men. There are more general assumptions as well about the major theme of African American history, the struggle for freedom. Freedom is perceived as such an overriding goal of all black people and race unity the best means to achieve it that it is assumed there is no particular woman's angle in need of telling.

The one very visible black woman in Revolutionary New England history is the young enslaved prodigy Phillis Wheatley. The best-known black person in all of the colonies, hailed as a poetic genius, widely praised for her literary talents, her life was in many ways the exception to the common condition of black women of her place and time. She was not the first black woman poet in New England but rather the first to have her work published. She was also another first as well, the first African in North America to use the word "freedom" in her poetry and the first to express her "love of *Freedom*" in print. A symbol of black intellectual and literary achievement, even amidst bondage, she was a slave who knew Greek and read Ovid in the

---

and put in boldface the word GOD because she regarded the word as holy. It is not completely clear who owned this letter at Phillis Wheatley's death. She may have left her correspondence with Susanna Wheatley's niece in Boston when she, her husband, and child moved briefly to Wilmington, Massachusetts, in the 1780s. The son of Susannah Wheatley's niece was a founder of the Massachusetts Historical Society, which acquired many of Phillis Wheatley's letters. However, at her death Wheatley's husband sold her possessions, including her letters, to pay her debts. Individual white Bostonians acquired and treasured these letters, but eventually donated many of them to the Massachusetts Historical Society. Phillis Wheatley, "A Poem on the Death of Charles Eliot, Age 12 Months" (manuscript copy), 1 September 1772 [2 pages], courtesy of the Massachusetts Historical Society

original Latin, and was a published author when she was thirteen or four-teen. Feted on a brief trip to England and hailed for her verse by Voltaire, her return to Boston received considerable notice. Many pieces are missing from her biography, especially the years of her marriage, the birth of her three children, and her early death in poverty at around age thirty. Still, her celebrated but tragic life and early death cannot serve as a proxy for the con-dition of black women in New England. She was a transatlantic figure who met the distinguished people of her day at a time when most black women, once they had been forced to cross the Atlantic, were much more defined by the local.

The documentary trail for other daughters of Africa is harder to fol-low. While there are letters of black men to their former masters, there are none from black women.[36] In colonial New England one enslaved husband and father recorded his daily thoughts and activities in a journal; another requested that a white man place his wedding announcement in the local newspaper, and a third kept his own account book.[37] An illiterate free black man from Haddam, Connecticut, dictated his thirty-two-page autobiogra-phy, *The Life and Adventures of Venture Smith* (1798) to a white schoolteacher and abolitionist who published his recollections in a local newspaper. No black woman kept an account book, a journal, a diary, or published her autobiography, to our knowledge, or succeeded in having her wedding announcement placed in a newspaper. Thus, the contemporaneous written record about black women is less substantial than that for black men, in large part because they were much less likely to be literate. Sadly, many of the let-ters written by the few literate black women have not survived. For example, while some of the correspondence of Phillis Wheatley to her female friend Obour Tanner, a slave in Newport, has been preserved, none of Tanner's let-ters to Wheatley have been found.

Still, black women's desire for freedom has survived, preserved in docu-ments written by others. The defining feature of this more indirect testi-mony was that it was "as told to" another person, usually white, usually male, with the other person not always clearly identified. An illiterate woman offered her testimony, which was copied down according to the linguistic conventions of the day and/or the format required for a particular kind of document. It is impossible to distinguish between the two voices in such collaborative efforts or discern the process that went into constructing a single account.[38] Moreover, the product of such collaboration was often written in the dominant literary styles of the day, from Enlightenment phrases about the rights of the individual, to sentimental language about the suffering of the family, to the language of sin and redemption used in conversion narratives. Still, there have been a couple of extremely impor-tant finds in recent years; these consist of a new poem and letter written by

Wheatley; conversion narratives of two enslaved women in Ipswich; and three additional lawsuits for freedom in New England courts brought by black women, two in New Hampshire, and one in Rhode Island.

Of course, it cannot be assumed that every enslaved woman in New England wanted to be free—some, especially the elderly, recognized that they were too weary to make a living on their own and were better off living with their owners.[39] Most of the women who testified about their desire to be free were English speaking and Christian; in the written record there are only a few sentences about women, usually born in Africa, who did not convert to Christianity and often retained some elements of African spiritual worship.[40] Certainly, adhering to African religious and sexual practices of healing and harming was a form of slave resistance—an oppositional culture—evident in fortune telling, magic, collecting shells, and in Bakongo symbols scratched on walls or found in a shoe hidden in a crevasse in the basement of the owner's house. Yet the women before 1700 about whom the most is known were Africans by birth and Christians by choice, usually born in what they called Angola and after that captured from further north in various inland parts and marched to the slave castles and ports of West Africa where they were forced onto ships sailing west.

Many black women in New England's colonial and revolutionary history are known because they told their stories to adult neighbors and their children who visited them in their humble dwellings. To be sure, New England African American abolitionists also published the history of blacks in the region, based on family accounts or reports they themselves learned from whites.[41] But white abolitionists left behind the largest number of recollections, personal reminiscences of servants or slaves in their family or family stories handed down to them. By the time of the Civil War, the occasional abolitionist preferred to portray an epic struggle between the evil South and virtuous New England, which obliterated the region's slave history. Most white abolitionists, however, took the position that the region's slavery was different—quite a few used the term "mild"—but still needed to be remembered. When Henry David Thoreau built his cabin at Walden Pond, the local freed slaves who had once lived there had disappeared. Nonetheless, Thoreau, who aided fugitive slaves en route to Canada, still collected anecdotes from local residents who knew free black settlers at Walden Pond and described their lives in his journal.[42]

The remembrance of individual enslaved men and women in New England was crucial to the abolitionist cause. Defenders of slavery argued that bondage was a natural condition for black people because they were mentally inferior to whites. At a time when there were no standard measures of intelligence, the best way for abolitionists to refute such views was to point to the one black individual who was the equal or the superior of whites in character and intelligence; by those standards, Wheatley certainly was at the top of the list. In addition, some abolitionists chose the example of a black man but others pointed to a black woman they had known since childhood. Although black men were more often remembered than black women, it was nonetheless the case that black women were recalled more fondly because of the children that they had "tenderly nursed."[43] In fact, some of these children became abolitionists because knowing a woman who had struggled to gain freedom had forever changed their racial attitudes. While the stories whites told about such women tended to place black family and friends in the background, they were not entirely missing.[44]

After New England abolitionists faded from the scene, the main interest in black family history came from descendants of African slaves. Well-educated men and women who were descended from men who fought in the Revolution or founded black churches took pride in their heritage. The black activist and civil rights leader, W. E. B. DuBois, traced his ancestry back to the free black community of Great Barrington at the time of the American Revolution. In the 1920s he wrote to his uncle to ask details about the family history and assembled his own family tree so he could apply for admission to the Massachusetts branch of the Sons of the American Revolution. In the midst of the Great Depression, war, and the struggle for civil rights, many black families lost interest in family history. Then in 1977 the quest of journalist Alex Haley for the story of his family, *Roots*, took him to a village in Gambia he believed was the home of his earliest African ancestor, Kunta Kinte. His published inquiry was made into an enormously popular television series aired over eight consecutive nights.[45] Awakened by this successful story of finding a lost past some black genealogists in New England began digging through collections of private letters and public documents in search of an ancestor's name or a Revolutionary War pension application.[46]

Local history sleuths, black or white, usually started with a single piece of information, a date of birth, marriage, or a land transaction, and followed leads to other documents. The most they could hope for was to find one further indication, often less than a sentence long, which they used to piece together a biography or family story. Schoolteachers or retirees who had flexible schedules and were living in New England towns made the best detectives; they devoted many years to research in archives, the records of local history societies, wills, and deeds kept by town clerks.[47] Professional historians adopted the same methods and examined the same kind of sources but saw their goal differently, as providing insight into the nature of New England slavery, offering historical context while arriving at broad generalizations about culture and society.

In the pre-DNA years, genealogy was quite separate from the field of archeology, although they are now closely allied. Those who conducted local digs lived in New England and worked at a single site, but their interest was somewhat similar to the professional historians—making large claims about general conditions of life or cultural survivals among slaves and free blacks in New England. Black historical archaeology in the region began at the end of World War II with a husband-wife team in 1945 who excavated the garden of Lucy Foster of Andover, Massachusetts. A Christianized slave, Foster became free with the general emancipation of slaves in Massachusetts but remained as the servant of her widowed former mistress. After her mistress's death she received a cow and an acre of land in town where she planted her garden. Perhaps there was not enough drama in Lucy Foster's life to inspire other investigations. Whatever the reason, black historical archeology did not really take off again until the appearance of *Roots*.

When it did, archaeologists began to excavate burial grounds, cemeteries, and the cellars of colonial houses. They found evidence of a few African artifacts such as quartz used for divining and filed hourglass teeth of men and women who in their youth had participated in a puberty ritual in Africa that required dental mutilation. They conducted digs at the settlement of former slaves in Plymouth, a slave quarters in Medford, a thousand-acre plantation, several houses, and burial places of slaves in Connecticut, and the "Negro burial ground" in Portsmouth, New Hampshire.[48] The recent boom in DNA testing has led to new inquiries, if not yet any new results. Descendants of Venture Smith and his wife Meg (Marget) gave scientists permission to excavate the Smith gravesite in Connecticut in order to perform DNA sampling of the bones and teeth of Smith, his wife, son, and granddaughter. No genetic material of Smith or his kin could be obtained; all the searchers were able to uncover was a bone of the lower arm of Marget Smith, too badly decomposed to provide any genetic clues.[49]

The next major stage in research about New England slavery occurred in the early twenty-first century as a result of the slave-reparations movement. Lawsuits seeking reparations for slavery identified individual corporations that profited from slavery, but in the process also singled out major New England universities that benefited from the slave trade. In 2001 Ruth Simmons, the newly appointed black woman president of Brown University, recognized in a swirling controversy over slave reparations at her school an opportunity to confront the University's history of participation in slavery and the slave trade. Elite New England colleges, it turns out, were not solely bastions of white abolitionism. Enslaved men helped to build University Hall, the first building of the university, and about thirty members of the corporation of Brown in its first fifty years were slave traders or captains of slave ships. Yale University followed Brown's example, revealing in a report the many buildings and scholarship funds at the school named in honor of slave owners. At Harvard two university presidents and a faculty member owned slaves and one of the wealthiest slave owners in Massachusetts endowed a professorship at the law school that endures to this day.[50] Newspaper reporters for the *Hartford Courant* wrote a series of articles about slavery in their city, and the newspaper apologized for printing fugitive slave ads; Aetna, also based in Hartford, confessed to its own complicity in issuing insurance policies on slaves in the 1850s.

The news that slavery had been a vital part of New England life and economy began to reach the public in various formats. Special issues of journals, conferences, exhibits, and teacher workshops were devoted to exploring the role New England played in the slave trade and the region's cultural amnesia about the history of slavery, an amnesia which dates to the nineteenth century. Journals of New England historical societies published special issues on slavery in New Hampshire or Connecticut; school teachers compiled curriculum units about New England's hidden past. Museum tour guides, who once pointed only to the English silver, chintz, and damask in the parlor, began to offer special tours of an attic recreated as a slave quarters or point out the spot behind the mansion where free blacks had built their cabin. An actor at the one surviving slave quarters in New England now portrays the story of the elderly enslaved woman who worked at the plantation for more than fifty years. A couple's seven-year search for the history of the Lucy Terry Prince, a former slave in Deerfield, Massachusetts, dubbed the first black woman poet in North America, resulted in *Mr. and Mrs. Prince: How an Extraordinary Eighteenth-Century Family Moved out of Slavery and into Legend.*[51] Filmmakers brought to the screen the family struggles of a black couple in Connecticut who fought off slave catchers. Descendants of New England's wealthiest slave-trading family wrote a book and then produced a film about the part of the family history many of the relatives were ashamed to reveal.[52]

Even as individual women who clearly wanted freedom are being rediscovered, the larger story of the significance of gender to the history of freedom and equality has yet to be told. It requires telling the stories of individuals and marriages in order to arrive at broader generalizations about the interrelationship of various identities, placed in the transatlantic contexts of the slave trade in Angola, West Africa, the West Indies as well as the evolution of slavery in New England, beginning with the Puritans. Chapter 1 examines the significance of the slave trade in New England from the time of English capture of Angolans in the 1600s to the larger importation of slaves mainly from further north along the West African coast in the next century. It shows the main ways that black men and women defined freedom even while enslaved, as well as the significance of the patriarchal ideal among New England slaves. Chapter 2 looks at the unique conditions of New England slavery for women, their social isolation in the countryside, health and work conditions, and the favorable circumstances afforded to them in New England criminal and civil law.

Chapters 3 to 6 examine women's quest for freedom in relation to black women's definition of freedom as property holding, religious identity, family, and legal self-ownership. Chapter 3 sketches the impact of property ownership on three black marriages in the eighteenth century. Detailed case studies of these unions prove the significance of the ideal of the propertied farmer or urban homeowner for women's definition of freedom and independence. No matter what the personal dynamics of individual marriages were, the outlines of patriarchy were always present. Chapter 4 reveals that black women's ideal of freedom through Christ strengthened the emphasis on personal character and sexual morality but also connected them to that part of the Christian world that condemned slavery as a grievous sin. Chapter 5 shows that while the slave trade destroyed African families, New England slaves created new ones and nurtured the desire for a household headed by a man who was a protector and provider for his family. Although some free black unions were long-enduring partnerships, the model of the family was not an egalitarian but a hierarchical unit. During the first moments of emancipation, beginning in the 1780s, conflicts between black men and women, already apparent in slavery, became quite visible precisely around issues of male authority and married women's employment. Black husbands in defense of their reputation, their honor, and their credit at the store strove to control their wives; as a result, some black wives fled their marriage. The primary focus of chapter 6 is the story of enslaved women who brought individual suits for emancipation in the courts; at the end of the Revolutionary War one woman made larger collective claims, that slavery was unconstitutional in the Commonwealth of Massachusetts based on the principles of the new state's constitution. Overall, winning legal freedom through the courts was the form of emancipation that most clearly involved interracial associations and the assistance of white abolitionists.

Chapters 7 through 9 trace the impact on black women of social and organizational changes that arose during and after Revolutionary War. Chapter 7 reveals that black men and women exploited the chaos of wartime and antislavery sympathy among whites to declare themselves free. There were many reasons why slavery ended in New England after the Revolution, but among them were the efforts of black women and men to secure it and take advantage of the spirit of liberty present among their white neighbors. As emancipated slaves, black women as well as men in New England became citizens of the newly founded New England states, even though their rights were circumscribed. As chapter 8 reveals, patriarchal principles limited black women's participation in free black institutions. Since black citizenship was defined in terms of the assertion of black manhood it was not clear what role women could play other than working for wages in menial jobs and caring for their homes. Despite being denied the full rights of citizens free black women tried to carve out their own, more-limited definition of citizenship. They sought to achieve concrete benefits for themselves and their families from free black institutions or in petitioning the governments of New England states. In pursuing these goals they also showed that they wanted respect from their neighbors, education for their children, economic security, religious fellowship, and a government that affirmed and enforced their claims for justice. Only in the early nineteenth century, as the epilogue indicates, did black women place great emphasis on gender as well as race, defining their role less as subordinates in a black patriarchal family and more as mothers of the race concerned both with home and family, and the abolition of slavery, while also confronting the "monster prejudice" they faced daily.

In some respects, it is necessary to concede that black men deserve their pride of place, because the definition of black manhood defined and circumscribed the definition of black womanhood. Black men's struggle to be men—propertied citizens who possessed the right to vote, heads of household, pious Christians, guardians of their family and providers—molded, channeled, and limited the struggle of black women for their liberty. Yet seizing freedom needs to be understood as occurring within the dynamics of the black family as well as in the founding of black organizations. There was always a crucial link between ideals of authority in the black family and black public life. Conceived in that way the story of black women in slavery and freedom is not simply the history of the minority of a minority but of abstract principles applied to life, namely, how the ideal of freedom was undercut by notions of hierarchy and male authority in the household.

1

The Uniqueness of New England

In all regions of British North America, patriarchy and slavery were combined, but in New England the combination retained for a longer time significant features of English common law. Masters in many colonies thought
of themselves as patriarchs who protected, guided, and cared for their slaves;
if anything, New England masters regarded themselves as more benevolent
masters than those elsewhere. It is true that many slaves in New England
received medical care or had warm cloaks to wear in the winter. Nonetheless, good treatment of New England slaves is also a powerful myth that has
to be seen for what it is, a form of denial of the reality of property ownership in human beings. Still, New England was indeed a special category of
slave society, "a society with slaves" and one in which English legal principles shaped a more complex definition of the enslaved as both persons and
property.[1] The historian Ira Berlin distinguishes between "slave societies"
and "societies with slaves." Slave societies were socially, economically, and
politically dependent on slave labor, had a fairly large enslaved population,
and allowed masters extensive power over their slaves unchecked by the law.
Almost everyone in such a society, free or slave, sought to own other human
beings because slaves were a major source of wealth. Moreover, the economy
of slave society was often dependent on the production of a labor-intensive
crop such as sugar, cotton, tobacco, indigo, or rice.

By definition, a society with slaves had a small slave population. The
New England society with slaves depended on maritime trade and diver-
sified agriculture, and did not rely on the cultivation of a single crop. The
courts upon occasion acted to check the power of the slave holders; human
bondage was only one of many forms of labor, with family labor, hired day
labor, wage labor, and indentured servitude far more common. In a society
with slaves the bondspeople often lived as ones or twos in the households of

their masters. The New England society with slaves depended for its prosperity on trade, especially with the West Indies, the largest export market for New England goods and the largest importer of New England goods. Thus, the two different kinds of slave societies were actually regional economies bound up with each other.[2]

The specific distinguishing consequences of this particular society with slaves for black women were that they had more opportunity to seek freedom than elsewhere because of the New England legal system, the frequency of manumission by owners, and chances for hiring out, especially among enslaved men, who seized the opportunity to earn enough money to purchase a wife and children. Free blacks who had been manumitted or moved from slavery to indenture to freedom appeared in small numbers by the 1650s. Exactly the size of this small free black population in New England is hard to tell. One estimate is that about a sixth of Connecticut's black population was free in 1750 and had grown to one quarter of the black population in a few decades. The size of the free black population was quite variable, however, and in 1774 only 13 percent of Newport's black population was free.[3]

However, the odds of gaining freedom cannot be used to infer what the actual conditions of slavery were like, other than to say that there was more reason for hope, since slaves could see the possibility for breaking their chains. As far as whites of conscience were concerned, New England abolitionists invoked the phrase "kind treatment" routinely, differentiating the form of slavery in their region from that of the benighted South. Masters and their descendants used the term, too, referring to an owner as an "uncommon kind and indulgent Master." These descriptions can never be taken at face value nor can kind treatment be reduced to a single factor. In fact, the whole question is in a sense irrelevant since it was not kindness but liberty that so many slaves desired. Yet it is still useful to examine an array of social and legal indicators of slave treatment and living conditions. Among these are the extent of an enslaved women's community; the exploitation of their labor; the enforcement of laws against crime; conditions of health, diet, and child bearing; access to the civil legal system; and the flexibility in the way the term race was defined. Because of all these differences in circumstance between regions, slavery in New England was much to be preferred to slavery elsewhere, say, at the opposite extreme, in the West Indies.

The first place to look for the condition of enslaved women in New England is the extent of a support network of other black women. In the New England countryside blacks lived isolated lives, dwelling miles from another black person. Michael Gomez has argued that a black community can take shape even without a shared work life or common residence, so long as "black folk could get from one farm to the next on a regular basis and within a reasonable time."[4] Even by this standard, a community did not exist for most blacks in rural New England since they encountered other black people only on an irregular basis. In seaport towns there was an interracial community of the poor, consisting of free blacks, slaves, Indians, and poor whites; the enslaved could sneak away from their owners' households at night as they danced and sang to the music of a black fiddler, gambled, and drank rum or punch at unlicensed taverns and dram shops that made their profit from violating the colony's prohibitions on selling liquor to blacks and Indians.[5]

Creating a community of black women was difficult due to the lopsided margin of black men to women. The small black population in Massachusetts Bay Colony and in the largest area of concentration, Boston (Suffolk County), was more heavily weighted toward men from early on (Table 1), because men's labor was more in demand. The percentage of women in major towns of New England remained much the same throughout most of the eighteenth century, irrespective of whether the black population was measured through an estate inventory or a census. Most slaves lived in the seafaring cities, which had a largely male enslaved population throughout the eighteenth century; Newport, with a female majority by 1774, was the exception. Many of the black men of Newport were sailors who left behind their families for months at a time. Some mariners were drowned at sea, died in wars or shipwrecks, or succumbed to scurvy, malaria, or yellow fever contracted in a tropical port of call. For the same reasons, white women of Newport appeared in the town census as the majority of the white residents of the town.[6]

Table 1. Percentage of Black Women in the Black Population of New England Towns, 1700–1774

	Percentage Female	No. of Blacks Enumerated
Boston, 1700–1750	41	820
Boston, 1751–1770	38	536
Salem, 1754	42	84
Salem, 1765	32	173
Portsmouth, 1767	33	87
Portsmouth, 1773	37	160
Newport, 1755	47	1755
Newport, 1774	52	1246

Sources: For Suffolk County, the percentage of women who were "Negro, Mulatto, Indian and Spanish" is based on Suffolk County inventories, Peter Benes, "Slavery in Boston Households, 1647–1770," in *Slavery/Antislavery* ed. Peter Benes and Jane Montague Benes (Boston: Boston University Scholarly Publications, 2005). All other figures are from Elaine Forman Crane, *Ebb Tide in New England: Women, Seaports, and Social Change, 1630–1800* (Boston: Northeastern University Press, 1998), 19 and are based on census figures.

The demographic character of the black population in New England was affected by local need as well as the changing nature of the international slave trade. Periodic construction booms in New England seaports and the shortage of white workers due to casualties at sea and in wars led to increased demand for African male labor. The end of the monopoly of the Royal African Company over the slave trade in 1698 opened the trade to the ships of New England merchants. With more New England entrants, the supply of slaves grew, and the price fell. In the 1720s world prices for Caribbean sugar plummeted and West Indian planters dumped surplus slaves on the market, lowering the average purchase price for a slave. In the 1760s Boston enjoyed a building boom after the Great Fire and the white laboring population had been reduced by casualties in war, smallpox, and the closing of the ports to British emigrants during the Seven Years War. Moreover, English slave traders, shut out of the Spanish slave market, were forced to lower their prices to be able to sell the slaves they had captured on the African coast.[7]

Always slave men cost more than slave women, but they were also considered more valuable, not simply because of their greater physical strength but also because they could be put to work in a greater variety of tasks in the countryside and the city.[8] On farms they worked in the fields alongside their owner or his son. Enslaved men rented out did the same kinds of work as white hired labor, visiting houses to sweep chimneys or going door to door to cobble shoes in the winter. Slave men repaired roads and fences, cared for horses, cleaned stables, cleared stones, dug clams, mowed hay, plowed, carted dung, butchered hogs and sheep; a master gave a hired slave considerable responsibility, such as allowing him to purchase horses or mind the household in his absence. Enslaved men dug graves or potatoes and delivered wood. During the long winter months they were needed to chop wood for their owner's fireplace. In the cities enslaved men worked in construction, the skilled trades, or in the individual household. At the docks they unloaded ships, cut sails, made anchors, cord, and ropes, and built ships' masts. Enslaved and free black men served on Nantucket whalers, schooners, oyster boats, ferries, privateers, and fishing boats. Black Jacks could be found on the ships that sailed north to the Newfoundland Grand Banks and south to the West Indies; a few were scattered among the crews destined for the Caribbean or slave ships headed for the West African coast. One Nantucket free black sailor left a modest estate that included his Bible, other books, and his compass.[9]

As the number of blacks increased, masters began to offer some enslaved men an opportunity to acquire a skill, training an occasional man for a craft. White owners believed that men, even African men, were the dominant sex, to be trusted with cash and respected for independent judgment; the black man who was taught a skill was worth more in the open market.

Nature her various Skill displays
In thousand Shapes a thousand Ways;
Tho' one Form differs from another,
She's still of all the common Mother:
Then Ladies, let not Pride refist her,
But own that NANNY is your Sister.

1.1. Jersey Negro, 1748. The woman in this portrait, Ann Arnold, may have been called the Jersey Nanny because she was the wet nurse of a child whose parents were born in the English isle of Jersey. John Greenwood's print was the first individual portrait of a black woman in North America and was advertised for sale in a Boston newspaper. In the poem at the bottom of the portrait Greenwood urges Ladies to remember that "Nanny is your sister" and that Arnold was a virtuous woman despite her heavy-set body and straggling hair, a symbol of the menial nature of her work. The pin around her blouse, and her large breasts, with nipples showing through, suggests a wet nurse but also reveals the intense observation of this feature of the body of black women by whites. The plaid kerchief around her shoulders did double service as humble adornment and napkin for a baby's spit up. Photo © 1748, Museum of Fine Arts, Boston

Soap boiler, blacksmith, or printer was suitable work for a slave man. Several black men were called "Doctor" because they helped their owner, an apothecary and physician, prepare compounds and visit patients. One bondsman in Newport was a master chocolate grinder who processed cocoa and sugar into chocolate readied for shipment to the European market. Enslaved men were butchers, bakers, and candlestick makers, as well as rum distillers, locksmiths, cabinet makers, stone polishers, and leather tanners. Male slaves served as apprentices to wig makers, who shaved their customers faces and heads and made their wigs. In households, there were many gender crossovers, with enslaved men and boys doing women's tasks, and women undertaking some men's tasks such as caring for horses and shoveling snow. Gender distinctions were minimal among enslaved children, since boys as well as girls cared for young children and did the cooking and cleaning. Still, black men and boys rarely spun, sewed, washed, or ironed, although there were some exceptions. Enslaved women were also hired out by the day, but were largely put to work in female occupations. For example, the local minister rented out his enslaved woman to nurse a sick woman in town.[10]

The New England system of slavery recognized the enslaved woman was most useful in doing menial or servile tasks considered women's work. In households of the elite a mistress assigned the enslaved woman or girl the task of polishing the family silver or the furniture.[11] The wealthier the woman, the more specialized the enslaved woman's tasks. A few wives of men of great wealth had an enslaved lady's maid who helped them with their clothes, hair, drew their baths, and mended their clothes. Some masters preferred to have the servant girl shave them rather than going to a barber. In town an enslaved woman might be sent to the store to pick up a skein of thread or a yard of ribbon. However, most mistresses used their woman slave not as their personal attendant but rather as a domestic menial, put to work sweeping, emptying chamber pots, carrying water, washing the dishes, brewing, looking after young children, cooking and baking, spinning, knitting, carding, and sewing. For most white women the greatest value of an enslaved woman was that she would do the laundry, the kind of work they did not want to do. The "good drudge" was the woman who could do this kind of unpleasant work steadfastly and without complaining. Raised in a wealthy Rhode Island family, Elizabeth Morgan claimed to have deserted her husband because she had to do all the housework, including the wash. In her petition for divorce she made clear that she considered heavy household work a form of *slavery*. Complaining that "she had been his slave long enough already" she was willing to return to her husband only if he bought "her a Negro wench" so that she did not have to get her hands wet or "anything of that nature."[12]

Few white women purchased their own slaves and instead received them as gifts or an inheritance. Among solicitous parents for whom price was not an object an enslaved woman made an excellent wedding or Christmas gift. In advance of a son's marriage, a father helped him purchase a female slave to assist his future bride in the work of the household. A Jamaica planter sent his mother the present of an enslaved girl. Owning an enslaved woman also made it possible for an elderly white woman to remain in her own home rather than live with her children. Although women received slaves rather than purchasing them, a wife could press her husband to make inquiries to purchase a maid for the household. For the married woman of means the enslaved woman or girl did the household chores while her mistress embroidered bedspreads, sheets, towels, dresses, or shoes. White women had the time to visit their kin and neighbors and attend quilting bees knowing that a female slave at home milked the cows, fed the chickens, washed the clothes, and ironed. But there was no such thing as an apprenticeship for a female slave; she had little room for advancement into skilled training because most owners wanted someone who knew little more than how to spin. If black men had greater self confidence and were more assertive because they had artisanal skills and had more opportunities for geographic mobility, then it follows that women's self-esteem was lower because they lacked access to such training and lived in a more confined world where they had little freedom of movement.[13]

Quite a few households were in fact small business operations: taverns located in the front parlor, a coffee house, a home that took in boarders, or a boardinghouse. An enslaved woman did the cooking, mending, washing, and ironing for the boarders. A husband could run his business with the help of his wife, but many widows operated taverns or boardinghouses who might benefit from the labor of a slave: one out of five Boston taverns in 1771 was operated by a woman. Black men and women seemed more interchangeable labor for tavern owners to serve customers, cook, sweep up, and wash the dishes and cutlery. Some taverns had licenses to lodge guests in the upstairs rooms and serve hot meals; a slave could be put to work cooking and making the beds. The tavern was also a hiring hall for seamen where they could meet a captain eager to assemble a crew. The great advantage for the land-bound slave of working in a tavern was coming into contact with mariners and ship's captains who provided news about the outside world and carried parcels or could be solicited to carry a message.[14]

The myth that New England slavery was benign has become so embedded in the region's view of itself that it forces the recital of evidence to the contrary, including evidence about the treatment of enslaved women. Black women, men, and children were cruelly treated in many similar ways, but with some distinctions as to gender and a few traces of the patriarchal principles New Englanders inherited from the mother country. The record of slaves who were branded by their owners, had their ears nailed, fled, committed suicide, suffered the dissolution of their families, or were sold secretly to new owners in Barbados in the last days of the Revolutionary War before they became worthless never seems sufficient to refute the myth of kindly masters. At the outset it needs to be said that owners of slaves often behaved in a manner not in keeping with their benevolent view of themselves. They lashed out at their slaves when they were angry, filled with rage, or had convenient access to a horsewhip.

Patriarchy also had an impact on punishments in the criminal law. The law of petit treason reflected a larger form of patriarchal thinking of the English colonists and concern about maintaining a hierarchical social order. It made two types of murder into a separate crime—a wife killing her husband or a servant killing a master or mistress. Petit treason was a lesser crime than high treason, the killing a king, but a more serious one than ordinary murder because the criminal had killed a husband, master, or mistress. The English scholar of Caribbean slavery Diana Paton notes the significance of "a violent act by a slave against a white person could never be just that; it always carried with it the implicit threat of slave rebellion and the overthrow of white power."[15] The penalty for petit treason in English law was being hung by the neck for women, and for men being dragged to the site of execution, disemboweled, castrated, beheaded, and the body sliced into four pieces. Thus, women were given what was thought of at the time the more humane penalty.[16] Two enslaved women in Massachusetts Bay found guilty of the crime of petit treason were Maria in 1681, and Phillis in 1755. Their corpses were set aflame to convey the message that the killing of a master was a blow against the state.

The significance of burning the criminal's body was not that it was common punishment—there were only two instances of it—but the strong impression made by the spectacle and leaving the bodies to rot. The pastor of North Church and president of Harvard College Increase Mather noted in his diary, using italics for emphasis: "*The Negro woman was burned to death*—the 1st yt has suffered such a death in N.E." The second enslaved woman whose body was burned at the stake, Phillis in Cambridge, Massachusetts, in 1755, had been convicted of the crime of petit treason for poisoning her master. An enslaved man, Mark, was probably the ringleader of a plot that involved him, Phillis, and another woman, who was punished by banishment to the West Indies. Since Mark did not actually commit the act, he was considered an accessory to Phillis's crime. The assembled crowd witnessed the death of Phillis "burnt then to bradishes" and went to hear Rev. Mr. Appleton deliver a sermon, "The Way of the Transgressor is Hard." Mark was hung, his body, covered in tar, was left for years to rot, suspended on chains at Charlestown Common, "an awesome icon" of the power of slave owners. Mark directed his *Last & Dying Words* to black women as the kind of weaker vessels who were especially suscep- tible to immorality. Confessing his sins he beseeched "my Fellow Servants, (especially the Women) to take warning from me, and shun those Vices which have prov'd my Ruin…"[17]

New England judges and juries employed a racial double standard with respect to murder—slaves who took the life of the master were treated as if they slayed a king; masters who killed their slaves were given the benefit of the doubt. Black women as well as men were among the victims of this racial double standard. Even though there were laws that made the murder of slave a capital crime, no white person was ever put to death for killing a slave. Jinny, a bondwoman in Hartford in the early eighteenth century, died of natural causes, but white witnesses at an inquest about her death testi- fied that she had been subjected to "terrible and unwarrantable thrashings."[18] After two days of hearing witnesses, an inquest panel ruled that she died "a natural death." The master of Jenny, a slave in Newport in 1767, flogged her so badly that she was crippled and had trouble walking. Her owner was never brought to trial and it was she who was hauled to court for the murder of her infant, a crime she could have committed as revenge against prior ill-treatment. A white owner in Maine who beat his enslaved girl to death was first indicted for murder; his charge was reduced to cruelty and he was released from jail after he paid a fine.[19] In 1761 a nine-year-old enslaved girl in New London who was punished with a two-foot-long horsewhip lived for four days before expiring; a court made her owner pay the costs of prosecu- tion but failed to exact any further punishment because they believed he had not intended to kill her.[20]

The treatment of enslaved women was unique in respect to one sexual matter, forced breeding. This was a form of racial punishment never inflicted upon white or Indian women servants. It involved a master deliberately choosing an African man he owned to impregnate one of his female slaves and commanding her to have sex with the man. The Anglican fur trader and landowner Samuel Maverick held the dubious distinction of being the first slave breeder in Massachusetts Bay colony as well as the first slave owner in the colony. In 1638 he held three Africans, two women and a man, and was living on a thousand-acre island in the Boston harbor, where he had plenty of room to house slaves and their offspring. Soon after the African man forced himself on the woman, she kicked him out of her bed. Refusing to accept her master's view that he was entitled to breed her, Mr. Maverick's woman appealed to John Josselyn, a thirty-year-old English traveler and guest in the Maverick house. In a high-pitched shrill cry the woman managed to convey to Josselyn that she viewed Maverick's demand as "in high disdain beyond her slavery."[21] Josselyn recorded her appeal but did not give any suggestion that he came to her aid.

The actual extent of forced breeding was limited since it made no economic sense to most urban New England slave owners to house infants along with their other slaves in an already-cramped house. Only a few masters in Boston such as Maverick had enough land to build their slaves separate cabins as was common practice among the planters in the Narragansett region of Rhode Island or southern Connecticut. Yeoman farmers in New England lived in a salt box house next to the barn and the outhouse and erected a slave cabin nearby. Advertisements of slaves for sale in eighteenth-century New England newspapers suggest greater interest in purchasing slave infants and children in the countryside precisely because of this difference in housing. In twelve advertisements of slaves the owner was getting rid of an overly fertile woman—breeds "like a rabbit" or reason for sale: "frequent pregnancy"—whereas in eight a woman was touted as "a notable breeder."[22] An advertisement in the *Boston Gazette* in 1745 hints as to why the "excellent breeder" was often not in high demand. A twenty-eight-year-old woman was offered for sale "only in town" who "had the Small Pox, but a very poor Breeder, therefore not fit for the Country...."[23]

Sexual coercion, as opposed to breeding, was a fact of life for a servant woman of any race, in town or in the country. A mistress rarely protected women or girls living in her household from the men in her family because she tended to view them as a sexual threat or a corrupting influence. In general, white men plotted to corner a woman servant or slave in the cellar, the fields, or waited until Sunday when a wife had gone to church. Joanna Negro, a slave in Woburn, testified in a county court in 1686 that the neighbor of her owner, Joseph Carter, had "gott her with child in the dyke nere the well" when his wife was out of town. To take the blame off himself Carter told Joanna Negro to say that Samson Negro was the father of her child. Carter warned her that "if she layd it to him he wold sett the divel to worke upon her and...she would never have a quiet life againe."[24] Carter's wife Bethiah was the midwife at Joanna Negro's childbirth. Bethiah Carter put her through the standard interrogation, asking Joanna the identity of the father of her child. Joanna Negro named Samson Negro because she thought otherwise Bethiah Carter "might hurt her."[25]

Enslaved women's daily toil in New England was less demanding than the field labor slave women in other regions were compelled to perform. Enslaved women in New England were not forced to harvest sugarcane in the ninth month of pregnancy or to lift a long five-to-ten-pound pestle to crush the hulls of rice in a huge wooden mortar. Even so, bones and muscles had to absorb the burdens of lifting, bending, and carrying. Archaeological evidence based on the study of skeletons found in New Hampshire and in

New York confirms the adverse effect of years spent at hard physical labor. Workers in Portsmouth, New Hampshire, repairing a sewer line in 2005, struck a pine coffin, thus happening on a three-hundred-year-old Negro Burying Ground. Although many slaves were interred on their owner's property, an outlying area of this seaport town was reserved for the burial of blacks. The adult skeletons unearthed included those of four males and one female, a sex ratio even more imbalanced than the actual black population in Portsmouth at that time. Most of the adults were in their thirties; no artifacts were found buried in the graves.[26] One of the bodies, that of a male, showed repetitive forearm rotation, which might have resulted from heavy lifting and daily rounds of shoveling snow in the winter.

Even though the work of black women in the North was not unduly long or harsh by West Indian standards, it nonetheless took its toll on their bodies. The African Burial Ground in New York City is the largest single burying ground discovered for Africans in the New World; more can be learned from the 421 skeletons found there than from all the gravesites in New England. The skeletons unearthed bear witness to poor living conditions, inadequate diet, and malnutrition for enslaved men, women, and children in that city—and by inference, in New England seaports, where work, living conditions, and climate were relatively similar. In 1991 a construction crew at work on a corner lot near City Hall came upon a skeleton, the first evidence of what had been at one time the place of internment for between ten thousand and twenty thousand Africans in Manhattan. Historical archeologists removed skeletons and artifacts from the site in order to analyze bones, DNA, and dental structure. The burial ground was first begun in the late seventeenth century because blacks were not permitted internment in the graveyards of Christian churches, even if they themselves had been converted to the faith. Most of the skeletons were of infants and children and the adults were more often male than female. Unlike in New England, Manhattan had a largely female black population; the preponderance of male skeletons at the burial ground probably reflects the influx of black men to Manhattan during the Revolutionary War when they were offered freedom in exchange for deserting their masters to enlist in the British army.[27]

Aches, pains, muscle tears, and the early onset of arthritis were the inevitable result of doing the heavy physical labor of the household required in early American households. Many women, even those in their thirties, had arthritis in their knees from daily kneeling to scrub floors. They strained and tore their muscles and broke their bones, producing lesions on the skeleton, and enlargements of the areas around the bones to which neck, arm, and leg muscles were attached. Skeletons from the African Burial Ground in Manhattan reveal that somewhat more men than women had such lesions because more men were engaged in heavy lifting and carrying burdensome loads on their shoulders or balancing them on their heads. But the decided majority of the skeletons of both men and women exhibited these lesions.[28]

The large number of skeletons of children and infants at the African Burial Ground also suggests that infant mortality was very high, due to poor health care, malnutrition, and infectious diseases (measles, smallpox, diphtheria, whooping cough, chicken pox, cholera, scarlet fever, and yellow fever). Infectious diseases arrived by ship but spread quickly in this dense, malnourished population, with weakened defenses to immunity. The skeletons of children reveal metabolic disease that resulted from anemia due to iron deficiency (poor nutrition) and infections such as meningitis and tonsillitis. An additional sign of malnutrition was hypoplasias or whitish or brownish grooves in the enamel of adult and children's teeth. The grooves result when the body is engaged in fighting fever or infection and provide proof that the individual suffered serious illness in childhood.

The archaeological evidence from the African Burial Ground further suggests that black children in New York City were routinely malnourished. They suffered from anemia, rickets, and hypoplasias because of deficiency of diet, particularly low levels of Vitamin D. The ultraviolent rays from the sun do not provide sufficient Vitamin D in northern climates during the winter months, especially for people with dark skin who are unable to process Vitamin D as efficiently as those with fair skin. Deficiency must be compensated for by foods such as egg yolks, tuna, liver, and milk.[29] When children do not get enough Vitamin D, their bones soften and they develop rickets, a disease that causes bow-leggedness.

Some slaves and free blacks ate well and others went hungry; some dined at the table with their owner's family, while others were fed scraps in the kitchen. All New Englanders enjoyed better nutrition in the summer when fresh fruit and vegetables were plentiful than in the winter when they survived on salted meat and dried peas made into soup. During the coldest months of the year a white New England family scraping the bottom of the meat barrel may have been less inclined to share their bounty with their slaves. Elizabeth Colson, a biracial indentured servant in Massachusetts, testified, "I was carry'd very hardly too by my Mistress, and suffer'd hunger and blows, and at least was tempted to steal."[30] Blacks in colonial Philadelphia were known to subsist on stale bread and watery broth, sometimes flavored with the bones of the less desirable parts of animals, such as cow's feet; they drank polluted water or perhaps beer or cider. Families who kept a cow served milk or used it in cooking for breakfast and supper; the poor who did not own a cow had no milk to drink. Women often ground corn into meal flavored with watery broth, and at other times mixed it with sour buttermilk. One enslaved family in revolutionary New York took its corn meal with three ounces of dark, often stale bread, slathered with hog's lard. Once a week the master gave them half a pound of beef and half a gallon of potatoes.[31]

Inadequate diet in New England and elsewhere affected enslaved women more than men since they required more iron to supplement what they lost through menstruation; pregnant women also needed more protein and calcium. A diet of corn meal, stale bread, and watery stew provided neither sufficient calories nor vitamins for pregnant women and lactating mothers. When mothers were malnourished, their children suffered as well. Masters who skimped on provisions for their slaves believed they were not only saving money but were subduing the baser instincts of their chattel so as to encourage their obedience.[32]

Black women's heaviest physical burdens were carrying water and lifting heavy cauldrons filled with boiling water to do the wash. As part of her morning chores an enslaved woman or a slave boy filled a large jar or bucket with ten or twenty gallons of water at a pump and carried it back to the family's quarters. If it took a hundred gallons of water a day to do the washing and cooking, some five trips a day to the pump were needed for these tasks. Black women were often balancing heavy loads on their heads, a carrying method known in Africa (but one which could cause skull fractures). A laundress built and stoked the fire, moved heavy wooden washtubs, and bent over a barrel or a cauldron filled with boiling hot water. She made laundry soap from lye and animal fat; wood ashes, hog dung, or hemlock were used to remove stains.[33] With her heavy wash stick the laundress stirred and lifted the clothes in the boiling water; she beat the excess lye and ash out of clothes with her stick. After she rinsed the clothes, she wrung them out by hand, and hung them up to dry. Laundry was done separately for each set of clothes, that is, flannels, whites, and colors; ironing required heating heavy irons in the fireplace.

The most visible effects of doing the laundry and the ironing were spinal column bones that were scalloped rather than smooth. Many of the women carrying heavy loads were pregnant; excess back strain in the early months of pregnancy is known to cause stillbirths and miscarriages. The deformation of the spine also suggests that in addition to heavy lifting, mothers were also carrying children on their backs as was common in West Africa, where women frequently nursed infants while walking and doing other chores.[34]

Even though slaves often lived in the same house as their master, they did not necessarily sleep in a heated room in the coldest of months. The best sleeping space in the winter for household slaves was the kitchen because of the heat from the fireplace or in the attic close to the chimney. Some houses had an ell or nook in the kitchen where the slave bedding was kept. The attic was reached by a separate entrance and stairways; the roof was not insulated so aside from the heat from the chimney there was no heat in the winter and no ventilation in the summer. More often slaves lived in the attic, where they slept on straw mattresses, perhaps with a blanket and sheets, a cradle for an infant, or a bed with sheets and a blanket; a mother and her child might share the same bed. In Boston one enslaved mother and her child slept in a curtained bed in a hallway, a highly unusual and genteel accommodation. Houses were often cramped, and the slaves living in the attic usually slept next to the tools or storage area. All attics were not created equal, and the ones in eighteenth-century homes with gambrel roofs were considerably roomier because the roof was sloped and the ceiling was higher. The fact that slaves made chalk drawings on the wood beams of the roof suggests that they made these spaces their own. Massachusetts owners of high social standing believed it was only "certain New York families" who housed their slaves in the cellar, which was of course damp and cold, but as with all distinctions between kindly and bad masters, these claims are unverifiable.[35]

As a result of heavy work, poor housing conditions, and inadequate diet, the average black woman did not live past forty; she might gain her freedom without many years to enjoy it.[36] Overall, the demographic facts of birth and death show that the conditions of life for black women in New England were quite poor. Women did not give birth to sufficient numbers of children who survived infancy for the native black population to grow. Since most urban masters discouraged slave fertility, the true test of whether the master's coercion caused the limited growth of the black population is the childbearing rate of freed black women, which remained quite low.[37] Year after year black deaths outstripped black births, a pattern that persisted in freedom as well as in slavery. A professor of divinity at Harvard, Edward Wigglesworth, put it most crudely in noting that "a large importation from Africa [was required] to keep the stock good."[38] The statistician and economist Jesse Chickering observed the persistence of this trend in antebellum Boston. He remarked in 1846 that "some have even supposed that, without immigration, and without mixture with the whites, the whole race would, in a few years, be extinct in the Commonwealth."[39] About fifteen years later the Boston city registrar recognized the same pattern, that black deaths exceeded births. He reached the conclusion "that this race among us is doomed to a speedy extinction, unless sustained by outside accessions."[40]

There is little reason to believe that enslaved women in New England were deliberately choosing not to reproduce as a form of resistance to their bondage and the possible future sale of their children.[41] To be sure, interest in and resort to abortion is impossible to know. Plants brought from Africa to the Americas such as okra and aloe could have been used as abortifacients; desperate women used sticks to induce a miscarriage. However, the one known instance of attempted abortion by an enslaved woman in New England was coerced, not freely chosen. Joseph Carter had threatened Joanna Negro if she revealed that he was the father of her child; he bought her savin, widely understood as an abortifacient. When he learned she was pregnant he instructed her to "take that and it wold kill the child." After she gave birth, he encouraged her to the kill the infant, suggesting that it was a guilty white man, not the enslaved woman, who had the greatest interest in slave abortion.[42]

Slave infanticide was very difficult to hide and what is known about the enslaved mothers who murdered their babies is that they were mainly servant girls trying to avoid punishment for fornication. One free black mother who had previously abandoned her first two children killed her third, shortly after giving birth clandestinely in a swamp; all the other African mothers who murdered their infants were slaves.[43] Black women had even fewer options than other household servants because they could not leave their employer to return to their relatives. Instead they faced certain punishment of whipping and possible sale of themselves and their child. Between 1663 and 1773 eight enslaved women in New England were accused of infanticide. Two out of the eight were hanged; four were acquitted; and two were punished by whipping or imprisonment.[44] While there were more black than white or Indian women accused and punished for infanticide, the actual rate of infanticide was somewhat higher among Indian women, since their culture accepted infanticide and abortion as forms of population control.[45] Enslaved women facing execution for infanticide were desperate, sometimes mentally ill; they had concealed their pregnancies, giving birth alone, killing their child, then hiding the dead body. If questioned, such women claimed their baby was stillborn and in some cases, they may have been telling the truth.

The reason enslaved women rarely engaged in abortion or infanticide was because pregnancy was an important source of pride, proof that a girl had become a woman and that life went on, despite the tragedy of enslavement. In West and Central African marriages the wife's task was to bear a child, preferably within the first year of her union. In such cultures children were a life force who aided their mother's spirit in merging with those of the ancestors. Women gained power when they brought the next generation of the lineage into the world. A black man took masculine pride in fathering a child; the husband who was impotent was not truly a man. An African man chose as his bride a woman he thought was fertile and sent away one who was childless; a barren woman brought shame on herself, her husband, and her lineage. Arranged in a hexagonal coffin, burials 335 and 336 at the Manhattan African Burial Ground were the skeletons of a mother and her infant cradled in her right arm.[46] Either the wish of the dying mother was to hold her child in her arms or those who buried her thought it fitting to arrange the bodies to express their belief in everlasting maternal love.

Nor is it likely that the explanation for black women's low fertility in New England was diminished capacity to conceive due to breastfeeding. It is true that women in West Africa prolonged breastfeeding, which has the effect of lengthening the interval between pregnancies. Nonetheless, white women in New England tended to breastfeed infants for an average of a year to a year and a half.[47] New England masters would not have permitted an enslaved woman to nurse for an interval longer than that accepted for their own wives and daughters, especially when she was needed in the kitchen, the barn, and the garden. Therefore it appears that the main reason for black women's low fertility was the poor health of mothers who tended to succumb to infectious disease and respiratory infections such as tuberculosis and pneumonia; Africans had no natural immunity to some of these diseases and the supposed immunities that Africans had developed against smallpox, virulent in West Africa, has been overestimated. In fact, blacks constituted one third of the dead during Boston's smallpox epidemic of 1764–65. Tuberculosis, a major killer of black adults, is known to cause sterility; the high level of childlessness among black women in New England even in the nineteenth century can be attributed in part to the effects of this disease.[48]

It was not health conditions but legal conditions that made New England a uniquely favorable environment for black women. An orderly society that made a visible display of punishing the rebellious slave was also one attuned to the discipline of white men, especially disreputable ones. British colonists, north and south, held that the law should enforce sexual morality and punish transgressions of the moral code. But in New England the colonists believed that such a standard of conduct should not allow exceptions because of the race of the victim. For that reason, the rape of an enslaved woman by a white man was prosecuted. Occasionally a white man in the antebellum South could be charged with the rape of a slave if the perpetrator was not the owner, a master or mistress pursued the matter, the rape was quite brutal, or the victim was very young, say, age six or younger. Even so, there do not appear to have been any such prosecutions in the colonial South.[49] To be accurate, justice prevailed not in all of New England but only in Plymouth where there were two cases of white men charged with the rape of black women before slavery came to an end in Massachusetts.

In 1717 a Plymouth court indicted Zebulon Thorp with "intent to ravish" an "Ethiopian" woman. The woman's mistress supported her in bringing her charge, creating the highly unusual situation of the mistress of the enslaved woman serving as her powerful protector. There are few details about the rape, and it was not clear whether the mistress had witnessed the attack or simply believed the story her "Ethiopian" woman told her. After being charged with rape, Thorp appeared in court inebriated and was sent to jail for twenty-four hours, perhaps to sober up, before he was released prior to his trial. Once out of jail, he started drinking again. While galloping on his horse one evening he was thrown off and died the next morning. Thorp may have committed suicide because he had previously stated that he would rather die than suffer conviction for ravishment. We will never know whether jurors in Plymouth Colony were prepared to put a noose around the neck of a white man found guilty of the rape of a slave woman. Still, Thorp's indictment reveals the importance of gender and reputation in Plymouth Colony; the word of a black woman, backed by her mistress, was believed over that of a white man of bad character.[50] James Studley was the second white man in colonial Plymouth accused of the rape of a black woman and, like Thorp, was poorly regarded by his neighbors. His trial in 1758 was a historic first in New England: the first trial of a white man indicted for the rape of a black woman. Studley was charged with forcing himself on his victim and trying to have sex with her in a public place. His assault was actually an acquaintance rape, since in the prior term he and the unnamed woman were issued warrants to appear in court. At that time the woman was fined for "confessed fornication" and Studley was also fined for an unnamed crime and ordered to pay court costs. Although in this second court case Studley was convicted of attempted rape it is not clear what punishment he faced.[51]

After the Revolution rape victims gained a hearing in jurisdictions other than Plymouth and a man accused of rape did not necessarily have to be a disreputable reprobate to be punished. The accused rapist in Lynn in 1786 was Calvin Newhall, a forty-one-year-old Revolutionary War veteran and married man; he was charged with assault and intent to ravish Deborah Sarker, a black woman. The jury split as to whether to convict him on the more serious charge of intent to ravish, which carried the death penalty. That they decided against the death penalty was to be expected since no white man had ever been executed for the rape of a black woman in any of the British colonies, let alone any of the thirteen states of the new nation. Unwilling to invoke the death penalty, the jury nonetheless found Newhall guilty of the lesser charge of assault. Newhall was whipped twenty times, required to post a bond for good behavior, placed on probation for three months, and ordered to pay court costs.[52] Black on black rape was not taken lightly in the Bay State, either. In 1791 a black man was charged with attempt to commit rape on a black woman walking in a public area in Boston in the evening. The case was remanded to the Massachusetts Superior Judicial Court for trial but its outcome was unclear.[53]

The way judges defined race showed the continuing impact of English patriarchal principles on New England law. Slavery was definitely an inherited legal status in Massachusetts Bay, but only after 1740 can it be said that slavery in New England was inherited through the mother's line and then not consistently.[54] No other region of British America hewed as closely to English rules about lineage in which a child inherited the father's legal status; as a consequence, in New England a black woman could give birth to a "white" child and that child was entitled to freedom. Moreover, the colonial assemblies of New England never passed legislation on the question of maternal inheritability of slavery and thus avoided making a deliberate statement reversing British principles. In the absence of such legislation, the matter was left up to the courts.

The freedom suit of Abda Duce, a slave in Connecticut, upheld a key rule of English patriarchy, that a father's legal status determined that of his children. In this case, Duce's father was English and his mother was African, and it was held that because his father was English, he, too, was an Englishman. The issue of slave status arose precisely in legal cases involving biracial adults who had two possible lineages and could be defined as English or African. Actually, the key term was not lineage, or even race, but blood; European peoples in the Middle Ages believed that all people were of one blood since they were common descendants of Adam—Eve was mentioned from time to time. The term blood referred mainly to high birth, as in noble blood, but was also used to describe the people of a nation such as English blood or French blood. In fact, English people were understood to share a common lineage based on their "blood."[55] No one ever mentioned African or Angolan or Senegambian blood, perhaps because slaves from these places were not seen as belonging to (powerful) nations. Although the French and the Spanish often spoke about the purity of blood, the English did not. To them blood was not a matter of purity or degrees of impurity (one eighth, one quarter, one drop) but of paternal lineage—the son of an Englishman was English and as such deserved his freedom.

At least in Massachusetts Bay Colony slavery became a hereditable condition by law in 1641, but how the condition was passed along from one generation to the next was not discussed. By adopting this code of laws, the first legal code in the New England colonies Massachusetts became the first colony of Britain to make slavery legal, using Biblical precedent in carving out the initial definition of a slave, and distinguishing between man stealing, the heinous crime, and the wholly acceptable transaction of acquiring captives through third-party purchase. Thus the Massachusetts Body of Liberties read: "That there shall never be any bondslavery, villainage or captivity amongst us, unless it be lawful captives taken in just wars, and such strangers as willingly sell themselves or are sold to us. And these shall have the liberties and christian usages which the law of God established in Israel concerning such persons doth morally require; provided this exempts none from servitude, who shall be judged thereto by authority."[56] Connecticut and Plymouth colonies adopted similar statutes. Did this legislation initiate slavery, that is, lifelong bondage, or merely sanction indentured servitude limited to a specified number of years of unpaid labor? Exactly who or how many Africans were considered indentured servants versus lifelong slaves will never be known; the umbrella term "servant," in common use at the time, masks precisely these distinctions. Whatever the rules, the colonists decided to tighten them by 1670; the word "strangers" was dropped from the law, apparently to deny automatic freedom to enslaved children and allow for the birth of children into slavery.

In many of the colonies, including those in New England, the matter of the status of biracial children was still unresolved. A test case emerged on the eastern shore of Virginia where sexual liaisons between Africans and the English were not infrequent. In 1655 Elizabeth Key, a biracial woman, the daughter of a white father and African mother, had grown up as an indentured servant; after her master died she successfully sued for her freedom in a county court. She won in this court but lost at the next level; her attorney then decided to petition on her behalf to the General Assembly of the colony of Virginia. They appointed a commission to investigate, which decided not to rule themselves but returned her case to the Virginia county court, which reaffirmed its original ruling. After gaining her freedom Key married the white man who had served as her attorney and had drafted her petition to the General Assembly. Precisely to foreclose similar suits of this kind the Virginia Assembly in 1662 passed a law specifying that the child of a slave mother was a slave. Making this descent rule explicit in law offered an economic advantage to the slave owner since his right to keep the children of his women slaves was upheld; the added advantage for the Virginia assembly and owners was that subsequent lawsuits from biracial children who might want to attempt this route to freedom were curbed. By passing this law and several others the Virginia Assembly aimed at nothing less than discouraging all interracial liaisons. Many other southern colonies devised their own unique rules to try to stamp out interracial sex, although several did not adopt the principle of maternal inheritability of slavery until much later.[57]

The freedom suit of Abda Duce of Hartford, Connecticut, also known as Abda Jennings, began in 1702 and ended in his freedom two years later. It involved the same legal question as that of Elizabeth Key, whether a biracial child was in fact born a free person. Duce had escaped from his master and was taken in by a prominent political leader in Hartford, Captain James Wadsworth. At the time he was a married man and his wife was expecting his child. His mother was Hannah Duce, a "slave for life" and his father was an Englishman, John Jennings, about whom nothing is known. Jennings and Hannah Duce had not married, and Hannah Duce and her son were owned by the same master. Abda argued in his lawsuit that he should be considered free and white because his father was an Englishman. Insisting that he was not a slave but rather an indentured servant whose term had ended, he claimed he was being wrongfully held in slavery. In county court he sought damages from his master's estate for keeping him enslaved past the age when his indenture came due. The jury agreed with him and ruled that Abda had "English blood in him" and therefore was entitled to his freedom.[58]

The arguments of the opposing lawyers in this case offered different views about everything from the immorality of slavery to the question of how slave status was inherited. The case was appealed by the son of Abda's legal owner who sought to claim him as part of his rightful inheritance. Losing his valuable property in a county court, the man appealed to the Governor and his Council in 1703. He hired as his lawyer the aristocratic landholder, prominent attorney, and noted New London Congregationalist minister Reverend Gurdon Saltonstall who had grown wealthy from transporting slaves from Barbados to Connecticut. Citing the law of Virginia of 1662, Saltonstall told the gentlemen assembled that "such persons as are born of Negro bond women are themselves in like condition."[59] He called several witnesses to the stand, including two women present when Hannah Duce gave birth to prove that Abda had been born of a slave mother. Pointing to an estate inventory that listed Abda as chattel, Saltonstall sought to show that an important legal document had classified Abda as his owner's property.

Saltonstall also cast aspersions on the reputation of Hannah Duce in hopes of damaging her son's character in the eyes of the jurors and implying that Jennings may not have been Abda's father. After all, Saltonstall pointed out that the "Negro bond woman" had several sexual partners, including Indian men. He added that she was not a Christian and suggested that her son did not appear to be one, either. Because she was a heathen Hannah Duce was prohibited from coming to court and swearing an oath on the Bible that Jennings was the father of her child. Saltonstall further claimed that even if Jennings was the father, he had not married his son's mother and therefore Abda was a bastard, not entitled to the privileges of inheritance extended to legitimate children. Abda also had a prominent attorney, Richard Edwards, a wealthy merchant who read widely in theological tracts and the law. Rather than refute directly these claims, Edwards offered his own arguments, including the important assertion that slavery was incompatible with the Christian faith. The General Assembly sided with Abda and upheld the county court ruling and awarded Abda damages for being held illegally in slavery. Abda Duce died in Hartford in 1708, a free man who had acquired a small amount of property and left behind a wife and seven-year-old son.[60]

In this legal contest between two definitions of slavery and race, the Virginia statutory approach was rejected in favor of a more English and flexible definition of race—a personal victory for Abda and an affirmation of the principle of patriarchy. The officials of Connecticut were not free from racial prejudice, however, since Connecticut, like the other New England colonies, was beginning to enact many laws to strengthen racial barriers, including a series of "black codes" that curbed the movements and freedom of slaves, Indians, and free blacks. However, a Connecticut court and the colony's General Assembly had chosen in this particular case to define slavery as inherited through the male line. Eventually judges in New England ruled in the opposite manner, but not consistently and without any legislative imprimatur.

Many slaves, no matter where they worked or lived, wanted liberty for themselves and their families. So far as we know they defined it in multiple ways, including wanting land, religious freedom, and opportunities for their children. There is no reason to suppose that black women in New England envisioned freedom any differently than other enslaved women. But in New England there were several avenues to achieving freedom and thus what made New England unique was that among these avenues to freedom was the legal one. The fact that there was a legal path to freedom should have affected black women's consciousness since it gave them a more positive view of the law, attorneys, and juries.

New England was both a society with slaves and a patriarchal society that retained fundamental English principles of inheritance rather than adapting them to slavery. At least initially in New England patriarchy shaped race more than race shaped patriarchy. In New England colonies no law, custom, or legal decision prior to 1739 defined slavery as a status inherited through the mother's line.[61] In this respect the colonies adhered to English common law, even as they departed from the rules of the mother country with respect to divorce, fornication proceedings, poor relief, and warning-out of strangers from town.[62] The reason that New England colonial legislatures never passed any legislation on the question of the inheritability of slavery is the importance of the idea of "English blood." Their notion of race was inseparable from their view of lineage as a blood line, especially descent from nobility. Because of the persistence of the idea of English blood, New England remained more English, less New World in its thinking about slavery for a much longer stretch of time. Thus, slavery in New England balanced novel legal adaptations with conformity to English rules of descent. As a result of this distinctive legal system New England law did not always and invariably protect owner's property rights above all other considerations. Yet one of the ways this transplanted English world was very new was the availability of land for almost every white man who wanted it. In New England, as we will see, owning land was a form of security, a means of financial speculation, and a symbol of political independence. Property ownership was not simply a man's form of freedom from which women were excluded, however, but important to black women as well, as an inquiry into the lives of several black women in eighteenth-century Massachusetts and Vermont will reveal.

2

PROPERTY AND PATRIARCHY

The man who owned land was an independent citizen; the landless man, a tenant or wage laborer, was seen as corruptible, capable of being coerced into doing the bidding of those who provided him with a living or dwelling place. It is often assumed that free blacks in the North were so poor and faced such persistent racial discrimination in wages that they did not possess the economic base for citizenship, since they had not the means to buy land, let alone acquire the livestock and equipment they would need to farm. In fact, many blacks acquired land by purchase and by means other than purchase, just as many whites did. At the end of their terms of service black indentured servants often received a few acres. A master might use the wages his hired-out slave received to buy land and a house for him, and put the deed in his slave's name. A benevolent slave owner might grant a slave some land at manumission or in his will; occasionally black men also received grants of town land, which were handed out freely to all male residents. Black men serving in the militia, the navy, or on a privateer received a lump sum for their service, which some used as a down payment for the purchase of land. Free black craftsmen also saved their money to buy land. In an accident of fate, the slave of the Governor of Massachusetts Bay rescued him from drowning in the Charles River and received as his reward a tiny parcel of land in Boston.[1]

In 1656 Boston Ken, a.k.a. Sebastian Kane, probably brought from Angola to Boston, became the first black landholder in Massachusetts Bay Colony. A free black sailor and Christian convert, he owned a one-third share in a fourteen-ton sailing ship; he also planted four acres of wheat on the small parcel of land he owned in Dorchester where he lived with his wife Grace and their children. Even a couple of *enslaved* men in New England acquired property and drew up wills, thus proving that it was possible to both simultaneously be property and own property.[2] In an urban area property holding might mean owning a house, a town lot, or a business. A free black man, Thomas of Boston, had his own chair-making establishment by the 1670s; he drew up a prenuptial contract leaving his shop and all of his property to his future wife, Katherine Negro. (Thus, he was free, owned his own workshop, and devised a contract without acquiring a surname). By the 1730s Emanuel and Mary Bernoon, a free black couple, managed their own oyster and alehouse in Providence; after her husband died Mary continued to live in their house, supporting herself by taking in washing.[3] It is no accident that Boston Ken or the Bernoons had Portuguese names; slaves from Angola proved quite entrepreneurial, often gaining their freedom and owning land or going into business by the last half of the seventeenth century. Moreover, some of their enterprises clearly appear to have involved the woman working alongside the man.

As property owners black men usually followed the unwritten land transfer customs of their white neighbors or English legal procedures for will-making. Free black husbands and fathers who drew up wills usually selected as executors white men known for their probity. They generally left their widow her thirds, prescribed by law, the one third of the life interest from a husband's real estate and a third of his personal property, even though in most cases, there was no personal property to divide. Usually, a widow was allowed to live in the family house during her lifetime but at her death her life share went to the designated owner of the property.[4] According to the law a widow was not allowed to sell her one-third life interest; instead, she was expected to pass it along intact to her husband's eventual heirs, usually their children. In adopting these principles of inheritance, free black men were demonstrating their belief in the idea that a widow was a husband's dependent for whom he should provide. She was to be taken care of so that she would not become a burden on the community but not given so much wealth that a man's children were robbed of their inheritance. Black men also adhered to legal norms about shares given to inheriting sons and daughters. According to Connecticut intestate law sons and daughters were supposed to receive an equal share of a father's estate, while the oldest son was entitled to a double share. Free black fathers, even those who drew up wills, followed this general rule. Thus the younger son and daughter of Ned Negro, who changed his name to Edward Willoughby after he was emancipated, received their father's house lot, cow, oxen, and horse but their oldest brother was granted a double share.[5]

The first black woman on record to acquire property on her own was a free woman, a widow and the beneficiary of unusual circumstances. Zipporah Done was born free in Boston around the 1650s to slave parents, because at the time of her birth Massachusetts did not have a law specifying that the children of slave parents would become slaves. Her father, born in Angola and a compatriot of Sebastian Kane, maneuvered his way out of slavery to become an indentured servant and after his term ended an independent landowner. Done gave birth to a stillborn child and was accused of murdering the baby. She was found innocent and sometime after that she came into some money, perhaps given to her by the son or nephew of a Boston Commissioner, who seems to have wanted to insure her silence as to the identity of her child's father. Done paid cash for land in Boston with a house on it; no will is extant, so it is unclear what happened to her property after her death.[6]

Making a will was the next major milestone for a property-owning black woman. The first to do so was the widow of a landholding husband in Hartford in 1699. Philip Moore (from the name probably Angolan), although illiterate, had become free, acquired several parcels of property, and built a house in East Hartford. He had a large family of adult children and grandchildren, and although some of his children were free, others were indentured servants. Most of his possessions were left to them but he gave his wife his moveable estate; she appears to have been living in the house with her daughter and grandchildren at the time of her husband's death. Rather than appointing a male executor Moore trusted his widow to handle his financial affairs. Accordingly, it made sense for Ruth Moore, although illiterate, to make a will the next year, in which she left everything to her daughter-in-law at her death.[7]

When women were able to come into their own land, they fought hard to be able to hold onto it, even going to court to claim their rights. In the 1760s Northampton widow Bathsheba Hull, the mother of four young children, bought three acres of land, assuming that the seller had clear title. The town of Northampton, however, claimed her land and house belonged to them and took her to court to evict her. Hull fought back but lost; nonetheless, Northampton voters at the town meeting decided to offer her a fair price for her house, so long as she agreed to sell. With no real options, Hull accepted the offer, left town, and went into service. Unable to care for all of her children she placed her son with black friends living in Stockbridge until she was able to come back for him.[8]

For blacks in New England property holding was central to their definition of freedom and their understanding of property was individual, not collective. Black farmers marked out the boundaries of their land with huge boulders to distinguish their property from their neighbors. Land represented wealth, security, independence; it conferred political power, since only white men who owned land possessed the right to vote. Free blacks were full participants in a neighborly credit system in which they were borrowers and lenders as well as speculators, eager parties who bid up the price of land and sold quickly, buyers of land often willing to take advantage of Indian sellers in frontier areas. However, in most cases, black landowners also had to work odd jobs, never becoming completely independent of the labor market. Because that was the case, wives in landowning couples were also expected to earn additional income for the family.[9]

Detailed case studies of the marriages of three black women who moved from slavery to freedom in New England provide insight into how deeply patriarchy was enmeshed with land ownership. It produced a great range of adaptations from economic partnership in marriage to possible theft of the wife's property and from dependence at a husband's death to economic competence as a widow, preserving and perhaps even expanding the family's wealth. Lucy Pernam, Lucy Terry Prince, and Chloe Spear were former slaves in eighteenth-century New England married to free black landowners. Prince and Spear had been captured in Africa and brought to New England as children; Lucy Pernam's origins are not known. As a widow Lucy Pernam inherited her husband's unimproved farmland in New Hampshire. Chloe Spear was an urban homeowner who saved some of her wages and with her husband purchased half of a house in a Boston neighborhood probably best known for its brothels, dance halls, and drunken sailors. Prince's husband had sufficient acreage for a working farm and supplemented his income by renting his oxen.

The story of these three marriages can be read as answering the question of whether marriage was compatible with and even necessary for a woman to achieve freedom. There seem to be three different answers to this question. One is that marriage robbed a woman of her property and left her penniless; a second that marriage was a true economic partnership for the accumulation of wealth and the care of minor and even adult children; and the third that marriage was an economic partnership but that widowhood provided a woman with the greatest degree of freedom; indeed, that a woman could enjoy true freedom only in widowhood. The limits of patriarchy appear most when things go wrong in a marriage, not when both members of the couple are able to harmonize their personalities and their interests. Yet there were patriarchal principles evident even in the best of these marriages. The stories of these three marriages need to be told from the point of view of the wives, as they entered marriage, lived with their husbands, separated from them, or became widows and as well as by following their property, as these women brought land to their marriage, accumulated it in marriage, or tried to secure it as separated wives or as widows.

The victim of a very bad marriage, Lucy Pernam was forced to scrounge much of her life. She had wed a fellow slave of her owner in Newbury when she was relatively young. After her husband died she married Robert Robin, the former slave of a minister and his wife. He had been freed at the death of his widowed mistress who had left him land in New Hampshire. Robin married Lucy in a ceremony at St. Paul's Anglican church in Newbury and sold some of his land in New Hampshire to buy her freedom. The land was unimproved and there is no evidence that the newlyweds considered moving there; instead, they settled into rented rooms in a largely white neighborhood in Newbury. Like most freed black couples living in town they depended on two incomes; Robin became a laborer and Lucy sold provisions. Their landlord was Lucy's former master, John Little, a truckman or businessman who engaged in the barter and exchange of goods.[10]

Robert Robin's relationship with John Little appears to have been a close one. When Robert Robin lay ill and on his deathbed John Little stood nearby. Robin named Little executor of his estate and specified in his will that his gun should go to him at his death. In his dying days Robert Robin worried about Lucy's depression and suicidal tendencies. Two months after his death, Lucy's neighbors witnessed her going through a phase "remarkably wild profane and obscene." Then she met Scipio Pernam, an illiterate but free black truckman from Ipswich, a tall, thirty-year-old bachelor who was well dressed, temperate, and had "a commanding appearance."[11] Lucy was a very eligible widow, having been left an estate of £202 in New Hampshire land, cash, and goods. Most young widows of the time, especially women who had never had any children, chose to remarry. Although she was twice widowed, Lucy's decision to marry again was not unusual and two months after her husband's death, she returned to St Paul's as a bride for the third time.[12] After her wedding she moved out of the rooms rented from John Little; perhaps Scipio used her money to buy their small house and lot in an alley in Newburyport.[13] Eleven months later Lucy gave birth to a daughter and after that her marriage deteriorated rapidly.

Scipio Pernam claimed he beat Lucy because she was raving, destroying their home, and provoking him. Lucy insisted that Scipio was hitting her because she demanded access to what was left of her money. Scipio, she said, controlled her inheritance from her late husband, her household belongings, and even her good clothes.[14] Under coverture a remarrying widow retained ownership of the real property she brought to the marriage but lost control over the management of it, and tendered outright control of the personal property held at the time of her marriage. Concern about her good clothes was not an idle inquiry; it was common for the poor to pawn or sell good clothes for cash. Lucy Pernam was not completely satisfied with her husband's financial stewardship. Initially he beat her with "two blows with a stick." The law of Massachusetts Bay Colony in 1641 punished a husband for unnatural severity toward his wife; there is no evidence that Massachusetts Bay ever recognized a husband's legal right to administer physical correction of his wife.[15] Nonetheless, Scipio Pernam's neighbors never challenged his right to beat his wife.[16] Lucy Pernam was not easily controlled, however, and two blows with a stick soon escalated into much more severe beatings. In fact, Scipio Pernam's abuse of Lucy was so severe that their neighbors could hear her crying out and she claimed that she felt her life was endangered.

The town of Newburyport exercised oversight over households in order to maintain proper authority and back up the husband's control over his wife. The town's selectmen and overseers of the poor ordered Lucy to the house of correction, apparently with Scipio's assent. The good woman was supposed to remain silent and only the truly bad one resorted to profanity; Lucy was clearly the bad woman, raving against her enemies, and threatening to reduce the town to ashes. Walking the streets alone, she had been charged with disturbing the peace, apparently engaged in prostitution. Free blacks, like slaves, were subject to a 9 P.M. curfew, which Lucy was violating. Scipio punished her for "night walking" and her violent outbursts with a whipping; the town flogged her at the whipping post, committed her to the workhouse, and confined her in irons in the town jail.[17]

The Pernam's white neighbors in Newburyport took Lucy's threat to burn down the town seriously because they lived in closely packed wooden houses and believed that many blacks, even those who were free and addressed them politely, secretly harbored desires for revenge. Because it did not require unusual physical strength, arson was a crime easy to commit and difficult to prevent. Although black women were seen as less prone to violence than black men, they were also perceived as unpredictable and volatile; masters went so far as to sell an enslaved woman because of her "furious temper."[18] Nonetheless, not every black person suspected of arson had dropped a hot coal into a pile of hay; the charge was easy to make, especially if one assumed malicious intent among almost every black or Indian in town.

Colonists had long regarded slave arson as an act that harmed individuals and their property and as a threat to the stability of the state. In Haverhill around 1700 an unnamed enslaved woman, previously whipped by her master for disobedience, placed gunpowder in his bedroom and lit a fuse with a piece of hot coal.[19] More threatening still were angry individual blacks who wanted to overthrow established authorities and select their own king and governor. The setting of ten mysterious fires and the torching of the homes of the elite during a time of war, drastic food shortage, and recession triggered the Great Conspiracy of 1741. White New York responded to the fear of revolt with a witch hunt and the most extensive series of trials of slaves in colonial American history. Black males charged as conspirators confessed and named names; soon over half of the enslaved men in the city were thrown into a dungeon underneath City Hall. The alleged ringleaders were hanged, along with seventeen black men and four white male accomplices; thirteen black men were burned alive at the stake.[20]

As local Massachusetts residents read in their newspapers of the great plot in Manhattan every theft and small fire in the neighborhood seemed to heighten their sense of panic. A white mob in Roxbury caught a slave accused of theft, stripped off his clothes, tied him to a tree, and thrashed him; after he was cut loose he was taken to his master's house where he soon died.[21] The atmosphere of hysteria led to the accusation and conviction of a black man and woman, belonging to two separate owners, for setting a fire in Charlestown; he was executed and she was condemned to death but managed to avoid the gallows.[22] None of Lucy Pernam's neighbors believed she had accomplices, but her actions raised the troubling question as to whether there were other free blacks as dangerous and desirous of revenge.[23]

Lucy Pernam's threats and railings appear to have arisen from her depression, brought on by a long history of domestic violence, racial prejudice, and perhaps an abusive childhood.[24] Her problems first appeared in the last years of her marriage to Robin, then subsided, and resurfaced after she married Scipio Pernam. Lucy Pernam may have found it especially difficult to cope with her second husband's illness and death or may have sunk into depression after the birth of her daughter. Whatever the sources of her problems, she seems to have exhibited all the characteristics of a mentally ill woman; she appeared normal at times and was raving at others, with rapid and unpredictable mood swings.[25]

A black woman, even if threatening and crazed, nonetheless elicited sympathy from her neighbors because of her physical suffering and abject condition. One couple and their slave in Newbury took pity on Lucy after she had been badly beaten by Scipio. During the fall or winter of the second year of her marriage Lucy and Scipio quarreled, and she broke the windows in their house. Scipio beat Lucy and threw her out of doors, a common tactic of husbands who sought to exert their authority over their wives. The Pernam's one-year-old daughter remained with her father. Why had Lucy left without her daughter when slave fugitive mothers often grabbed their children when they fled? She may not have had any choice, or may have calculated that a child could not survive if thrust out into the cold.

Lucy had no relatives to turn to and apparently could not consider her mother-in-law her ally. Instead, her neighbors, Ebenezer and Sarah Knap, took her in. Their slave, Cesar, knew her and might have played a role in pleading on her behalf. She was so ill when she appeared at their door that Knap had to hire a nurse to care for her for two weeks; after that Sarah Knap and family took care of her until she regained her health. Perhaps Lucy promised Knap she would pay for the nurse as soon as she had access to her assets. Knap, like most neighbors in Newburyport, assumed that Lucy should return home to her husband and her daughter. He visited Scipio several times, asking him if he would take Lucy back (and, one expects, looking for payment of the debt Lucy had incurred); Scipio Pernam repeatedly refused to allow Lucy in the door. The town authorities, hoping to resolve the couple's dispute, pressed Scipio to reconcile with Lucy but he told them, "she will never come under my Roof again and I wish she was dead."[26]

Scipio had no intention of repaying Knap for caring for Lucy and took steps to insure that he had no continuing legal responsibility for Lucy's support. He posted a notice on a tavern door in Newburyport, which disclaimed any obligation to pay his wife's debts.[27] Under coverture, Scipio Pernam was required to support his wife in a manner appropriate to his station in life. If he refused to provide for her, she could go to court and sue him. While a wife's suit was pending, a husband was responsible for her support, which meant that she was permitted to run up charges in his account at a store or tavern. If a wife abandoned her husband, however, the law allowed him to refuse to pay her debts so long as he posted a public notice of her desertion.[28]

Scipio Pernam decided he did not want Lucy to remain in town, even if he was not responsible to pay her debts. He sold Lucy to a local butcher, who, finding her recalcitrant, bound and gagged her, and offered her to another buyer headed for New York.[29] A husband selling his wife to a male buyer was not as extraordinary as it might seem. In England husbands were known to sell their wives to other men in what constituted informal divorce. A husband and wife in Hartford in 1645 and another couple in Boston in 1736 engaged in such unwritten but nonetheless binding agreements.[30] To think the Pernams reached a mutually satisfactory agreement of this kind requires assuming that the local butcher was Lucy's lover. If he was, then why did he turn around and sell her a couple of days later and why did he have to gag her? Self-divorce was unprecedented among free blacks, but it was not unknown for a free black man to threaten to sell his woman into slavery, as was the case with a free black man in Warwick, Rhode Island, who purchased an enslaved woman from her owner. They lived together without marrying and he often told her that if she did not obey him, he would "put her in his pocket" (that is, sell her). Lucy was not obeying Scipio and he appears to have sold her and kept the proceeds. Realizing that he had purchased a mad woman, the butcher offered Lucy for sale to a new buyer who forcibly carried her out of the state to New York.[31]

Lucy managed to escape from her owner in New York and make her way to Boston where she stayed with her friends, Tobias and Margaret Locker. A free black couple who owned their own home, the Lockers were among the relatively few free black property owners in Boston. Exactly how Lucy met the Lockers is not clear, but it is important to note that a woman considered insane in Newburyport had upstanding black friends in another city. Six months later, she returned to Newburyport either because she wanted to visit her daughter or because the authorities in Boston had forced her to leave. Back in Newburyport Lucy was convicted of disturbing the peace and sent to the house of correction. After her release, she left for Boston again to live with her friends.[32] The authorities in Boston acted as they had before, disqualifying Lucy from receiving public charity and sent her back to Newburyport, the town of her legal residence.

Facing the prospect of having to pay for Lucy's relief Newburyport town officials concluded that she should live with Scipio since he had a legal obligation to support her. They insisted that Scipio take Lucy back, which he did—or was forced to do—despite his previous protestations. Several months later a male neighbor found Lucy bloody from another beating. She filed a libel for "divorce from bed and board," a legal separation that did not grant the right to remarry. The Governor and his Council followed their typical procedure in such cases: they appointed a panel of three justices of the peace to hear testimony of witnesses in Newburyport. Scipio also replied to Lucy's libel by refuting her claims point by point, and requesting that she should be punished for her disobedience. Four months later he seemed willing to concede to her divorce petition but not before claiming he should not have to pay alimony because Lucy had been a slave and therefore had learned to support herself. He also offered the standard argument of the time of a husband who did not want to pay alimony, that his wife was about "his own age" and "as strong of mind as well as strength of body" as he. Already supporting an elderly mother and his daughter he claimed that he could not bear an additional financial burden. Nonetheless he indicated to the court that he was willing to pay reasonable alimony because he wanted to be separated from "so bad a woman."[33]

Lucy was the only mother in Massachusetts prior to 1786 who sought custody of her child in a divorce suit; divorcing wives in other New England colonies did upon occasion end up with child custody, but very rarely. On the matter of child custody, any good Boston lawyer would have told Lucy she had no chance; a free black father, like a white father, had a common-law right to custody of minor children. Nonetheless, even though she lost custody of her daughter, the Governor and his Council in Massachusetts granted Lucy a separation with alimony, thereby affirming the view that the free black married woman, just like the white married woman, was a femme covert—a married woman whose husband was responsible for her financial support.[34] What is even more remarkable is that they ruled in favor of an angry and profane black woman who broke the windows in her home, seems to have engaged in prostitution, and threatened to set her town ablaze.

Perhaps the Governor and his Council had been persuaded by Ebenezer Knap's testimony that Lucy had suffered severe abuse.[35] Whatever the reasons for their decision, they ordered Scipio to pay six shillings a month in alimony, but like most separated husbands at this time, he did not pay. Lucy, with the assistance of her Boston attorney, sued to try to secure the money Scipio owed her.[36] Her lawyer Benjamin Kent drafted a petition complaining of nonpayment of alimony, becoming in the process only the third black woman in New England to submit a petition to a Governor and Council.[37] He stood by her and probably paid the small filing fee required of a petitioner, but Lucy never saw a shilling of the money awarded her.[38]

Lucy was in and out of jails and the workhouse the last fifteen years of her life, back and forth between Essex County and the city of Boston. At the onset of the Revolutionary War she was in Boston, swearing as usual, threatening "to set the Town on fire." Dumped in a Boston jail cell with thieves and prisoners of war, many of them quite ill, she probably existed on little more than bread and water. Warned out of Boston she was sent back to Newburyport.[39] After a time she was confined in irons to the workhouse and then released to live with a town official, paid to house her. Discharged and on her own she found work in nearby Rowley, Massachusetts, during the war. (The local courts were closed during the last years of the conflict, which probably meant that any threats of arson Lucy tended to make were ignored.)

After the war ended Lucy was accused of burning a widow's barn filled with hay and grain in Rowley.[40] Once again she was able to secure legal assistance; the court appointed two distinguished attorneys who successfully argued her case before a twelve-man jury, which pronounced her not guilty. After living without incident for six years she was confined in chains at the Newburyport jail in 1787. Two weeks before Christmas that year she set fire to the straw in her cage, apparently trying to take her life. The town built a sturdier wooden pen with a padlock to confine her; she spent her final years thus confined; it is not known when or how she died.[41] Scipio, who does not seem to have remarried, may have been caring for his elderly mother and raising his daughter. In his last years he was forced to sell the house on Bartlet's Lane at auction but still had a small amount of property. When the money was gone he entered the town's almshouse where he died in 1814; the whereabouts of his daughter are unknown.[42]

Few other black women in Massachusetts could claim to have spent as much time in Massachusetts courtrooms and jail cells as Lucy Pernam. The downward trajectory in her unhappy life began in her twenties when she married in haste for the third time. She brought to this marriage land, household belongings, and good clothes and at last had become a mother. Within the year she was turned out of doors, separated from her child, and was sold into slavery and taken to New York state. Suffering from depression, rage, and self hatred throughout her life she finally committed the arson she always threatened, almost killing herself in the process. Losing control of the property she brought to her marriage, she was often dependent on town relief. A desperate fugitive wife who fled to the homes of her neighbors and friends, she was a victim as well as a resilient survivor, who escaped from a new master in New York and although warned out of Boston, managed to find her way back there several times. While she resorted to flight and ignored town authorities, she also turned to the law, with the aid of several different lawyers who defended her despite her threats or arson and coarse language. They helped her gain a legal separation, try to get an order for alimony enforced, and saved her from being convicted of arson, and possibly from hanging. If she was raving, threatening, and apparently mad, she nonetheless made sense when she met with her attorneys, appeared in court, or explained her plight to her friends.

Scipio Pernam supported coverture and also opposed it, depending on the privileges or the obligations it imposed upon him. He believed in patriarchy and sought to exercise his privileges under it, including administering moderate correction of his wife and going well beyond that when he felt she was out of control. Town officials sided with him, even though Massachusetts law did not recognize a husband's right to physically discipline his wife. The white Newburyport community intervened in the Pernam family not to protect Lucy from abuse but rather in encouraging reconciliation and a husband's obligation to support his wife. Newburyport selectmen also pressured Scipio to take Lucy back and support her because otherwise they would have had to do so. Scipio Pernam escalated his tactics from defense (posting a notice that he was not obligated to support his wife) to offense, selling his wife into slavery as a means of getting rid of her and making some money in the process. In his divorce suit he offered a long list of reasons as to why he should not have to pay alimony, including his argument that he was not responsible for his wife's support because slavery had rendered the black woman independent. The Massachusetts Governor and his Council threw out this self-serving claim and ordered Scipio to pay alimony, which he, like most separated husbands, did not do. He seems to have had legal custody of his daughter, not because he fought for it, but as a matter of default, although he also appears to have been a dutiful son supporting his elderly mother. Still, he never possessed ultimate authority in his own household because he had to submit to the entreaties of worried neighbors and the demands of the town selectmen. Sympathetic to this "gentleman of color," neighbors in Newburyport believed Scipio Pernam had borne the suffering of his hapless "matrimonial connexion" "with real resignation."[43]

Bars Fight by Lucy Terry

August 'twas the twenty-fifth,
Seventeen hundred forty-six;
The Indians did in ambush lay,
Some very valiant men to slay,
The names of whom I'll not leave out.
Samuel Allen like a hero fout,
And though he was so brave and bold,
His face no more shalt we behold
Eleazer Hawks was killed outright,
Before he had time to fight,
Before he did the Indians see,
Was shot and killed immediately.
Oliver Amsden he was slain,
Which caused his friends much grief and pain.
Simeon Amsden they found dead,
Not many rods distant from his head.
Adonijah Gillett we do hear
Did lose his life which was so dear.
John Sadler fled across the water,
And thus escaped the dreadful slaughter.
Eunice Allen see the Indians coming,
And hopes to save herself by running,
And had not her petticoats stopped her,
The awful creatures had not catched her,
Nor tommy hawked her on the head,
And left her on the ground for dead.
Young Samuel Allen, Oh lack-a-day!
Was taken and carried to Canada.[44]

Lucy Terry, a young woman enslaved in the frontier town of Deerfield, Massachusetts, related the tale of her settlement decimated by a wartime Indian attack. Storyteller, wife, and mother of six—Lucy Terry was hardworking, virtuous, the good Christian woman, everything Lucy Pernam was not. The visible outlines of patriarchy recede in examining her marriage, since she and her husband, Abijah Prince, were long-time partners in a family economic enterprise. She suffered no legal disabilities from coverture because her husband was a good provider, protector, and an excellent and trusted companion. Lucy and Abijah Prince and their sons fought very hard to acquire land and hold onto it despite being swindled and harassed by a prejudiced white neighbor. Several times Abijah took matters into his own hands, but he also recognized the benefit of hiring a lawyer, bringing various cases to court many times and usually winning.[45]

Years before Lucy Terry married she composed a ballad after an Indian attack on Deerfield in 1746. The ballad was intended to be memorized and sung and although Lucy knew how to read and write, she never transcribed her composition. Instead, her neighbors sang her ballad and passed it along until it was published in the *Springfield Republican* in 1854.[46] Because "Bars Fight" eventually appeared in print, Lucy Terry is now often considered the first African American poet in North America, even though Jupiter Hammon was once referred to as the first published African American poet because a poem of his appeared in print in 1760. In employing this rhymed musical form of English society and telling the tale of suffering on the frontier against Indian foes Lucy Terry enjoyed popularity in Deerfield during her lifetime and long after it. Describing for her neighbors the saga of death and survival, Lucy entertained those who gathered in her master's home, local boys who came to warm themselves by the fire as they listened to her stories and rhymes.[47]

Early eighteenth-century Deerfield was a stockaded town of two hundred residents in western Massachusetts, an English settlement on Indian land. King George's War between England and France broke out in 1745, with the Abenaki Indians, who had been displaced from Massachusetts to northern New England and Canada, allying with the French. The Abenaki succeeded in overtaking a fort in western Massachusetts and without detection crept eastward to launch attacks against fortified settlements in the Connecticut River Valley. Reaching Deerfield they hid in the Bars, a meadow area south of town named for the moveable wooden bars that acted as a gate to keep cattle from getting into the cornfields. Lucy Terry, a slave in the town at the time of the attack, knew many who died, were wounded, or taken captive. In her ballad she used "I'll" to indicate that she had the authority to recite the names of the dead and wounded. She employed the phrase "we do hear" to incorporate whites and blacks of Deerfield, although she did not mention by name any of the more than twenty slaves in town because they were not in the Bars when the attack occurred.

An orphaned African captive, Lucy empathized with young white children, who, like herself, suffered or were taken away from their families at any early age. Recapitulating her own kidnapping in west Africa, she told the story of the young Samuel Allen, forced to march along the trail with the Abenaki several hundred miles to their settlement in Canada. In "Bars Fight," she took the side of settlers in whose midst she dwelled, and seems not to have had any Indian friends. The families who lived on the main street of Deerfield were her neighbors—and her superiors. According to oral tradition Lucy, as an old woman, returned from her home in southern Vermont to visit white friends in Deerfield. One woman urged her to sit with her at the kitchen table to which she replied, "No, Missy, no, I know my place."[48]

The legend of Lucy Terry contributed to the making of the myth of New England as an especially congenial region for enslaved and free blacks, where bondage was mild and social relations with a former mistress were close. White local historians retold her saga to their children and then repeated it in published articles and books. Lucy Terry became living proof of the intellectual capacity of black people, a striking example of the reasoning abilities thought to be lacking in women of all races and black people. Pliny Arms, the first of several local chroniclers in Deerfield, wrote an unpublished report on the town's history in 1819. He opposed racial discrimination in the North and saw Terry's speaking ability and balladry as proof of black intellect, just as others had taken Phillis Wheatley's verses as demonstrable evidence of her genius.[49] Local historian Rodney Field derived his information from Arms, the stories his grandmother told him, and his memories of conversations with Lucy's sons when he was a young boy. Field, who grew up in the Vermont town where Lucy died, also actively corresponded with other genealogists in Vermont and Massachusetts. Amateur historian George Sheldon, a Deerfield descendant of slave owners who relied on the oral history developed by Arms and Field, published an article, "Negro Slavery in Old New England" in 1893. Sheldon reprinted "Bars Fight" and inserted stories about Lucy Terry Prince in his article amidst information about blacks in Deerfield.[50]

These New England amateur historians garbled the family stories unintentionally and ended up making Lucy's husband seem less assertive than he really was. A couple of dubious anecdotes weighted the scales on Lucy's side. According to legend, Terry pleaded with the trustees of Williams College for three hours to have her son admitted to the school but was turned down because of racism. If she spoke without interruption for that length of time, she would have been the only American woman of her day to have done so. To be sure, Lucy's daughter was living as a servant in the home of a trustee of the College and she and Abijah were well acquainted with the founder of the school. However, two of Lucy's sons were in their thirties at the time she is alleged to have made her entreaty and her third son, although twenty-five at the time and of an age appropriate to attend college, had already married and moved to Glastonbury, Connecticut. There are strong reasons to doubt that such an event occurred. The letters of the first president of the college, the archives of the school, and the records of the trustees do not reveal any plea from Lucy.[51] Moreover, in her impassioned oratory Lucy would have had to make the case for an applicant who could not read the Greek or French required for admission. Sheldon's second inaccuracy came closer to the truth: Lucy had argued for her family's legal claims to land not before the

United States Supreme Court in 1796, as he claimed, but instead before the Vermont Supreme Court in 1803.

In defense of his property Abijah Prince spent many more days in courtrooms and attending town meetings in central Massachusetts and southern Vermont than his wife. Over the course of several decades he acquired the family's three parcels of land in Guilford and Sunderland, Vermont, and Northfield, Massachusetts; he had also hired a lawyer to take a man to court for cheating his son out of his wages. Abijah had financial acumen since he kept an accurate record of all his credits and debits in an account book. With his sons at his side he took the law into his own hands, retaliating against his wealthy neighbor across the road after an attack on his farm.

Yet the basic story remains as the local historians told it, a captured African girl becomes free, a wife, mother, legal advocate, and Christian, and reveals herself to be hungry for land, learning, and salvation. Like most other slaves in New England Lucy Terry's life began in Africa where she had been kidnapped at any early age and brought to New England, perhaps to Bristol, Rhode Island, or Boston, where she was sold at auction. She could not remember anything about her kin or the ship that brought her to a distant shore. In the new land she was purchased by Samuel Terry, Jr., a man of considerable means who planned to become a clergyman. He gave the young slave girl his surname—as was common among owners in New England at this time. Falling into debt Terry began liquidating his property, selling the young girl to a farmer and tavern owner in the frontier town of Deerfield, Massachusetts.[52]

Lucy grew to womanhood in the household of Ebenezer Wells and his wife Abigail. Like most slave owners in town, Ebenezer Wells was a self-described "gentleman," who had a good library, held a number of town offices, and belonged to the local church. Wells, like Samuel Terry, wanted a slave girl who could be raised properly to meet the family's exacting requirements. He and his wife may also have enjoyed having a young person in the house, since they were childless. Soldiers boarded in their home and men stopped at the tavern in their parlor for rum or cider after a day's work. Abigail and Ebenezer Wells needed a servant who could wait on their patrons, sweep, cook, make the beds, and do the washing for their boarders; Lucy was put to work at all those tasks and was also expected to sew, spin, tend the vegetable garden, do the washing and ironing, and help her mistress make the cheese.

As a child reared in the household of a religious family, Lucy Terry attended her master's congregation, the First Church of Christ in Deerfield. In Deerfield it was routine for enslaved children to be baptized as infants or as young children. Lucy, probably eleven years old at the time, was brought to the baptismal font by Ebenezer or Abigail Wells during the 1730s. Cesar, the other slave of Welles, was baptized at the same time and became a full church member, along with four other Deerfield slaves; Cesar, a religious man, also purchased a psalm book for himself at the local store.[53] Lucy became a full member of First Church in 1744 when she was about twenty years old, at a time of religious enthusiasm in the Valley.[54]

Most of Lucy's future life was intertwined with the freedom seeking, entrepreneurship, and litigiousness of her future husband, Abijah Prince, a former slave brought from Connecticut to Massachusetts by Benjamin and Lydia Doolittle. Prince was born in Africa around 1706 and like Lucy had been snatched from his relatives, never to see them again. Exactly how Abijah came to acquire his surname of Prince is not clear, although there were two ship captains near New Haven with that last name and Prince was a common New England surname.[55] His owner, Reverend Benjamin Doolittle of Wallingford, Connecticut, took a position as the minister of a congregation in Northfield, Massachusetts. Reverend Doolittle, a Yale alumnus and minister, had inadvertently brought his slave to a town which included abolitionist Christians, making the minister—who was not well liked to begin with—quite unpopular. Doolittle had at least three other jobs: minister to a second congregation at Fort Drummer, Vermont; part-time physician, with a practice extending as far as Springfield; and proprietor's clerk in a neighboring town. His Northfield congregation resented his long absences and what they considered his excessive demands for salary and firewood, especially in light of his other sources of income.[56]

The Great Awakening, which kindled religious fires across the entire Connecticut River Valley, also ignited abolitionist sentiments among Doolittle's congregation.[57] The families of Northfield were fairly wealthy but there was only one other slaveholder in town.[58] Seized by the moral imperatives of their faith, twenty of Doolittle's parishioners, including several church deacons, denounced him as a greedy slaveholder and urged him to emancipate Abijah. One of them lambasted Doolittle so blisteringly in private for owning a slave that he could not think of a reply. Doolittle's congregation did not oppose slavery simply on moral grounds, but also thought it made Yankees lazy, unable to do their own menial work. Black people in bondage, they held, were cheap labor who threatened hard-working free white men. The dispute grew so heated that the Hampshire ministerial association, including the noted minister Jonathan Edwards from nearby Northampton, was called in to mediate. Edwards drafted a statement of compromise, arguing that the real grievous sin was not slave ownership, which after all brought Africans to Christianity, but rather the slave trade, which he saw as an immoral means of stealing human beings from their families. The controversy died down and Doolittle retained his position; while mending a fence in his yard one day, he felt a sharp pain in his breast and dropped dead of a heart attack.[59]

Lydia Doolittle, the minister's widow, inherited her husband's slave Abijah at his death. He had her permission to hire himself out, probably with the assumption that he could keep part of his earnings and she would receive the rest. During King George's War between the English and the French Deerfield commanders were desperate for recruits, whom they enticed with the offer of a lump sum payment at the end of their service. Abijah returned from the war but apparently without enough money to buy his freedom outright from Lydia Doolittle. Instead he persuaded a weaver in Northfield he had known many years to purchase him from Doolittle, with the understanding that he could buy his freedom from this man, but at a price lower than Lydia Doolittle would have asked. Abijah returned to Northfield in time to qualify for the town's offer of unimproved land to male residents. He then moved to Northampton, a larger town with a more sizable black community, and boarded with a young black couple while he worked for a hatter and church deacon.[60]

For almost ten years Abijah took various odd jobs but remained a bachelor. It seems that Abijah had his own priorities—freedom, land, then marriage and children. He selected as his bride an enslaved woman in Deerfield whom he must have seen grow from a girl into a woman. Many free black men took an enslaved wife and lived separately, visiting her at her master's quarters. Abijah did not want to father children born into slavery; he waited until he had a chance to buy the freedom of his bride. As for Lucy there were a few black men who lived in town or passed through and although Abijah was not young, he was healthy, free, literate, honest, hard working, and had no bad habits.

Lucy prepared for her marriage in a manner similar to white girls of her age. Like many slaves and free blacks in Deerfield and in other small New England towns she had a small account at the local store.[61] Purchasing a thimble and pins she sewed her trousseau, buying about 1/8 yard of cambric, a fine linen cloth used for making underwear, ruffles, a handkerchief, yards of trim, some ribbon, and for a treat to serve her suitor, a "cake of chocolat."[62] Wells allowed Lucy to spin or otherwise hire herself out so that she could accumulate credits in her store account and assemble some of the goods she would need for housekeeping. Abijah Prince was also making preparations for his marriage, purchasing items at the store with proceeds from the salmon he caught and buying fabric, which Lucy may have used to sew him a shirt. By reenlisting in the militia Abijah earned a second lump sum, large enough so that he could purchase Lucy's freedom. They sealed their bargain in a familiar way; Lucy was one month pregnant at the time of her wedding in May of 1756; she and Abijah settled into a cabin on the outskirts of town, tenants of Ebenezer Wells, awaiting the birth of their first child.[63]

The couple displayed all the qualities of thrift and industry expected of Yankee farmers. Abijah hired himself out to Reverend Jonathan Ashley and was paid with the use of two of Ashley's slaves, Cato and Titus. These men helped him plow in the fall, plant in the spring, thrash wheat, dress flax, cut wood, slaughter hogs, and tap trees for maple sugar. Like most slaves in Deerfield Cato and Titus were often hired out, sometimes to farmers as far away as Greenfield. Abijah bought a small boat, which he used to ferry men, livestock, and supplies up and down the Connecticut River. Lucy matched her husband in industry to bring in extra income by spinning. Some owners gave a former slave woman a spinning wheel so she could make extra income. As a married woman Lucy no longer had a separate account at the country store but instead charged goods in her husband's name.[64]

Lucy and Abijah also conformed to the racial mores of the "river gods," as the slave-owning gentry of the Connecticut Valley were called. The names they chose for their six children reflected the highly unusual Biblical names or ironic choice of the names of Roman emperors owners liked to select for their slaves.[65] Abijah and Lucy named their sons and daughters Cesar, Duroxsa, Drusillla, Festus, Tatnai, and Abijah. Cesar was a common name among slaves in New England, including that of the other slave in the Wells household, but as the name of a Roman emperor also represented a kind of ironic mocking of the slave's decidedly unimperial status. They named their oldest daughter Duroxsa after the daughter of Herod, the Roman governor of Judea at the time of Jesus. Drusilla was a female version of a Roman clan name in the New Testament. They called their second son Festus after the Roman governor described in Acts who placed the Apostle Paul on trial. The third son, Tatnai, was named for a Persian governor who, at the command of Darius, assisted Jews in rebuilding the temple. They named their youngest son Abijah after his father, a common practice among Deerfield residents, slave or free.[66]

Naming a boy for a Roman emperor was something the local gentry of the Valley liked to do. On the street in Deerfield where Lucy grew up were five slaves named Cesar and one Titus.[67] Most other emancipated slaves selected English names for their children and a few stubbornly refused to give up their African day names. Slaves also resisted their masters by insisting on retaining their African names, seeking to retain their African identity. For example, Quasho, a newly imported slave from Africa living in Plymouth, defied his owner who wanted to call him Julius Caesar.[68] Quite a few free blacks saw taking new first or last names as one of their first opportunities to shed the stigma of slavery. However, Abijah and Lucy were concerned with practical, not symbolic matters; they thought of themselves as Christian Yankee property owners who saw no reason to challenge the cultural practices of their neighbors in the naming of their children or in hiring slave labor.

After two decades in Deerfield Lucy and Abijah were ready to move to their own farm. To the north of Deerfield lay a vast green wilderness of Indian land being carved up for development by the Crown. Proprietors, as the designated owners of options on land were called, were granted huge tracts of territory with the promise that they could keep one hundred acres for every five they improved. Abijah's militia officer in King George's War, Elijah Williams, received a vast tract of undeveloped property in Vermont but did not have the time to clear it. With the pay he received from Elijah Williams Abijah took out a mortgage on one of Williams's hundred-acre plots. From spring to the end of summer Abijah was in Guilford felling trees, moving boulders of rock, draining the swamp, and fencing his property. Perhaps with the help of his son he was able to build a house and erect the outbuildings at his farm. With war looming, he and Lucy, their daughters and sons moved to their own place.[69]

In Guilford they found that their wealthy white neighbor, John Noyes, wanted them to leave. Noyes was faced with the prospect of two black neighbors, Abijah across the way and Darby, a man from Connecticut, next to Abijah. The first racial incident was that one of Noyes's male relatives assaulted Abijah's two young sons, Tatnai and Abijah. The next year his men broke down the gates of the Princes' farm, cut down a dozen of their trees, and set loose his cows and pigs to destroy their crops; Abijah retaliated by letting his livestock graze on Noyes' crops. Abijah engaged a lawyer, suing Noyes and his male relatives for the assault on his sons; Noyes countersued for the damage Abijah's livestock inflicted on his crops. Meanwhile, perhaps afraid that living in Guilford was untenable or to secure patrimony for his sons, Abijah returned to Northfield to press his option to purchase a small parcel of town land. That opportunity, however, had vanished in a wave of speculation by the town, but officials in Northfield decided Abijah had not received notice of the sale of his land option and offered him instead a cash settlement in lieu of his right to buy land from the town.[70]

As the dispute with Noyes escalated, Abijah's lawyer may have encouraged him to appeal to the Governor and his Council in Norwich, the state capitol of Vermont. Abijah remained in Guilford while Lucy traveled to Norwich to press the family's case. The opening of the fall session of the Vermont state legislature was an impressive pageant Lucy witnessed, as she waited five days before she could present her petition to the Governor and his Council. The petition emphasized that the Prince family was "greatly oppressed & injured" by John Noyes and his brother Amos.[71] The Governor and his Council were sympathetic; they decided to write to the selectmen of the town of Guilford asking them to protect the Princes from being harassed by the Noyes family, investigate the dispute, and reach an equitable settlement.

Lucy was known for her eloquence since the days she had first sung her ballad, but it had always been Abijah who had taken the family's case to court, with Lucy and her sons serving as witnesses. The demeanor of a petitioner to the Governor, such as Hagar Wright or Lucy Pernam, was supposed to be humble, not argumentative. [72] Abijah at eighty may have been too old to travel to Norwich or may have elected to remain in Guilford to protect their home and crops.[73] Although the Governor and his Council believed that the Princes were the injured parties, they also wanted to prevent them from becoming dependent on public charity.[74] Despite the warning he received from the state three months later John Noyes hired young thugs armed with clubs who broke down the door of the Prince home, beat their black hired man, and burned their hayricks. The family escaped without injury but their crops were destroyed. The state of Vermont sided with Lucy and Abijah and prosecuted the young men for trespass. Lucy, Abijah, and their son Abijah, Jr., testified at a series of trials about the assaults, which the state won. Nonetheless, they could not hold onto the biggest prize of all; Abijah's crops failed and he had to sell his land in Guilford. He and his family were extended the standard right of the elderly—a right to remain on their land as tenants for another eight years.

At home on the farm he had developed out of the wilderness Abijah died in his eighty-eighth year and was buried on his own land.[75] The savvy farmer who had hired his own lawyer and often went to court had made no will. Intestacy was a common occurrence among black men: nine out of ten black men with probated estates in western Massachusetts in the 1840s died intestate, four times the rate for white men in the area. Still, Abijah had shown himself well acquainted with the law and eager to protect his right to his property. Perhaps he was satisfied with the rules of intestacy, but if that was so, it means that he was also content to leave his widow as the economic dependent of her adult sons. A probate court in Brattleboro added Festus as a second executor alongside Lucy, thus, reducing Lucy's status to that of a coequal with her oldest boy.[76]

Festus and his brother took charge of the family's quest for land after their father's death. They asserted a more than thirty-year-old claim to a small parcel of land and options to purchase additional acres in nearby Sunderland. Back in the 1760s, the speculators who developed Sunderland assessed proprietors exorbitant taxes for the paving of roads. Abijah had never received notices of the tax he owed, and his land and rights to purchase additional land had been quickly sold and resold without his knowledge. His sons brought suit in Sunderland claiming that their father's estate retained ownership of the land because the town had not properly notified their father that he was delinquent in paying his taxes. Lucy at age seventy-nine traveled to Norwich once again to argue the family's claim before the Vermont Supreme Court.[77] The Court offered her monetary compensation but did not restore her right to her land. Not content with this settlement Lucy appeared before the Sunderland town meeting and was threatening to bring another suit. After listening to her plea Sunderland voters decided to grant Lucy and her heirs eighteen acres in town and build her a house on it, thus ending the family's eight-year legal battle.[78]

Living out her remaining years in Sunderland, Lucy rode horseback over the Green Mountains to Guilford once a year to see friends and visit Abijah's grave.[79] At her death at age ninety-seven she was praised for an "assemblage of qualities" and revered as a community elder. *The Franklin Herald*, the *Vermont Gazette*, and the Greenfield, Massachusetts, newspaper remembered her fondly. The obituary in the *Franklin Herald* of August 21, 1821, stated, "Her volubility was exceeded by none, and in general the fluency of her speech was not destitute of instruction and education. She was much respected among her acquaintance, who treated her with a degree of deference."[80] Whatever condescension betrayed in the first sentence of the obituary was balanced by its length and its praise for a woman whose life was "devoted to the service of God." Suitable respect was shown at her internment as Reverend Lemuel Haynes, the first ordained black minister in America, delivered the funeral sermon. The son of a black father and a white mother, he had been raised by a white family, fought in the revolution, and served a white congregation in Manchester. If defense of land had been stronger in Lucy's vocabulary than abolitionism, it was more than made up for by the fiery tone of Haynes's funeral oration. He used his sermon as an opportunity to launch a blistering attack on the Missouri Compromise as an unholy bargain with the slaveholding South.[81]

A third woman of property, Chloe Spear of Boston, resembled Lucy Terry Prince more than Lucy Pernam in that her marriage was long lasting and, if not affectionate, at least based on mutual regard. She pursued a landowning strategy in the city, where land had to be acquired with cash. Although it can be said that Chloe Spear accepted patriarchy and the racial etiquette of postwar Boston, she also possessed determination, entrepreneurial spirit, and ambition. *The Memoir of Mrs. Chloe Spear, A Native of Africa, who was Enslaved in Childhood, and Died in Boston*, whose author was an anonymous white woman, was published in Boston in 1832. It merged the abolitionist narrative of being stolen from relatives in slavery, the Christian story of spiritual rebirth, with the rags-to-riches tale of "personal effort" to "rise in the world" through the purchase of real estate. Like many subsequent slave narratives, the *Memoir* focused on being denied the right to read and write and the quest for schooling as part of seeking freedom. It portrayed the horror

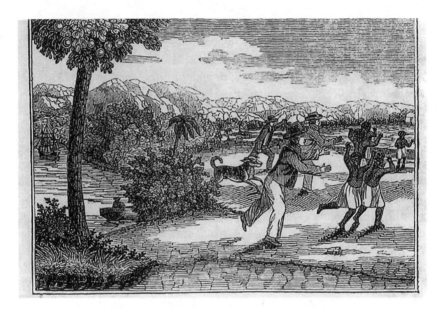

2.1. Chloe and Her Playmates Taken Captive by the Slave-Dealers. Illustrations of the West African slave trade, such as this frontispiece that adorned *The Memoir of Mrs. Chloe Spear* (1831) appeared regularly in newspapers, journals, or pamphlets. Abolitionist whites in New England hung engravings of the capture of slaves on their parlor walls. It was important that the slave dealers were well dressed men, wearing hats to reveal that true gentility came from right principles, not from appropriate dress

of the Middle Passage, replete with the "piteous cries and tears of these poor defenceless children" and "terrifying weeping victims packed on board the floating prison."[82] Chloe Spear defined freedom in several ways: spiritual freedom through baptism, communion, and membership in a church; personal freedom through manumission; and freedom to learn; property ownership was a form of freedom connected to all the others.

The anonymous white female author of *The Memoir of Chloe Spear* called herself a Lady of Boston, but revealed two telling details about herself: that she belonged to the same Baptist church as Chloe Spear and lived near her neighborhood.[83] A copy of the memoir lists Mary Webb, the daughter of a bookbinder who supported herself by taking paid positions with various benevolent societies, as the author.[84] Webb dedicated her life to Baptist missionary work among Indians in the United States and the people of India and other foreign countries. At about age five she suffered from a mysterious illness and became a paraplegic who for the rest of her life had to be carried when she was unable to maneuver in a wheelchair.[85] In her early thirties Webb founded the first women's missionary society in the world, an organization of Baptist and Congregational women, and two years later, started a second women's missionary organization for Baptists. She was director of the Sunday school of her church and established a separate Sunday school for black children, which white women of abolitionist sympathies saw as an important effort on their part to promote black education. Black children as well as adults eagerly attended such schools where they learned their catechism, listened to Bible stories, and were taught to read and write. Webb, who had overcome enormous handicaps in her own life, could easily identify with a Christian sister who had surmounted her own tragedies.[86]

By the 1830s abolitionist publishers were seeking inspirational articles about black heroes geared for adult readers and stories especially written for children. The *Liberator* reprinted Wheatley's poems and a Boston abolitionist printer issued a biography of Spear. Two years later a Boston press published a biography of Phillis Wheatley, written by a grandniece of her former mistress along with a children's biography of Wheatley, the first of many generations of children's biographies about black heroes. When the *Memoir* first appeared, the *Liberator* gave it a full page review, and reprinted the illustration, "Chloe and her playmates taken captive by the Slave Dealer." The paper also carried ads for the *Memoir* for sale at an abolitionist bookstore in downtown Boston. The story was compelling enough that the standard children's magazine of the day with no clear abolitionist ties, *The Youth's Companion,* reprinted it in its entirety.[87] Webb had wanted Sunday schools in the U.S. to buy the book and use it as instructional material for children, hoping that American sales would subsidize its distribution among Baptist missionaries in Africa. She also hoped her book would serve as inspirational reading for children being taught to read the Holy Scriptures.[88] The *Memoir* included a couple of details especially interesting to juvenile readers: a tale that Chloe was taken captive when playing with her friends and that one of the great losses she suffered was in being separated from a companion to whom she had become so attached on board the slave ship.

All stories published during the antebellum age involving the creative faculty of slaves or their suffering in bondage seemed to require some kind of attestation of authenticity. Affixing a white imprimatur to a black voice created the irony of a document of freedom circumscribed and dependent on a stamp of approval from white authorities.[89] Composed seventeen years after the subject's death, the anonymous author of the *Memoir* provided verification of the details of Chloe Spear's life in two ways. The first was by dialect speech (the author said she spoke in broken English) interspersed with elements to suggest authenticity—"she said" as well as sentimentality: "she sighed." The author added verification with phrases such as "according to the statement from her own lips to the writer."[90] The author also proved the accuracy of her account by quoting from Spear's manumission certificate and an article written about her at the time of her death.[91]

Other documents in Boston corroborate the details of the *Memoir*. Chloe Spear had been owned by Captain Bradford (referred to in the memoir as Mr. B), a mariner and one of the less prominent members of a family that could trace its origins to Governor Bradford of Plymouth Colony.[92] Cesar Spear was the slave of a cooper, that is, a barrel maker, in the same neighborhood. His owner had faced considerable pressure from abolitionist whites to emancipate his slaves during the war; he did so reluctantly and not before threatening to sell one of his truant slaves.[93] In 1798 the Spears paid $700 for half of a three-story newly built house with a small yard on White Bread Alley in the North End of Boston. The deed was in both names: "Ceasar Spear of Boston aforesaid Cooper and Cloe his wife" but even so, Chloe Spear did not have an enforceable right to the property separate from her husband.[94] In 1800 the Boston Overseers of the Poor placed an indentured servant with them, a girl who was "to learn housewifery, reading, writing, and ciphering." It was assumed that Chloe Spear would teach the girl to read or send her to the Sunday school Webb ran for instruction.[95] Chloe Spear survived her husband by nine years; whereas once she had sat in the balcony of the church, at her death she owned her own pew on the ground floor of Second Baptist.[96]

At her death in 1815 Spear was memorialized in five obituaries in Boston newspapers and in a biography of her by her minister published in a Baptist missionary magazine.[97] Filled with the usual praise for a woman of deep piety, her minister's account also mentioned that she spent weeks out of town attending religious revivals and had been something of a church shopper, choosing an experimental church in the North End before deciding upon the First Baptist and leaving it for Second Baptist. Chloe Spear also had died the wealthiest black woman of her day, leaving an estate of about $1500; the things she acquired in life were mentioned only in passing—her beds, bedding, and table linen. Instead her will reflected her values—an inheritance for her grandson, money left for black friends who belonged to Second Baptist, and funds for poor relief at the church and for the Baptist missionary society. Before her death she gave money to her minister; the will is completely consistent with Webb's characterization of Spear—in fact, Webb included a copy of it in the *Memoir*.[98]

Webb wrote within a particular genre, abolitionist juvenile literature, which invariably portrayed an edenic Africa and a child robbed or stolen from tender parents, but was a bit more didactic than adult nonfiction in making clear the moral lessons a pious life offered. The format was not a straightjacket, however, and would have certainly allowed for a few details about Spear as a mother. For some reason, Webb did not portray Chloe Spear as a grieving mother, bereft at the loss of her children. Instead, her sons and daughters are mentioned twice and quite briefly. Cesar Spear is more of a presence than her children, although not a highly esteemed one. In 1787 he was one of a small group of black men in Boston, many of whom were Freemasons, who presented a petition to the Massachusetts state legislature for the state to fund emigration of local blacks to return to Africa. The men who signed the petition seemed embittered and alienated, describing themselves "in many respects, in very disagreeable and disadvantageous circumstances; most of which must attend us, as long as we and our children live in America." [99] Nonetheless, like most advocates of emigration, he remained in the United States and prospered. Cesar Spear, along with Prince Hall and another black man, was trusted enough for his financial acumen to be named one of three executors of the will of a deceased lodge member. [100] Since black men prior to the war had usually chosen white men of standing as executors of their estates, Spear's designation was a sign of the respect in which he was held by a brother Mason as well as evidence of his long and close association with the black community leader, Prince Hall. In sum, there is evidence that Cesar Spear was regarded by his fellow lodge brothers as prudent, responsible, and fiscally competent.

Is the relatively unflattering portrait of Cesar Spear in the *Memoir* a fair representation of his wife's views or those of Mary Webb? In the 1830s several white abolitionist women wrote biographies or memoirs of black women in New England in which the subjects were portrayed as women who preferred not to marry or their husbands were presented in a negative light. The gender dynamics of black autobiography or memoir were predictable: men rarely devoted more than a sentence to their wives and the memoirs of black women written by white women similarly repaid the favor by giving men little attention, and what they received was somewhat unfavorable. Certainly in the *Memoir* Cesar Spear is pictured as an easily fooled helpmate unworthy of his wife since "he possessed none of the refinement, or economy, for which his companion was remarkable." [101] At his death Chloe Spear "did not make a display of grief, and pretend that she had lost one of the best husbands, as is the case with some persons after their friends are dead, but who were not very ardently attached to them while they lived." [102]

There could have been specific reasons why Webb took Chloe Spear's side. She was a committed evangelical, whereas Cesar Spear had belonged to the Freemasons, whom Baptists held to be almost as secular as atheists. If Mary Webb had not already reached unfavorable conclusions about Cesar Spear, it is equally likely that she was repeating the sentiments of Chloe Spear. He had preferred a wife more fashionable than the practical, unfashionable wife "rather above the common size" he had married; while he socialized with his friends in Boston, perhaps his fellow lodge members, she liked to spend weeks attending revivals outside of Boston. Then, too, temperate Baptists probably frowned upon the drunken feasts for which lodges were widely known.

The Memoir presents patriarchy as a system easily circumvented by a clever wife, with great benefit for the entire family. Chloe Spear manages to maneuver easily around her husband's requests but to do so she cannot be forthcoming or completely transparent. Wanting his wife to dress more stylishly Cesar Spear gave her money to purchase a silk gown "like udder colour women" but instead she bought a "cheap" and "comfortable" dress. Discovering that Chloe still had no fashionable clothes he gave her funds a second time to buy a silk gown, which she used to purchase another cheap frock. Cesar Spear did not ask for an accounting of the funds he offered, nor did he expect his wife to buy her own silk gowns even though she had her own earnings as a laundress.[103]

Chloe Spear deceived her husband about her savings as part of a strategy to acquire income-producing real estate. She knew that the property she wanted to buy had to be purchased by her husband "cause he de *head*."[104] She scouted out a house but it was Cesar who had to approve the purchase. When she told him she found a suitable half of a house in the North End she wanted to buy, he laughed and asked how much it cost. After Cesar Spear told Chloe he did not have the money for the purchase she replied that she had enough savings to do so. Disbelieving at first, Cesar Spear, not upset about his wife's secret cache of funds or discovering that his gifts had not led to the purchase of silk gowns, instead "was pleased, and very readily agreed to the purchase...."[105] After they bought the house Chloe Spear proposed a way to increase their cash flow. She told Cesar that they could occupy the least attractive rooms and rent out the rest, using rental income to fix up one room at a time and then raising the rent on each.[106]

Cesar Spear was the head of the household, and his wife was his economic dependent, even if she had the big plans, made her own income, and seemed to keep (some) of her money separate from his. The gender division of labor in their home reveals the dynamics of power in their marriage. During the day Chloe Spear worked for Boston families as a laundress but returned home by the evening to cook dinner for her husband and the boarders. Then she washed and ironed well into the night, "while her husband was taking his rest."[107] If anything, the *Memoir* underestimated the laundry work she did at home since it is likely she was also making the soap she used to do her washing. Her husband took on something of the female role during the day while she was at work, cooking lunch for the boarders. No one expected him to do the laundry or help with it, since it was considered his wife's domain. Who then resented Cesar getting a good night's sleep—his wife or her memoirist? At any rate, Chloe Spear slept little; in the evening after she came home from work she made "ready a good supper" and prepared breakfast for her husband before leaving for work. The point of view of the *Memoir* is that when Chloe cooked dinner or breakfast at home, she was performing the gender role expected of a dutiful black wife, engaged in a strategic gesture to reassure her husband that he was the head of the household. Nonetheless, she found it necessary to keep secrets from him until she was ready with her fait accompli.

In addition to deferential behavior toward her husband, Chloe Spear also engaged in courteous, perhaps even reverential, behavior toward white Christian women—and more than likely, the two sorts of gestures were related. In both cases, however, she altered her initial pose. At first when white religious women visited they sat at her ebony tea table but she did not join them; at their invitation she began to pull up her chair to the table, crossing a racial boundary to achieve social integration.[108] White women were willing to visit her house in her North End neighborhood, known for its "Nymphs Negroes e&c" because of their respect for her. Years later Chloe Spear seemed to feel guilty about the pleasure she derived from entertaining her white women guests.[109] Another white woman member of her church relayed her own anecdote about Spear in her dying days. She had been extremely grateful to the black women neighbors who were taking care of her. As she approached her end she regretted that she had made an "idol" of the wealthy white women who had come to visit, setting "them up above the neighbor and the colored friend."[110] However gratifying it had been to entertain her visitors at her tea table she found that when she needed it most her greatest support came from females of her own race.

The stories of these three marriages reveal the strength of principles of patriarchy and respectability, even among women we would consider quite independent. Their marriages were patriarchal in terms of beliefs, legal principles, and the gendered division of labor, despite the economic contributions these wives made to their households. Certainly Lucy Pernam did not enjoy greater independence and authority in her marriage because she sold provisions—such a woman, it turns out, was beaten, driven from her home, sold into slavery, and denied custody of her child. Scipio Pernam controlled his wife's major financial assets and used physical violence to control her. Far from sensing that his masculinity was imperiled because his wife earned her way, Scipio Pernam believed that slavery had made the black married woman independent and self-reliant, so that she did not require her husband's support. It was Lucy who upheld the position that her work history did not in any way disqualify her for alimony and that a black husband, like a white one, should shoulder the responsibility for providing for his dependents. In

Lucy Pernam's divorce the Massachusetts Governor and his council affirmed this view. Nor did Scipio Pernam's neighbors in Newburyport believe that female wage earning somehow granted women autonomy from the control of a husband or town officials.

Equally problematic is the idea of unalloyed female independence as applied to Lucy Terry Prince. Superficially the word seems appropriate for a woman who appeared before the Vermont Governor and his Council, the State Supreme Court, and the Sunderland town meeting. Yet Lucy was also a dependent who remained in Deerfield while her husband improved their land in Guilford and lost her own store account when she married; as a widow she was not the sole executor of her husband's estate but instead a co-executor with her adult son. In her marriage there was a clear gender division of labor, with Abijah responsible for keeping the financial accounts and the labor of the home and farm divided by gender. It seems useful to distinguish between industry in a shared enterprise and fiscal competence and responsibility, which were her husband's domain.

Abijah spoke for the family in legal dealings with the larger world except at the end of his life. In securing land, going to the courts, or seeking revenge against his neighbors, he took the initiative, and his wife and sons followed his lead. If not making a will was simply a failure to plan, it still had the result of leaving Lucy halfway between dependence and independence. Thus, of these three women, Chloe Spear who never argued a case before a court still appears the most independent—as well as the most manipulative. She came and went freely, spending weeks out of town at revivals, but also adopted the belief that limited disclosure of one's savings or spending to one's husband was the best marital strategy. A wife who did not allow her husband to play the part of the master of his house, she seemed to believe, was not very clever. She kept her own wages but also kept secrets from her husband. Engaging in subterfuge, she did not want to challenge Cesar Spear's authority, ordained by God and law.[111] Unlike Lucy Terry Prince, however, she received all of the couple's property when her husband died. Although Abijah Prince was the savvy and litigious entrepreneur, it was actually Cesar Spear who made the most thorough financial plans in the event of his death and trusted his wife the most.

In a society so concerned with vice and virtue, reputation—that is, the regard in which one was held by others—was a form of property, of great value. Two of these women were good wives married to good husbands, regarded by members of their communities as respectable Christians. Lucy Pernam, by contrast, was a bad wife married to a respectable man. However much she may have been cheated out her property her husband and her neighbors looked on her as threatening and immoral. A wife was bad not simply because she violated curfew, threatened her neighbors, swore, and seemed to be a prostitute, but also because she was a woman who refused to willingly submit to her husband's authority. Similarly, a husband who supported his infant and his elderly mother was reputable, even a long-suffering family man. Lucy Pernam's neighbors may have come to her aid when she appeared bloodied at their door but most of them were sympathetic to her husband. New England judges did not simply endorse this notion of reputation, however, awarding a separation with alimony to a bad wife condemned by so many of her white neighbors.

Respectability was a concept equally applied to interracial relationships, especially the efforts of black men and women to win esteem and regard among whites as a means of securing their place in society. Chloe Spear in her last days turned to her black women neighbors to care for her, bolster her pillows, and listen to her stories; she had begun to doubt the importance of placing so much stock in the regard of white women. Having lived by the belief that respectability was a suitable goal, her statements at the end of her life suggest that she had decided such a strategy lacked sufficient racial consciousness. Taking pleasure in the social calls of white Christian women, she concluded, had been a sin. Her black women neighbors, she finally decided, had been the most steadfast of friends, teaching her the true meaning of Christian charity.

3

Spiritual Thirsting

Even before emancipation, a few masters paid for their slaves to receive private instruction in reading and writing and an occasional slave or black indentured servant attended the town school. The *Memoir*, a personal and spiritual narrative, also described Chloe Spear's quest for education as well as religious enlightenment.[1] When she was thirteen years old, her master refused her request to send her to a schoolmistress so she could learn how to read. Unwilling to give up she bought a condensed version of the Bible to teach herself the alphabet. Discovering her with book in hand her master threatened to hang her by both thumbs and deliver a severe whipping because "it made negroes saucy to know how to read." She persisted in studying her Bible and found the effort well worthwhile. Psalm 25:1 was providential: "Plead my cause, O Lord, with them that strive with me: fight against them that fight against me." Psalm 71:4 spoke to her greatest hope, "Deliver me, O my God, out of the hand of the wicked, out of the hand of the unrighteous and cruel man." The Bible as a source of moral wisdom was ambiguous as to the status of the institution of slavery; passages from it could be cited to uphold the will of masters or subvert it; yet invariably enslaved girls and women selected portions that spoke to their identity as exiles from their homeland, spiritual friends with Jesus and freedom seekers.[2]

New England's slaves were not merely attracted to Christianity but to one specific form of it, evangelical Protestantism. Probably the key defining features of evangelical Christianity was a belief that the individual could experience God's saving grace by undergoing a spiritual rebirth.[3] An occasional Catholic priest wandered into Boston and was rumored to be saying mass but there was no Catholic church in Boston until 1788. Most New England Jews were merchant families living in Newport or New Haven; there is no record of slaves of Jewish owners or any free blacks joining the Truro synagogue;

no males other than those of Sephardic heritage were circumcised. Blacks showed up at Quaker meetings when they knew that a Friend, perhaps from out of town, was going to speak out against the slave trade. On a regular basis, however, black women and men sought eternal salvation through evangelical Protestant Christianity both because the style of worship bore some resemblance to African practice and because they preferred to listen to dynamic preachers. In the process of conversion they could testify about their personal experience of captivity and loss and they felt welcomed by the message that the meek shall inherit the earth. The Holy Spirit stirred to life most visibly in two major religious revivals in the eighteenth century, the first in the 1740s, the second in the 1760s; in ordinary times Christian ministers spoke words of comfort to grieving mothers, and in the extraordinary era of the American Revolution Phillis Wheatley understood, as did many others, that slavery was a violation of Christian beliefs and assumed that those who committed the sin of slavery would not be admitted to heaven. In sum, the path of black women's Christianity begins with an implicit understanding of the freedom implied in their faith and leads to an explicit statement of it during the Revolution.

From Christianity black women acquired two different but compatible ideas of freedom, the equality of souls and the importance of respectability among committed Christians as proof of their adherence to Christian religious beliefs. Christianity also offered clear definitions of gender roles; it prohibited women from speaking in public, becoming ministers, and preaching to men, and it was used to justify the subordination of women—and slaves. Black women often correctly apprehended these mixed messages of Christianity. To be sure, central and West Africans had their own spiritual traditions, moral code, and rules for proper conduct, but these did not include a concept of sin, of heaven and hell, or of the Devil. It was the moral power to condemn sin—power held by women as well as men—that was unique to evangelical Christianity. Like many other believers, Phillis Wheatley employed this power to point out the hypocrisy of Christians who professed a love of freedom while keeping their fellow human beings in bondage; true repentance for sin could only come with the manumission of slaves. She believed that the god she worshipped would turn against the Patriot's cause if they continued to hold their fellow human beings in bondage. Because of Wheatley's fame, a letter she wrote stating these views was reprinted in many New England newspapers, and during the revolutionary period it constituted her entry into ongoing debates in the region about the incompatibility of Christianity and slavery.

Many of the Africans kidnapped from Angola had converted to Catholicism before they were herded onto ships destined for the West Indies; those few who were brought to New England quickly figured out that the colonists detested Catholics and feared conspiracies of the Pope. Nothing was to be gained from practicing the Catholic faith or praying to a saint or the Virgin Mary and much to be lost from owning up to having been baptized a Catholic. Savvy operators like Sebastian Kane (and presumably his wife Grace) converted to the Protestant faith of their neighbors. Whether the decidedly different form of worship of the Puritans appealed to former Catholics is an open question. As the slave trade shifted northward along the African coast, the number of African Catholics fell sharply. Protestant missionary work in this region did not begin in earnest until the 1760s. The war captives and the abducted brought from West Africa did not believe in monotheism, although there were a few Muslims who knew Arabic and could read the Koran; most worshipped hundreds of minor gods as well as one major deity, thus combining polytheism and monotheism in a manner repulsive to Christians.[4]

Quite a few Africans who had not been Christianized in Africa saw no particular incentive in converting to the Protestant faith in New England, in part because many of their owners were opposed to their religious conversion. In addition, many Africans discerned a considerable number of unappealing features in Christian worship. Usually the sermons preached to them emphasized the importance of obedience and faithfulness of servants to masters.[5] In their first years after arrival in New England Africans who did not speak English well may not have understood the sermon. Their attention may have wandered during the hour-long sermon as well as the two required services on Sunday, one in the morning, the other in the afternoon. Women servants looking after the master's children were the only black people who occupied the family pew, there to quiet the children. Since churches were unheated white women often brought foot warmers to ward off the cold; black congregants would not have had any in the balcony where they sat with other black women (and black men were seated separately from the women on opposite sides of the balcony). Ministers usually referred to black people as "poor Negroes" and sometimes "dark souls"; some offered catechism to blacks with the white children, since all groups were seen as operating on the same religious plane. One could not fail to notice that ministers offered communion to blacks not during the service but after its conclusion.[6] Cotton Mather managed to imply a belief in the lesser intellectual ability of blacks in devising two catechisms for black Christians, one for those of "smaller capacity" and another for those of "bigger capacity." The records of First Baptist Church in Providence noted "Colored" next to the name of black members of the congregation, thus designating and defining by race members who should have been united in their faith.[7]

Even so, there was a long tradition of black interest in Christian teaching and of acceptance of blacks into New England Protestant churches. According to John Winthrop the first black in New England who converted to Christianity in 1641 was a woman, the unnamed slave of Rev. John Stoughton of Dorchester whom he baptized.[8] In these early years baptism was not merely initiation into the faith but an attempt to gain freedom since at this time it was believed that a slave who was baptized should be manumitted. In another possible bid for freedom, a mother who herself had been a long-time member of Boston's First Church brought her son for baptism about a decade later.[9]

The most fervent and devoted religious converts in Protestant New England were women who by the middle of the seventeenth century formed the majority of church members. There are a few clues to this pattern among blacks as well as whites. A godly church woman, Sarah Osborn of Newport, held Sunday evening meetings at her home attended solely by slaves in town. In 1766 she noted that thirty-five black women and forty-five black men were present at one of these Sunday evening meetings. However, black men may have had more permission to move about on the Sabbath, with black women expected to return to the master's home by sundown. The extant records from the First Baptist Church of Providence from 1775 to 1800 show that more than three out of five black members were female. The majority of the founding members of the first black church in New England, the African Baptist in Boston, established in 1805, were women.[10] On balance, it seems likely that black women were the more religiously committed members of the race.

Still, joining a church does not reveal the full extent of black commitment to Christianity because many blacks attended white churches without becoming members and met separately in their own religious meetings.[11] The separate meeting, called the Negro society, was held for two hours on Sunday evenings when slaves were given a day of rest and were allowed to move about; it was both a separate black service and a slave institution that enforced Christian discipline. White churches expelled errant members for drunkenness or sexual sin, and restored those who showed repentance. Negro societies operated according the same principle, except that blacks themselves were imposing the punishments. Cotton Mather, the noted Puritan minister in Boston, held such meetings for slaves as early as 1693 and twelve years later wrote his pamphlet, *The Negro Christianized*, hoping that others would adopt the system of religious instruction he had devised. The "rules for the society of Negroes" in Boston clearly distinguish between Mather, referred to as "the minister of God" and the members of the society (as in "our meeting"). The sins that were punished tipped the scale in favor of the control of masters over their slaves—no drunkenness, swearing, cursing, lying, stealing, or disobedience to masters; members of the society also swore not to shelter fugitive slaves. Nonetheless, it was the Society, not Mather, who punished errant members: "if any of our Number fall into Sin…we will *Admonish him*." No church societies at this time granted women the power of punishment; therefore, Christian male converts at the Negro societies were temporarily expelling known sinners, taking on the role of moral arbiters of their people.[12]

The First Great Awakening of the 1740s made Christianity more interdenominational, exciting, and democratic and thus more appealing to black women and men. It involved highly emotional preaching and intense religious expression that attracted new converts and fanned religious embers among those whose faith had flickered. The root cause of the Awakening was imperial rivalry with Catholic France, which stoked fears that devout Protestants had to experience a renewal of their faith to stave off the Catholic threat. Newspapers and books spread the word that the religiously faithful sensed the Holy Spirit loose in the land.[13] The Great Awakening began at revival meetings held out of doors, in private homes, the lodgings of itinerant ministers, and churches. During it more slaves and free blacks were being baptized, admitted to full communion, and became full members. In Freetown, Rhode Island, a black male slave was one of the five founders of an evangelical church begun as a result of the revivals.[14]

Above all else, the appeal of these awakenings to black women and men was the style of worship. At these revivals black women prayed, sang, shouted, fainted, testified, fell on their knees or collapsed on the ground, or went into trances in a manner that felt more African, less constrained, and thus more free. As Lois and James Oliver Horton note, "the 'shouting,' physical gyrations, 'holy laughter,' the dancing, and the singing that was common at camp meetings would have been familiar to the West African ancestors of the blacks who took part in this religious ritual."[15] The humblest of people, preachers held, could experience God's healing grace directly, without ministerial intervention or deep knowledge of the Bible; unlike at regular church services it was permissible to cry out during the preaching. In fact, black worshippers clapping, shouting, and interrupting the preacher with expressions of holy joy heightened the emotional intensity for all at the gathering.[16]

The Great Awakening attracted black men and women to churches in numbers never before seen. The breakaway Chebacco congregation in Ipswich, a seaport town thirty miles north of Boston, was regarded as one of the most evangelical in Massachusetts. All of New England was alive with the Holy Spirit, but Ipswich more so; the meetinghouse remained open all night, packed with as many as a thousand people, many of them going into trances. White women broke into the minister's sermon to cry out, including a Mrs. Whipple, who began to call herself "Mary Magdalene."[17] Addressing their fellow worshippers black male converts were so eloquent that white congregants followed them out of doors to listen to them preach.[18] Flora, an enslaved woman in her twenties in this congregation, became a lay exhorter, the one documented example of a black woman itinerant preacher in colonial New England.[19] Unfortunately the record of her religious conversion only mentions her call to preaching in a few words.

During the Great Awakening the outbreaks of conscience among New England whites were limited and local; at the same time in Northfield a few believers stood by their opposition to the slave trade and slave ownership. However, moral fervor evaporated quickly; the Great Awakening came to an end because of war with French Catholics to the north in Canada. With the fate of the empire at stake, the colonials apparently had less time to devote to the state of their souls or those of their slave-owning neighbors. A smaller revival from 1763 to 1764, dubbed the Seacoast Revival by one historian, brought Christianity to blacks living in Ipswich, Newport, and Providence but without the publicity the first Great Awakening enjoyed. This revival occurred in some of the same areas as the Great Awakening, led by many of the same preachers where some had found their faith twenty years before and then lost their way. There were no direct confrontations between abolitionist churchgoers and slave-owning ministers, as had been true in Northfield.[20] But some church elders and deacons who were brought to their faith during the revival did decide to emancipate their slaves in their wills.

In the season of revivals the Fourth Church in the sea coast town of Ipswich began to hold meetings on Tuesday and Thursday nights to allow new converts to testify to their "soul concerns." People traveled many miles to listen to the hellfire-and-brimstone preaching of its minister, the Reverend John Cleaveland. Tall and well built, Cleaveland was known for his deep voice, eloquence, and extemporaneous preaching. Among his personal papers were the conversion narratives of two enslaved women who joined his congregation in the 1760s. After Cleaveland listened to the women's testimony, he translated it into his own vocabulary, since it is unlikely that an enslaved woman would have used the word "concupiscence" (meaning sexual desire) in ordinary speech. The conversion narrative is thus a perfect metaphor for black Christianity, a negotiated product in a white format in which black women were able to inject personal experience and outline their own definition of freedom.[21]

The overflow of potential converts at Fourth Church was so great that Cleaveland held a one-day mass "registration" at the parsonage. The converts were lined up at 10 A.M.; by the evening, some had spent hours waiting in the outer room to be interviewed by Cleaveland and the deacons praying "either for themselves, or over some particular person or other in distress."

In the interview Cleaveland and the deacons asked the convert a series of questions. He wrote down their answers in his standard format, which consisted of a description of the convert's sin, a profession of religious faith, and the story of the conversion experience. Later candidates stood silently at the front of the church while Cleaveland read the narrative and then the converts responded to questions from the assembled worshippers who voted whether to accept them for full membership.[22]

Phillis Cogswell and Flora were slaves and converts at Fourth Church who experienced conversion. Both were in their forties and were about to marry brothers from a religious slave family, long-time members of the church. They seem to have favored the same passages from the Bible (albeit ones many others had selected as well). Both had been moved by the Great Awakening to join the Fourth Church and had then lost their religious enthusiasm. Two decades later they sought to renew their membership in the church just prior to their weddings, officiated by Reverend Cleaveland. It was common for women, whatever their color, to join the church prior to their marriage; Cleaveland or the in-laws of these women may have encouraged them to convert. Converts were also expected to raise their baptized children according to religious principles. To make sure that true faith was practiced, ruling elders policed the faithful, visiting each member of the church twice a year to "examine them in respect to their state, & growth in grace."[23]

Flora, born in 1723, most likely in Ipswich, had been an itinerant preacher during the Great Awakening. After being disciplined by the church for "her fall," she confessed her sin and was readmitted to the church; then she lost her faith. She belonged to the Choate family, two wealthy landowning brothers who built fishing boats and ran a commercial fishing business. Flora seems to have been illiterate, since she signed her conversion narrative with a mark. Because of their involvement in the Seacoast Revival the Choates had decided to emancipate their slaves in their wills. Flora seems to have been manumitted after her master died in 1767 when she married Titus, the slave of her master's brother, the same year. Titus's parents, who joined the church at the time of the First Great Awakening, were known among their neighbors for their devotion in attending religious meetings; his father, Ned, was born in Africa but it is unclear where his mother was born. After Titus gained his freedom at his master's death he and Flora took as their new last name, Nedson, as in son of Ned, following the African practice of adopting the father's first name as a surname.[24] That Christianized former slaves had retained an African naming practice suggests there was more compatibility between African custom and Protestant Christian identity than has previously been thought.

Upon listening to Flora's conversion narrative, the congregation examined her to confirm that she understood the implications of her statement.

Satisfied with her answers they voted to include her in "our Charity and Fellowship." She became a member of Fourth Church and her three children were subsequently baptized by Reverend Cleaveland as well. There was nothing specifically racial about confession of sexual sin, whether premarital fornication, cohabitation, or adultery; Cleaveland's own daughter was an unmarried single mother.[25] Flora in her statement told Reverend Cleaveland that God had abandoned her to Satan and "to her own lusts," since Satan could provoke a person toward "wantonness and concupiscence." Worried that her sinning could be used to discredit the religious revival as a "delusion of Satan," she acknowledged that she wanted to behave correctly "so as to declare God's Glory abroad," signaling that she wanted to resume her itinerant preaching.[26]

Although evangelical Christianity discouraged sex outside of marriage, it also permitted converts, including Flora, to express love of Jesus in a distinctly sexual manner. In her conversion narrative Flora selected the clearly erotic passage from the Song of Solomon in which Shulamite, the daughter of Pharaoh, marries King Solomon and describes their wedding night. The passage reads, "He ran to my Relief, he kissed me with the Kisses of his mouth and I found his love to be better than wine." Some commentators, embarrassed by a frank statement of sexual passion, have preferred to interpret this passage as a statement of God's love for the individual believer. If no sexual meaning was intended, it is nonetheless hard to miss the racial implications of her choice of this passage. Shulamite refers to herself as "black" because the sun had tanned her skin while she was working in the vineyards; it is easy to conclude that Flora sensed common bonds of race and gender with this Egyptian woman.

Phillis Cogswell, the other enslaved woman convert at Cleaveland's church, related a fairly conventional tale of spiritual reawakening, with no overt sexual overtones. Instead, she stated that at a time of religious enthusiasm, she did not want to be left behind. Like many converts she received her call to God in a dream, having fallen asleep thinking of Isaac Watts's "Cradle Hymn." The first stanza of the hymn, often sung in North American churches, was "Hush, my dear, lay down and slumber, Holy Angels guard thy Bed." Awakening with an awareness of her sins, Phillis engaged in a week of soul-searching and concluded that God had saved her from hell and was offering her a second chance for an eternal life.[27]

Unmoved by services at church, Phillis Cogswell experienced spiritual rebirth from her dream followed by reading Scripture. She cited her favorite Biblical passage, Isaiah 55:1 which read: "Ho, every one that thirsteth, come ye to the waters, and he that hath no money; come ye, buy and eat; yea, come, buy wine and milk without money and without price."[28] Originally addressed to exiles torn from their homeland, the prophet Isaiah invites the poor to a lavish banquet at no cost; he requires only that the person should be hungry and thirsty enough to drink from the cup of salvation. This passage had an obvious appeal to captured Africans who were poor and also adhered to the African belief that the spirit had to cross a great body of water to unite with those that dwelled in the African homeland. The passage also shows that Phillis Cogswell conceived of conversion as an intellectual as well as an emotional process, thus refuting the view that blacks were incapable of sustained thought. Phillis explained that "at first I was not sensible of much spiritual thirsting, but soon after they were bro't with power to my mind, I found some thirsting…"[29]

Slaveholders often selected as a justification for bondage Matthew 11:29, which Phillis had chosen as well. It read, "Take my yoke upon you, and learn of me; for I am meek and lowly in heart: and ye shall find rest unto your souls."[30] In offering the congregation a statement they expected to hear from slave converts, Phillis appeared to concur with the belief that bondage was justified because Africans were brought from heathen lands where they might receive the Christian message. She added more standard imagery when she related that "my Burden was immediately taken away and I felt as if I could fly." West Africans often interpreted dreams of flying as a signal from the spirits or a sign of good fortune; even Christians in New England could appreciate that flight was a form of escape from suffering and hardship.[31]

Three months after Phillis was baptized, she carried her infant to the baptismal font to receive Cleaveland's blessing. Members of the congregation usually had their children baptized right after they joined the Fourth Church. Phillis, however, did not bring her son for baptism until four months after she became a member of the congregation, which suggests that she was six months pregnant when she stood before the congregation to be admitted into its fellowship. A year after her son's birth she married Cesar, the brother of Titus in 1767; her husband was granted his freedom at his master's death during the Revolutionary War. Exactly how and when Phillis gained her freedom is unclear, although she was definitely free by the time courts declared slavery unconstitutional in 1783. After her husband died, Phillis remarried, outlived her second husband, and died when she was about seventy years old.[32]

The Seacoast Revival spread to Newport where Sarah Osborn was holding religious meetings for blacks in her home on Sunday evenings. Osborn began a prayer group for young women who belonged to her church in Newport in 1740 or 1741 after being inspired by two celebrity itinerant preachers of the day, George Whitefield and Gilbert Tennent. Because her husband was unable to work, perhaps disabled, she became the sole support for her family, running a school in her home with as many as seventy students at a time and taking in eight to ten boarders. During the height of the revival she held prayer meetings at her house six nights a week; slaves and free blacks began to attend family prayers at her home on Sunday evenings in 1765, which soon became so popular that they became full-blown Negro societies.[33] Osborn hosted these meetings and offered slaves instruction in reading and writing; visiting white Baptist ministers stopped in on Sunday evenings to preach. Some of those who attended began prayer groups of their own in their master's households.[34] Free blacks organized an Ethiopian society that met in her kitchen every Tuesday evening, with as many as eighty men and women crowding in.[35] The main difference between the Ethiopian society and the Sunday evening group was that the former consisted of free blacks, able to move about freely on a weeknight rather than just on a Sunday.

Sarah Osborn stood decidedly in favor of Christian respectability—no drinking, gambling, swearing, Sabbath breaking, or "uncleanness." Acting as a kind of personal advisor she counseled black women who attended the Sunday evening services. Two women regulars told her they wept day and night because they knew they had committed a great sin in living with a man outside of marriage, hoping for forgiveness now that they had legally married.[36] It was always possible that enslaved women pretended to believe in sexual fidelity while conducting their personal lives according to a more flexible moral code. The profuse weeping of these two women demonstrated their sincere commitment to legal marriage and their understanding that cohabitation was a sin against God, occasioning in them anguish and emotional soul-searching.

A minister who was a close friend of Osborn as well as of her husband tried to stop her from holding these meetings, but without success. Newport masters feared that she was fomenting "disturbance and disorder" among their slaves. Attacked for her "Negro house," she justified her work among "Ethiopians" as the suitable form of religious mission for a woman, acceptable because she was not delivering sermons and was not taking on the role of a minister. She argued that black men and women, although adult, were similar to children in their need for religious instruction, a common prejudice of the time, but one effective in permitting her to continue her meetings.[37] She soon quieted her critics, who concluded that slaves who attended the Sunday evening meetings were "reform'd" under her influence, becoming "diligent and condescending" to their masters. In her correspondence she never stated any opposition to slavery—the only New England woman of her age to do so was Abigail Adams in a letter to her husband, John. Osborn had been careful to require the slaves who attended the Sunday evening meetings to ask their master's permission to attend. Moreover, she continued to own a slave, the daughter of one of the members of her prayer group, even though her minister Reverend Samuel Hopkins had time and again denounced slave owning from his pulpit.[38] In her circle in Newport others had more advanced views. At least among the Quakers in Newport there had been a long history of abolitionist stirring. A few years before the Negro society had formed, the Quaker minister John Woolman had visited. Shocked by the extent of the slave trade in Newport he drew up a petition to abolish the trade that he wanted to present before the state assembly, then meeting in town. Instead he delivered a draft of it before the Friends Yearly Meeting in Newport and some Friends then presented it to the assembly. Woolman also met with individual Quaker slaveholders and their wives to persuade them to manumit themselves. Osborn had Quaker women friends and would have known about the agitation caused by Woolman's visit.[39]

With the end of the Seacoast Revival many of the members of Osborn's Sunday evening prayer group drifted toward her church, the First Congregational, and its minister, Rev. Samuel Hopkins, whom Osborn had backed for the post over considerable opposition. For twenty-five years Hopkins served a congregation in Great Barrington but was dismissed because of his vocal opposition to the Tories during the Stamp Act crisis; before leaving town he sold the slave woman he owned. Like Woolman, Hopkins was shocked by the human suffering he saw at the wharves of Newport, concluding that the "town is the most guilty" of "a sin of crimson die." Hopkins came to hold that it was a denial of divine law "to hold mankind as my property." Losing hope for emancipation in New England he observed that freed blacks were treated as "underlings" in education and employment and would never be able to escape white racial prejudice. By returning to Africa, Hopkins believed that the blacks of New England could develop their own settlements and businesses, and spread the gospel to their African brethren. Discerning the hand of God in the crisis with Britain, Hopkins found the Patriots guilty of the greatest hypocrisy in demanding their own freedom while owning slaves and bringing them to American shores in "stinking ships."

By the time of the American Revolution Hopkins was preaching that the new nation had "blood on its hands," which could be wiped away only by abolishing the slave trade and eliminating the institution of slavery. He called on the delegates to the Continental Congress gathered in Philadelphia to end human bondage and beseeched the members of his congregation to emancipate their slaves. Later that year, selecting religious passages and quoting from the Declaration of Independence he fervently urged his fellow clergy to speak out against human bondage. Hopkins did succeed in persuading Reverend Joseph Bellamy of Litchfield, Connecticut, to emancipate his slave. Not a good speaker, he nonetheless attracted to his congregation many black men and women in Newport because of his principles, including Obour Tanner, John Quamino and his wife, Duchess, and several native-born Africans who shared his belief that they should return to Africa, resettle, and preach Christianity to their people.[40] Hopkins visited Boston frequently, sometimes to preach. Although it was not clear when Phillis Wheatley first met him, she was corresponding with him by 1774.[41]

Long after the seasons of religious revivals had come to a close other black women turned to spiritual faith for consolation during a time of personal grief. Despite having been for many years the slave of the most famous minister in colonial America, the wife of a professing Christian, and the mother of four baptized daughters, Rose Binney of Northampton had not herself experienced God's saving grace. She was an African who kept her memory of her homeland alive by retelling her story of how she was captured when she was drawing water from a spring. She seems to have become the slave of the Northampton preacher Jonathan Edwards when she was given to his wife Sarah as a wedding gift in 1727. Edwards had lost his post in Northampton in 1750 because he opposed the lax admission standards to church membership of the previous minister, his grandfather, Solomon Stoddard, whose membership reform policies have been termed the halfway covenant. Edwards moved west, to a relatively obscure position as the minister to a Mohican Christian mission that also had a few English families. So delighted was Joab Binney's owner that the divine was being forced from his pulpit that he manumitted him, allowing him to follow his sweetheart Rose to Stockbridge. The couple married in Stockbridge and started a family. Edwards either freed Rose—or Joab purchased her freedom—but he kept their son, Titus, as his slave. In Stockbridge Joab Binney became a leather tanner and blacksmith and bought a farm along the Housatonic River and another piece of land in nearby West Stockbridge.[42]

Although Edwards left his pastorate for the College of New Jersey (Princeton) in 1757, the Binneys settled into their home in Stockbridge. Later in life Rose Binney found it comforting to speak with the Reverend Stephen West, a long-time local minister in town who came to visit her. Five feet tall, dressed all in black, his hair thinning, he was an unimpressive figure. People varied in their assessment of the dynamism of his preaching, but his subject was invariably God's punishment of Adam and Eve for their sins in the Garden of Eden. No one doubted Reverend West's pastoral care, however; he made weekly calls at the abodes of many in the congregation, including those of free blacks in the Binneys' neighborhood. Years after her conversion West described Rose Binney as a "poor African woman" who spoke in dialect and worked every day at chores such as milking cows and building a fire.[43]

Rose Binney believed that the deaths of her daughters were God's punishment of her because she had not joined the church. In converting she hoped she could save herself and her surviving daughter. Because of her stated motivation West initially rejected Binney, believing her to be an insincere candidate for conversion. But he patiently waited until she achieved a deeper understanding of her faith. She visited his rectory and conversed with him, and West maintained his usual pattern of friendly visits. As these meetings proceeded Rose Binney no longer described an angry god but one who dwelled in nature. West asked Binney to repeat her story, that she found god in the sunshine, the clouds, the trees, in all of nature, "ful of God, evry where!"[44] West decided Rose was ready for conversion and baptism. Visiting her deathbed many years later he described her as a contented Christian prepared for her end. It is hard to overlook the way West reduces the status of the wife of a craftsman, farmer, and landowner to that of a "poor African woman." Yet for Rose Binney her minister's gentle manner and periodic visits may have more than compensated for any condescension she perceived.[45]

As the Seacoast Revival wound down, the career of a young evangelical prodigy in Boston was just beginning. A signed poem of "Phillis Wheatley" appeared in *The Newport Mercury* of 1767, which recounted the story of two Quaker merchants from Nantucket who had almost died at sea. In real life two men had stayed at the home of Boston merchant, John Wheatley, and probably related their harrowing tale during their visit, perhaps while the Wheatley's slave was waiting on them. Tutored in English by her mistress and her mistress' daughter, Wheatley wrote a poem about the "Fear and Danger the men faced." It is not clear who sent her poem to the *Newport Mercury*, although an unsigned letter forwarding it appeared in the paper referred to John Wheatley in the third person so it was likely not him.[46] Sarah Osborn lived in Newport and was known not to sign her name to any of the works she published. Sharing the religious faith of Susannah Wheatley, with whom she was acquainted, Osborn may have given the young poet her literary start.

During her brief lifetime Phillis Wheatley was heralded as a genius by the New England public and the European and black Atlantic world. Wheatley had been seized when she was seven or eight and brought on the brig *Phillis* to the Boston harbor. In 1761 Boston tailor and merchant John Wheatley and his wife Susannah purchased her and promptly decided to name her after the ship on which she arrived. An evangelical Christian who knew the Bible, classical mythology, and neoclassical literary forms, Phillis Wheatley sided with Patriots during the revolutionary era. Writing for an audience of mainly elite Christian whites who populated the social circles of her mistress she also had enthusiastic black readers. Jupiter Hammon, a slave on Long Island who was sent by his master to school to learn to read and write, paid tribute to his fellow black writer in his "Address to Phillis Wheatley, Ethiopian poetess" in 1778. Ignatius Sancho, a free black grocer and playwright in London, wrote to a Philadelphia Quaker to thank him for sending him the volume of Wheatley's poems. Not knowing that Wheatley had been manumitted five years earlier, Sancho praised her as a "genius in bondage" but criticized the injustice he believed kept her enslaved.[47]

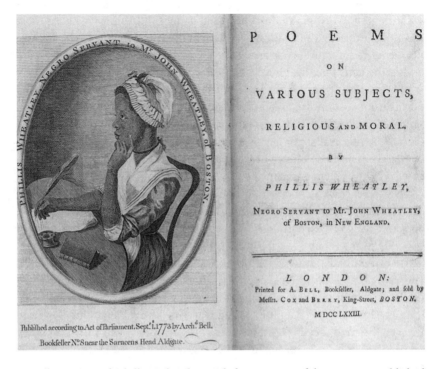

3.1. Illustration of Phillis Wheatley and frontispiece of her poems published in London in 1773. The English sponsor of Wheatley's poems, the Countess of Huntingdon, ordered an engraving of Wheatley as a means of showing that the poems were authentic since a white audience at this time believed a black slave incapable of poetic genius. Wheatley wrote a poem of praise "to S.M., a young African Painter," indicating that the artist was Scipio Moorhead, the slave of Reverend John Moorhead, a Presbyterian minister in Boston. The inscription on the engraving identified Wheatley in relation to her owner. The pose, left elbow on the table, chin in the left hand, was the standard one of the time for religious converts and poets. The paper, the writing desk, the quill pen, the inkwell, and leisure time to write were rare privileges for an enslaved woman. Phillis Wheatley. *Poems on Various Subjects, Religious and Moral. Frontispiece.* London: printed for A. Bell, 1773, courtesy of the Massachusetts Historical Society

   In her poetry Wheatley affirmed her various identities: she described herself as a Christian, an African, an Ethiopian, referred to herself as an "Afric' Muse" and when circulating her proposal for a second volume of poems after she had been emancipated and married John Peters, "a female African."[48] Her sense of her African identity was quite strong, which she fused with self-identification as an Ethiopian, the African people and ancient civilization often mentioned in the Old Testament. In the Bible Ethiopians were described as Christian redeemers—in the most generous view, as future rulers of the world who were spreading the faith. Many whites from Samuel Sewall to Sarah Osborn had also referred to black people as Ethiopians, a generally favorable term. However, when black people claimed to be Ethiopians they were stating their race pride in a rich religious heritage older than that of western Europe. The most significant phrase in the Bible about Ethiopians, found in a song of David, was a prophecy about their messianic role. Psalms 6:31 stated, "Princes shall come out of Egypt: Ethiopia shall stretch forth her hands unto God." In the King James Version of the Bible the princes of Egypt were men, whereas Ethiopia was gendered female.[49]

Although she called herself a "female African," Wheatley more often stated the African part of her identity. Nonetheless, as a young female author she never apologized for the failing or weaknesses of her sex. The recipients of her poems about death were grieving men and women, but David Grimsted argues that she gave "greater weight" to women's sense of grief.[50] Wheatley's frequent use of imagery about the sun appears to express her grief over losing her mother.[51] Wheatley's one memory of her mother was of her pouring out water in a libation as the sun rose in the east and then prostrating herself in the direction of the rising sun. Some have suggested that Wheatley's mother could have been a Muslim who was performing the first prayer of the day, which is supposed to take place before sunrise; in bowing to the east her mother was indeed praying in the direction of Mecca.

Wheatley was also conscious of gender because her literary patrons, beginning with Susannah Wheatley and her daughter Mary, were women. Susannah Wheatley encouraged Mary to tutor the young slave, teaching her to read and write in English and assisting her in learning history, geography, the Bible and Latin. Susannah Wheatley corresponded with the British Methodist Selina, the Countess of Huntingdon, who encouraged the precocious Phillis. The Countess was the financial backer for the publication of Wheatley's poems by a London printer; she made sure that there was an illustration of Wheatley at the front of the volume.[52]

Wheatley is most famous and most excoriated for a poem she wrote when she was fourteen, "On Being Brought from Africa to America." Its eight lines of rhyme express Christian religious piety, but seemingly offer justification for slavery.

> 'Twas mercy brought me from my Pagan land,
> Taught my benighted soul to understand
> That there's a God, that there's a Saviour too:
> Once I redemption neither sought nor knew.
> Some view our sable race with scornful eye,

"Their colour is a diabolic die."
Remember, Christians, Negros, black as Cain,
May be refin'd, and join th' angelic train.[53]

Black nationalists of the 1960s regarded Wheatley as a young female sell-out who parroted Christian apologies for slavery and the slave trade. Their standard reading of this poem was that Wheatley was suggesting that Africans were better off enslaved in the New World because they benefited by being brought from paganism to Christianity. For black nationalists of that era this poem constituted sufficient proof that Wheatley was guilty of racial self-hatred. Her references to her "benighted soul" and her "pagan land" have often been cited as evidence of her derogatory attitude toward Africa. Fortunately, in the last two decades, literary critics as well as historians have closely scrutinized the full body of her work, including this poem and found "On Being Brought" to be more subtle and more ironic than previously thought. In that sense, the poem resembled the nuanced message of Phillis Cogswell, offering whites the justification for slavery they expected to hear and inserting more subtle meaning into the text.

Wheatley converted to Christianity as a young girl and soon began to define heaven as a realm of freedom, a place of escape from the sins of the world. There is no doubt that Wheatley believed that Christianity was a superior religion and supported missionary efforts to bring the faith to the African continent.[54] Nonetheless, in her poem Wheatley described blacks as a "sable" race, emphasizing the color of a small brown mammal valued highly for its rich fur. In not choosing the word dark or black to refer to color of the African's skin, she avoided the colonists' easy association between the color black and evil or sin.[55] Wheatley also tackled racist views, by putting them in quotes, and then refuting them. The "some" who "view our sable race with scornful eye" were sinners, those who failed to acknowledge that God was engaged in saving the souls of Africans. Racists believed that the black skin of Africans proved that they were "diabolical"—that is, prone to doing wrong and in league with Satan, a view she criticized and mocked.[56] She addresses her largely white audience as a voice of authority (even at age fourteen), telling her readers to "remember" that "Negros" could be "refin'd," meaning educated, and just as likely to go to heaven as white people.

Wheatley's métier was the elegy, a respectful poem written upon someone's death and the favorite genre of Christian evangelicals. John Shields, one of the most well known of the literary scholars who has studied Wheatley's writings, asserts that in her elegies she looked to death and the afterlife as a place free from slavery. He argues that "the goal of her elegiac meditations was to discover a realm where men did not enslave their black brothers and sisters."[57] Moreover, many of her elegies ask her readers to live up to noble ideals rather than simply enumerating the good qualities of the deceased.[58] Among the most significant of these was Wheatley's elegy for the British evangelical itinerant preacher George Whitefield, which made her famous in Britain as well as in America because it was addressed to Selina Hastings, the Countess of Huntingdon who had selected Whitefield as her personal chaplain. Eventually it was through Huntingdon's patronage that Wheatley's volume of poems was published in England.

Whitefield, one of the most celebrated preachers of his day, made seven separate tours to the colonies, and managed to persuade the Deist Benjamin Franklin to empty his pockets into the collection plate. The "son of Thunder" visited Massachusetts frequently, once attracting a crowd of thirty thousand to Boston Common—the largest public gathering in colonial America up to that time. An anonymous poem written about one of his visits to Boston decades before hailed him as a preacher who welcomed "the *Black* as well as *White* and says for them there's room." Whitefield spoke in a style that appealed to a black audience—in the middle of preaching he broke down in tears and he moved his audience to weep. Some anti-revivalists discouraged slaves in town from going to hear Whitefield preach but their entreaties went unheeded.[59]

In August of 1770 Whitefield spent three weeks preaching in the Boston area, probably visited the Wheatleys, and may have stayed at their home. The next month, while spreading the gospel in Newburyport, he died from a heart attack.[60] In her elegy for Whitefield, "On the Death of Reverend George Whitefield" Wheatley wrote, "Take him, ye Africans, he longs for you, Impartial Saviour is his title due." Whitefield had a large black following but he was not an abolitionist. When in Boston he frequently stayed at the home of Jacob Royall, the largest slave trader in Boston. At the orphanage in Georgia he established he owned the slaves who did the institution's menial labor. When Wheatley wrote this poem at age seventeen what mattered to her was Whitefield's reputation among local blacks, Susannah Wheatley, and her religious circle. Moreover, she liked the way Whitefield had moved his audiences: she mentioned "the music of thy tongue" and the electric effect he had on his hearers: "Thou didst in strains of eloquence refin'd/ Inflame the heart, and captivate the mind."[61]

The first inkling that Wheatley's evangelical Christianity had endowed her with the power to stand in moral judgment of others, including white men of much superior social standing, appeared in "To the University of Cambridge in New England," written in 1767. She did not need to visit Harvard to witness the behavior of these college students who frequently came to Boston. George Whitefield had labeled Harvard a den of iniquity, which had forced the president of the College to defend the university and its students. Wheatley, repeating views common in evangelical circles, lectured the students on their disreputable conduct, hoping her appeals would shame them into reforming. She invokes her racial/religious identity as an "Ethiop" who "tells you," the Harvard students, about sexual sin, urging them to suppress "the deadly serpent" in its egg.[62] Telling them to "improve your privileges" while in school, she hints that she had been denied the advanced education the young men took for granted.[63]

Wheatley defined freedom in the context of being kidnapped and taken from her parents in Senegambia, the struggle of the colonists against British tyranny, and her Christian religious faith. She capitalized and put the word *Freedom* in italics three times in a poem "to the Right Honourable William, Earl of Dartmouth" (1772). She begins the poem portraying New England as it saw itself, as the birthplace of "Fair *Freedom*." Knowing something of Dartmouth's connections with a charitable school for Indians in New Hampshire and with British abolitionists, Wheatley appealed to him to support ending the slave trade. Her poem suggested that Dartmouth, curious about the muse singing his praises, might want to learn "from when my love of *Freedom* sprung." She explains that it originated not in New England but rather in being "snatched from *Afric's fancy'd happy seat*" as a young child. In language intended to convey the emotional impact of the slave trade on an African father whose child was kidnapped, she writes "what pangs excruciating must molest, what sorrows labor in my parent's Breast?" Committed to the Patriot cause, even when she congratulated George III for an act of political moderation, the repeal of the hated Stamp Act, she wrote "a monarch's smile can set his subjects free!"

"Goliath of Gath" was the longest work in her collection of poems, and one of the two epics in the volume. It told the story of young David of the Old Testament in his struggle against Goliath, literally the tale of a courageous representative of the meek overtaking the strong in a bid to win freedom for his people. Wheatley had crossed the gender divide to identify with a young man who had left his homeland behind, was possessed of "warlike courage far beyond his years," and had great pride in his race ("small is my tribe, but valiant is the gift"). She represented the young David, "Jesse's heir," as a servant, charged with protecting his father's flock. Before David took on Goliath his brother reminded him that he was a humble shepherd of his people. Thus emboldened, the boy confronted and slew the giant and was designated as the one who "freedom in *Israel* for his house shall gain." Wheatley's poem in her day could be read in two ways, as the colonists successfully attacking British rule or as a slave fighting for his freedom and that of his people. Either way, she identified with the young shepherd, his triumph against the odds, and his courageous one-man stand in the cause of freedom. David Grimsted also sees in the description of "blood gushing in torrents" after Goliath's decapitation Wheatley's attraction to violence as an expression of God's wrath against injustice.[64]

In May of 1773 Wheatley sailed to England, a young woman of nineteen or twenty, sent there ostensibly for her health but also to promote the publication of this and other poems in her volume, having failed to secure a publisher in the colonies. Many enslaved men had traveled to Britain with their masters and more than a few black sailors on New England ships had docked there. Wheatley, however, was the first enslaved woman from North America to make a journey of this kind, accompanied as she was by the son of her master. The British abolitionist Granville Sharp acted as a chaperone and guide, taking her to see the tourist attractions. Benjamin Franklin paid a call at her lodgings and she was finally able to meet Lord Dartmouth, to whom she had dedicated her poem against the slave trade. An American merchant in London gave her a folio edition of *Paradise Lost* and she carefully wrapped for home the books she bought (all of Pope's poems, a copy of *Don Quixote*). The British abolitionists who met Wheatley may have shamed her owner into promising to manumit her. Apparently having obtained a promise that she would be free if she returned to Boston and having worked out an arrangement to receive the money from the sale of her poems, Wheatley decided to sail back to America to nurse her dying mistress; she was manumitted the month after her arrival, and Susannah Wheatley died the following year.[65]

Wheatley's abolitionist voice became much stronger as a free woman living in Boston in revolutionary times, communicating her antislavery views in a personal letter to Rev. Samson Occom, the Mohican Presbyterian minister. Reverend Occom probably stayed at the Wheatley home on King Street before embarking on his first ministerial speaking tour of England in 1766 when Phillis could not have been more than thirteen. The Wheatleys may have encouraged the young woman to write to Occom during his visit to England. Part of the Whitefield religious circle in which Susannah Wheatley moved, Occom was fond of "the little Miss" and thought she would make a good missionary to West Africa. Like the most forward-thinking evangelical ministers of the revolutionary age, Occom, in 1774 in a letter to Wheatley that has not survived, appears to have denounced ministers for owning slaves and claiming that they did so because it was "very fashionable." He seems to have concluded by stating that the Gospel of Jesus reflected the mind of God and that God believed in True Liberty in "both Temporal and Spiritual" realms since Wheatley repeated his views in her response to him.[66]

Wheatley wrote to Occom about the hypocrisy of slave owners, not just that of slave-owning ministers. Although Wheatley had referred to the house of Israel in "Goliath of Gath" she had not specifically invoked Moses and his people in previous poems. Now she called slave owners "modern Egyptians," underlining the deep impression reading the Book of Exodus had made on her poetic and political understanding of slavery. Insisting there was no distinction between "civil and religious liberty," she agreed with Occom that liberty was the goal in both realms. Wheatley's English publisher had been willing to publish her volume of poems provided that the book contain an attestation from prominent dignitaries in Boston who certified that the young enslaved woman had indeed written the poems. Of the eighteen men who signed their names to this statement, presented in the introduction to her volume of poetry, the majority were slaveholders. Some, such as the governor of the colony and his lieutenant governor, were Loyalists, but James Bowdoin was a Patriot.[67] Wheatley refused to give up on men such as Bowdoin. Instead she wrote to Occom that she hoped to "*convince* them [emphasis added] of the strange Absurdity of their Conduct whose Words and Actions are so diametrically opposite." Believing that God had intended to redeem Africans, she wrote:

> In every human Breast, God has implanted a Principle, which we call Love
> of Freedom; it is impatient of Oppression, and pants for Deliverance, and by
> the Leave of our modern Egyptians I will assert, that the same Principle lives
> in us. God grant Deliverance. in his own Way and Time, and get him honour
> upon all those whose Avarice impels them to countenance and help forward
> the Calamities of their fellow Creatures. This. I desire not for their Hurt, and
> but to convince them of the strange Absurdity of their Conduct whose Words
> and Actions are so diametrically opposite. How well the Cry for Liberty,
> and the reverse Disposition for the exercise of oppressive Power over others
> agree,—I humbly think it does not require the Penetration of a Philosopher to
> determine.[68]

The appeal of Wheatley's letter was in the elegance of her expression and her fame. Since Occom lived in Mohegan, Connecticut, near New London, he probably forwarded her letter to the local newspaper, the *Connecticut Gazette*, which reprinted it on March 11, 1774. Within a month her letter appeared in ten more newspapers in Connecticut, Massachusetts, and Rhode Island. In revolutionary times Wheatley had found an anonymous publicist who was eager to circulate her views to the New England press.[69] Then the war that everyone had been anticipating finally arrived. The Patriots trapped British troops inside the city; John Wheatley headed out of town and Phillis Wheatley fled to Providence where Mary Wheatley had gone with her husband, who had found a post as a minister to a poor congregation.[70] Meanwhile, the British fleet was anchored outside the island city of Newport and the British had sent an army of several thousand troops to occupy the town. Ferries and small boats were bringing some food to the stranded islanders but the General Assembly of Rhode Island had issued a warning for residents to leave. Wheatley's friend, Obour Tanner, remained in Newport, but was able to send a letter to her in Providence.[71] Wheatley responded, describing herself as a "mere spectator" during the war because she was safe in Providence while the fighting was transpiring to the south.

Her letter mentions that she had passed "very agreeably" in conversation with Mr. Lingo and John Quamino. Nothing is known about a man named Lingo; Quamino, no longer a young acolyte of Osborn and Hopkins, had returned from his theological training at Princeton seeking funds to purchase the freedom of his wife and surviving daughters and pursue the goal Hopkins had proposed of sending black missionaries to West Africa.[72] His wife Duchess and their children were in Providence as well, since her owners, the Channings, had fled there. It has always been claimed that Susannah Wheatley kept Phillis from associating with other blacks and that her slave's correspondence was censured by whites. This evening conversation, however, suggests that as a free woman Phillis Wheatley was meeting on her own with the black evangelical community that revolved around Sarah Osborn and Reverend Samuel Hopkins.[73]

In her letter to Obour Tanner, Wheatley expressed shock at the behavior of British troops in Boston. She had seen the pattern before, going back to the Boston Massacre. Her appreciative audience had raised her status from that of "an uncultivated barbarian" to a "poetical genius" but even if she was held to be an exception, the African people were still regarded as barbarians. The poles of savagery versus civilization were used to condemn the religions and peoples brought to New England by the slave trade. She certainly accepted the enlightenment that Christianity brought. However, even after having been feted in her trip to England, she was beginning to doubt the secular ranking system, now considering the British uncivilized. She wrote to Tanner, "Possibly the ambition & thirst of Dominion in some is design'd as the punishment of the national views of others, tho' it bears the appearance of greater Barbariety than that of the unciviliz'd part of mankind."[74]

The evangelical Christianity that black women adopted appealed precisely because it resembled aspects of African worship, even though there could not be an official recognition of this resemblance. Instead, black Christians held that African spiritual practice was sinful in its worship of "trees, and streams, and fountains or water, and reptiles."[75] Not only was it believed that animism was sinful but so, too, were common African sexual and marital practices, such as polygamy and cohabitation outside of legal marriage. While Christianity vigorously condemned these sins, it also offered spiritual rebirth and forgiveness for sin. For women such as Flora and Phillis Cogswell conversion was a quest "to be made free in Christ." Flora, imbued with the Holy Spirit, was called upon to preach—an unprecedented position of authority for an enslaved woman.

The Protestant Christianity enslaved women adopted was filled with jus-
tifications for slave obedience and slavery itself as well as with empowering
messages. It is true that Phillis Cogswell offered a justification for slavery as
part of her conversion to Christianity. But the enhanced meaning in her life
that came from becoming a member of the Fourth Church is unmistakable.
Similarly, Christianity was both the religion of slaveholders and of abolitionists. In the latter group were the white members of Fourth Church who
believed their newly found faith required them to emancipate their slaves
in their wills. The abolitionist implications of Christianity became clearer to
more of the public as the revolution approached. Phillis Wheatley shared the
views of Occom, Hopkins, and many others of her age who held that slavery
was a profound violation of Christian religious beliefs. In the revolutionary
age many Christians understood slavery as a sin requiring immediate and
total redress through the emancipation of slaves since there could be no
compromise with the evil of slavery.[76] An opponent of personal immorality and slavery, Wheatley saw political and spiritual liberty as inseparable,
adding her voice to those who regarded the abolition of human bondage as
a religious and moral issue.

4

MARRIAGE AND THE FAMILY

Jin Cole, an enslaved woman in Deerfield, stolen from her family in Guinea when she was about twelve years old, said that as a result of her capture "we nebber see our mudders any more."[1] Repeating the critique of slavery that black women had been voicing since Hagar Blackmore, she attributed her great suffering to the loss of her kin. Some New England black men and women like Cole or Hagar Blackmore were still able to call to mind their lost relatives in Africa, but the extensive kinship obligations and more variegated types of marriage of their African worlds were destroyed by New England slavery. In patrilineal societies of west and Central Africa the husband and his clan exercised authority; in matrilineal societies the mother's brother did so. In many West and Central African cultures the first born always had higher status than the other children. In New England, the mother's brother played no role whatsoever; there is no evidence that a first born had higher rank than other children; indeed, the whole concept of lineage, which gave senior women a powerful role, had disappeared.[2] Not to be found in New England were coming-of-age rituals or negotiations prior to a marriage between families. If there were kin related by blood and marriage who managed to be captured together, it is likely that they were separated on American shores. Although on board the slave ship the stolen Africans began to call each other brother and sister, such relationships were severed because slaves were sold separately in ones or twos. The imbalance of black women to men virtually ruled out the West and Central African practice of polygamy; if anything, the excess of black men encouraged marriage between native American women and African men. In fact, there was substantial mixing of the races occurring, including occasional interracial marriages between black men and white women and informal marriages between white men and black women. Moreover, because of the limited life expectancy of the black population, great-grandmothers were relatively rare while orphans were quite common.[3]

During slavery love of family persisted despite frequent sale and separation of children from their parents and husbands from wives. Slaves created new families in New England, marrying and having children. In many cases bonds to a child or a spouse survived despite living in separate residences, especially when families lived in the same town or in regular visiting distance. Husbands planned escape attempts to free their wives and children or negotiated with the owners of wives to secure their freedom; mothers ran away with their sons and daughters to keep from being separated from them; fathers and mothers went to court to win freedom for themselves and their families.

In law enslaved and free black men had some legal rights but their rights were fewer than those of free white men and those they had were inferior in many ways. An enslaved man and woman had the right to marry but a master retained the right of sale; a slave husband could divorce his wife but he did not have custody rights over his children; a slave could marry an Indian or a black person but not a white person. The right to marry was one of the unique legal rights slaves in New England enjoyed that defined them as both persons and property before the law. They came to enjoy this right because many owners, especially Christian ministers, were ambivalent about completely denying a family life to their slaves. Masters sought to reconcile their religious beliefs in Christian marriage with their economic interest, offering a form of second-class union for slaves—the style but not the substance of legal Christian marriage, making clear that they protected their rights of ownership and their right to sell their human property. Beginning in the 1760s free black husbands tested the question of whether a husband's rights over his slave wife trumped those of her owner; they learned time and again that they did not.

Freedom meant reuniting the family, but ideas about freedom for the family were also shaped by African notions of honor, the Christian concept of respectability, and the disgrace and deprivations black men experienced in slavery. The family living together under one roof was to be a patriarchal household with the husband as the main provider and protector, his wife as his subordinate, and their relationship as a monogamous marriage sanctioned in religion and law. Free black couples such as the Princes, the Pernams, and the Spears lived by these ideals but also maneuvered around them. During the decades of emancipation, tensions in black marriages, evident even in slavery, spilled out into newspaper advertisements of free black husbands disowning the debts incurred by runaway wives. Jealousy and fears of dishonor created a combustible mix for black marriages at the moment of emancipation. Free black men, acquiring the rights of white patriarchs, quickly realized they had assumed the new obligation to support a dependent wife. They wanted to command the movements of their wives but also believed that women had to work to support the family. Black women tended to think that a husband should support his family but did not want a man who was too controlling. This chapter tells the story of this conflict, as it emerged in public sight at the end of the Revolutionary War.

In fact, free black husbands, faced with runaway wives, responded, seeking to damage the reputation of their wives in the widest possible community, that of the newspaper-reading public. By doing so, they were rendering black domestic dramas into entertainment and scandal for white readers of these papers. In singling out for derision the unfaithful wife, they were abetting one of the oldest stereotypes about the race, that black women were licentious. Placing black private troubles before a white public, they believed, was a necessary price to pay to defend their honor. The voices of the wives of these men were muted because they had less honor to defend and more interest in holding onto their respectability by keeping silent. The wives who did speak out against their husband's charges seem to have been seeking greater personal freedom while also believing that a husband should be responsible for the economic support of his wife.

Most black mothers, free or slave, died an early death; those who survived faced the likelihood that sale would separate family members. Enslaved black children, no doubt, were more likely to be living with their mothers than with their fathers. Yet many children grew up without parents or kin; enslaved mothers as well as fathers were often missing from the lives of black children; some parents were dead, but it was not unusual for husband and wife to be residing separately and for a young child to be living apart from both of them.[4] How many slave families were intact and living in the master's household is impossible to know. There are no censuses of households before the 1790s; historians have had to estimate familial relationships based on the next best source, inventories of the estates of slave owners. Such inventories compiled for Boston from 1685 to 1775 give some sense of slave residential patterns, although not of family relationships. In these Boston inventories about 35 percent of slaves in Boston were living in a white household without another slave, 30 percent were living as a pair, 17 percent were one of three slaves, 8 percent were one of four, and 10 percent were residing in a group of five or more slaves. Many of these pairs were an adult couple, but one cannot be sure. In seaport towns with a very small black population, slaves were parceled out to households one by one. Thus, in Portsmouth, New Hampshire in 1727, four out of five slaves were the single slave in the household.[5] In the 1750s even at the largest slave "plantation" in Massachusetts, Isaac Royall's Ten Hills Farm in Medford, which had its own separate slave quarter, there were no black couples among the thirty-eight slaves living there.[6]

By far the major reason for the separation of slaves was sale but there is no way of knowing how common it was. To many masters breaking up families was a matter of profit, although some had moral qualms. Owners ended up selling slaves to free up funds, pay their debts or their rent, or as a means of cutting expenses; at the master's bankruptcy his slaves were auctioned off. For the most part, masters sold their slaves because of reduced economic circumstances. But they also sold those who were obdurate, rebellious, threatened to kill them, or were seen as immoral (as in the mother sold with her infant because she had given birth to a biracial child).[7] Some slaves were inherited by family members or owned by sets of brothers who lived within visiting distance of kin. There is surely a different meaning of "sale" when a child lives within walking distance of the residence of both parents than when the slave was sent to another region, never to be seen again. Even when the new owner lived nearby, it is impossible to tell whether a mother saw her child every day or once a week at church. Despite the fact that parents lived close by, it still seems likely that the master and mistress were defined as the primary authority. Yet if for no other reason than that such slave children had no right to inherit, it was doubtful that they perceived their owners as "parents."

Some owners refused to sell a mother and child separately, while others advertised for sale the mother "with or without child"; similarly, infants, even when the mother was alive, were sold separately from the mother. In Boston a slave owner mounted his horse, put the infant he just purchased in his saddle bag, and headed home for Woburn. After the birth of a twin boy and girl, the wife's owner kept the girl, and the enslaved father, living nearby, claimed the boy, but the father's owner quickly sold the baby boy to wealthy neighbors. The price of an infant for sale was minimal; purchasers were bearing some expense in acquiring a slave infant since it would be several years before the child could do any work; families who bought infants were often fairly well-to-do childless couples who could afford the care of a baby and wanted to raise a child who could eventually be put to work on their farm or in their business. During the revolution the Reverend Jeremy Belknap visited local slave owners in Dover, New Hampshire, trying to persuade them to emancipate their slaves, and served as a witness to manumission agreements they devised. After moving to Boston he recalled the days in slavery when infants were separated from their families, when "Negro children were reckoned an incumbrance in a family; and, when weaned were given away like puppies."[8] Belknap was certainly correct that "Negro children" were given away at a very young age; yet some were disposed of much before they were weaned, such as one nine-day-old baby. Infants were first advertised as available free of charge in a Boston newspaper in 1706. Another ad described "a Negro Infant Girl About Six weeks Old, to be Given for the Bringing

Up."[9] Such advertisements were most common in the 1740s, when eighteen separate owners in Massachusetts offered slave children "to be given away," even an infant "about three weeks old." The apparent reason for the appearance of so many ads was the economic hardship of owners, who did not want to assume the expense of caring for an infant. Enslaved men spoke for themselves and one suspects for women as well in a petition for freedom in Massachusetts in 1774. They wrote, "Our children are also taken from us by force and sent maney miles from us wear we seldom or ever see them again there to be made slaves of for Life which sumtimes is very short by Reson of Being dragged from their mothers Breest."[10]

Many enslaved husbands and fathers devised legal strategies, made escape plans, and/or saved to purchase their relatives, even though they were living separately from their families for many years. The man took the initiative because he was free, was able to hire himself out and keep some of his money for himself, or worked a piece of land to make enough money to afford his owner's purchase price. He also had a special opportunity to gain a large sum of money if he enlisted in the militia. Men like Abijah Prince who were much older than the women they courted were nonetheless highly eligible if it was known that they were able to purchase the freedom of their brides. If the husband buying his wife's freedom was a slave, his owner sometimes allowed him to hire himself out one or two days a week to earn the money to buy his freedom and that of his family. Some husbands were able to buy a wife and children at the same time, whereas others bought their sons first, since children were cheaper and could be put to work to earn enough money for the purchase of the rest of the family.[11]

Venture Smith, who excelled at negotiating with his owners, belonged to the latter group. Seized in West Africa and taken to Rhode Island at age eight he married Marget, a fellow slave of his owner, at twenty-two. Soon thereafter Smith, said to weigh three hundred pounds and to possess enormous physical strength, intervened in a quarrel between his wife and her mistress. He tried to get Marget to apologize to her mistress, but instead the woman went for her horsewhip. Unwilling to stand idly by, Smith "received the blows of the whip" but turned around and threw "the whip to the devouring fire." While Smith negotiated his own sale to another master, his wife and children remained behind. Living apart from his family he continued to visit them and fathered two more children. He had a clear plan to gain freedom for his family, which involved buying his sons first so that they could help him in his various enterprises, including his business of carrying freight on small boats between Rhode Island, eastern Connecticut, and Long Island. Slowly he acquired enough funds to purchase his wife and daughter, deliberately timing his purchase of his wife to occur before she gave birth so that he would not have to pay for his youngest child.[12] Smith's effort to protect his

4.1. Headstone of Meg (Marget) Smith, 1809, Haddam, Connecticut. Meg (Marget) Smith lived out her remaining years on the hundred-acre farm her husband owned in East Haddam, Connecticut. She survived her husband by four years and was buried next to him in the graveyard of the First Congregational Church in East Haddam. Her son and granddaughter were also buried there. Her husband's gravestone told the dramatic story of his kidnapping in Africa and self purchase; her gravestone, either chosen by her husband before her death or by her surviving children, related no story and defined her solely in relationship to her status as a widow. Photo by Karl Stofko wife and his financial acumen, first in slavery, and then in freedom, showed that an African-born husband aspired to be the protector of his wife, even in slavery, and wanted to be her provider as well, by negotiating for her purchase.[13]

Actually, the slaves most likely to be sold were adolescent boys, who often grew up separately from their families. Young boys and men, useful as general farm labor, were treated more like hard currency than lifelong property, easily liquidated when their masters did not need their labor and required cash. Even if sons had been initially raised by their mothers, they were quickly removed from them. Enslaved boys were sold several times; the lucky ones were purchased or given as gifts to owners within the same town. Others were sold to new masters who took them away and as a result, were shuffled around quite often in their youth. Thus, when Edom London was thirteen years old he was first sold, and he was purchased ten more times by owners in Massachusetts and Connecticut over the next twenty years. He was sometimes owned by a master for as little as a few weeks. At age thirty-three he became free, several years after he was discharged from the Continental Army.[14] Other young men were orphaned Africans who arrived in New England without kin. One youth brought from Mali was first owned by a master in New Haven who in the winter did not give him shoes. He had six subsequent owners in Milford, Connecticut, some of whom owned him for only a few months. Black women were less in demand as laborers and were sold less frequently, except when they were bought for purposes of speculation.[15]

The prospect of a life in slavery was hardest for a boy as he grew into a young man: he wanted to assert his manly independence and was willing to take risks to achieve it. The typical slave runaway was an adolescent boy who had no responsibilities to a wife and children and fled on his own, although some of these young men were merely "playing truant." Some young men were running away because they were in search of sexual or marital partners; others sought escape because they knew their masters were planning to sell them—or that they were of such an age that they were likely to be sold. Fugitive young men scattered in all directions, some toward the large seaports and others toward Indian towns where they might settle, avoid English law, and find an Indian wife who had some land of her own. Abolitionist sea captains knowingly enlisted runaways as crew; other captains were desperate for healthy, strong young men and did not ask too many questions of those willing to enroll for a long and dangerous voyage. There are no examples of advertisements for enslaved women who dressed as men so that they could sail away to freedom. Among the 649 advertisements for runaways in several Connecticut newspapers between 1763 and 1820, 87 percent were male. Advertisements for runaway slaves in Rhode Island newspapers from 1732 to 1800 show that 85 percent of slave runaways were adult males and boys.[16]

A wife might steal a horse to visit her husband and child on the neighboring farm, but it was rare for her to engage in escape attempts so that she could reunite with her family. Most of the women who did take flight were young, often unmarried; some were fleeing to cities; one runaway from Newport was hoping to take shelter with her mother. Only two of the enslaved women fugitives advertised in Rhode Island newspapers between 1732 and 1800 were mothers—at least according to the advertisements, which after all did not routinely describe maternal status; the ads mentioned motherhood only if a woman was traveling with her children. Some mothers ran away and left their children behind; however, many women did not want to flee unless they could take their children with them. It was much more difficult to escape with children in tow; women were slowed down because young children took small steps, were too heavy to carry, were hungry, and cried out or made other noises, thus alerting patrollers. An enslaved woman stopped on the road might not be able to easily explain why she had left her master's place. Even a mother who was able to reach a new town and escape detection would have had difficulty finding work because employers did not want to house a woman and her children.[17]

A few mothers took flight rather than accept being parted from their children. In 1764 Lillie, thirty-four years old, fled her owner in New London with her two daughters, perhaps because she feared being sold away from them. Lillie and her daughters were captured and returned to her master. Eight years later Lillie, pregnant with another child, was sold to Joseph Miner of Coventry, and was thus separated from her children (perhaps by then one of her children was dead). Her four-year-old daughter Susan was still living in the household of her first owner in New London. In Coventry Lillie gave birth to a son, Tony. In April of 1773 she took him with her as she fled, fearing an impending sale. Headed back to New London, she walked a distance of thirty-one miles; arriving in New London at her old master's house, she grabbed her daughter Susan and disappeared. There is no evidence that Lillie was captured; instead she appears to have become a noted fortuneteller and died in 1786 at age fifty-one.[18]

Slave marriages persisted despite the threat of sale and the frequency of couples living separately; it is the permanence and legality of these relationships that is in question. Masters knew that slaves had relationships, called "Negro marriages," for no other reason than the obvious one, that enslaved women had children with a man who often lived nearby and came around to visit. With or without ritual, a couple consented "to take each other for better or worse in their own way."[19] The question was how masters and courts regarded such relationships. Some wanted to sell a woman because she was immoral, others thought it was preferable to look the other way, and still others wanted to negotiate a sale so that the couple could live together as husband and wife. In most cases, masters had granted permission for these arrangements. "Negro marriages" appear in New England criminal records in two contradictory ways. Slave husbands and wives, who were not legally married but wed according to the standards of "Negro marriage" were fined for fornication. There were few such prosecutions, however, because it was not the slave but the master who ended up paying the fines.[20] A Negro marriage also appears in a prosecution of an enslaved woman for killing her baby. A jury in Massachusetts found Flora not guilty of the crime of infanticide because she was tried under an obscure statute that punished with hanging a mother who had murdered her "bastard" child. The prosecution charged Flora with giving birth alone to a baby and throwing the infant into the pit of an outhouse. The jury decided that Flora had not given birth to a "bastard" because she was a married woman, even though she had not been married by a clergyman. This jury was not trying to make a broad statement about the validity of "Negro marriage" but instead was reluctant to send a woman to her death and seized on a technicality to declare Flora not guilty.[21]

Probably the most puzzling attitude toward "Negro marriage" was that of Rev. James MacSparran, an Anglican minister and large landholder in southern Rhode Island noted for his efforts to baptize slaves in the region. As a man of the cloth, one might have expected him to encourage the marriage of his slaves. Perhaps he disliked Mingo, the potential husband for his slave Maroca who lived on a neighboring plantation, or he did not want his slaves to marry "abroad." Previously Maroca had a daughter with a fellow slave of MacSparran's, but the father of the child had died or been sold. Then she had two children with Mingo. A convert to Christianity, she had promised MacSparran to break off the relationship but when he caught her "receiving presents from Mingo," he knew she had deceived him. Going against his wife's views, MacSparran punished Maroca with one or two lashes. Maroca had been willing to lie to MacSparran because she wanted to continue to see Mingo, even though she risked a whipping. However, MacSparran retaliated against both of them by selling their child soon after the baby was baptized.[22]

The Reverend Samuel Sewall of Boston, known both as the judge who regretted his decisions at Salem witchcraft trials and the author of a pamphlet denouncing the slave trade and slavery, officiated at black marriages in Boston as early as 1700. In order for these marriages to take place Sewall sometimes involved himself in negotiations between the respective owners of the couple. A case in point was the marriage of Jane to an Angolan slave, Sebastian, who was Sewall's hired laborer. Jane and her mistress wanted Sebastian's master to indenture him so that he could buy Jane's freedom; the owner refused, but was willing to provide some money to Jane if she had children with Sebastian. Sewall urged Jane and her mistress to accept this offer, which they did; the couple were legally married, and the next year their child was born and baptized in Sewall's church. In Massachusetts in 1705 the legislature adopted a proposal of Sewall that no master could "deny marriage to his Negro with one of the same nation, any law, usage or custom to the contrary notwithstanding."[23] Sewall appears to have pressed for a law because he sensed public uneasiness about slave marriage. Even though Massachusetts was the only New England colony to pass a provision expressly providing for legal marriage of slaves, slaves in Rhode Island, Connecticut, and New Hampshire were often married by ministers or justices of the peace.[24]

In order to secure the legality of slave marriage Sewall was forced to accept a ban on interracial marriage. (English law had no restrictions on interracial marriage.) As was true in coastal Virginia, interracial sex was more common than anyone was willing to admit and prior to the ban, there was at least one instance of an interracial marriage—a white mistress and her African slave in Scituate in 1690. The purpose of the ban on interracial marriage was to prevent blacks from mixing freely with whites, including the most dangerous kind of interracial association, marriage. Whites feared interracial marriage more than any other form of interracial association because it symbolized social equality and threatened white men's sense that they held exclusive ownership of their women's sexuality. In order to further police the color line white owners threatened to punish black men found having sex with white women with banishment to other colonies.[25] It was not interracial sex or even marriage that was the issue so much as the hierarchy that preserved white woman as the sexual property of white men. Thus, there was no policing of sex or marriage between blacks and Indians nor any attempt to curb the liaisons between white men and black women.

De facto interracial marriages, which offered routes to freedom for the woman, existed despite the law and suggest that on the frontier no one paid much attention to legal statutes about marriage. The first woman who achieved her freedom in this manner was Nana Negro, the concubine of Dutch fur trader Elias Van Shaack. The Dutch bought African slaves from New York City to their large tracts of land along the Hudson where they traded liquor to the Mohicans in exchange for beaver and deer pelts. Van Shaack left the area of Dutch settlement on the eastern side of the Hudson and headed for fur-trading territory across the Massachusetts border. He brought with him Nana; she gave birth to their son Cuffee, who was raised to learn the languages of trade, English, Dutch, and Mohican. A Massachusetts legislative committee decided that Van Shaack's liquor sales to the Mohicans were disturbing the peace among the Indians and required him to move to the town of Stockbridge, populated mainly by Christianized Indians living in English-style homes as well as wigwams. Van Shaack speculated in land, traded horses, made plans to build a saw mill, and bought more furs. Nana nursed him through his many years of decline; preparing for his dependents in the event of his death Van Shaack deposited a deed of manumission for his wife and child in 1746. After his father's death Cuffee Van Shaack, like his father, speculated in Indian land; he also honored his father's wishes to look after his mother. In his own will he specified that his mother should be allowed to live in her house and gave the balance of his property to his partner for his mother's care.[26]

French Huguenots seemed to have been surprisingly French in their personal conduct, taking African women as their mistresses. Slave owning was fairly rare in the seaport town of Milford, Connecticut; the Huguenot émigré Lewis Lyron with his six slaves was by far the largest owner in town. He maintained his ties with France, importing wine as well as trading with the West Indies. A widower, Lyron chose not to remarry; instead, he took as his mistress his slave Bess who cared for him in his last years. In his will he deeded five of his slaves to his relatives, but manumitted Bess and made special provision for her. She received use of the house and the land during his lifetime, which reverted to his nephew at her death. He also left her an iron still and various pewter items so that she could make her living from brewing liquor.[27] Lyron's nephew, as executor of the will, clearly knew about Bess and was trusted by his uncle to distribute property to her.

The largest number of legally married slaves were owned by ministers and church deacons who believed their religious principles enjoined them to encourage Christian marriage among their slaves. They were especially likely to favor the marriage of a couple who lived in their home. Many ministers, believing that the purpose of Christian union was to prevent fornication, saw marriage as a religiously acceptable way to permit sexual intercourse under their roof between the slaves they owned. Seeing themselves as members of a godly community, ministers also wanted to encourage the proper formation of families. They held that the family was the primary institution for enforcing order and that a stable marriage, even among slaves, served as a barrier against resistance and outright rebellion.[28]

It would seem that the frequent separation of husband and wife in slavery encouraged taking new partners. Actually enslaved husbands and wives regarded adultery as a serious ground for divorce. Neither an enslaved husband nor his enslaved wife was expected to have to endure a spouse's interracial liaison; interracial sex was not simply a stigma for a white woman but a reason for black men or women to assert rights to legally terminate a marriage. In fact, marital unhappiness caused by interracial sex precipitated the first two divorce suits brought by New England blacks, an enslaved wife in Bolton, Connecticut, in 1725, and an enslaved husband in Boston in 1741.

These unhappy spouses would have needed an attorney to draft a petition to a governor and his council; in granting these divorces a governor and his council indicated that they believed that slave married couples were entitled to the same remedies as free couples and that enslaved men and women had the same delicacy of feelings as white people. It also might be added that white colonists believed that a black or white spouse should not have to accept a spouse's infidelity when it involved interracial sex.[29]

The actual process slaves went through in marrying combined paternalism with acknowledgment of the humanity of the slaves, precisely the same mixed messages as in New England law. A man visited his sweetheart and to express the seriousness of his intent brought her a present, such as the earrings the slave Jack in Boston made for his beloved Juliet. A slave suitor asked for the master's permission to marry the bride. If the owner assented, the couple posted banns, that is, asked a minister to announce the planned marriage in a church three Sundays in a row to determine if there were any impediments to the union. An enslaved couple was married by a minister or justice of the peace. Sometimes the bride wore a special dress given to her by her mistress and the groom might be given a suit of clothes by his master. The husband was expected to pay a fee to the minister for performing the service, but some masters paid the minister's fee or a minister returned the payment to the bride as a wedding present. After the ceremony guests danced to the music of a fiddle player, feasted, and toasted the happy couple with rum or cider. Some of these marriages were then legally registered in the town records.[30]

New England ministers recognized potential problems in the marriage vows slaves took, but seemed to vary in which passages they found most contradictory. The Reverend Robert Hubbard in Greenfield, Massachusetts, consulted his colleague before revising the wedding vows for two slaves owned by different owners to omit the phrase "you promise to live together."[31] One Congregational minister eliminated to "till death to us part" so as to make clear the temporary nature of slave marriage. The slave bride was asked to pledge obedience to her husband, but the groom was told that he and his wife would remain true to each other "*so* long as God, in his Providence, shall continue you and her abode in such Place (or Places) as that you conveniently come together."[32]

Reverend Samuel Phillips, a slaveowning minister in Andover, Massachusetts and later the founder of Phillips Academy, created special vows for slaves. These emphasized that the master had the right of sale and asked each of the parties to swear obedience to their owners in his special "Form for a Negroe Marriage." Before pronouncing the couple married, he said, "I then agreeable to your Request, and wth ye Consent your Masters & Mistesses, do Declare, that you have License given you to be conversant and familiar together, as *Husband and Wife*, so long as God shall continue your Places of abode as aforesaid; and so long as you shall behave your-selves as it becometh Servants to doe: For you must, both of you, bear in mind, that you Remain Still as really and truly as ever, your Master's Property, and therefore it will be justly expected, both by God and Man, that you behave and conduct your-selves, as Obedient and faithfull Servants towards your respective Masters & Mistresses for the Time being."[33]

While the legal rights of the enslaved husband were limited to the right to divorce, the free black husband had many of the same rights as a free white man, except when his legal rights came into conflict with those of a slave owner. A free black husband married to a free wife was permitted to exercise a right of moderate chastisement (even though there was a law against wife assault), had legal custody of his children, and had the right to determine the residence of his wife and children. Moreover, the principle of coverture was tested and affirmed in the divorce of Lucy and Scipio Pernam. However, a free black man married to an enslaved wife had much more limited rights than a white husband because the master's right to control his property invariably trumped the rights of a husband under coverture.[34]

In the 1760s a black husband for the first time tried to use the principle of coverture as a means of gaining his wife's freedom. Fortunatas Sharper, who was free and living separately from his enslaved wife, was probably motivated both by his belief in the rights of a husband and his desire not to have to purchase his wife's freedom. His owner, a Quaker in Barnstable, had honored a pledge to emancipate him made before the Sandwich Friends Meeting, which had been encouraging members to manumit their slaves. Sharper wrote to Colonel James Otis, the eminent lawyer and member of the Governor's Council who lived in Barnstable, asking for (free) legal advice. He wrote, "I have married a slave with her masters and mistresses free consent with Righting from under their bans." He wanted to know "whether ano I cant taker a way and hold hur By Law."[35] There is no record of a reply, and since court records in Barnstable County were destroyed in a fire, it is not known whether Sharper was able to bring suit for his wife's freedom.[36]

During the Revolutionary War black husbands tested several other legal strategies to gain freedom for a wife. In 1773 Peter Hanson, an illiterate free black man in southern New Hampshire, was residing in Nottingham and his wife and six children were living with her master in the neighboring town of Dover. Hanson had been making trouble with his wife's master and mistress for not allowing him to visit his family freely. An African brought to New England, Hanson had been baptized as a young man by the Rev. Jeremy Belknap and had brought all of his children to baptism. Like Wheatley, he saw slavery as a violation of his Christian beliefs, arguing that he should be permitted to divorce because "making Slaves of any of the human Race is unrighteous in the sight of God…" The fact that Belknap was also antislavery strengthened Hanson's views of the incompatibility of his faith and slavery. Petitioning the New Hampshire legislators as men who dwelled in "the land of Liberty," he hoped to show them that the kind of marriage he was forced to endure violated their principles. Making clear his quarrel was not with his wife but with the nature of slave marriage he argued that it "would be very Wicked" to father slave children and that any offspring conceived in bondage would curse him forever. Remarkably, the House of Representatives of New Hampshire voted to hear Hanson's petition before the state's General Assembly thought better of the matter and ignored his plea.[37]

Another somewhat less innovative legal strategy was for a husband to bring suit against his wife's owner for damages in depriving him of his rights as a husband under coverture. At the end of the Revolutionary War, Exeter, aided by Northampton abolitionist lawyer Caleb Strong, sued Oliver Hanchett for the huge sum of £600 damages and for the loss of his wife's company. Strong had helped to draft the Bill of Rights to the Massachusetts Constitution and had been the lawyer for Quock Walker who sued for his freedom the same year. Strong believed that the general language of the Bill of Rights, which stated that all men were created equal, had rendered slavery in Massachusetts unconstitutional. *Exeter a Negro v. Oliver Hanchett* (1783) was also an interstate dispute, since Exeter was free and residing in a Massachusetts town, while his wife Flora, the slave of Oliver Hanchett, lived across the border in Suffield, Connecticut, a town that had originally been part of Massachusetts. Strong may have surmised that a jury would rule in favor of Exeter because Hanchett, a former captain in the Revolutionary Army and tavern owner, was described by his neighbors as "a desperate character, and the terror of the region."[38] Exeter's suit also raised the question of "comity," whether one state was required to honor the law of another when it conflicted with its own.

Exeter and Flora had been legally married for more than a decade and had two young daughters but had been living apart. When Flora was about to be sold by Hanchett, she ran away with the help of her husband and a female friend. Hanchett offered two major arguments in the lower court. The first was that he held legal title to the ownership of Flora; the second was that Flora and Exeter had "consented" to limit their marital rights in their wedding vows by assenting to one of the standard marriage vows ministers offered slaves. Hanchett stooped so low as to call as his witness the minister at their marriage who testified that Flora vowed to remain a "servant" obligated to her respective master.[39] The assumption here is that the free black man had the legal right to enter into a contract, and since marriage was a form of legal contract, Exeter had voluntarily limited his rights as a husband.

The court of common pleas in Hampshire County, Massachusetts, found on behalf of Exeter but reduced the damage award to £65 and court costs. Hanchett appealed to the Massachusetts Superior Court, which ruled on his behalf. The higher court seemed to have made its decision based on Hanchett's legal title to Flora and avoided the question whether coverture affected her status as a slave. The court ruled that it was inappropriate for the Commonwealth of Massachusetts to harbor the fugitive slave of an owner from another state. The judges of the Court distinguished between their desire to eliminate slavery in Massachusetts and their respect for the property rights of an owner from outside the state. In vain Exeter searched for his wife and daughters after Hanchett sold them but died not knowing their whereabouts. They had been taken to New York City and purchased by a new owner who brought them to a small farming area in western Virginia near Roanoke; their heirs kept alive the family's love of liberty. Four sets of grandchildren of Exeter and Flora in coordinated lawsuits tried to win their freedom in the courts of Virginia, alleging that their mother and grandmother were free.[40] They lost all of these suits, however, and gained their freedom only as a result of the Emancipation Proclamation.

Never satisfied with individual legal strategies to gain freedom, however novel, black men also pursued collective means of gaining freedom through petitions to colonial and state legislatures, in which they expressed the importance of patriarchal ideas in their definition of freedom. Felix, no last name given at the time, probably Felix Holbrook, signed the "humble petition" of several enslaved men in Boston in 1773, which requested compensated emancipation—asking for time to work several days a week so that they could purchase their freedom. To Felix real property was the foundation of political rights, but ownership of wives and children came next; all of these rights then served as the basis for political rights. Felix wrote, "We have no Property. We have no wives. No Children. We have no City. No Country."[41] In May of 1774 "a Grate Number of Blackes" in Massachusetts specifically addressed the second-class nature of black marriage. They wrote that they were deprived of liberty because "the endearing ties of husband and wife are strangers for we are no longer man and wife than our masters or Mestresses thinkes proper marred or onmarred." The men imbued this petition with notions of hierarchy and submission to proper authority. Black men had been denied their proper masculine dominance in the family because of slavery, they argued. They demanded to know, "[H]ow can a Slave perform the duties of a husband to a wife or a parent to his child [?] How can a husband leave master and work and Cleave to his wife [?} How can the wife submit themselves to there Husbands in all things [?] How can the child obey thear parents in all things [?]"[42] Like other petitions, this one was not acted on, although it prompted discussion in the Massachusetts legislature.

Freedom for the black family in the post-revolutionary era led many couples to seek legal marriages and move out of white households into their own quarters. The percentage of blacks living with whites plummeted dramatically in city after city; in Newport it fell from 86 percent in 1774 to 59 percent in 1780. Black families in Providence and New Haven had to delay their goal of family reunification because of gradual emancipation—in 1790, only 23 percent of blacks in Providence were living in their households, and the figure was 40 percent in New Haven. Meanwhile in Boston, where slavery had been unconstitutional for seven years by the time of the census, two-thirds of blacks were living in their own households.[43]

Before a man went off to war, he often legally married his sweetheart, or he went before a minister when he was home on furlough. After fighting for their country black veterans returned home to build a cabin, find a job, and start a new life; in the meantime some couples had grown apart.[44] In the new atmosphere of freedom free black husbands were restricting the movements of their wives or insisting that their wives must go out to work. *How can wives submit themselves to their husbands in all things?* Some wives were refusing to submit themselves to their husbands in many things. Among white as well as black wives a "female spirit of independence" had been nurtured by war and the rhetoric of the revolution. A few couples took their marital disputes to court, generally seeking a divorce on grounds of adultery or bigamy; others separated but reconciled at the behest of neighbors.

Beginning in 1781 free black men began to take out newspaper advertisements, refusing to pay for the debts of errant wives; these ads rather than occasional divorce suits of couples serve as the best barometers of racial identity, black male patriarchy, and conflict between the sexes in the post-emancipation era. The twenty-seven black husbands who paid for advertisements in New England newspapers between 1781 and 1800 found themselves forced to admit that they had been unable to live according to the ideal of patriarchy.[45] In these advertisements a husband presented his wife as a reprobate, a "bad woman" who did not know her place—and refused to stay at home where she belonged. Conflict in black marriages appears to have been related to sex, money, the physical mobility of women during and after the war, and a husband's desire to control his wife; in sum, it was not simply a man's credit but his honor and manhood that were at stake.[46]

Among the most common of complaints of these husbands was adultery. For a married woman the dictionary definition of "elope" was "to run away from one's husband with a lover." Fourteen out of twenty-seven husbands charged their wives with elopement and another six with more specific ways of saying the same thing: Abigail Ingersoll had "behaved herself in a manner not becoming a virtuous woman"; Rebecca King had "behaved unworthily"; Sylvia Hall had "violated the Marriage Covenant and thereby rendered herself unworthy of any confidence." Primus Grant was the most explicit of the husbands in assailing his wife for "having left his dwelling [and cohabiting] with other men."[47]

A wife's adultery had powerful resonances in African and New England cultures—in both cases, it represented the greatest form of dishonor for a man, and a threat to patriarchy. The religious traditions from which New England's Africans came were quite diverse: polytheist spirituality, Christianity, Islam, and various combinations of these. African cultures also varied greatly in the severity of the punishment for adultery and the degree to which adulterous men and women were punished for infidelity in a relatively equal manner. In some of these cultures adultery was a reason for divorce; cultures also varied as to the importance of a bride's virginity at marriage.[48] Nonetheless, in all of these cultures there was no greater dishonor for a husband than to be a cuckold. The experience of freedom only exacerbated this sense of violation because adultery rendered a free black husband unmanly and threatened his belief that he had affirmed his manhood in winning his freedom. Adultery, as historian Toby Ditz points out, was "a crime against the husband who was master of his wife. And in the eighteenth century, a man who was not a master ... was not a full member of the civil community of adult men."[49]

The punishment for failure to pay one's creditors was being sent to debtor's prison—an experience unknown among enslaved men since they had not been responsible for their own debts. Bound by the rules of coverture, a free husband was responsible for the debts his wife incurred. In the first years of emancipation some black men were beginning to learn what debtor's prison was like. Six years after his marriage to the beautiful and talented Phillis Wheatley John Peters found himself locked in a cell in debtor's prison in Boston, considered to be a "derdfull Place." He had owned a grocery store on Court Street in Boston but apparently could not pay his creditors. One of the most distinguished young gentlemen of his race in Boston, Peters wore a powdered wig and carried a cane. If an enterprising representative of the race with such a celebrated wife could be brought so low, what might happen to other more humble Africans? In some jails debtors were separated from common criminals in a separate room, but mostly they were thrown in with them. Usually debtors were sentenced to a two- or three-month term, although some were allowed to leave prison after a week or two. A mariner could also be forced into debt peonage, compelled to make one voyage after another until a wife's debts were paid off.[50]

Were these husbands also trying to get their wives to return home by cutting off their credit? Some white husbands explicitly stated in their advertisements that they wanted a wife to come home; black husbands offered no such an entreaty. Nonetheless, the "harboring provision" in nine of these advertisements threatened those who sheltered a fugitive with a damage suit; by making it risky to help an absconding wife, a husband increased the chances that his wife would recognize that she had no other option but to reunite with him.[51] However, since most of these advertisements did not include statements of this kind, it can be assumed that the majority of black husbands were not explicitly trying to secure the return of their wives. Moreover, a husband who stated in print that his wife had committed misconduct or indecency does not appear to have been ready to settle his marital differences amicably. The one couple who seemed to negotiate their parting on friendly terms was Sarah and Joseph Nightingale of Providence who notified merchants and other creditors that they had ended their marriage and had "mutually agreed to part from each other."[52]

Some insight into the general nature of marital tensions can be gained from examining these advertisements more broadly. A few white husbands had begun taking out such ads in New England newspapers by the 1740s (and in Pennsylvania as early as the 1720s). The first Indian husband who took out such an advertisement was the English-educated Indian sachem, Thomas Sinigret ("King Tom"). Over the objections of his tribe, he had married Mary, a biracial woman, at the local Anglican church. Mary had taken as her lover Benjamin Cross, an English settler, and was not discreet, since her servant had caught her having sex with him. She had left her husband for Cross, but Sinigret showed up at Cross's house drunk and assaulted her. Already in debt because of his lavish spending, he advertised his wife in the local paper, *The Newport Mercury* and followed up by petitioning for a divorce.[53]

Sinigret was the relatively atypical husband who took out an advertisement because he had had a great deal of property to protect; most men had none, but instead wanted to safeguard their credit and stave off being sent to debtor's prison. After the first newspaper advertisement of a black husband appeared in a Boston newspaper at the end of the war postings spread throughout New England to other major cities such as Providence, Salem, and Hartford and to the small towns in western Massachusetts; later on posting caught on among the small black populations in Vermont or Maine. Even though black men were late to the game, they were overrepresented among husbands who posted their wives. In Boston in the 1780s there were eight advertisements placed by black men in Boston newspapers out of a total of fifty-seven, or 14 percent of the total postings for runaway wives in the city in which blacks were 3 percent of the population.

The husbands who posted these ads—at least the ones about whom information can be found—were black men who exemplified the ideal of respectability. Five signed their advertisements with their mark; presumably the rest were literate, and if that was the case, their rate of literacy was much higher than that for the average black male of their day. An equal number were veterans of the Revolutionary War and one, Salem Poor, had been recognized by white troops "as a brave and valiant soldier" who fought with them at the Battle of Bunker Hill.[54] In fact, Salem Poor and Prince Hull (not to be confused with the leader of the Boston black community Prince Hall), had been comrades in arms at the Battle of Bunker Hill and served side by side in the Continental Army at the Battle of Saratoga. Another veteran, Pomp Magus, had fought off the redcoats with a pitchfork when they invaded Reading. After enlisting in the Continental Army he took part in the attack on the supply depot at Fort Ticonderoga, served three years under General Washington, and was held as a prisoner of war by the British in New York City. Cato Gardner and Cato Gray were comrades of a different sort, belonging to the African Lodge in Boston, the first organization of black Freemasons in North America. Two of the husbands had petitioned unsuccessfully to the Massachusetts legislature to fund black emigration to West Africa; these men took pride in their race. Veteran Cato Freeman had taken a new surname to symbolize his new legal status. Another five husbands called attention to their race in their advertisement, by referring to themselves as "a black man," including Cesar Hall of Providence who signed his advertisement as "a free black man."[55]

Less is known about the fugitive wives than their husbands, except for Sally Larnard Prince, the daughter-in-law of Abijah and Lucy Terry Prince. She left her husband Cesar, a tenant farmer and Revolutionary War veteran, after eight years of marriage. She and Cesar had married in Hadley, Massachusetts, when she was four months pregnant but their child had died. Like most free couples, they had moved from town to town in search of work, ending up in Manchester, Vermont.[56] It is true that the typical black soldier in the Continental Army was away from home for an average of four years, leaving a young wife behind, but the Princes were married after the war. Nor did Cesar Prince come from a dysfunctional family with poor role models of marital stability. The thirty-year partnership of his parents exemplified the ideal of commitment to family worthy of imitation by any young man. Although there is little information about these women the whereabouts of a few of them can be discerned from the information their husbands provided. Amas Cambridge fled with her children to New Marlborough; Catherine Gray left Boston to take shelter with a black woman in Westford, a town twenty-three miles to the north.[57]

Cato Gardner of Boston, the first black husband in New England to post an ad for his wife, was one of the most eminent free black men in post-revolutionary Boston and a close personal associate of the black leader Prince Hall. Gardner was one of a group of seventy-five black men, including Cesar Spear who signed a petition urging the state of Massachusetts to fund black emigration to Africa. In 1797 he helped to establish the second black organization in Boston, the African Society, which, among other things, provided benefits to widows of member, but only those deemed respectable by the Society. In 1805 he withdrew from the First Baptist Church to help organize the first black church in Boston, African Baptist, and solicited $1500 from friends and personal contacts to complete the project. A marker above the front door of the church, still standing, reads: "To Cato Gardner first promoter of this building."[58]

Two years after they were married in Boston in 1779, Violet and Cato Gardner were having problems. A husband who thought in terms of "my family," not "our family," he complained that his wife neglected "her duty in my family, going abroad and idling her time, to my great Damage..." Recently freed from slavery, it appears that Violet had "Company" who tempted her "to go abroad." Cato Gardner thought his neighbors encouraged Violet and decided that they should move to another neighborhood "where she may have less Company." Under coverture a husband had the right to determine the domicile of a couple; nonetheless, Violet refused to move.

Meanwhile Boston's African Lodge had placed Cato Gardner on trial for "carnal dueling" with an unnamed lodge brother. The lodge expelled him temporarily until he cleared himself of the charges by vote of his brother Masons. The most likely reason Gardner had engaged in a duel was because he suspected a fellow lodge brother was keeping Company with his wife. Violet Gardner's apparent infidelity had caused her husband's "Ruin," a word he used three times in his advertisement, which conveyed not merely his fear of financial difficulties but also his sense of disgrace and dishonor.[59] The African Lodge, like the public officials of Boston, did not approve of dueling, believing that black men should display respectability as law-abiding citizens. But while the African Lodge disapproved of the duel, it was not unknown among the larger public—Boston Common had a reputation as the place where duels took place, even though Massachusetts had tried to crack down, fining or imprisoning men caught dueling. In eighteenth-century Boston gentlemen quarreling over cards or men who had too much to drink at a tavern challenged each other to these fights to the death. In 1742 two enslaved men, accompanied by their seconds, had been arrested on the Boston Common before they could raise their swords and were sent to jail.[60] It is not necessary to say that black men wanted to be gentlemen, like white men, since combat to the death also fit with an African sense of masculine honor defended through a test of wills and physical strength. But it is important to point out that men such as Cato Gardner could see that the entire standing of the race depended on black men holding themselves to a high standard of personal conduct. Thus his honor as an African and as a respectable Christian gentleman was at stake.

The second husband to complain in print was Boston Paul, whose quarrel with his his wife Ruter had to do with money. He complained that she was refusing "to labour or do any thing to support herself, and is running me in Debt, more than I am able to pay." There are subsequent examples of emancipated slave woman who also refused to labor. After the Civil War former enslaved women in the South sometimes withdrew from full-time work in the fields, preferring to devote themselves to their families. In most cases, their husbands concurred with their decision, but some women hoped to remain at home, despite their husbands' wishes to the contrary. Southern whites complained that former enslaved women "wanted to play the lady," an aspiration they thought much above the station of former slaves, to be condemned as "putting on airs." Maybe Ruter Paul did not want to work as a domestic and hoped to avoid having to take in laundry at home.[61] Her wishes, however, ran contrary to her husband's belief that she needed to earn an income—as well as the stated view of a free husband like Scipio Pernam that the black woman had been fitted by slavery to support herself.

Only one black husband, Prince Hull of Hartford, had some doubts about the black man defending his honor by damaging the reputation of his wife. Hull's background was quite similar to that of other disgruntled husbands. He had grown up in Pittsfield and at age twenty-five joined a Massachusetts militia company, which fought at the Battle of Bunker Hill. Enlisting in the Continental Army three separate times he was discharged honorably in 1777 after being wounded at the Battle of Saratoga. At the war's end he was in his early thirties, employed as a laborer, and living with his wife Lucy in Hartford. Two successive weeks he advertised for Lucy in 1783. He stated that she had eloped, suggesting that he believed she had committed adultery, and perhaps had run off with her lover. She returned home at some point, however, since seven years later, Hull was forced to advertise for her once again. The following year Prince Hull married a free black woman in Middletown, Connecticut, and had a child with her, even though he had not been legally divorced and there is no evidence that Lucy had died.[62]

Hull claimed his task was "disagreeable" in an advertisement in 1791, but pointed out somewhat defensively that white husbands posted their wives, too. He believed that his marital troubles should be hidden from public view, and that family privacy was especially important to black people who should "not declare them [their troubles] to the world." His ad read, "With regret, and shame, the Subscriber finds himself under the necessity of advertising his wife, —Although it is practiced by some white people, yet he (tho black) blushes at the thoughts of declaring to the world that his wife has run away."[63] Hull raised the ante from his previous advertisements seven years before by forbidding "all persons harboring or trusting [his wife Lucy]."[64] He seems to have been trying to force Lucy to return home but since he had "remarried" a year after she left, he may not have been successful in his effort.

The marriages of Lucy Pernam and Mary Sinigret suggest that some of the wives who were posted had been battered by their husbands. Still it cannot be known whether a wife was leaving her husband for another man, defying him on her own, or was so physically mistreated that she was running for her life. Several of the white women of New England whose husbands took out advertisements against them did respond in their own advertisements. Among the white Vermont women who did so, a little less than half complained that the husband was physically abusive or severely neglected the family by failing to provide for them.[65] Countering the charge of adultery they claimed their husbands were insanely jealous. There is every reason to think that black wives had a similar story to tell about husbands so eager to control their movements and decide what company they could keep. Other black wives in eighteenth-century Massachusetts experienced domestic violence; prior to 1760 two wives were the victims of axe murders committed by their husbands. Empowered by a sense of her rights, one free black woman in Boston in 1797 called the night watch to "take her Husband for abusing her" one evening. As the watchmen entered the couple's room the husband drove a fork into the side of one of the men but caused "little damage"; it is not clear if the man was punished by the courts.[66] In Nantucket at about the same time a black husband who assaulted his wife and threatened her life was found guilty by a jury and was whipped with fifteen stripes and ordered to post a bond for good behavior.[67]

Very few white or black women took out advertisements responding to their husband's printed version of events because a woman was not supposed to bring private matters before the public. The two black women who did defend themselves against their husband's charges in their own advertisements had strikingly different views about the matter of female independence.[68] At age twenty-one Phebe Price had married Samuel Cesar, a young free black man who had moved to Bennington, Vermont, from Providence. Five months after they were married Samuel took out an advertisement complaining that his wife was "contracting heavy debts to his injury." Phebe Cesar took out two advertisements in successive weeks in the Vermont Gazette in 1802 refuting her husband's charges. She insisted that she had not deserted their home and that the heavy debts her husband alluded to consisted of "one case of necessity only" in which she had charged a trifling sum on his account." If Samuel thought she had engaged in an unpardonable sin, she offered to repay him "to the last cent." She added the proviso that she would give her husband his money if he "provided he will on his part return to the duties of a husband: and that I do not refuse or mean to refuse to live with him as a wife; but that I shall demand the support and attention due to me, in that character, on every proper occasion, from him as my husband."[69] Desiring respectable dependence, not independence, she was willing to return to Bennington and accept a subordinate position in her home in exchange for her husband's financial support.

Believing in her own rights to property, not in patriarchy, Dorcas Sampson of Providence, Rhode Island, responded to her husband's complaint that she had abandoned him by claiming that he had in fact left her. Her ad stated that "instead of my absenting his bed and board, he has absented from my bed (not having any of his own)." She seems to have referred to her husband's race ("James Sampson a black man") so that the white readership of the *Providence Phoenix* could identify him, not as a positive statement of racial identity. Her posting reveals a strong sense of individual, not mutual ownership of their place of residence, clearly distinguishing his bed from hers. Her voice was not that of the pious Christian woman, the humble supplicant to the legislature, the partner in the family enterprise, or the runaway willing to return home but instead an angry, even sarcastic wife telling the world that she had lost confidence in her husband. Revealing her bitterness she wrote "as he cannot get trusted on his own account, I forbid any one trusting him on mine—and in future he may make his old great coat answer for a bed."[70]

There is a commemorative stamp in honor of Salem Poor but no one remembers Mary Poor; Cato Gardner is regarded as a founding father of Boston's black community and Violet Gardner is entirely unknown. It may never be clear whether these women should be claimed as heroes or victims, independent women or unhappy and unfaithful wives. Whether a wife fighting for her freedom from her husband is the same kind of rebel as a fugitive slave running away from an owner is a question nineteenth-century feminists always liked to pose. The point of recounting their lives is to note that within a few short years some black women might have been both. Beneath the façade of unity in the newly established free black community were tensions within black marriages visible to the readers of the *New London Gazette* or the *Columbian Centinel*. The ideal of patriarchy and marital fidelity cannot be dismissed merely as unsuitable for the reality of free black life, poor choices for women and men who might have found it easier to live with egalitarian gender roles and sexual liberalism. Instead, black men were willing to fight to the death to avenge the wrong to their honor. They not only went to great lengths to defend their standing in the community but also willingly publicized the wrongs they believed they suffered.

5

Seeking Possession of Her Liberty

Joan Jackson was declared free in 1716 in Cambridge, Massachusetts, the first enslaved woman to win her freedom in the courts of New England. She and her husband John spent the rest of their lives seeking to free their children from slavery. Similarly, three other women, one in South Kingstown, Rhode Island, and two in Portsmouth, New Hampshire, succeeded in winning legal freedom by 1750. The New England freedom suit was a civil lawsuit brought by an enslaved person that culminated in a trial in a local court, often decided by a jury.[1] The freedom suit did not begin in colonial New England but it was nonetheless mainly found there. The first such suits appeared in colonial Virginia where there were six of them, one brought by a woman, prior to 1670. Thereafter, such suits disappeared because laws in Virginia closed the legal loopholes that made it possible to sue for freedom. Free black women in Virginia, however, in rare instances did petition the court to hold onto their freedom. There were no freedom suits prior to the end of the Revolutionary War in Pennsylvania or New Jersey. In New York slaves who claimed to be captives of the Spanish and thus prisoners of the war could sue for their freedom in the admiralty courts but there were no civil suits of slaves in New York courts seeking freedom.[2] In New England enslaved women went to court to gain their freedom and free black women did so in order to hold onto theirs. In sum, the New England legal system was unique in the access of slaves as well as free blacks to the courts and in the assistance they received from the region's attorneys.

All told, fourteen black women brought civil lawsuits to win their freedom beginning in 1716 and ending in 1783. Not content with negotiating better terms in slavery, black women took their case to court because they wanted self-ownership. As in all other aspects of black history, the record is scanty and uneven. Local historians and genealogists have not combed through the documents of every county. That one suit came to be known because of references to it in a subsequent one and another from lawyer's notes suggests that court records do not reveal the full extent of litigation.[3] The life stories of six of these women will be recounted here (three prior to the Stamp Act Crisis, three after that) to prove that black woman's desire for freedom preceded by many decades the revolutionary sentiments of white colonists. The Stamp Act Crisis forms a chronological dividing line because as a result of revolutionary fervor that began then more slaves felt emboldened to sue for their freedom in the courts of New England.

Women's freedom suits were brought on the basis of one of three technicalities in the law: that there had been a fraudulent sale, perhaps because the owner had no legal title to his slave; that the plaintiff was not black (by virtue of having a white or Indian mother); or that the owner had entered into a manumission agreement but the document had disappeared. These lawsuits represented a retail rather than wholesale approach to ending slavery, a bid for freedom one person at a time. Nonetheless, a woman testifying in a courtroom crowded with her neighbors was letting them know that she wanted her freedom, even if she and her lawyer did not utter an impassioned appeal against the institution of slavery. Still, by the time of the American Revolution black women plaintiffs did refer to Liberty in their lawsuits and were making more explicit political connections between their pleas for freedom and the American ideal of liberty.

The life stories of a few of these plaintiffs also reveal that these women thought about freedom much more broadly than legal ownership of the self. The last of the fourteen and the best known, Elizabeth Freeman, brought the first legal test of the constitutionality of slavery in Massachusetts in 1781. Like so many other women, she had a many-stranded definition of liberty, which included her belief in the ideals of the Declaration of Independence as well as in the opportunity to buy land, reunite her family, and live a Christian life. In freedom she found ways to express and combine multiple identities (racial, religious, familial, and occupational). No newspaper mentioned her suit at the time, but subsequently her neighbors and employers remembered her for her sterling character; other than Wheatley, Elizabeth Freeman is the most famous black woman Patriot of the revolutionary era. For abolitionists her personal story of courage and extraordinary personal qualities undermined the argument that black people were intellectually inferior to whites and proved that blacks, just like whites, achieved their greatest potential from a life of freedom. The local people who recounted her life were important writers and abolitionists who supplied the words to prove that she believed in the abstract principle of inalienable rights of the individual.

Because judges and juries were more sympathetic to the cause of the slave in Massachusetts than elsewhere, there were more freedom suits there and great chances of success for the plaintiffs.[4] The largest number of such suits initiated by black women, eight, were brought in Massachusetts courts, from the first in 1716 to the last in 1783. Seven of the eight were brought by a woman, acting alone; one was initiated by a husband and wife against the wife's owner. Seven of the suits resulted in freedom and in the eighth the outcome is unknown. Black women brought three additional suits in Rhode Island, the first in 1729 and the last in 1772; two out of these three were successful.[5] There were two freedom suits of black women in New Hampshire, the first in 1742, the second in 1750, and both plaintiffs won.[6] The one black woman who sued for her freedom in Connecticut lost her suit.[7] Black men brought their freedom suits on the basis of one additional ground never found in women's suits, violation of a contract to purchase one's freedom. In Massachusetts between the 1760s and the end of the Revolutionary War six men brought freedom suits on these grounds; they were uniquely situated to sue for freedom on this ground because they were far more likely to be hired out and were therefore able to enter into a purchase agreement with their owners. Thus, these men were placed in a position enslaved women never experienced, negotiating a contract with an owner who subsequently reneged.[8]

In other ways as well, enslaved women confronted greater obstacles in seeking their freedom. Marital status was a major barrier for enslaved women who wanted to bring a civil suit seeking freedom. Because of coverture a married woman was prohibited from suing on her own behalf. Lawyers paid a great deal of attention to whether a woman was single or married and therefore had the ability to sue in her own right. Thus, a married woman (such as Joan Jackson) probably had to claim to be single in order to proceed with a lawsuit. Lawyers for owners in two separate suits contended that the black woman plaintiff was married and therefore had no legal standing to sue. In both cases, however, the attorney's claim failed to persuade, perhaps because the enslaved woman in question was not legally married. However, coverture did allow for a married woman to join with her husband in bringing a lawsuit—and there was one instance of this kind in Massachusetts in 1777.

The procedures for filing a lawsuit reveal the importance of attorneys in subsidizing a woman's litigation and coming to her aid over a period of several years. The standard fee for an attorney was two pounds, which was not an impossible expense for the time. Matthew Robinson of South Kingstown waived his fees for one of his two black women clients and may have done likewise for the other woman, who clearly had very little money. Fees for the clerks, the justices, and the notices that had to be served prior to bringing a case may have cost more than the actual services of a lawyer. The attorney filed these papers in a civil suit in the four-judge Inferior Court of Common

Pleas, which met quarterly. To bring a civil suit required the purchase of a writ from the local justice of peace who notified the defendant of the charges filed and the damages claimed. The plaintiff had to pay for serving the notice and either the attorney or the plaintiff had to endorse the writ, indicating liability for court costs if the suit was lost. Since enslaved women did not have the money or property to pledge as a bond, their attorneys had to be willing to be held liable for court costs if the suit was lost.[9] Most lawyers did not have a local practice but instead rode the circuit to make their income. In traveling from Boston to Salem on behalf of an indigent client an attorney was demonstrating his commitment to justice, the law, or both. Oral tradition has it that blacks in Cambridge contributed to the funding of one man's suit in 1769 but it seems likely that the other plaintiffs received free legal services.[10]

We do not know how these women went about locating a lawyer, but the background of the attorneys reveal that these men were rather typical members of the bar. Most of the lawyers who handled these cases were Loyalists. Benjamin Kent of Boston, who wrote the divorce petition for Lucy Pernam and argued the freedom suit of Jenny Slew joined the Stamp Act protests in Boston but switched his support to the Crown as the revolution approached. Like many other Loyalists he sailed for Halifax, Nova Scotia, after at the end of the war where he went to live with his daughter, who had married a Boston Tory. The two Robinson cousins, lawyers in Rhode Island, were long-time Quaker abolitionists who also sided with the Crown. Thomas Robinson of Newport ("Quaker Tom") was a merchant and shop owner who manufactured and exported spermaceti candles and did legal work on the side. He took his first case on behalf of enslaved women in 1772; three years later he negotiated the personal manumission of Binah, an enslaved woman in Newport. The Nantucket whaling merchant and Quaker William Rotch had offered Binah an interest-free loan so she could buy her freedom from her master. Robinson persuaded Binah's owner to lower his price by threatening to help her flee to Nantucket where Rotch promised to back her in a freedom suit. The promise was not an idle one, since five years previously Rotch had engaged the eminent attorney and future president of the United States John Adams to argue on behalf of the freedom of Prince Boston, a fugitive slave in Nantucket. After the war Robinson crusaded for the end of the slave trade and gradual emancipation in Rhode Island, kept track of the number of black people illegally enslaved in Rhode Island, and was accused by owners of aiding fugitive slaves.[11] Engaging in a personal rescue mission in Newport harbor, he rowed from shore to board a ship destined for the West Indies to demand the release of a kidnapped black man. His cousin, Matthew Robinson, considered one of the most learned members of the Rhode Island bar, sheltered fugitive slaves on his large estate in

SEEKING POSSESSION OF HER LIBERTY 131

South Kingstown, practiced law in Newport and had an even longer record of activism beginning with his successful suit on behalf of Sarah Chauqum in 1732 and ending with another one on behalf of Esther, initiated thirty-six years later. Matthew Robinson took cases for Indians facing the loss of their land, fugitive slaves, and blacks accused of violating the criminal law. For his needy clients he paid all court costs, including any fines or damages they incurred, and pursued their cases for many years.[12]

The story of the Jacksons belongs to the early history of New England abolitionism, since they took advantage of an alliance with white religious people of conscience to pursue their bid for freedom for themselves and their children. Joan Jackson is known to us because of her daring deeds rather than her words.[13] Jackson, her husband, and adult children were involved in forty-five lawsuits over several decades in New London, Connecticut, and Middlesex County, Massachusetts, making them the most litigious black family in colonial New England history, even more litigious than Lucy and Abijah Prince. Separated by many sales, living in separate colonies, this family fought for their freedom by daring intercolony flight, hiding, and bringing suit after suit in the courts for decades. The year after Joan Jackson won her freedom her husband failed in his bid for the emancipation of their son in a New London county court in what may have been a legal effort timed to coincide with hers. Thereafter, her purported owner and his heirs brought at least four separate suits to claim her children as slaves, which her husband and children fought. One of her sons, inheriting his love of liberty from his mother and father, tried to run away from his owner, and sued unsuccessfully for his emancipation in the New London courts. Joan Jackson's own success confirms the fact that Massachusetts was a friendlier legal environment for an enslaved plaintiff than Connecticut, where slave ownership was more prevalent. Yet the couple doggedly pursued their freedom in the courts of both colonies.[14]

Joan Jackson and her husband John belonged to the Rogerenes, a religious sect numbering less than fifty people in 1730. The Rogerenes were similar to Baptists in some respects and Quakers in others. Like Baptists they believed in adult baptism in water; their worship service resembled that of Quakers in that adherents spoke when the spirit moved them. The Rogerenes, also like the Quakers, rejected the idea of a learned ministry since they held that all people were born with a conscience. Openly and loudly they opposed the established church in the colony, the Congregational Church. Proclaiming their faith in the streets, they often barged into their neighbors' religious services to argue with the minister. By deliberately engaging in civil disobedience, they hoped to get arrested in order to mount challenges to established religious and political authority in court. On the Sabbath, the day of rest, the Rogerenes went out of their way to annoy their neighbors. The interracial character of their group reflected their beliefs in fair dealings with Indians and manumission for slaves. The interracial sex that occurred among Rogerenes—Indian men and African women, black men and white women—indicates they were also violating the sexual taboos of their neighbors. Not abolitionists in the modern sense, the Rogerenes held that slaves should be emancipated after completing a term of indentured service.[15] They helped the Jacksons over many years as well as another black woman, Hagar Wright, who had lost her manumission papers and had to petition the governor and his council to claim her freedom.[16]

For the Jacksons legal consciousness was embedded in family ties and interracial community and their struggle in the courtroom was an extension of the family's efforts to live together in New London and secure freedom for their children. Joan Jackson's ideas of freedom were reunification of the family, ownership of land, expression of religious principles, and legal self-ownership. The Jacksons were able to seek their freedom in the courts because of their personal connections to several generations of the largely white members of their religious fellowship. It took an indignant husband, a couple who wanted to live together, and a wealthy interracial community that believed in the value of dissent and had its own lawyers to sustain so many suits over so many years. It is therefore fitting that we know a great deal about the Jackson family and their pursuit of freedom, although unfortunately almost nothing is known about Joan Jackson's successful day in court. As in many of these legal cases, the masters of Joan Jackson are characters in their own right; one of her owners, Samuel Beebe, was among the most tenacious slaveholders in New England because of the length to which he and his heirs were willing to go to hold onto their human property.

The father of the Rogers clan was a wealthy English emigrant, James Rogers, who became the richest man in New London from trading with the Indians, establishing a flour mill, and making biscuits for the navy. He had intended to manumit his slaves at his death, perhaps after they had completed a term of service. Rogers named his adult son John and his grown daughter Bathsheba as the executors of his will with this object in mind, but the language of his will was somewhat ambiguous. Joan and her mother, Maria, a deaf mute, were among the several slaves James Rogers owned. Joan's father was never mentioned in the records but since she was described as a mulatto woman; her father was probably a white man, perhaps even James Rogers himself, especially since there was another former slave of James Rogers—possibly Joan's brother—who was also a mulatto. John and Bathsheba Rogers, acting in accord with what they believed was their father's intent, treated Joan as a free woman; Joan lived with Bathsheba and cared for her children. She had probably known John Jackson, her senior by many years, for a long time. He had been purchased by John Rogers, Jr., manumitted by him, but resided among the Rogerenes as an indentured servant. As a young man he had been arrested along with other Rogerenes for working on the Sabbath. He had fathered a child with a white girl, the daughter of a Rogerene follower, and was required by a New London county court to pay support for his child for four years. Joan and John Jackson seem to have married according to Rogerene principles, which did not involve a minister or a justice of the peace. They did not immediately go into housekeeping, it appears, but eventually began to share a rented house with an English family and then moved into their own cabin in the Rogerene settlement.[17]

The sworn enemy of Joan and John Jackson was Samuel Beebe, the son-in-law of James Rogers. He was a wealthy and litigious slave owner who argued that his father-in-law's will was ambiguous and produced documents in court showing that his wife had been given legal ownership of Joan and her children. In his younger days Beebe had also been a Rogerene, who, along with his fellow dissenters, had broken the Sabbath and been punished with forty stripes. As he matured "King Beebe," as he was known, became one of the wealthiest men in the county, obsessed with securing his wife's inheritance. His wife had apparently agreed that she would not claim her slave Joan until her mother's death. When Elizabeth's mother died Beebe went after Joan; the Rogers' family lawyer implied that Beebe faked legal documents to prove his wife's claim.[18]

After winning his lawsuit, Beebe took Joan and her two-year-old son Jack to his large farm on Plum Island, an 840-acre island in Long Island Sound where he raised sheep. Joan was pregnant at the time and gave birth to her eighth child, her daughter Rachel. In June of 1711 John Jackson, along with John Rogers, rowed twelve miles across the choppy waters of Long Island Sound to seize Joan and his two children. In the middle of the night they rowed back across the Sound to the Connecticut shore and made their way to the Jackson cabin. With Beebe in hot pursuit John took his wife and children to hide in the homes of sympathizers of the Rogerenes in Rhode Island, probably Quakers or Baptists, since they, too, were religious dissenters. Beebe hired three bounty hunters to help him track down Joan and her children. They found them hiding in Rhode Island; within twenty-four hours someone alerted the authorities and the governor of Rhode Island ordered Joan and her children returned to Beebe.[19]

Rogers and Jackson deliberately chose a bench trial rather than a trial by jury to illustrate the evils of injustice in Connecticut. The judge was Reverend Gurdon Saltonstall, not only the nemesis of Abda Duce and a friend of Samuel Beebe but a long-standing enemy of John Rogers. Saltonstall had won a defamation suit for slander against Rogers seventeen years before and there is no reason to believe that the mutual animosity of the two men had cooled in the intervening years. John Jackson and John Rogers, Jr., were charged with trespass; Jackson took the stand and testified that Joan "was taken away from me wrongfully," a phrase that reverberated with that of Hagar Blackmore fifty years earlier.[20] He was thus the first husband to attempt to make the argument that under coverture he had the right to determine his wife's domicile. Saltonstall sentenced the two men to pay Beebe twice the value of Joan and her children and the costs of prosecution. Since John Jackson could not afford to pay his share of these costs, he was forced to indenture himself to Beebe. In turn, Beebe sold the indenture to his lawyer, Colonel John Livingston. Both John Jackson and John Rogers cried out in the courtroom that the sentence was unfair; for his outburst John Rogers was sent to prison for six months and John Jackson, instead of being imprisoned, went to work on the farm of Colonel John Livingston.[21]

Joan and John lived together on the estate of Colonel Livingston in New London with their youngest child while their other children were dispersed in households of the Rogers clan in New London. Livingston presided over Mount Livingston, a huge mansion and lands in New London with African, Indian, and European household workers, farm laborers, and mill hands. It seems likely that John helped on the farm and that the couple resided in a cabin on the grounds. Joan became pregnant again and gave birth to a son Jeremiah. After remarrying Livingston was liquidating his assets before moving to London with his new wife. He took Joan and her baby Jerry to Boston where he sold them at a slave auction to John Stone of Framingham, Massachusetts, in 1714; about two and a half years later Joan brought a lawsuit for her freedom in Middlesex county court.[22] What exactly prompted the suit and who helped her is unclear, although in order to appear in court Joan would have had to allege that she was a "spinster." Like other early freedom cases, hers was probably argued on technical grounds. Although the actual legal record is missing, the most likely legal argument was fraudulent sale, that Stone did not have clear title to ownership of her and her son. Such an argument is consistent with Stone's subsequent actions. After he lost in Middlesex county court he tried to get his money back by suing Colonel Livingston, claiming that Livingston did not hold clear title to Joan and Jeremiah when he sold them to him.[23] (Defect in title was a common argument both sides used in a lawsuit involving a slave).

After Joan Jackson won her freedom in the courts of Massachusetts she and Jeremiah returned to New London. John Jackson appears to have completed his term of service with Colonel Livingston. Soon thereafter he went to court to pursue two lawsuits, suggesting that his cases were part of a coordinated legal effort on behalf of his family. He sued Livingston for defrauding him of four acres of land promised at the end of his indenture; he won this suit and twenty pounds.[24] He then sued for the freedom of his son, John

Jr., whom Livingston had sold to a new owner in Norwich; his son's owner won the case, claiming he had a clear bill of sale.[25] Many of the other Jackson children remained slaves, living in New London or nearby. Subsequently some of the children ran away from their owners and tried to gain their freedom in the courts. Joan and her husband spent their remaining years together, with Joan dying first. After the two of them had died, the heirs of Samuel Beebe continued to go to court to try to claim the Jackson children as their slaves.

The other early abolitionists who assisted blacks seeking their freedom were Quakers. Among those they helped were Sarah Chauqum of South Kingstown, the daughter of an Indian mother and an African father, who claimed that she was an indentured servant who had been illegally enslaved. Unscrupulous whites in New England left to care for free black orphaned children realized a quick profit from selling the child into slavery. Children who had living parents could still be kidnapped and sold, not just to the South or the West Indies, but within New England. Kidnappers targeted Sarah Chauqum as a brown-skinned young girl working as an indentured servant in a South Kingstown household without any powerful local patrons or neighbors to intercede on her behalf. They pocketed a quick profit from selling her into slavery; for four years she served a shopkeeper in New London, Connecticut, mainly spinning wool. Finally she escaped to South Kingstown; her mother successfully pleaded with Matthew Robinson, the Quaker attorney and large landowner in town, to take her daughter's case and waive his legal fees. Robinson successfully won suits in various courts on Sarah's behalf, first securing her freedom in a justice court in South Kingstown, and then winning three successive appeals. He handed over the legal responsibility of the case to the state's attorney general of Rhode Island who won substantial damages for Sarah for the four years she had been enslaved.[26]

If the Rogerenes of New London and the Quakers of South Kingstown help explain the backing needed to bring the earliest freedom suits, it is not as easy to locate any abolitionist connections behind the six successful freedom suits of black men and women in New Hampshire prior to 1750. There were no abolitionist lawyers in New Hampshire, even though prominent attorneys were willing to take these suits. Two of the six were women living in the seacoast town of Portsmouth, the first in 1739 and the second in 1750. A few Quakers dotted throughout the colony manumitted their slaves after a term of service but Portsmouth itself was a northern outpost of the slave trade; ships destined for the West Indies or the slave trade along the coast of West Africa were built in the local harbor. Schooners and sloops from Portsmouth, making stops in Philadelphia, New York, and the eastern shore of Virginia, carried "Jamaica" fish to the island to feed the slaves, as well as lumber and naval supplies.[27]

The first black woman to sue for her freedom in Portsmouth was Elisha Webb, born in freedom in Virginia, the daughter of an African father and a white mother. She had been taught to read and write by her Quaker mistress, who placed her in an indenture so that she could learn a trade before her term of service ended. There were several interracial couples living in eastern Virginia as well as a substantial number of free black landowners; the region was also the port of call for ships headed south to the West Indies and north to New England. Elisha's master to whom she was indentured sold her time to a Portsmouth sea captain who brought her to his home port. He pretended Elisha was his slave and thus profited from selling her to a local shopkeeper. Elisha used her literacy to secure her freedom, finding a sympathetic party in Portsmouth who conveyed a letter of hers to the Virginia county judge who had processed her indenture papers. She informed the judge of her lawsuit and requested that he send a document indicating the facts of her situation. It took eight months to receive his written response because the mail was very slow. He told Elisha to show his letter to her owner, who would assuredly set her free; he sent regards ("their blessing") from her parents, still living in Virginia.[28]

The Portsmouth shopkeeper, possessed of a legal bill of sale for a slave, was not easily persuaded to give up valuable property merely because of a letter from a judge in Virginia. Nonetheless, Elisha's lawyer, the first college-educated attorney in New Hampshire, took her case to court. The New Hampshire court of quarter sessions, confronted with conflicting evidence, decided to write to the judge in Virginia for sworn proof of Elisha's status. He replied by sending many documents, including his sworn statement, along with those from Elisha's former mistress, the mistress's daughter, and the mistress's son, a Virginia justice of the peace. A Portsmouth jury decided in Elisha's favor, but the shopkeeper appealed to the colony's Superior Court; in the meantime he seems to have abandoned his effort because he failed to appear when the case came to trial.[29] As a free woman in Portsmouth, Elisha and her partner Cesar, the father of her seven children, lived together, apparently without ever legally marrying.

The Stamp Act Crisis and revolutionary ferment following it increased the overall number of freedom suits, and as a result, the stories of the women seeking legal freedom appear less idiosyncratic and more connected to a larger political narrative. Among the fourteen freedom suits of black women, nine were brought after 1763. The black desire for self-ownership and family reunification began to intersect with white colonist's resentment against British rule and frequent resort to the metaphor of slavery, describing themselves as reduced to the abject condition of slaves. It was no longer acceptable to conduct slave auctions in taverns; buyers instead had to make discreet inquiries of the printer of the advertisement if they wanted to purchase a slave.

Across New England advocates of freedom were confronting slaveholders and demanding they free their slaves; more owners were emancipating their slaves in their wills. Most juries in Massachusetts, largely comprised of non-slaveholders, had always decided in favor of enslaved plaintiffs seeking their freedom. Success was contagious with revolutionary and abolitionist rhetoric in the air; slaves were encouraged to sue and lawyers decided the respect they gained from their peers was worth the lost time and money it took to prosecute these cases.[30]

Jenny Slew's lawyer Benjamin Kent (Lucy Pernam's divorce attorney in Boston) deliberately avoided attacking the institution of slavery in her freedom suit because he wanted to win his case. Kent's actual argument in *Slew v. Whipple* was that Jenny Slew was white and therefore should not be enslaved because of her race. Slew's mother was a white woman, Betty Slew, and her father was black. At the time she brought her suit the flexible rules of race of the founding generations of New England colonists had disappeared. In the Abda case, Connecticut followed the principle that paternal lineage determined freedom: a son of a free man was himself free. In New Hampshire in 1750 a judge in a freedom suit had ruled that the colony followed the Roman principle of "partus sequiture ventrem" (lineage follows the mother). Judge William Cushing in Slew's case fifteen years later scribbled in his notes "partus sequiture ventrem. Colour is a Presumption."[31] His Latin/English shorthand indicated that he was inclined to think that Jenny Slew was white because she was the daughter of a white mother.[32]

In the first stage of Jenny Slew's suit the major issue was not her race but her marital status and whether she had legal standing to sue. Her attorney offered the standard trespass argument, that Slew had been kidnapped and held against her will for three years, while John Whipple, Jr., her owner and a sea captain in Ipswich, forced her to work for him. Slew demanded her freedom and £25 in damages from Whipple. Whipple's lawyer contended that Slew was legally married, but there is no information as to whether he introduced any documentation to prove that she was.[33] The brief transcript of her trial indicates that she had been married twice, both times to black men. In reaching its decision the court was split evenly: two judges thought Slew had legal standing and two did not, and because there was a tie, she lost her case. As was the common practice, the loser had to pay the winner's court costs. It seems likely that Kent paid these costs as well as those for her appeal. Whipple's lawyers at the appeal stage again claimed that Slew was a married woman and had no right to sue but this time the court asked for proof of Whipple's ownership and he was unable to furnish a valid bill of sale.

Kent reassured the judges that the suit was a standard trespass claim and that he did not intend to challenge the legality of slavery. He insisted, "I shall not enter into the Right of some Men to enslave others."[34] Kent cannot be faulted for deciding on such a strategy when faced with a Superior Court judge who himself owned slaves. Judge Peter Oliver, loyal to the Crown, owned several slaves as did his son. Nonetheless, he seemed to enjoy exposing the hypocrisy of the Patriots. The lawyer from Braintree, John Adams, taking notes in the courtroom when Judge Oliver announced his ruling, wrote that Oliver looked upon the suit as "a contest between liberty and property—both of great consequence, but liberty of most importance of the two."[35] Jenny Slew won her freedom but nothing is known about her life subsequent to her appearance in court.

When Juno Larcom of nearby Beverly used the word Liberty in a Salem courtroom in 1774, she signaled that she understood that broad principles were at stake. On its face, her freedom suit resembled that of Jenny Slew nine years earlier and was heard by the same Superior Court. The only one of the slaves of David Larcom to sue for her freedom, she claimed that she was not a slave because her mother was an Indian. Her mother was brought by ship from North Carolina to Portsmouth and from there to Beverly where she became one of the many slaves of a local sea captain; there is no information about Juno's father, although presumably he was an African. The sea captain at his death willed Juno to his daughter. When the daughter, a widow, remarried, she brought her slave with her as part of her dowry. Juno's new master was David Larcom, a wealthy landowner in Beverly and nearby Manchester, a man very much concerned about wringing the last ounce of profit out of his human assets.[36]

In court Juno Larcom's lawyer offered the standard trespass argument, that she had been kidnapped into slavery. She also claimed that she was a spinster, even though it was clear that she had a living husband—who resided separately from her in a nearby town. Indeed, these similarities with Slew's case suggest that the reason Juno Larcom found a lawyer willing to take her case is that it closely resembled Slew's and thus it appeared winnable in the Salem courts. Larcom was luckier than Slew in that the opposing lawyer did not question her marital status. After David Larcom died Juno Larcom's suit was dismissed because there was no defendant. In the midst of the war her longtime mistress chose not to impede her and the other Larcom slaves from claiming their freedom. Instead, her former mistress gave her a small house next to hers where she, her children, and some of her grandchildren lived; Juno Larcom died there in 1816 at the age of ninety-two.[37]

At the time she had brought her suit Juno Larcom had been deeply worried about the sale of her children into slavery in the South, fearing that she would never see them again. She and Jethro Thistle had four children before they were called to their faith, married in the First Church of Beverly, underwent adult baptism, and had seven more children, all of whom they had baptized in the church. David Larcom had sold Juno's son Cesar to a shoreman of Beverly when he was seven and sold their twelve-year-old son, Reuben, to a local owner. But Larcom and his brother, Rufus, were selling off the rest of their slaves to the South, fearing that general emancipation would render their property worthless.[38] David Larcom owed interest on a loan and preferred not to liquidate land to pay his debts. Fearing her children would be lost to her and her husband forever Juno Larcom told the court, "now I am oneasy By reason of selling my Children." With considerable emotional intensity she described how "my Master Larcom had sold two or three of my Children for 7–04–10 and now I am on easy by reason for selling my Children." She conveyed the price, denominated in pounds, shillings, and pence to indicate that in his haste Larcom was taking much less than the going price. Turning to the judges and jury she said to them "jentlemen of the jury and judges judge ye Weather or noe I hadent ort to Be set at Liberty."[39]

The Massachusetts legislature never passed a law outlawing slavery but the Bill of Rights of the Constitution of Massachusetts, drafted in 1780, declared all men free and equal. Elizabeth Freeman used this language to challenge the constitutionality of slavery in Massachusetts and her struggle remains one of the great attempts to put the ideals of inalienable rights into practice. Born into slavery, Elizabeth Freeman and her sister seem to have been owned by wealthy Dutch landowners who lived in Claverack, New York on the border with Massachusetts. Their daughter married a wealthy Englishman who received at her marriage or the death of her father two of the family's slaves.[40] Before the Revolution Elizabeth, or as she was called in slavery, Bett, had given birth to a daughter, Little Bett. Nothing is known about her husband, although one story has it that he was killed in the Revolutionary War. The other plaintiff in *Brom & Bett v. J. Ashley Esq.* was Brom, an enslaved man without a surname described only as "a Negro Man...of Sheffield" and a "Labourer," who may have been a slave in the household of John Ashley's son.[41]

The two lawyers for Brom and Bett were highly influential patriots, Theodore Sedgwick and Tapping Reeve. For generations the Sedgwicks had been storekeepers and farmers in New England. Young Theodore had been kicked out of Yale his senior year for "boyish gayeties" during a season of student riots against tuition hikes and British rule. Considering their punishment excessively harsh, school officials later reinstated him. Maturing quickly he settled down to study law in the office of a relative in Sheffield. A social conservative who gradually moved to the Patriot side, he served briefly in the Revolutionary War as a general's aide to a military expedition to Canada and then made his money furnishing military supplies for the Continental Army.[42] His children later claimed that he had purchased a slave mother and young daughter during the war to save them from a "hard taskmaster." Not long after his victory on behalf of Elizabeth Freeman and Brom he negotiated for the freedom of a woman fugitive slave who had fled from nearby Lenox to Sheffield and pleaded with him to help her.[43]

Sedgwick's position on emancipation was both limited and ambiguous. He saw himself advancing the cause of slaves in Massachusetts while not seeking to eliminate slavery throughout the nation. Later the same year after his victory in *Brom & Bett* he served as the lawyer for Oliver Hanchett, the Connecticut slave owner who defeated the lawsuit of Exeter seeking to win freedom for his wife. Sedgwick was also an early member of the leading abolitionist organization of its day, the Pennsylvania Abolition Society. Later on as a U.S. Senator he sponsored a fugitive slave bill to return escaped slaves to their owners. The one attorney willing to argue either side in a freedom suit, he found it easy to reconcile his commitments to personhood and property. Sedgwick recognized no inconsistency: he saw himself respecting property rights, upholding those of masters from other states in which slavery was legal, but attacking the institution within the Commonwealth of Massachusetts, where the Bill of Rights of the state's constitution had declared all men free and equal. Elizabeth Freeman's other lawyer was a prominent Connecticut attorney, Tapping Reeve. The son of a minister and a Princeton graduate, Reeve had taught school and earned his living as a tutor. During the Revolution he recruited soldiers for the Continental Army and briefly served as an officer; at the end of the war he had begun to establish a law practice in Litchfield.

The defendant, Colonel John Ashley, the wealthiest and most influential man in Sheffield, Massachusetts, was, as the owner of five slaves in 1771, one of the largest slaveholders in the entire colony. Bett and her sister probably lived in the attic of his house.[44] Ashley had acquired his military rank when he was promoted to colonel during the French and Indian War. He owned the general store, directly across the street from his home, as well as a warehouse, a grist and cider mill, tanneries, a potash works, an iron forge, thousands of acres of land, and the houses of his tenant farmers. A Yale graduate and lawyer he became a local judge of the Court of Common Pleas. In fact, he had to recuse himself from the bench because this case was being brought in his court. Initially a defender of the Crown and a conservative voice in radical times, he, too, had joined the Patriot cause. Along with other prominent men of the town, including Sedgwick, Ashley had drafted the Sheffield Declaration in his upstairs study, perhaps with Elizabeth Freeman listening in or serving the men while they deliberated. The declaration, one of the many local manifestos of the day, reaffirmed the revolutionary rhetoric that "God and Nature have made us free." Zach Mullen, a third Ashley slave, also sued for his freedom, contending that the colonel had beaten, wounded, and imprisoned him; his case had been postponed while the courts attended to *Brom & Bett*. Ashley was represented by two prominent attorneys, one from

Lanesboro, Massachusetts, and a trustee of Williams College and the other a noted attorney from Sharon, Connecticut.[45]

Elizabeth Freeman's suit arose, according to one version, when she heard the words of the Declaration of Independence and felt that they applied to her.[46] The other version is that a group of local abolitionist whites were looking for a test case and selected Freeman and the laborer Brom as the plaintiffs. Even if the second version of the story is correct, it is still not clear why only two of the Ashley slaves joined the suit. The possible answer is that Brom and Elizabeth Freeman lived independently, not subject to coercion by their owner. Sedgwick and Reeve began by filing a writ of replevin, which argued that Brom and Freeman were not the legitimate property of Ashley and should be released from being held by him (because the constitution forbade the ownership of people as property). Ashley refused to comply with the writ, saying that Brom and Elizabeth Freeman were his slaves for life. Sedgwick and Reeve tried two more times to get writs to free Brom and Freeman but still Ashley refused. The court ordered a trial; Brom and Freeman were allowed to live freely so long as they furnished a bond that they intended to prosecute their case. A Berkshire County jury decided that they were not slaves; Ashley was assessed thirty shillings damages and court costs. He dropped his appeal, perhaps because a few weeks earlier the Supreme Court of the Commonwealth had ruled that slavery was unconstitutional in another freedom suit.[47] Ashley also settled the first case against him still pending, that of his slave Zach Mullen.[48]

After winning her freedom Elizabeth Freeman sought to support her family and acquire property. A free woman and a widow with a daughter needed an income and a place to live. Elizabeth Freeman became the head servant in the Sedgwick household, who presided over a retinue which included three other blacks, including her daughter, and part-time, often Irish, local help. The mistress of the household, Pamela Sedgwick, sank into a depression punctuated by fits of raving after the birth of her tenth child. Elizabeth Freeman, "a dear friend," was the only one in the household who could comfort "the crazed woman."[49] The family not only depended on Mumbet's skills as a nurse but also as a midwife. She presided over the births of the last of Pamela Sedgwick's children and at the births of the Sedgwick grandchildren. After Pamela Sedgwick died Mumbet wanted to leave the employ of the Sedgwicks. She may not have liked the judge's new wife, who could not abide country life and had a brandy and laudanum problem.[50] Freeman had slowly taken steps toward personal independence, first by moving into her own quarters and working for the Sedgwicks during the day and then becoming a midwife and nurse in town.

Freeman was one of the few black midwives in New England at this time. Midwifery was the highest paid female occupation; a woman succeeded in it only because she was truly trusted by her neighbors who could count on her to come to their home even during a snowstorm or in the middle of the night. With enough savings from her midwifery practice Freeman bought a five-acre lot with her son-in-law on which to build a small home on Cherry Hill Road overlooking the verdant green of Monument Mountain. Four years later she bought another 12.5 acres to augment her property from her son-in-law's brother; then she bought out her son-in-law's share of her house and land in 1811.[51] Perhaps she purchased her son-in-law's share as some kind of separation or divorce agreement for her daughter; the couple may have split up sometime before he joined a small number of free blacks who sailed for Liberia.[52] Elizabeth Freeman was one of the few women of any race who could claim to be a taxpayer in Stockbridge. She was also a churchgoer, a member of the local Congregational Church across the street from the Sedgwick mansion. When one of her granddaughters died in childbirth, she was consoled by her deep faith, knowing that the death was God's will.[53]

Freeman played a minor part in Shays' Rebellion, the farmer's revolt against foreclosure, in which at first it appears she assumed the role of the loyal household domestic, defending the employer's home, even when he himself was not present.She sided with the Federalist opponents of Shays' Rebellion, as did most free blacks in Massachusetts. Although the Republican and Federalist parties vied for the black vote, most black enfranchised men voted Federalist because they were the party of abolitionists and opponents of the slave trade. It is true that most Federalists had not been abolitionists, but all abolitionists with political affilliations were Federalists. The immediate cause for the farmer's revolt was a transatlantic financial crisis that led the Commonwealth of Massachusetts to raise property taxes, to be paid in gold and silver, which farmers did not possess. Armed soldiers, loyal to the central government, patrolled the streets of Stockbridge in 1786, but rebel farmers with bayonets broke through, going house to house, pillaging, looking for firearms as well as valuables. They targeted the Sedgwick home because they knew that the master had helped send their compatriots to prison. Alone in the Sedgwick manse, the family away in Boston, Freeman had picked up a shovel from the kitchen to defend herself. When the marauding men demanded the family silver she led them to the basement where she had hidden it in her chest. About to accede to the men's demands she said to them, "Oh, you had better search *that* . . . an old nigger's chest." Shamed by her comment the men retreated up the stairs, grabbing some of Theodore Sedgwick's silk stockings and ruffled shirts as they left. When they tried to steal the old gray mare Freeman liked to ride she hit the horse with its halter, and it galloped away before the men had a chance to secure it.[54]

5.1. Miniature watercolor portrait on ivory of Elizabeth "Mumbet" Freeman (ca. 1742–1829) by Susan Anne Livingstone Ridley Sedgwick, 1811. Elizabeth Freeman was in her seventies when she posed for this watercolor portrait by Susan Sedgwick, the wife of Theodore Jr., whom Elizabeth Freeman had helped to raise. Elizabeth Freeman wears the gold necklace Catharine Sedgwick gave her. Susan Sedgwick was twenty-three when she painted this miniature and had given birth to her first child the same year. Since miniatures were often painted to commemorate a key event in the life cycle, it seems likely that Sedgwick painted this portrait after the birth of her child and Freeman might have been her midwife. Sedgwick kin donated letters and other materials to the Massachusetts Historical Society in the 1920s. Courtesy of the Massachusetts Historical Society

Still a practicing midwife at age seventy-six Elizabeth Freeman posed for a miniature portrait painted by Susan Sedgwick in 1811. The portrait shows a highly respectable woman whose furrowed brow and deep pockets under her eyes reveal her advanced age. She represents the living embodiment of the ideal of respectability for an elderly woman. Mumbet's white hair peeks out from under the front of a white cap, a standard head covering for a woman of advanced age. No longer a sign of aristocratic status, the portrait had become a commonplace; prosperous families even in rural areas paid an amateur artist to paint their likenesses, which hung in their parlors.[55] Although Freeman was a heavy-set woman, she appears to have been wearing a corset. Like many matrons of a certain age she chose a white scarf to cover a bare neck.[56] Wheatley had been portrayed in a standard pose for a contemplative evangelical, but the original drawing designated her "as a servant" of the Wheatley family. Freeman was not a slave or a servant but a midwife in Stockbridge, churchgoer, homeowner, mother, and grandmother. Susan Sedgwick, the young wife of the Sedgwick son who may have loved Mumbet the most, painted the tiny portrait on ivory using watercolors. In this miniature the subject looked directly at the artist, not gazing heavenward or demurely staring away.

Freeman had dressed carefully for her portrait to reveal her occupational and racial identities as well as her affection for the Sedgwick family. The vivid blue dress she was wearing could have been made by hand or by a local gown maker. Archaeological sites from the antebellum South as well as Newport have consistently found blue glass beads among the small personal artifacts remaining. Blue was not a distinctively African color, but instead an African American one, which, it was thought, symbolized curative qualities used to prevent illness—a form of protection from misfortune and sickness.[57] A midwife and nurse who cared for mothers and their young children, she had chosen to wear a dress conveying the healing power of blue. In the portrait Elizabeth Freeman was wearing a gold necklace, a gift from Catharine Sedgwick.[58] Other black women in New England also owned gold jewelry but what was distinctive in this case was that the necklace was a gift from the sister-in-law of the artist.

In great pain at the end, Freeman was looked after by four separate physicians the Sedgwicks sent for her care. She suffered a series of small strokes, but was still able to speak.[59] Near her death she devised a plan to protect her children from their spendthrift ways; she asked Charles Sedgwick to create a trust and named him as trustee, thereby becoming the first black person in New England to rely on such a legal device. Catharine and her older sister Frances witnessed the document and Freeman signed it with her mark.[60] Half of her real estate she left in trust for her daughter Betty and her heirs and the other half she gave to her great-grandchildren.

Elizabeth Freeman, daughter of the American Revolution, revered midwife and nurse, died at home in her own bed in 1829, buried in the Sedgwick family plot. She had amassed certain luxuries over the years, such as the gold watch she left for her grandson, bits of velvet and lace and her silk gowns, as well as savings of $1000. Her will was a statement about her doubts as to the financial acumen of her kin as well as a map of her emotional ties, the record of her success in achieving propertied freedom, and proof that she collected and preserved objects of memory. She left all her household furniture, gowns, a shawl, and a linen pocket handkerchief to her daughter. The ownership of a "large chest writing desk" by a woman who could not read or write marked her ambition. Among the fifty-two cherished family items she enumerated

5.2. Elizabeth Freeman's Headstone, Sedgwick Family Pie, 1829. Like many other beloved former domestics, Elizabeth Freeman was buried in the family plot of the family she worked for. It is thought that Catharine Sedgwick composed the epitaph for her headstone (far left). It read: "She was born a slave and remained a slave for nearly thirty years. She could neither read nor write yet in her own sphere she had no superior nor equal. In every situation of domestic trial, she was the most efficient helper, and the tenderest friend. Good mother, farewell." Photo Courtesy of Paul Rocheleau were two that preserved the memory of her parents, a black silk gown "recd of my father" and a short gown that had belonged to her mother.[61]

In 1829 Elizabeth Freeman passed from history into memory and from a Patriot of the Revolution to a role model for antebellum abolitionism. Her struggle to gain her freedom and first-person sentences attributed to her come from two Sedgwick children she raised and the English novelist, Harriet Martineau, who visited Stockbridge and knew the Sedgwicks; there is thus no "voice" of Elizabeth Freeman without the Sedgwick records. Catharine Sedgwick, the youngest Sedgwick daughter who became a noted author, wrote a journal entry about Mumbet two months after her death. Catharine did not like her stepmother very much and preferred to call Freeman "mother." The young Catharine often listened to Elizabeth Freeman chronicle her struggle against Ashley.[62] Engaging in revolutionary rhetoric, akin to Patrick Henry—and the black Minuteman, Lemuel Haynes— Freeman said she much preferred liberty over death. Freeman told the young Catharine, "I would have been willing,... I would have been willing if I could have had one minute of freedom—just to say, 'I am free'. I would have been willing to die at the end of that minute." Catharine recorded Freeman's exact words when she heard the Declaration of Independence. She said, 'If all are free and equal... Why are we slaves?' "[63]

By his mid forties Theodore, Jr., had retired from his law practice in Albany, New York, and with his wife Susan had moved back to Stockbridge, and became an abolitionist speaker in town. In front of his neighbors at the lyceum in Stockbridge in 1831 he delivered a lengthy lecture. Later that year Sedgwick published his lecture as a pamphlet, *The Practicability of the Abolition of Slavery*. Some of the members of his audience were familiar with Elizabeth Freeman as a midwife or the family's nurse. When he stood on the lyceum stage Sedgwick repeated the stories Mumbet had told him— about her parents, her Dutch owners in New York, her sale and that of her sister to Colonel Ashley and his wife, and the death of her husband during the war.

Sedgwick had crafted his own version of the slave narrative, the dramatic story of slavery to freedom told in the first person. In this literary format a slave engages in a physical struggle with the master (or mistress) and gains psychological as well as physical mastery over domination. Thus he related the dramatic tale of Mumbet's struggle—shielding her sister from being struck by a hot kitchen shovel made of iron wielded by Mrs. Ashley, she was struck on her arm and permanently scarred, a bodily badge of honor she bore for the rest of her life. Many New England white abolitionists believed in the mental and physical inferiority of black people but not Theodore Sedgwick, Jr. He did not adhere to the modern concept of generalizability based on a number of cases, either; instead, he believed it was possible to

5.3. Bracelet made of gold beads from the necklace of Elizabeth "Mumbet" Freeman, by an unidentified goldsmith, late eighteenth century. Catharine Sedgwick gave Elizabeth Freeman a gift of a single strand of gold beads. Before her death Freeman gave the necklace to Sedgwick, who had it made into a double stranded bracelet in the 1840s, with "Mumbet" engraved on the clasp. The bracelet was passed down within the Sedgwick family until the husband of Sedgwick's grandniece donated it to the Massachusetts Historical Society in 1884. This donor believed the bracelet symbolized slave emancipation in Massachusetts, "an epoch in our social and political progress." Courtesy of the Massachusetts Historical Society

arrive at a conclusion based on one case truly well known. Because of his intimacy and familiarity with Mumbet he had reached the understanding that black people were equal to whites.[64] He told his listeners, "Having known this woman as familiarly as I knew either of my parents, I *cannot* believe in the moral or physical inferiority of the race to which she belonged."[65]

What the English novelist Harriet Martineau added to the public record was pithy first person quotations from Elizabeth Freeman that gave her a New England dialect. A close friend of the Sedgwicks, Martineau visited Stockbridge and may have collected their stories about Mumbet. She related the tale about the lawyer who asked Elizabeth Freeman how she learned about legal doctrine for her freedom suit. This Freeman dropped her g's, and speaking as a country woman, is said to have replied, "By keepin' still and mindin' things." The lawyer pursued the matter and asked her, "What things?" While "waiting at table," she overheard men talking about the Bill of Rights and the Constitution of Massachusetts. She then resolved that "she would try whether she did come in among them."[66]

The huge success of *Uncle Tom's Cabin* inspired Catharine Sedgwick to publish a brief biography of Elizabeth Freeman in *Bentley's Miscellany* in 1853. She had previously written a novel whose main character Meta, a noble and dignified enslaved woman, resembled Elizabeth Freeman, but had never published it. Catharine Sedgwick had loved Mumbet as "mother" but unlike her brother, did not believe in equality between the races. In a private recollection of the family history written for her niece she revealed that she thought of Freeman as "a remarkable exception to the general character of her race." Fortunately for her own later reputation, Stowe's novel and her brother's speech many decades before seemed to have constrained her from expressing this view.[67] Instead, she included the same quotations of Mumbet's she had recorded in her journal twenty-four years before. Censuring her private thoughts she wrote instead that Freeman's life was proof of racial equality. Taking a page from her brother's lecture she wrote that if "you could establish the equality of the slave with a master in a single instance," it disproved arguments about racial inferiority.[68]

During her life Elizabeth Freeman was respected most for her strength of character. Immediately after her death she was placed in the pantheon of Patriots, remembered for her "inextinguishable love of freedom," her fervent belief in the principles of the American Revolution.[69] Her owner Jonathan Ashley believed in the principles of liberty as well but it was Elizabeth Freeman who had taught him what they really meant. Like so many other black women in New England, Freeman never separated her belief in the inalienable rights of the individual from her identity as an African American, Christian, mother, and midwife. Her life revealed how black women understood freedom, what they accomplished after gaining it, and how they achieved respectability. Her life in freedom was interconnected with the Sedgwick family but she was not defined by them, instead, stepping outside of their home into her own. After she acquired the house on Cherry Hill Road she could look out from her front porch at the yellow field of rye, the mist covering the base of Monument Mountain, the blue of the undulating hills and Housatonic River flowing through the valley merging with the azure of the sky and ponder all that she had been able to accomplish for herself, her family, and her neighbors.

6

Spirit of Freedom

Before the war enslaved women probably had more restricted opportunities for travel than any other group in the New England colonies. Like Juno Larcom, many women and men were not awaiting favorable court decisions but were simply declaring themselves to be free. Even before Elizabeth Freeman fled from the Ashleys' home, other women during the war were taking their freedom by escaping their owners, seeking work doing the laundry for the troops, leaving the countryside for town, and moving from there to larger seaports in search of work, lost relatives, and community. Once settled, women had more room to ponder how they wanted to combine African custom, patriarchy, and opportunity for independence in matters from choosing a last name to buying a piece of property. In an atmosphere of contagious liberty blacks often received aid from their white neighbors in dramatic rescues.

After slaves won their freedom many towns as well as the Commonwealth of Massachusetts passed new legislation and stepped up enforcement of rules of inhabitancy as a means of controlling the free black population. While town officials recognized that some deserving black neighbors might upon occasion require assistance, they were equally likely to look upon emancipated slaves as burdensome charity cases. In a state of panic state legislators as well as town authorities identified as a special target slave refugees coming to New England from other states. Equally dangerous in the public mind were black prostitutes and the occasional black madam; black men marrying white women seemed to disturb the public imagination in direct proportion to their numbers in the local population. Black women living with a white man provoked condemnation but not the same level of fear because there were no instances of legal marriage between black women and white men.[1]

The idea of patriarchy was that the woman was dependent on her husband for support; the idea of town patriarchy was that a poor woman could become dependent on her town fathers to provide for her. Just as there were individual patriarchs who did not want to assume responsibility for a wife's debts or pay alimony, so, too, town governments were under pressure from taxpayers to reduce the population eligible for relief. Surveillance and roundups of transients and people who were not legal inhabitants of a town were long-standing New England traditions, by no means racially motivated. Faced with a larger relief problem than elsewhere in New England, Rhode Island officials took more dramatic actions, not merely questioning black single mothers but renting a horse and carriage to escort them and their children out of town. Fear of black freedom was expressed in economic as well as sexual terms. Cities used the warning-out procedure to get rid of poor women and as a way to run prostitutes out of town. While some women refused to go along, more found a way to circumvent the rules, following the same pattern as Lucy Pernam, leaving town, as ordered, but soon returning.

Parents whose chose to name a son George Washington Freeman left no doubt as to their political allegiances. By the time she wrote her poem about the Boston Massacre, Phillis Wheatley, although still in her teens, regarded freedom for the former British colonies as "the cause of liberty." If she omitted a few of her patriotic poems for a volume published in England, her sentiments remained unchanged. While a refugee in Providence during the war she sent her poem "His Excellency, the Commander" to General Washington at his headquarters in Cambridge. A bit embarrassed by the lavishness of her praise (she called him a "great chief") Washington invited her to visit him in Cambridge if she was in town. Washington did not record her visit in his journals, but a subsequent biography indicated that Wheatley met with the General at the Vassal mansion for about half an hour, probably in March of 1776, as British troops were evacuating Boston. Wheatley was not alone in her fidelity to the rebels. The husbands and sons of quite a few women left behind in New England fought on the Patriot side in the Revolution. Rose Binney, Lucy Terry Prince, and Meg Smith sent their sons to the battlefield; word reached Juno Larcom that her husband died at Valley Forge and she learned as well that her son was killed on a privateer somewhere off the New England coast.[2] There was one practical reason to welcome a husband or son's enlistment; a man who joined the Continental Army received a bounty, which could be used to buy a woman's freedom. In burning towns and spreading smallpox among the local population, occupying British troops made enemies among black as well as white women. Surry, a free black household servant of Patriot Samuel Adams, was trapped in Boston by the redcoats during the British siege of the town, as was Adams's son, a medical student. She finally made her way to safety outside the city and returned to live with the Adams family.[3]

American troops aided several black women seeking their freedom, encouraging in them the view that the true promise of freedom lay with the Patriots committed to "a spirit of liberty." Ebenezer Allen's Green Mountain Boys captured about fifty prisoners of war at the battle of Ticonderoga at a fort on Lake Champlain in neighboring New York. (There were quite a few Allens from Vermont at the battle, including the famous colonel of the militia, Ethan Allen.) Among the captured prisoners were Dinah Mattis and her two-month-old daughter, slaves of a British officer at the battle. Allen wanted to free the captives because he believed "it is not right in the Sight of God to keep slaves." He asked for the assent of his troops, which they willingly gave; then he offered Mattis an emancipation certificate and safe-conduct pass to Vermont.[4] Close to the end of the war Colonel Ethan Allen returned home from the battlefield to Bennington. The new minister, a gentleman from Connecticut, had brought his woman slave with him to a congregation that refused membership to slave owners. Allen convinced the woman she should sue for her freedom; her owner was dismissed from his post and she seems to have been allowed to take her liberty without having to go to court.[5]

White sailors, who often worked side by side on board deck with their black counterparts, also displayed abolitionist sympathies. In 1777 Connecticut sailors seized Cuba, a twenty-five-year-old woman from Jamaica from a British ship. Assuring her that the new country was "a land of liberty," the sailors told her she could gain freedom in Massachusetts. During the revolution the legislature of the Commonwealth had passed a resolution declaring that slaves captured in the state were to be held temporarily until they could be returned to the masters in the South as part of a prisoner exchange. Fortunately, an unknown patriot drafted a petition on Cuba's behalf to the state's legislature, which resulted in her freedom.[6]

Some black women decided to throw in their lot with the redcoats because they believed the British offered them more opportunities for gaining their freedom. There were always rumors that blacks in Boston were planning to fight for the British for precisely this reason. In the beginning of the war Lord Dunmore, the British commander in Virginia, held out the promise of emancipation to enslaved men willing to bear arms for the king. As the war dragged on, British General Henry Clinton (whom Wheatley had met when she was in London) offered manumission to any slave who ran away from a rebel master—women, children, as well as men—but also threatened to sell into slavery any black person found to be fighting for the Americans. Clinton advanced on Newport in 1779, accompanied by a small group of Black

Pioneers, a regiment of black men commanded by a white officer. Enslaved mothers with their children ran toward his troops, where they found work as cooks and laundresses. When the British withdrew their ships from Newport harbor, seven out of ten black refugees on board were mothers and their children. Other refugees sailed with the British to their stronghold in New York City where they remained for several years until they, too, were evacuated to Nova Scotia with defeated British troops and other civilians.[7]

Black Loyalists had made themselves unpopular in Boston before the war even broke out. Phillis Prince and her husband, Newton, were free, belonged to the Patriot church at Old South (along with Wheatley), and had their own business, catering to assembly balls, making pastries, and selling lemons. Newton Prince testified on behalf of British soldiers who were put on trial in Boston for shooting into a crowd in 1770 (what the Americans called the Boston Massacre). The Patriots retaliated against him by boycotting his business. When the British evacuated troops and about a thousand refugees loyal to their side in March of 1776, much of the city was destroyed and his business prospects were dashed. The Princes decided to sail with the Loyalists for Halifax where they became cooks and servants for a Tory Boston merchant; they followed him to London opening a shop selling provisions for sailors. While Phillis Prince was in poor health, her husband, with the help of several prominent white Boston Loyalists, applied and received a tiny pension from the British government to supplement their income.[8]

As the war dragged on in New England, enslaved women fled to the American side and provided information about the British positions to the Patriot armies. Three slaves—Jane Coggeshall, Violet Pease, and William Carpenter—stole a boat and rowed twelve miles to patriot territory at Point Judith in 1777. An armed guard escorted them to South Kingstown, where the General Assembly of Rhode Island was meeting. In return for information about the size of the British contingent in Newport and its fortifications, they were granted their freedom and given a pass to head safely through American lines. Carpenter moved to Philadelphia to find work, Violet Pease disappeared, and Jane Coggeshall took several jobs in domestic service before moving to Providence. Worried that the heirs of her owner might try to re-enslave her, she successfully petitioned the state of Rhode Island after the war to declare her free.[9]

While laying siege to an army of ten thousand British soldiers they had trapped within the city of Boston, General Washington's troops encountered an even worse enemy: smallpox. British troops developed immunities to the disease from early exposure in England. But the embattled farmers and militia men from small New England towns who had never experienced smallpox before came down with fevers and rashes on their face at an alarming rate. Washington asked the Continental Congress to establish a "hospital department" which provided tents, supplies, surgeons, and makeshift nurses for the troops; abandoned Loyalist mansions, the almshouse, and the workhouse were turned into hospitals for his army. Enslaved couples were hired from their masters to work in these makeshift hospitals; the husband served as a waiter or a laborer and his wife as the laundress, who cared for the soiled linen of the sufferers.[10]

In establishing his headquarters in the Vassal mansion in Cambridge George Washington assembled a local staff of eight, white and black, including two slaves named Dinah and Peter, and a literate local free black woman, Margaret Thomas. When Washington evacuated Cambridge he took Margaret Thomas with him to do the laundry and mending for him and his staff, even though after the end of the war he confessed he "never wished to see her more." If his opinion had already formed in Cambridge, he may have been persuaded to bring Thomas with the army by his valet and favorite slave, William Lee, who had formed an attachment to her. Thomas remained with the Continental Army at Germantown, then traveled with them to the winter encampment at Morristown, and the winter quarters during "the starving times" at Valley Forge. She left the army for Philadelphia where she boarded with a black couple who worked as cooks for white families. Lee followed her to Philadelphia and they lived together, apparently unmarried. At the end of the war Lee, who had returned to Mount Vernon, requested that Thomas should be allowed to reside there as well—a request that seems not to have come to fruition.[11] Other women who did not accompany the troops found that the war offered more of a chance to work for pay. With British imports of cloth entirely cut off by sea, black women were able to earn a living by making homespun cloth. The wife of the deputy governor of Rhode Island employed six black women to spin and weave, perhaps to make cloth for shirts or uniforms for Rhode Island soldiers.[12]

Masters such as David Larcom had tried to seize their last opportunity for a profit by selling their slaves to an owner in the South. Learning of plans such as these, white town residents helped slaves to escape their master or fought off a paid kidnapper sent to seize them. In several Rhode Island and Connecticut towns white residents intervened to help enslaved families escape and threatened the lives of their abductors.[13] The residents of Hebron, Connecticut, conducted the most dramatic rescue of a local slave family. Cesar and Lowis Peters and their eight children, the youngest of whom was still being breastfed, were the property of a Loyalist who had fled to England. To settle his debts the owner had sold the Peters family to a South Carolina master who attempted to ship them to his plantation. While the men of Hebron were away from town on militia muster, kidnappers grabbed the Peters and loaded them into a wagon headed for the port of Norwich. The women of the town ran quickly to tell their men. Six townsmen from

Hebron and a constable rode all night to Norwich and grabbed the Peters family from the dock before they were loaded onto a ship sailing for South Carolina. Two years later Cesar and Lowis Peters petitioned the Connecticut legislature for their freedom. In their petition they expressed their anxieties about being sold, perhaps to the West Indies, their "continual fear of being secretly taken with their Children and sold out of this to some foreign Country."[14]

Some Boston owners who did not want to remain trapped in the city took their slaves with them as they fled. The Bradfords escaped Boston for Andover where they squeezed into a friend's home; the great advantage for their slave Chloe was that the owner of the house, a schoolmaster, offered to help her improve her reading. In the wartime chaos some enslaved mothers chose to head in one direction, while their owners were too busy fleeing in the other direction to notice. Abigail and her children, including an infant, were living with Captain Blevin and his family in New London, a center for privateering against British ships. The British retaliated against the seizure of their ships by invading the town, setting fire to the marauding ships and warehouses at the waterfront and torching houses. The Blevins loaded their belongings in a wagon and fled; Abigail scooped up her children, stole a wagon, and set out for South Kingstown where she had previously lived with a different owner. Eventually Captain Blevin came to retrieve her and her children but she refused to go with him; by war's end it was unclear whether she had become free.[15]

New England townspeople were especially sympathetic to a slave transported from a slave to a free state, usually slaves from Connecticut. Dinah Mason's owner, a former Connecticut resident who moved to Vermont and became the judge of the Superior Court of Vermont, convinced her that she was still a slave, telling her that her legal status was governed by the gradual emancipation law of Connecticut. Mason continued as the slave of the judge two years after the Vermont state constitution had abolished slavery until the judge's neighbors persuaded her that Vermont law governed her situation. Under the state's constitution, they told her, she could go free; the judge chose not to stand in her way when she left his household and found lodgings elsewhere.[16]

Legal emancipation in Vermont, New Hampshire, and Massachusetts created the division between completely free states in the northern part of New England and states that offered gradual emancipation in southern New England. According to the federal census of 1790, there were no slaves in Massachusetts or Vermont, 157 in New Hampshire, 958 in Rhode Island, and 2648 in Connecticut. By 1810, the census reported that the number of slaves in all the New England states had shrunk to 418. The actual number of slaves may have been somewhat higher than these figures because officials underestimated the actual number of slaves in the region. Census takers in Massachusetts in 1790, for example, encouraged the few remaining slave owners in the state not to claim their chattel so as to further the impression that the Commonwealth was truly a land of liberty.[17]

In Connecticut and Rhode Island emancipation was gradual and enacted by statute; in fact, the laws of these two states resembled each other because white abolitionists in both states cooperated in framing their legislative proposals.[18] The statutes in these states freed slaves over a course of years; the laws specified that newborn children born to enslaved women were emancipated only when they reached the age of maturity; those born before 1784 were left in a permanent state of bondage. The purpose of such laws was to phase out slavery gradually and emancipate one slave at a time, rather than free a whole class of people. The effect of gradual emancipation was to provide some compensation to owners by offering them the unpaid labor of enslaved children into young adulthood. In these two states some parents who had been freed saved up the money to buy the freedom of their children; others chose to indenture themselves to buy their own freedom or that of a family member.

Seizing the moment a few free black women purchased land or started businesses, often catering to the families of former owners and other members of the elite. Phillis, who appears not to have taken a surname when she was freed, bought land in Killingly, Connecticut, as did Hazel Blossom in Pittsfield, Massachusetts. The first black woman to purchase property in Newport after the Revolution was a widow, Bess Brown, who had two married daughters. In her will in 1794 she left the actual ownership of her house to her married daughter and allowed her other daughter, who was separated from her husband, to live in another part of the house with her two children.[19] Black women, especially widows, sought to claim economic freedom by starting a small business cooking and baking, since preparation of food had been part of their work in slavery. Mareer's Quaker owner manumitted her before his Friends' meeting the first year of the war; subsequently she opened a shop on the main street of town to sell beer, candy, and cakes.[20] Dinah Gibson, a former slave in Portsmouth, New Hampshire, famous for her fruit cake and spiced cocoa, catered balls and banquets in the town's assembly hall her former owners managed. Not only did these women draw their patrons from the families of their former owners but such families often assisted them in starting their business. Dinah, once a slave in Exeter, New Hampshire, opened "Dinah's Cottage" outside of town where she served cake and ale; the daughter of her former mistress helped her buy the land so that she could have her own place.[21]

Whereas most female heads of household headed for the city, black couples often went in the opposite direction because they hoped to become independent farmers. Black men and women were looking for cheap land in out-of-the-way-places where the local whites might be less prejudiced or at least leave them alone. While many veterans returned home at the end of the war, others were moving to islands off the mainland or rural areas of New Hampshire and Vermont; former slaves who could not afford to buy land squatted on rocky points near the sea or barren hills next to the road to town. Some of the squatters were in fact "family" settlements. After her owners fled the country, Zilpha White built a tiny house at Walden Pond on the road leading into town of Concord and supported herself by spinning. Her brother, sister-in-law, and their children lived in the hut next to hers. War veterans who headed to more-isolated locations included the families that established a small black colony near the summit of a mountain in New Hampshire. After the war Violate Fortune and her husband Amos, former slaves from Massachusetts, had close black friends in Jaffrey, New Hampshire, who helped convince them to move there. They built a house and a barn on twenty-five acres of land in Jaffrey and adopted a daughter; he established a tannery and she set up a handloom and became a weaver.[22]

In the seaport cities black women were marrying, baptizing their children, and joining white churches in even greater numbers than before the war. The evangelical and the experimental drew the greatest and most enthusiastic of black followers; Baptists were poorer and less well educated than other denominations and attracted more than their share of black worshippers. At the Sabbatarian church in Newport, a small Baptist church that held its weekly services on Saturday, blacks were 11 percent of total communicants. Many black people in the maritime towns were loyal to ministers they had known for decades. Like most of Newport, Samuel Hopkins had fled the town when it was occupied by the British. Redcoat occupiers, desperate for firewood, had torn down houses and stripped old ships in the harbor. Hopkins returned to find his church ransacked; his congregation, which always had more than its share of poor people, did not have the money for repairs. In the winters the interior was "as cold as a barn" and Newport Gardner had to help the aging Hopkins climb the steps to the pulpit. Black religious women and men continued to stand by Hopkins, listening to his dull sermons, contributing to the costs of publishing his theological work.[23] White congregations were choosing black men and women for honors previously reserved for whites: a black man to ring the church bell, a black woman to sweep the church, an assignment usually given to a church deacon. Still black men and women met as "Negro societies" on Sunday evenings in the homes of black families. In Boston blacks were permitted to assemble at Faneuil Hall but only during the day—provided they did not make a disturbance. Thus it was more convenient and less restrictive to meet at a schoolhouse in the West End of Boston on Sunday afternoons.[24]

Freedom for the black family, as we have already seen, brought private quarrels into public view, exacerabated by frequent separations. A husband who was a sailor was often away from home for six or seven months a year, engaging in what was a relatively lucrative but nonetheless dangerous occupation. His wife hoped to make enough from washing and spinning at home so that she did not have to make the rounds of the homes of white women. Sailor's wives lived near one another so that they could help each other with child care and daily chores. Nonetheless, such women were often dependent on town charity and if desperate enough turned to prostitution. Some couples were forced back into live-in domestic service, such as one husband and wife who took out an ad seeking employment together as live-in servants, but indicated "if no person appears desirous of employing them together, they will live separately."[25] A couple might work for pay for a former master but also agree to indenture their children to him.[26] An ideal situation was to serve as caretakers for a family in their absence. Single mothers were often forced to become live-in domestics and looked for a black family or benevolent white one that promised to teach their children to read and write. Some parents tried to specify that a child would be educated, but for the most part, black children in indentures were less likely to receive instruction in literacy than white children.[27] The most desperate of mothers abandoned their children in a doorway, the street, or a shed, especially if the children were biracial, perhaps the product of coerced sex. Such children were sometimes placed out in indentured service but were also raised by the white families that found them.

Black men could change their surname as a symbol of emancipation, whereas for the most part, black married women took the last name of their husbands. Free blacks before the revolution had often selected new surnames, but there was a rush to do during the war. Some men took a new surname, symbolic of citizenship, as in Liberty, Free, Freeman, Freedom, Freeborn, or Citizen; symbolic of race pride, as in Blackman or Brown; or symbolic of masculinity as in Newman, Beman, Fullman, and Manjoy. Cesar Isham changed his surname to Beaman because he wanted to "be a man." The preference for English names varied from the historical (Oliver Cromwell) to the geographically specific (Butterfield Scotland). For the most part, black men expressed their freedom through the adoption of a new surname, but some created new first names (Newman) or reverted to an African first name (from Primus to Zingo). Other black men continued to follow the west African tradition of adopting the father's first name as their surname. After Cuff Cousins returned from the war, he took as his surname Tindy, the first name of his father; the son of Primus adopted his father's first name as his last name.

Women also chose names that included free or man in them to symbolize their independence from slavery. In 1790 Juno Larcom was a widow, going by the name of Freeman and Fullman, but later reverted to Larcom—a switch in surname common among free blacks who depended on the patronage of former owners.[28] Many widows also took the husband's (or father's) first name as a surname, which indicated that they, too, affirmed West African naming practice. Dinah Ned, a free black woman, who married Hartford Turner in Boston in 1783, exemplified this pattern. When her husband took the name of his new employer, she adopted his new surname as her own; when he changed his surname a second time, she followed his lead. After he died, she took as her surname Hartford, her husband's first name.[29]

Nonetheless, a few married women made choices independent of their husbands. Rosanna Freeborn kept her own new surname, separate from her husband's surname of Elio, which perhaps was the last name of his master.[30] Women had more choice over their first name than their surname: choosing an English first name reflected acculturation to English norms as well as a desire to escape the stigma of having a slave woman's name. Bett, a woman without a husband to consult, changed both her surname and first name, selecting the surname Freeman and preferring to be called Elizabeth rather than the affectionate diminutive of Bett.[31]

On their own women, especially the young and the husbandless, were fleeing to New England seaports where they could find work at war's end. The increase in manumissions and black migration from smaller towns or the countryside to seaports resulted in a growing population of free blacks faced with limited job opportunities in the 1780s.[32] The decline in overseas demand for the agricultural products of North America and the closing of West Indian ports to U.S. ships as retaliation for British defeat in the Revolutionary War shattered the maritime trade. While the New England economy slowed to a halt, the black seaport population was swelling, and included slave fugitives, most from nearby slave states.[33]

One particular fugitive of the revolutionary age became known not just for her daring exploits but for the fame of her owners. Ona Judge escaped to Portsmouth, New Hampshire, and arrived there by concealing herself on a boat from Philadelphia, probably with the assistance of the ship's captain. She was the twenty-five-year-old former slave of Martha Washington, and coolly walked out of the Executive Mansion in Philadelphia one spring evening in 1793 while the president and his wife were eating dinner. Probably with the help of free blacks in Philadelphia, she secured passage on a ship to Portsmouth. She may also have been the first black woman stowaway, because there is no record of other women who boarded a ship and reached safety in New England. While he was president Washington had discreetly tried to enlist a customs official in Portsmouth, a former slave owner himself, to secure Judge's return. Aware of Northern sentiment, Washington chose not to risk adverse publicity and abandoned the effort to retrieve Judge during his presidency.

Meanwhile, Judge married a free man in Portsmouth, a sailor in town, gave birth to a daughter, and was helping to support the family as a seamstress. After Washington finished his second term and retired to Mount Vernon his wife Martha continued to pressure him to retrieve one of her favored slaves. Washington importuned his nephew, planning a trip to Portsmouth, to secure the return of Judge and her young daughter to Mount Vernon. Pounding on the door of Judge's cabin the nephew tried several times unsuccessfully to persuade Judge to accompany him to Virginia. Sensing that the nephew was about to abduct her, Judge hired a boy with a horse and carriage who took her and her daughter to the cabin of friends, a black veteran and his wife who lived in the countryside. Townspeople of all stripes must have supported her because no one divulged where she was hiding. After Washington's nephew abandoned his search, Judge came out of hiding. Deliberately avoiding interviews for many years, she had nonetheless became a local celebrity, known in town as Washington's fugitive slave. In her seventies, she gave an interview to a New Hampshire abolitionist minister, which appeared in a local newspaper, and a second to *The Liberator*, knowing full well that she was aiding the abolitionist cause by helping to damage the reputation of George and Martha Washington.[34]

After emancipation New England states as well as individual towns were fearful that former slaves, especially the elderly, would become dependent on the public purse. The sizable proportion, if not the majority, of the inmates of almshouses of Boston, Salem, and Charlestown were "the state poor," paid for by the state, rather than towns. The state feared the problem would grow larger since other towns were seeking to pass along to them their welfare burden. In 1788 Massachusetts responded to public fears of dependent slaves by passing legislation to force former slave refugees to leave the state within two months or face imprisonment and whipping. Passed the day after the legislature enacted a bill outlawing the slave trade, the legislature appears to have been acting on conscience with one hand and responding to xenophobia with the other. However, the common denominator in both pieces of legislation was that the Commonwealth of Massachusetts was restricting the number of blacks who could enter the state. Seven years later Gabriel's Rebellion in Virginia ignited fears of impending black revolt, prompting authorities in Boston to activate the anti-immigration law of 1788. On the list of potential black deportees were several long-time residents of Boston such as Cato Gardner as well as propertied black men, some of whom were founders of Boston's black self-help organization, the African Society.[35] Cato Gardner never left Boston, and one suspects, neither did many of the others slated for deportation. The point of the legislation was to notify potential applicants not to expect relief.[36]

Warning out in towns was largely a symbolic process of notification, more bark than bite, although the ratio of bark to bite is not at all clear. A constable served a notice upon newcomers that they could not claim poor relief from the town. Only the disorderly were made to leave town; thus, many of those who were warned out remained where they had been living. The towns were concerned with providing relief for those who had a legal settlement in town; those who did not had to be notified they were ineligible for relief. Large towns paid for outdoor relief to the poor, aid to those who remained in their homes, and indoor relief at an almshouse; smaller towns never built an almshouse and thus their relief was entirely of the outdoor variety (firewood, funds for the care of a dying woman, wet nurses for black orphans, burial money, payments to local residents for the boarding of a black orphan).[37] Legal settlement was the local equivalent of citizenship, a way of defining the obligations a town had for the individual and the right of an individual, in Kunal Parker's words, to "resources by reason of age, illness, disability, and poverty."[38] There were many rules for determining town inhabitancy but prior condition of servitude and marital status were among them. A free married woman took her place of residence from that of her husband, whereas a husband could not derive his residence from his wife. Even if a woman was separated, she was still a resident of her husband's town. As always, slavery trumped coverture: an enslaved married woman was an inhabitant of her master's town, not her husband's town.[39]

All newcomers were subject to the warning-out process; those warned out were not all beggars and even a few slave owners were subject to these notices. The warning out of blacks prior to emancipation was actually quite limited. Blacks had been warned out of New England towns as early as 1683, but in relatively small numbers. Free blacks were less than one percent of those warned out in Worcester County, Massachusetts, from 1737 to 1789 and were about equally balanced between the sexes.[40] Slaves were not subject to the warning-out process because their movement was controlled by their masters.

In the 1790s Massachusetts towns were extending their dragnets quite widely, sometimes based on race, more often based on class. In 1790 a list of "warnings to Negroes" of Salem enumerated virtually every black in town; the next year the list included mostly white inhabitants. During the winter of 1792 town officials in Boston engaged in the largest sweep ever conducted in Massachusetts, subjecting two thousand people to warnings, with single women vastly overrepresented. In the winter work was hard to find and officials in Boston wanted to notify people they termed transients not to expect town support. By no means were warnings limited to newcomers. On the list in Boston were Cesar and Chloe Spear, long-time residents, warned that they were ineligible for relief but never forced to leave Boston. When Stock-bridge undertook its own warnings out in 1793, Rose Binney and Elizabeth Freeman received notices. What is not known is the extent of subsequent surveillance over their lives or how they felt about being singled out by town officials. By the middle of the middle of the 1790s, all the states except Rhode Island assumed responsibility for the relief of migrants and warnings out by towns were eliminated.[41]

Unlike other New England states Rhode Island retained responsibility for relief and took more action to expel possible dependents. Town authorities in Rhode Island always took the process more seriously than their counterparts elsewhere, because many Rhode Island men were injured or killed at sea or in naval warfare—or did not return to their wives and children, thereby creating a larger dependent population of single mothers, widows, and orphans. In addition, the black transient population of the state had increased dramatically with emancipation, the destruction of Newport, and the mass emigration of Narragansett slaves to Newport and Providence. Only one percent of the transient population in Providence in the 1730s was black; in the 1780s the figure was 21 percent.[42] Are you a legal resident of the town? was the first question Rhode Island town authorities asked of an applicant for poor relief. The town council of Greenwich in 1780 ordered all blacks, mulattoes, and Indians to leave town immediately. Six years later the town council of Tiverton decided that all black people had to leave town within a month or face internment at the workhouse or assignment at hard labor. In these cases the town constable or sergeant kept a supply of blank forms and added in the name of any black person he encountered.[43]

As Rhode Island recovered from the economic hard times of the 1780s, the white welfare population fell, leaving blacks and Indians a larger percentage of the dependent poor. By 1800 blacks and Indians were half of all those warned out in Rhode Island but only 5 percent of the total population.[44] Rhode Island towns especially targeted single mothers: about half of the transient heads of household authorities questioned were single mothers, Indian or black.[45] Moreover, poor mothers were forced to find an indenture for their children when they became dependent on town relief—or they were warned out. The legal residence of a child born out of wedlock was not that of the mother, but instead the town where the child was born.[46] Often mothers had their children taken from them involuntarily and placed in an indenture.[47] Such a system of forcible separation of children from their mothers looked uncannily like the system of slavery from which they had just received deliverance.

Black women fought back against the patriarchy of town fathers and the limitations on their newly found freedom of movement, sometimes with the help of local whites.[48] Some women went into hiding and did not show up when they were ordered to appear before a town council; a few refused to sign transcriptions of their testimony. Still others were warned out of a town and went to live elsewhere temporarily or squatted on a tract of vacant and unincorporated land for a few years before they managed to find their way back to the town from which had been expelled. Judah, a mother in her fifties, living in the Providence workhouse, declined to affix her mark to her testimony before the town council in 1780. She and her daughter, Raney (Urania) in her mid-twenties, were living at the workhouse as inmates. Both had been former slaves in the plantation areas of southern Rhode Island. Judah, who had been emancipated by her owner in the 1750s, moved to Newport, where she had relatives. Her daughter's master had allowed her to move there, live with her mother, and hire herself out. Judah's husband may have been a free black sailor often away at sea. When the British bombarded Newport and occupied the town, Judah and Raney, like many other residents, fled to safety in Providence. After a few years on their own they were confined to the town's almshouse, probably because of ill health.

As part of the warning-out process the Providence town clerk appeared at the almshouse and asked Judah and Raney to testify about their history and legal residence. He did not interview the women in the home of a respectable family, the standard procedure, perhaps out of fear that they might bring fleas or spread disease. After reading them a transcript of their testimony he asked them to affix their marks. Judah refused to sign, saying that she "never did sign any writing." The town council branded her and her daughter as persons "of bad character and reputation," terms usually applied to brothel owners, prostitutes, and runaway wives. Mother and daughter were permanently separated; Judah was sent to North Kingstown and Raney to the overseers of the poor in West Greenwich. Even though Judah had not lived in North Kingstown for thirty years it was considered her town of habitation because her legal residence was the town of her former owner. Similarly, Providence officials defined Raney as an inhabitant of West Greenwich despite the fact that she had not lived there for more than a decade.[49]

Local whites often assumed that a woman of bad character and reputation had to be a prostitute. Mobs attacked brothels operated by black women, fearful that black women living in their midst were bringing disorder to the neighborhood. After arriving in Providence during the war and living in various parts of town Margaret Bowler Fairchild, a former slave from Newport, rented the old jail and converted it into a boardinghouse, with rooms rented out for sexual commerce. The prostitutes at the boardinghouse were black, biracial, and white women, servicing white and black sailors. White neighbors in a warehouse district close to the docks, although accustomed to drunken sailors, were upset by Bowler's interracial clientele.[50]

The authorities targeted Bowler, her women neighbors, and the women in her employ, not the white mob who leveled her property. After her boarding-house had been completely destroyed the deputy governor of Rhode Island, sensing public support for the mob, recommended a crackdown on all "bad houses" as part of a general effort to restore "order and virtue" in Providence. The town council issued a warrant to force Bowler, her female lodgers, and other neighbors suspected of prostitution to testify before them. Apparently not finding all the women who lodged with Bowler, the councilmen made Bowler name names. Was she trying to bargain for a lighter punishment or none at all? Despite her cooperation, the councilmen of Providence gave her ten days to leave town, which for the times was generous. She left Providence temporarily but returned to the city within a couple of years. Other mobs in Providence destroyed brothels operated by black women in the next two years. Subsequently a local white minister in Boston noted that rioters in the city were also "pulling down" brothels in which white women served a black clientele.[51]

Black women during the early years of emancipation displayed a certain resilience because as hard as the authorities tried to control them, they never quite managed to do so. The black poor were welcome in their communities so long as they were clearly notified that they were ineligible for relief. Only in Rhode Island did officials round up the local black population rather than merely issue warnings. But free blacks had sought to assert their respectabil-ity, shield themselves from racial prejudice, and help raise the entire regard in which the race was held. No matter how long they had lived in town, or how many neighbors they knew, free black men and women were a suspect class; town officials were allowed to put them under surveillance. True free-dom and independence, free blacks might well have thought, would only emerge if black people organized among themselves to help their own—the problem, it turned out, was that such a promising development also turned out to restrict the civic participation of black women.

7

CITIZENSHIP

In the age of emancipation free blacks were deeply involved in living out their ideas of citizenship, independence, and asserting their identity as Africans. Conscious of their rights, aware of the barriers to racial equality, black men at the end of the war founded fraternal lodges, the burial organizations known as African societies, and informal black militias. Although both black women and men claimed for themselves the rights of citizens and the identity of Africans, women were excluded from membership in these free black institutions.[1] Even before the Revolution in Election Day festivals black men followed one principle of exclusion: that only men could vote. Part of building the new institutions of freedom was that black men now had the power to make their own decisions about membership. The basis for exclusion were the general ideas of gender held by New England society. These dictated that the propertied men in the new republic looked out for dependent widows, that men shared special bonds in their own associations, and that women could not fight for the town or their state and thus were not deserving of the full rights of citizenship.

It is a measure of the limited definition of equality and the influence of white models of politics on free blacks that black women, who had been so active in gaining their freedom, remained so marginal to the life of free black communities. Blacks in New England had defined freedom in terms of patriarchy, regarding men as heads of household and as the natural leaders of their communities who acted as the representatives of the family. Only a few black men were actually enfranchised—those who owned property, and some of them were not allowed to vote until after they went to court and demanded their rights. Most black men were excluded from jury service, the judiciary, the constabulary, local and state elective offices; there were no black college graduates. But there was one black man who was a judge and tax collector, and in fact, was an appointed judge and a justice of the peace decades before the American Revolution. Wentworth Cheswell, the son of a biracial father and a white mother, landowner and schoolmaster, was appointed justice of the peace in Exeter, New Hampshire in 1768, hearing minor legal cases that came before him. After the Revolution he was not only a taxpayer but the town's tax assessor and was elected multiple times as town selectman, auditor, and coroner. Another New Hampshire war veteran, Sampson Battis, commanded a battalion of largely white soldiers in the New Hampshire state militia by 1800. Thus very light-skinned black men were able to circumnavigate the burdens of race; very light-skinned black women were unable to escape the barriers of gender. The occasional black women landowners of the time were denied the right to vote not because they were black but because they were women. The same rationale for political disenfranchisement applied to black as to white women, irrespective of race: they did not deserve the suffrage because their husbands and fathers represented their interests in civic affairs.[2]

Many free black men who joined these early organizations of the free black community were veterans of the Revolutionary War who returned from battle with the letters "U.S.A." printed on the buttons of their uniform. Black men, not women, had demonstrated against the Stamp Act and stood with whites at Lexington and Concord. Military service strengthened the connection between black male identity and political rights since black male veterans believed they had earned the right to be citizens and speak on behalf of their communities. In peacetime black men regarded service in the militia as a means of proving themselves good citizens. In 1786 Prince Hall, the founder of African Lodge No. 1, probably a war veteran himself, offered seven hundred troops to the Governor of Massachusetts to put down Shays' rebellion. Hall was making a grand, even grandiose, gesture, since seven hundred black men of fighting age approached the entire adult black population of greater Boston at the time. Hall had concluded that free blacks had more to gain from siding with Governor Bowdoin than with the rebels. After all, Freemasons were suspected of rebel sympathies since Daniel Shays was a member of the order. In his petition Prince Hall described the men of his lodge as "peaceable subjects" who were "members of [a] fraternity," law-abiding black brothers ready to stand up for proper authority. Elizabeth Freeman had yielded a shovel when the Shaysite rebels pillaged the Sedgwick house, but she could not don a uniform and fight.[3] Without a second thought Governor Bowdoin turned down Hall's offer. Neither the commanders of troops nor the Governor welcomed the prospect of gigantic black phalanx marching west from Boston.

Because of the attitudes of black people and white society as well, black women played a limited role in the development of free black institutions. Women's civic efforts in the post-revolutionary era ranged from an elderly woman telling her story of enslavement and demanding back pay for her unpaid work in bondage to women participating and challenging black men's organizations or founding ones of their own; in these attempts black women were seeking to define the meaning of justice as well as their place in the free black community. Economic need, assertion of African identity, and familial consciousness were far stronger than race and gender consciousness, which, as might be expected, appeared first among black literate women.

Invariably these early women leaders were husbandless, most often widows. Holding the legal status of femme soles, these women had the same rights to own property, control their wages, and sign a contract as a man; they, too, were heads of households. Thus these widows enjoyed far more independence of action than other black women, endowed with a legal standing greater than that of a married woman. The widow was a multivalent figure, of course: she could be needy and helpless, independent, or troublesome; in the annals of the free black community widows appear in all of these guises in the early years after emancipation. But the very fact that there were so few married women participants in free black life reveals the extent to which the ideal of patriarchy limited black women's freedom of action.

A sole black woman named Belinda forced the newly formed state of Massachusetts to reckon with questions of economic justice for former slaves. In her petition to the Massachusetts legislature Belinda made the first public demand by a former slave for reparations in the United States. An enslaved mother emancipated by the will of her master, Isaac Royall, Jr. she sought a yearly pension from her former owner's holdings confiscated by the state of Massachusetts. Belinda was a black woman citizen much ahead of her times, even though she was not a member of a free black organization nor a founder of a social movement. Unlike subsequent efforts to gain reparations, Belinda's demand was not greeted by disrespect but in fact passed the Massachusetts legislature with the imprimatur of Patriot heroes Samuel Adams and John Hancock. Her petition to the state legislature argued that reparations did not violate basic principles of liberty but were in fact a matter of simple justice. A strong supporter of the American side in the Revolution, she considered the Revolutionary War an armed conflict in "the cause of freedom." Like Phillis Wheatley, a woman of the Enlightenment, Belinda believed that freedom originated as a gift from "the Almighty Father."[4] Her thinking about labor was quite capitalist and modern, that work had to be remunerated and a worker should be compensated for previously unpaid labor.

In Massachusetts the idea of reparations for slavery was broached several times before Belinda's petition to the Massachusetts legislature.[5] James Swan, a young, radical eighteen-year-old Scotsman who found work as an apprentice in a Boston counting house, first raised the idea, mentioning it briefly in his *A Disuasion to Great Britain* (1772). The next year Felix Holbrook and three compatriots, the authors of a petition to the Massachusetts legislative assembly seeking additional opportunities to purchase their freedom, included Swan's pamphlet along with their petition. Unwilling to press the idea of reparations themselves they were nonetheless eager to forward Swan's views. Timothy Pickering, an aging deacon of the Presbyterian Church of Salem, made the religious argument for reparations in a public letter addressed "to my brethren in the 13 United American Colonys or States" in 1777. Previously Pickering had brought a petition tabled by the Massachusetts General Assembly to end the colony's participation in the slave trade and had also tried to change the law so that slaves would be taxed as persons rather than property, a subtle maneuver to end the legal status of slavery. Citing Old Testament passages to justify reparations for slavery, Pickering wrote that "Our Slavers are advised to pay their Africans for their Past Services and to Let Them Goe Free. Jer'h 22. 13. Isaiah 58.6."[6]

In 1781 another Royall former slave, Anthony Vassal, petitioned the state's General Assembly for something similar to reparations on behalf of himself and his wife. He wanted title to his house, the one and a half acres of confiscated land on which he was growing crops, and exemption from future taxes; his request was denied. However, the Massachusetts legislature approved an annual pension for him derived from rents on the estates of his former owner. Anthony, the coachman, had married one of the slaves of his mistress (a Royall daughter) brought to her marriage. The couple had to live separately in a nearby Cambridge mansion when Anthony's owner sold his pregnant wife and children to nephew who lived nearby. Cuba and Tony's infant son was given to a new owner in South Woburn. When the war ended, the family, reunited, dwelled in a small cabin behind the mansion where Cuba had been living, then serving as the headquarters of George Washington. During that time Anthony Vassal was employed as a day laborer at the Royall estate in Medford and he certainly met Belinda, if he had not known her before, and must have revealed his plans to her.[7]

Belinda was granted reparations from the state of Massachusetts not because she was a slave who had been denied wages but because her owner took the wrong side in the American Revolution. Isaac Royall, Jr., the largest slave owner in Massachusetts, fled Boston soon after the Battle of Lexington. He was one of the English landed gentry of Massachusetts, men who could trace their wealth to the plantations of the West Indies. His father, the upwardly mobile son of a New England carpenter, owned sugar plantations

7.1. White Clay pipe, with Letter M. Enslaved women as well as men sought to rest from work by sitting down and smoking tobacco in a pipe. Archaeologists from Boston University, excavating the grounds of Royall House in Medford, Massachusetts, between 1999 and 2001, found this commercially produced pipe, with the letter M carved on it. The one slave owned by Isaac Royall, Jr., whose name began with M was Mira, identified in the Massachusetts census in 1754; there were no whites at the house with the first name of M. Photo © 2006, Royall House Association, used by permission and a rum distillery in Antigua, and was a slave trader. Born on his father's Antigua estate (near Royalls Bay) in 1719 he was sent to Boston for private tutoring when he was young. After enduring drought, hurricanes, outbreaks of yellow fever, and a possible slave uprising thwarted at the last moment, his father decided to turn over the management of his plantation to overseers and retire to Medford. Planning his move gradually, Isaac, Sr., had bought an estate in Medford and asked one of his older brothers, Jacob, a merchant and slave trader in Boston, to supervise a huge remodeling project, refashioning an old New England farmhouse into a Georgian brick mansion. Royall, Sr., gradually shipped some of his slaves to the estate, finally leaving the island with his wife, the younger children, and some of his slaves in 1737.[8]

Isaac Royall, Jr., at age twenty-two took as his bride a fifteen-year-old girl who brought to her marriage a plantation in Dutch-controlled Surinam and an estate in Rhode Island. Isaac Royall, Sr., died the next year and his sons came into their inheritances. As an absentee owner of lands in Antigua, Royall, Jr., traveled to the islands from time to time to check on the management of his holdings.[9] Royall had been a bit of a conniver in his younger days, engaging in a secret but unsuccessful plot to become the governor of New Hampshire. After that effort failed he led the genteel life, finding suitable husbands for his daughters, a wealthy young man from Boston and another from Kittery, Maine, who came to call at the mansion and courted his girls at the gazebo under the statue of the god Mercury. He involved himself in Massachusetts politics and philanthropy, donating funds to public education in Medford, serving as moderator of the town meeting and as justice of the peace of Suffolk County. The Governor came to dine at Ten Hill Farm, and found it advantageous to hire out several of Royall's slaves.[10] An Overseer of Harvard College, Royall contributed to the restoration of the Harvard library and laboratory after it was damaged by fire in 1764. The proprietor of a large tract of land near Worcester, Royall decided to donate some money and a folio Bible to the new meetinghouse; as a result, the local farmers decided to name the town after him (Royalshire, then Royalton). In the years before the revolution Royall was a moderate, who thought British troops quartered in Boston inflamed the militants on the American side and urged appointment of colonial governors who could calm the troubled waters. After his wife and his brother Jacob died he lost interest in the political controversies of the day. By the time the first shots were fired at Concord and Lexington, Royall, like many Tories, fled from the countryside to safety among the besieged British troops with their backs to the sea in Boston. The city may have been safe from the Patriots but not from the smallpox, since his older daughter died there from the disease while they were refugees in town.

After British troops evacuated Boston in 1776 Royall made his way to Salem. Failing to secure passage to the family plantation in Antigua he decided to take the first English ship headed out, sailing to Halifax, Nova Scotia.[11] One of his other daughters and her wealthy husband joined him there. As Royall was leaving, George, one of his elderly slaves at Ten Hill Farm, committed suicide, anticipating (correctly) that his master was planning to send instructions to sell him. Royall's estate manager Dr. Simon Tufts urged the New Hampshire general commanding the Continental Army to use the mansion as his headquarters since an otherwise deserted house would be vandalized and completely destroyed. Even so, the general and his officers helped themselves to the fine old wines in the cellar. The American general, his lady, and his officers moved in, with the Royall slaves taking care of their needs, fetching water, cooking, doing laundry, and mending.[12]

7.2. Slave Quarters, Isaac Royall House, Medford, Massachusetts. Some of the Royall slaves slept in the hall of the mansion next to the master's bedroom or in the attic of the house; the rest occupied the second floor of this two-story brick building next to the mansion. Isaac Royall Sr., designed the original one-story building and his son added onto it. Slaves did the cooking for everyone at the farm in the huge walk-in fireplace on the first floor of the quarters. The area around the quarters was used for dumping trash and waste and was thus the foul-smelling part of the Royal estate. Photo © 2006, Royall House Association, used by permission

While living in Halifax Royall was persuaded by his son-in-law to abandon returning to Antigua and sail for London. Once there he took several measures to redeem himself in the eyes of Massachusetts politicians, hoping to stop the Commonwealth from confiscating his property. He donated over 2000 acres of land in Royalton and elsewhere to fund a professorship at Harvard in law, physics, or anatomy. He also deeded a 600-acre tract of land for building a hospital for the poor in Medford. Nonetheless, the Commonwealth of Massachusetts designated him as one of its 308 "Great Enemies" and forbade him from ever returning to the state. Unimpressed with his largesse, politicians confiscated quite a bit of Royall's vast wealth and he was forced to claim penury in a petition for a temporary allowance from British government. Having suffered a stroke, he spent his last years in Brighton living with his son-in-law and died of smallpox in 1781.[13] In his will Royall manumitted Belinda; the executor of his will was instructed to pay her "for 3 years, £30."[14]

When Belinda submitted a petition to the Massachusetts legislature, she wrote a brief personal history of her capture in Africa and of her life as a Royall slave. In addition, Royall's estate inventories and Medford church records also provide a few details about a woman who appears to have been a pious Christian mother as well as a long-time slave of the Royalls. Belinda had two children, a son Joseph and a daughter, Prine, both baptized on the same day in August of 1768.[15] Since Belinda was fifty-five at the time of her children's baptisms at the First Church of Medford their enrollment in the church had not occurred at the time of their births but instead at a moment of her choosing. A little more is known about her daughter than her son. There were two slaves named Joseph at Ten Acres and only one survived; it is not clear whether the Joseph in the records of the plantation is her son. At the time of her petition Prine, Belinda's "infirm daughter," would probably have been in her thirties.

Belinda's petition combined the now-familiar theme of being stolen from the African homeland with a sketch of her owner's style of living so as to make the point that he was a Loyalist and landed gentry who had profited handsomely from the exploitation of his slaves. Despite contributing to Royall's bounty she had not shared in it. His riches were like food denied to her, her petition stated, since she had not been allowed "the employment of one morsel of that immense wealth." The walls of the second floor of Royall's mansion were decorated with flowers and birds painted on a leather wall hanging imported from China. Playing on the public's knowledge of Royall's genteel consumerism—and the new frugality of the republican era—the petition asked, "what did it avail her that the walls of her lord were hung with Splendor." Robbed of her time, she "never had...a moment at her own disposal." Royall was not a moderate, she claimed, but a full-fledged Tory and traitor, "pouring blood and vengeance on all who dare to be free," fleeing to England, "a land where lawless dominion sits enthroned."[16] In Medford Royall was generally known as the Colonel because of his service in the militia; the petition chose to refer to Royall's military rank to emphasize that he had been a British officer.

The British and American audience was eager to hear the testimony of an enslaved woman; her petition was the first time an African woman had described her capture in Africa and ruptured family ties along with her suffering on board a slave ship. Like other abolitionist documents of the day, Belinda's petition began with the portrayal of an idyllic childhood in Africa and the two tender parents left behind. Abolitionists, seeking to refute the view of Africa as barbaric, picked up the same themes as Wheatley, that Africa was not "a dark and ignorant land" but instead a "country" of great natural beauty, a Garden of Eden. Belinda remembered the area where she came from, the "mountains covered in spicy forests... yallies, loaded with the richest fruits... that happy temperature of air..."[17] The petition stated that "each hand in that of a tender parent, was paying devotion to the great Orisa," the name for a major Yoruba deity. Kidnapped from her village on the banks of the Rio de Volta (in what appears to have been present-day eastern Ghana) Belinda referred to herself not in terms of tribal identity but instead as an African. Reacting to seeing whites for the first time, she used the words "white" and "Europeans." Unlike other slave autobiographers, Belinda made clear that she had been enslaved not by Africans, but by whites.[18] The petition described an "armed band of white men," men whose round light-skinned "faces were like the moon," "the most dreadful of all enemies," motivated by greed for West African gold, robbers and thieves who "placed their happiness in the yellow dust."[19] Taken to the coast she was forced to board a slave ship with three hundred tormented Africans, some of whom were contemplating suicide as the only way for their spirits to return home.[20]

Not since Wheatley's letter denouncing slave-owning Patriots a decade before had a document in a black woman's name circulated so widely. The petition was reprinted in four Massachusetts newspapers and in a Quaker-edited newspaper in New Jersey and in Philadelphia, the home of the first abolitionist society.[21] It also appeared in a Bristol, England, newspaper, edited by a Quaker and also in an English popular magazine. An anonymous editor rewrote the English version of the petition and asserted that Belinda was raped when she was young. The new version reads, "One of his meanest servants robbed me of my innocence by force, and at an age when my youth should have been my security from pollution." The story of rape in her youth underscored the special suffering of the African woman and may have been a tale a British abolitionist audience was waiting to hear. In this particular version of the petition Isaac Royall was not identified by name, but instead described as a "cruel ungrateful master," perhaps because his son-in-law, a Loyalist refugee from Maine, Sir William Pepperell, was living in reduced circumstances in England but still had some influential friends.[22]

The person who wrote Belinda's petition probably served as her publicist, forwarding it to newspapers and magazines. Since Belinda was illiterate, historians have speculated about the amanuensis who wrote in such an elegant but sentimental abolitionist style, and probably stood by her for seven years as she struggled to receive the money awarded her. The most likely author is Prince Hall, who at one time lived in Medford; he had the literary ability to narrate the slave plight in terms of "weeping eyes and aching hearts" and wrote by hand several petitions of blacks forwarded to the Massachusetts legislature. The acknowledged leader of blacks in the Boston area he took seriously his responsibility to come to the aid of helpless women and their children. Hall knew as a brother Mason a former slave at Ten Hills Farm, Fortune Howard, who had become a cooper, moved to Boston, and joined him and thirteen other black men in being initiated as Freemasons just before the war broke out. Hall was also well connected with abolitionist Quakers in Boston, important clergy in the city, and state legislators. He was also acquainted with influential people in Britain: black seamen, some of them members of the lodge, hand carried his correspondence with evangelicals or British Freemasons to England.[23]

The executor of Royall's will, who probably paid Belinda for three years from the funds of the estate, witnessed the petition. Willis Hall, the courtly town clerk in Medford and a church deacon, added his signature as the first witness and his nineteen-year-old son was the second. Willis Hall had been Royall's good friend, who, probably acting upon his friend's instructions, had been able to save some of Royall's land from being confiscated. (The land was sold many times, but acquired by Dr. Tufts, and is now part of College Hill, near Tufts University.) Why had Willis Hall, a former slave owner himself, signed his name to a document that characterized his old friend as a bloodthirsty and vengeful Tory? He seems to have concluded that Royall's reputation had already been ruined and that so long as the Commonwealth was accumulating the income from the Royall properties, Belinda might as well receive a share.[24]

Black women such as Lucy Pernam had learned painfully that legal victories were worth considerably less than the paper they were written on. Over a course of seven years Belinda fought to receive a pension, beginning with her petition to the Massachusetts legislature in 1783. That year she was awarded recompense of fifteen pounds, twelve shillings to be paid out of Royall's estate—more per year than her master had been willing to provide—and received one payment. Three years later she applied to Isaac Royall's daughter, Mary, who had returned from England and was living with her husband in Boston. In 1786 Mary's husband, William, paid Belinda two pounds and two shillings—a fraction of the amount specified by the Commonwealth. The scene of Belinda's encounter with William Erving cannot be known, but the main character was a seventy-three-year-old mother with a curved back and a furrowed brow. Showing up at Erving's stately home in Boston—perhaps taken there by Hall—she was handed a sum of money, and signed a document of receipt with her mark. Desperate for some income she may have begged, but then again persistence was her truly defining characteristic. Mary Royall Erving and her husband left Boston again for England where she died soon after her arrival. Belinda resumed petitioning the Massachusetts legislature the next year; as part of her effort the Philadelphia magazine editor Matthew Carey was persuaded to reprint a copy of her petition.[25] She succeeded in getting the Massachusetts legislature to order an annual payment for her, which she received for three years.[26] In 1790 the executor of the Royall estate refused to pay the pension "without a further imposition" from the Massachusetts legislature.[27] The legislature appointed a committee to investigate and ordered resumption of the payments; after that there is no further evidence about Belinda or Prine.[28]

Belinda believed that the Massachusetts legislature had a moral responsibility to her and her daughter. In her view the Revolution required a reckoning with New England slavery, a monetary recompense for the wrongs she and her children had suffered. Yet for her justice was more than a matter of money; she wanted to tell her story and affirm her identity as a captured African and vulnerable mother and reveal the gross misdeeds of the several white men who had wronged her. Class- and race-conscious, sentimental in her attachment to her parents, and desperate in her need for support for herself and Prine, her petition was presented to the Massachusetts legislature three times. The great Patriots of the Revolution, Samuel Adams and John Hancock, one of whom refused to own a fellow human being, the other an owner who had emancipated his slaves, signed and approved the petition in 1783, thereby tacitly endorsing the idea of reparations. When her petition reached England it was transformed into one of the first tales of rape of a young African woman, unwilling to be shamed into silence. In the mid-nineteenth century Belinda had not yet lost the contest of remembrance, since British and American abolitionists heralded her "eloquent petition," even though Royall was also remembered in the name of a town near Worcester and by a professorship in his name at Harvard Law School.[29]

Robert Feke, a good provincial painter, and the greatest artist of the colonies, John Singleton Copley, both portrayed Isaac Royall as the very model of an English gentleman in his youth and his mature years. His former slave, who had known him much better and longer, drew a much more unfavorable picture, turning his acquisition of great wealth against him. She pictured for her audience the interior decoration of her master's mansion, a world of silver pitchers, mahogany desks and chests, and imported Turkish carpets. If anything, her indictment was not scathing enough—a father who burned at the stake a rebellious slave in Antigua, one brother auctioning off slaves in Boston coffeehouses, another who secretly hired a gang of men to abduct his remaining slaves and sell them to Barbados before they became worthless, yet another whose efforts at last minute sale contributed to slave suicide—the only ones surprised to learn about the Royalls would have been those who subscribed to the myth of the kindly owner and faithful master.[30] Unlike so many other women who struggled to sever their chains, unnoticed in the press, Belinda received considerable hearing for her views in her own day as well as after her death. Her arguments were emotional, not technical ones; she was a kidnapped African who denounced white slavers as greedy, a mother concerned about providing for her disabled daughter, a woman who believed that freedom was nothing if not coupled with justice to undo great wrongs.

The first two black institutions founded in New England were the African Lodge, established in 1775 under Prince Hall's leadership in Boston and chartered by an English Masonic organization twelve years later, and the African Union of Newport, established in 1780. Boston's African Lodge was a male secret society incorporated as part of the international network of lodges of Freemasonry. Freemasonry, while it had some medieval roots, blossomed in the eighteenth century, and found adherents both in England and in the colonies; throughout the colonies many Patriots of the Revolution such as George Washington and Benjamin Franklin were Freemasons. The black men of Boston under Hall's leadership were administered the oath as Masons (in return for payment) by a member of an Irish regiment quartered in Boston willing to initiate them.

The Freemasons under Hall symbolized the way masculinity, African identity, and freedom were joined; in the African Lodge brotherhood and fraternity affirmed the special bonds of black men with each other, made more so because of secret codes and passwords. Just as the rituals of Election Day were a performance of gender, so, too, the rituals of the African Lodge expressed the ideal of the free black man deserving of respect. Thus, the lodge placed its own distinctive stamp on the most significant ritual of them all, the funeral. A Mason had a right to a burial led by a funeral band followed by his lodge brothers dressed in their special costumes, carrying the insignia of the order. On St. John's Day, an annual feast day for Masons, the men in their regalia staged their annual procession on the streets of Boston, followed by a banquet at Hall's home. The African Union of Newport had no secret rituals but was rather an independent, unaffiliated organization, begun as a dues-paying burial society, which backed emigration to Africa. The African Union met separately as a Negro society on Sunday evenings; it, too, staged burials for its members. Unlike the Masons, it also acted as a bank, providing loans against the property of its members, several of whom owned small pieces of land. From these organizations in Boston and Newport free black societies spread to a few of the other New England seaports. Hall's African Lodge of Boston established in 1797 an additional lodge for its members who lived in Providence[31] The Newport society successfully helped black men in Providence to start a similar organization in 1783. Two other African societies were founded in 1796, the first in Boston and a second in Portsmouth. These organizations provided their dues-paying members with disability benefits, helped defray the costs of a funeral, and offered payments for widows of members.

Freemasonry resembled West African secret societies in the emphasis on "cooperative assurance," funerals, and special signs and passwords known only to members. In West African secret societies initiates swore a blood oath on joining. Many African secret societies had their own banners and staged their own public processions, especially for a funeral. The societies also provided for the sick and buried the dead; members progressed by ranks to positions of the highest status. In West Africa women's societies were open to all women, who underwent an initiation ritual through which they acquired separate names other than their birth names. The women's societies had their own leaders, who controlled rituals for women, a significant African tradition not transferred to New England less because owners actively discouraged it than because women's secret societies and the sense of solidarity underlying them had disappeared.[32] Thus, the crucial gendered aspect of these free black organizations, the exclusion of women and the absence of separate societies for women, was not an African tradition but rather a distinctive New England one.

The rules of membership of the African Union of Newport reflected the ideals of patriarchy, citizenship, and independence. Membership in the society was limited to free black men, with the exception of Newport Gardner, a community leader, born in West Africa who retained his African name (Occramer Marycoo) and native language and always made clear that he was planning to return to his homeland. Nonetheless, all the other members of the society were free, identified by the designation of Mr. before their name. Political independence of the male citizen rested on his ownership of property, which entitled him to represent the interests of his dependents. In creating formal associations black men were adopting the political model of their white male counterparts, relying on what historian J. R. Pole refers to as "the basic economic presupposition that the ownership of a specified amount of property was an essential guarantee of political competence."[33]

Members of the African Union had to be free, male, and a freeholder, with the exception of Gardner, but nonmembers also signed one piece of correspondence of the Union as part of their effort to encourage a similar organization in Providence.[34] The secretary of the African Union in Newport drafted a letter to the men in Providence in 1789 outlining the rules for starting their own organization. A freeholder was a landowner and legal resident of a town and could be female as well as male; however, only male freeholders were allowed to vote in town government and elect a representative to the General Court. Six members of the Union and five "freeholders" who were not members signed the letter. One of them was Rebecca Folger, whose husband may have left with the British for Nova Scotia during the war. As a freeholder she owned property in Newport but as a woman she was not allowed to vote and therefore was not eligible to belong to the African Union.[35] It is not clear what circumstances led the men to encourage Folger to sign the letter, but they may have regarded her situation as unique since she did not live in a household headed by a man.

The Union's responsibility for the conduct of the funerals of its members eventually led to the inclusion of a black woman in their funeral rental business. Since colonial days Newport masters in an unusual act of paternalism had established a separate section in the Common Burial Ground for the graves of their slaves. In most of New England slaves were buried in unmarked graves or given wooden grave markers often destroyed by wind and weather. Newport masters paid for the granite headstones for their slaves, many quite expensive and beautifully carved with heads of angels with African features. Pall bearers lifted the coffin to their shoulders and led the slow procession to the gravesite. In freedom black people of Newport were conducting their own funerals and purchasing their own carved headstones for the graves of their loved ones. Black dignity depended on free people of African descent organizing their own funerals and paying for these burial markers rather than relying solely on the generosity of former owners.[36]

The African Union established a separate business for the rental of equipment needed for burials, called the Palls and Biers Society, in which "proprietors" purchased a share of the pall and bier, rented for funerals. (A bier was a wheeled wooden cart on which the coffin was placed and the pall was the cloth covering the coffin). The proprietors were entitled to a share of the profits from the rental of the pall and bier at the funeral of members of the society. Since there was no black undertaker at this time, a master of ceremonies organized the funeral and, as was the custom of the day, sent white gloves to friends and neighbors as invitations to the event.

While the coffin remained in the home the society served tea and rum to those assembled. The funeral procession followed, the family and the members of the Society walking behind the bier. The Society issued stern reminders to its members that it was their solemn obligation to march in the burial procession of every deceased member of the organization.[37]

In 1792 the Palls and Biers Society of the African Union sold Duchess Quamino a one-sixth share in their business, thereby making her the first black woman invited to join a black male organization in New England. Trusted for her business acumen she had sterling personal qualities as well as good connections. Quamino was called Duchess because she claimed to be the daughter of an African prince and "had much of the bearing of royalty" about her.[38] Her husband, the missionary-in-training John Quamino, had died during the war, trying to make enough money as a privateer to purchase the freedom of his wife and two daughters. Serving on a privateer was not the same as being a pirate; instead, Quamino had signed up for the crew of a ship whose mission it was to carry an enemy ship back to port and sell off the cargo. The proceeds, which could be considerable, were divided between the owners of the vessel and the members of the crew. Quamino was willing to risk his life for a quick profit so he could buy the freedom of his wife and children.

Widowed at age forty, Duchess Quamino and her four children returned to Newport from Providence to live in the home of William and Lucy Channing; he was the attorney general of Rhode Island and she was the daughter of a wealthy family that made their money from the slave trade in West Africa. The Channings manumitted Quamino the year after her husband died, but she continued to live with them, serve as their cook and the nanny for their nine children, and cook for the balls and parties they held in their home. They allowed her to use their kitchen to make plum cake and other pastries, which she sold from their home and at the Newport market on Sundays. Dubbed "the pastry queen of Newport" Quamino eventually saved enough money to buy a small house in town.[39]

Duchess Quamino brought the sensibility of a grieving mother to a black men's organization. At the time she was made a member of Palls and Biers the society purchased a new smaller pall, suitable to cover the coffin of a child. It seems likely that the idea of the child's pall was Quamino's since she knew how much mothers wanted a dignified funeral for a child; she may even have located the seamstress who could sew the pall.[40] Her decision appears not to have been an act of charity, however, since she was sharing in the rental income from the pall.

Why had the men of Palls and Biers invited Quamino to become a member, when black men's institutions excluded women? They may have decided that a deserving widow could benefit from an additional opportunity to make money. A sympathetic figure known to all, Duchess Quamino was well acquainted with grief since she had lost three daughters, one at birth, a second at age fifteen, and a third who died at eighteen just a few months earlier.[41] Since one of her daughters was buried at the Common Burying Ground, she was clearly committed to the dignity of ceremonies held there. She enjoyed high status among free blacks in Newport not only as the widow of a man well respected among them but also as African royalty. Moreover, as a widow she could engage in business as a femme sole; she could sue and be sued and own property in her own name. More practically, the society needed the capital she was willing to provide.[42]

A widow could also make trouble for Newport's African Union, especially when her word could not be easily discounted. Several years after Quamino became a proprietor of Palls and Biers, another widow, Dinah Sisson, queried the members of the Union about the account of her late husband, Neptune Sisson. He had been a slave who made extra money from growing crops and selling them at the Newport market; he did well enough to spend money on his wardrobe, including linen and silk handkerchiefs. Dinah Sisson and her husband had been friends of several members of the Union for many decades.[43] At the time of his death Neptune Sisson had been a member of the Society for five years; the Union had organized his funeral.

Dinah Sisson seemed to think that the men of the Society had not recorded all of her husband's contributions and/or that they were cheating her out of money to which she was entitled. At her request, the Society supplied her with a record of her husband's payments of dues to the general fund, which in fact showed that he was delinquent in his remittances. Nonetheless, Dinah Sisson was gossiping among blacks in Newport, perhaps threatening a lawsuit. The members of the Union do not appear to have been antagonistic toward her, but nonetheless free black men were deeply sensitive about their reputations. Concerned about being given "a bad name by the widow," they voted to disband their organization and returned the dues to each member.[44] Thus, they had to suspend temporarily their system of providing death and disability benefits to their members because of her challenge. Thereafter they incorporated the Society under its new name so that members would be protected from any future liabilities.[45]

While Duchess Quamino had formal power in Palls and Biers, Dinah Sisson was exercising informal power. Gossiping among neighbors women could form public opinion, in favor of or against male leaders of the black community. As historian Mary Beth Norton notes, "gossip for all its negative connotations, was a crucial mechanism of social control—one used by ordinary people themselves, and especially by women, who lacked men's easy access to…other forums."[46] Dinah Sisson intended to damage the reputation of the men of the African Society, knowing full well that black men were extremely concerned about how others viewed them. She did not have the power to demand inclusion in the society but she could rattle its members sufficiently so that they were forced to disband.

The male members of these African societies formed in New England had more than a passing interest in emigration to Africa. No slaves pursued a petition for reparations subsequent to Belinda, while black petitioners kept up steady pressure on state legislatures in New England on behalf of emigration to Africa. None of these petitions to state legislatures succeeded and therefore, emigration had no greater chances of success than reparations. Nonetheless, the idea of emigration had greater appeal to emancipated slaves, especially those born in Africa, because it was a collective undertaking that expressed their sense of the futility in attaining equality and justice in the new republic. Slaves had already made the collective petition their major political tool in seeking the end of slavery and civil rights in New England. Seeking to escape suffocating white contempt in the United States, they also sought to bring the Christian religion to their fellow Africans, establish their own farms and settlements ruled by a constitution, and engage in commercial trade with Americans and the British. Prince Hall and Cesar Spear were among those free black men of Boston who regarded themselves as "strangers in strange land," African by birth and identity, stranded in a new nation that would never grant them equality. Such men as these managed to combine contradictory positions, that they were engaged in a quest for citizenship, making demands of a New England state, while others were renouncing their citizenship in favor of returning to their homeland.

One of the key definitions of freedom for blacks in New England was private ownership of land. Ironically, free blacks believed they could best realize their goal by returning to Africa where they could acquire property for themselves and their families. Four black men, presenting a petition to the Massachusetts legislature in 1773, first broached the idea of emigration to "some part of the coast of Africa." They sought assistance from the government of Massachusetts because they needed money to charter a vessel and purchase land. It was always clear that black men intended a settlement of families, but black women's sentiments were more difficult to discern. Before his death at sea John Quamino was planning his return; presumably his wife Duchess, also born in West Africa, and his daughters would have joined him eventually. Nonetheless, as a widow, she never participated in emigration plans or joined any endeavors to further such an aim. When Quaker abolitionist John Thornton was trying to drum up interest among Boston blacks in a proposed settlement in West Africa, he turned to Phillis Wheatley. She supported Christian missionary efforts for that region, including sending black missionaries there and inquired of Samuel Hopkins about the success of a black Anglican missionary in the Gold Coast. Nonetheless, she did not want to marry a black missionary or accompany him to Africa. She preferred to live in Boston—and may already have found a suitor there whom she subsequently married. Wheatley demurred, replying to Thornton that she did not speak the local language and added that "this undertaking appears to be hazardous."[47]

While a woman as distinguished as Wheatley did not want to return to Africa and sensed the practical difficulties in establishing a new settlement, it does not follow that all black women in New England shared her reluctance. In 1798 a small group of blacks, born in Africa, several of whom lived in Salem, delivered yet another (the third) petition to the Massachusetts legislature requesting state subsidy for emigration to Africa. They recycled some phrases from previous emigration petitions, including that of Newport blacks nine years before, indicating that the same petition was circulating among free blacks in Rhode Island, Massachusetts, and Pennsylvania. Many of the men were illiterate, signing the petition with their mark. The first and only black woman to put her name on a petition for emigration was Deliverance Taylor, who was literate and signed the petition on behalf of her "family."[48] As a femme sole she was an independent actor and could represent her household; as a woman, presumably of African birth, she sought to join a planned settlement in West Africa; as a single mother she, too, may have wanted land of her own.[49]

Much stronger was the impulse to build new institutions in the New England town a woman called home. Early black women's organizations were entirely local efforts, with no direct communication between women in one city and another. A small group of women banded together to found the first black women's organization in New England, the Ladies African Charitable Society of Portsmouth, an auxiliary of a local black men's organization in 1796.[50] The Ladies Society was a highly practical undertaking initiated by a widow, designed to provide financial backing for a school two sisters-in-law ran out of their home—and to raise funds to pay the tuition of poor students who attended the school. An entirely local endeavor, the founding of the Ladies Society did not lead to the establishment of similar organizations in other cities. Although black women were migrating from town to town, the cosmopolitans remained black men who were sailors or preachers who traveled from one major city to another. Yet the Ladies Society does provide the evidence that even within the more local world they inhabited black women were carving out their own role and that education of black children was their major concern.

The founder of the society was a thirty-six-year-old widow and mother of seven, Dinah Chase Whipple.[51] Like Duchess Quamino, she was little known outside her seaport community, where she was well connected with religious whites and the town's former slaveholding elite, and was a member of the town's predominantly white church. She had been taught to read and write during slavery, educated by her owner, a New Hampshire minister (or his wife) and as a free woman subscribed to the local newspaper. At age twenty-one in 1781 Dinah Chase was married to Prince Whipple in a local church in Portsmouth; her owner manumitted her the day of her wedding.[52]

A large, "well proportioned" man, Prince Whipple, like Duchess Quamino, claimed regal heritage, and like her had a first name that indicated his royal birth.[53] Whipple and his brother Cuffee were brought to Portsmouth from West Africa as young boys.[54] Prince Whipple accompanied his master to war as his valet or butler, tending to his owner's clothes, delivering messages, and waiting on him at meals. After Prince Whipple returned to Portsmouth he began to meet with other African-born enslaved men in town who wanted their freedom. They drafted a petition to the New Hampshire General Assembly in 1779 that asserted "that the God of Nature gave them Life and Freedom," but their petition was tabled; William Whipple, a signer of the Declaration of Independence, did not emancipate Prince Whipple until 1783.[55]

At the end of the war Prince Whipple became, in modern terms, an event planner. He arranged the musicians, hired the caterer, and served as the waiter at weddings, dinners, balls, and evening parties of the Portsmouth elite at the local assembly hall. He went into business with his brother Cuffe, who, installed in a sunken orchestra pit, serenaded guests by playing his fiddle, while a local former slave Dinah Gibson made the sandwiches and punch.[56] William Whipple promised his former slave Prince a house for himself and his family, but died before fulfilling his pledge. Honoring her late husband's wishes his widow (known to her neighbors as Madam Whipple) allowed the two brothers to move a two-story wooden house into her backyard, where the garden plot had been. When Prince Whipple died of a fever in 1796, he left behind his widow Dinah and seven children, the oldest of whom was twelve; his brother, his wife, and two children continued to share the house with them.[57] Many widows of black Revolutionary War veterans, young women of childbearing age, did remarry, but a mother of seven, the youngest of whom was one month old, had few marital prospects. In Portsmouth Dinah Whipple was respected as the widow of the major black leader of the community. Her sister-in-law, Rebecca Daverson Whipple, four years her senior, was also a founding member of the society.[58] The most likely other members were neighbors, the wives of men who belonged to the African Society.[59]

Black parents who hungered for learning pressed for access to tax-supported schools for their youngsters, or if that failed, formed their own African schools. Dinah Chase Whipple and her sister-in-law Rebecca, educating children, including their own, in their own home, were the first black women schoolteachers in New England, although they never laid claim to the title. After the Revolution more towns were funding schools with town taxes— supplemented by tuition paid by parents—and more free black pupils were enrolled in these schools; other black students were receiving instruction in small private schools. The curriculum at most of these schools consisted of instruction in reading and writing but black girls, like white girls, were expected to demonstrate their knowledge of the alphabet in their samplers. The charitable designation of this society suggests that the school may have been one for poor children who could not afford to pay tuition. Another possibility is that Whipple had established a dame school for infants and small children of both sexes, which provided child care for employed mothers as well as rudimentary instruction in the alphabet and sewing.[60]

For most of the residents of New England a lady was a genteel white woman who owned a considerable number of silk gowns and enjoyed a certain amount of leisure, someone like Madam Whipple or the Royall daughters. Black women had never been referred to as African ladies; if anything, they were derided as "sable ladies," appearing comical when they tried to pose as "a person of quality." It was ironic then that black women would appropriate the ideal associated with the gentility of the landed aristocracy, a style of living Belinda had denounced. Yet the African lady was a new model for black womanhood that accepted class privileges associated with a former mistress while implicitly challenging racial and gender stereotypes circumscribing the women of the race. Since black people had an insecure foothold on prosperity, it was always understood that the African lady could be a respectable woman of modest circumstances who aspired to learning rather than a female born to gentility and wealth. In her last years Whipple was dependent on her church, the town, and the charity of the Portsmouth Female Humane Society; nonetheless she was a lady in terms of her education, dress, religious piety, manners, her character, her reputation, and the social standing of her daughters.[61]

Epilogue

Being stolen from kin and homeland was the central wrong African men and women cited time and again, going as far back as Hagar Blackmore's appearance in Middlesex County Court in 1651. All routes to freedom involved overcoming the injustice of that theft. The New England legal system, the abundance of land, participation in evangelical Protestantism, and the rhetoric of the Enlightenment about God-given natural rights added new layers to this original definition of freedom. In so doing, notions of freedom emerged not only from the slave trade but also from denial of access to liberties New England whites enjoyed. Some of the early Angolans in the 1600s were able to maneuver their way from slavery to indentured servitude to freedom and independent family life. As the option of serving as an indentured servant for a limited period began to disappear, enslaved women and men turned to the courts to seek their freedom, undertaking a legal process that might take several years. Bringing suit for one's freedom was also a unique benefit of life in New England, since in no other colony were there were so many men and women who successfully sued for their freedom in the courts. Some women and men also took advantage of legal loopholes provided by the complex and changing rules of race in New England. Claiming an English father or an Indian or white mother was a means of asserting the right to be free. Moreover, black men and women were able to pursue these lawsuits because they had white attorneys who took their cases and waived their fees. Men and women also owed their freedom to white townsmen who listened to their testimony, served as jurors, and ruled in their favor.

Salvation through Christ and a passport to heaven was not a substitute for freedom won through the courts but a complement to it. The Great Awakening of the 1740s vastly expanded the number of African converts to Christianity and added Christian inflections to women's definitions of freedom.

Evangelical Protestantism appealed to African women because it blended African and Christian elements, offered dynamic preaching, and provided religious services in which women could express their spiritual joy and personal anguish. Black female converts were also extraordinarily loyal toward the revivalist preachers who welcomed them into their services, both the famous fiery speakers and the dull ones, many of whom were principled opponents of slavery and the slave trade. It is extremely difficult to pull apart the injunctions of Christianity that women should be subordinate to their husbands, as ordained by God, and remain silent in the churches from the positive appeal of the rituals of baptism, communion, legal marriage, a respectful funeral sermon, and a decent burial. In becoming devout Christians some women gained the power to police each other's behavior as well as to pass moral judgment on the personal conduct of those who might be deemed their social betters. A few white believers in the seventeenth century understood that it was a grievous sin to enslave a fellow Christian; the atmosphere of the American Revolution made it possible for enslaved blacks in New England to join the chorus of those who were speaking this truth and circulate their opinions in New England newspapers.

Freedom for the family and property passed down to one's patrimony were one and the same thing. The ideal of a property-owning black family was a radically new one, since privately held property, to which one held legal title, was unknown in the African societies from which the captives in New England had been seized. Free black women were eager to have a home of their own. A few realized their dream on their own and a larger group as married women engaged in a common enterprise with their husbands. These women saw their home both as an economic asset and a place where daughters, grandchildren, and even great-grandchildren might come to live if they had nowhere else to go.

After their deaths the memory of several black women continued to influence a subsequent generation of abolitionists. Theodore Sedgwick, Jr., William Ellery Channing, and the Buffums of Rhode Island all credited their antislavery commitment to the black women who raised them. Early nineteenth-century abolitionist newspapers reprinted stories of black heroes— Phillis Wheatley and Crispus Attucks were the two most common—but they also told the tale of "Ona Judge, Washington's Runaway Slave" to expose the truth that the father of his country, even while serving as the president of the United States, was a slave hunter. Abolitionists believed that the central doctrine undergirding racism in the North and the institution of slavery in the South was the belief in black intellectual inferiority. It was thus absolutely central for them to provide individual examples of black men and women who refuted such a belief; the lives of Phillis Wheatley, Elizabeth Freeman, and Lucy Terry Prince offered shining examples of true learning, creative genius, courage, dignity, patriotism, and women's skill at reasoning and argumentation.

If New England was a Christian hierarchical society that revered English law, it was also a neighborly one. Some whites believed that black people made excellent neighbors, so long as they were self-supporting and did not move next door or, in some places, attempt to send their children to the town school. It seems to have been acceptable for a black man to marry a white woman in New Hampshire, Vermont, and parts of Massachusetts, although perhaps more so if he were part Native American, light skinned, and a good provider. Still, the casualness of racial prejudice was evident in names given to New England geography: Negro Brook, Negro Pond, Black Joe's Pond, Negro Island, Negro Lane, Negro Alley, "Nigger Point," "Nigger Pasture" and the many New Guinea neighborhoods.[1] At the same time, a free black woman who lived on the other side of Negro Pond was well respected for her knowledge of the Bible, her skills as a midwife or nurse for the black and white families in town, or the damask roses she grew in her garden.[2] Banding together to protect blacks whom they had known for years, local whites took in a wife badly beaten by her husband, raised an abandoned black child from infancy, and saved their black neighbors from thugs ready to ship them to slavery in the South, Barbados, or another island in the Caribbean. While some white farmers made it clear that black neighbors were unwelcome, others served on juries that awarded damages for the harm white ruffians had caused to black property. White neighbors embued with revolutionary ideals often came to the defense of local blacks during the war. Many townspeople turned more conservative in their attitudes after the war because of racial backlash, economic depression, and anxiety about the place of emancipated slaves in free society.

Black people engaged in gestures of deference to white people of high social rank, but they also engaged in gestures of deference to their own people, the ones they recognized as princes, princesses, or duchesses in Africa or elected as their governors on Election Day. The sense of deference to whites of high social standing was part of New England racial etiquette. Slaves entered the house through the side entrance or the door to the kitchen rather than the main door. Free black men bowed before entreating a white gentleman to read a petition, and both sexes addressed white people of higher social standing as Missy, Massa, or Master. In the city slaves often chose their own churches, separate from those of their master, but in the countryside they usually attended the master's church, walking behind him and his family during the procession on Sunday morning. As household servants they also absorbed rules about the deference ladies could expect. The lady was an English gender ideal, not an African one. But the notion that a woman should be accorded a level of dignity and respect because of her high status had its origins on both sides of the Atlantic, in notions of African royalty as well as in English ideals of decorum. Nonetheless, the ways that the lady showed her gentility—attending a ball, drinking tea, educating herself and her children—were formed from the ideals of slave owners. Playing the lady meant not getting one's hands dirty and entertaining women guests. Thus for the free black woman the ultimate symbol of higher status was sitting across from her white guests at her own tea table, cup in hand, immersed in conversation.

Black men of the revolutionary age wanted freedom, independence, property, and equality with white men, as well as respect from black women and their white neighbors. It is true that even in slavery black men enjoyed some of the privileges of masculine authority, but they were often denied the respect and rights free white men routinely enjoyed; patriarchy was their model for all social relations, in the family and in the black community. They believed that in order to be the equals of white men they had to rule at home. Free black women were thought of as partners and subordinates of their husbands, or some combination of both, but the husband was expected to hold the reins of power, even if his wife earned wages and may even have kept her savings separately. The Achilles heel of free black men was their vulnerability to any threat to their reputation. Alongside jealous husbands were the ones who wanted to control their wives' movements. Emancipation brought to public view a contest of power in black marriages, in which wives were asserting more independence than their husbands permitted and husbands were seeking to control their wives in a manner they found disagreeable. A true area of conflict between men and women was about married women's employment, with some women hoping that freedom meant that a black wife and mother could become a housewife and no longer have to take in washing and husbands insisting that their wives must contribute to household income and submit to their authority.

The widows of political leaders of the free black community were the first black women leaders, women who enjoyed enhanced standing derived in part from admiration for their husbands. To be sure, most widows and single mothers were "as poor as the Devil," eking out a living, often having to place their children with other families or indenture them while they entered domestic service. Many were required to demonstrate to officials their means of support, lest they be ordered to leave town. Yet the occasional ambitious widow who did not remarry prospered, buying land and a small house. Such women strove to attain their own version of propertied citizenship—minus the formal legal rights only men could enjoy. They engaged in civic life with a highly practical intent, seeking a tangible economic benefit for themselves and their families, yet also managing to assert their beliefs in racial equality and economic justice.

The definition and emphasis on idealized womanhood—the lady or the noble mother—emerged as free blacks increased their bid for respectability in the eyes of white society and their demands for the education of their children. Female gender consciousness was a product of emancipation, not slavery, and was associated with pious and literate Christian women who also asserted an identity as Africans. The founding of the Ladies African Charitable Society in Portsmouth in 1796 joined the ideal of the African lady with the goal of educating black children and fused identities based on race and gender with the notion of respectability. Blacks and whites invoked the ideal of the African lady or the subsequent one, the "respectable colored woman," as a way of asserting the sterling character of black women. Such terms secured for individual women protection from the pernicious stereotype that all black women were prostitutes, instead advancing the idea that they should be judged not on the basis of their race or economic status, but on their excellent personal qualities, demeanor, and sexual virtue. In sum, designating herself as a lady or anglicizing her first name were ways a black woman distanced herself from being defined as a lewd woman.

The small number of new black women's organizations in New England established between 1800 and 1830 were connected to the cause of education for children and adults—others provided charity in the form of mutual benefit payments in times of need and confronted racial prejudice in the North. The women who began these organizations were among the most respectable members of the Christian elite in their towns; their societies invariably included black women schoolteachers, literate woman undertaking a task appropriate for a black woman, the education of the young children of her race. The second black woman's organization in New England, the African Female Benevolent Society in Newport, begun in 1809, was created to provide funding for an African School, organized by blacks with assistance from whites. An Anglican woman in town had operated a school for black children in her house until 1799; the African school was a successor to the institution located in the same house. A black woman's organization to support the school, the African Female Benevolent Society, emerged out of an organization of men and women (called the African Benevolent Society) in which the women were not allowed to vote at its meetings. By this time, New England had a black church, which had female as well as male members; the precedent had thus been set for women to belong to a free black organization. There is no evidence that black women, beginning this society of their own, were protesting being denied the vote, since several of them were the wives and daughters of the men in the ABS; instead it appears that the women had formed an independent female auxiliary, including among their members the female assistant instructor at the school. Yet they clearly had attained more power since they could elect their own officers and control their own treasury.[3]

As schoolteachers in all-black schools women gained status among free blacks because of their literacy and dedication to the cause of children's education; they were thus in a position to be recognized as leaders of black women. Widowed schoolteacher Chloe Minns of Salem emerged as a women's organization founder in Salem precisely for this reason. She became a schoolteacher after black children had been thrown out of the Salem public schools when poor white parents objected to racial integration. A local evangelical minister, known for his "loud and animated" style of preaching, had many blacks in his congregation, including Minns. He persuaded the Salem School Committee to establish an all-black school and hire her as the teacher. A widow with two children she knew how to read and taught herself to write so as to be able to instruct her students. In 1817 she married Schuyler Lawrence, a black man and widower with five children. Lawrence was an enterprising cook who started his own chimney-sweeping business and employed several black boys. Upon marrying Chloe Minns became Chloe Lawrence, casting off her slave woman's name, Chloe, and choosing Clarissa as a suitable English first name for the wife of a Salem business owner.[4]

Perhaps because the couple had two incomes, Lawrence felt able to serve as president of the Colored Female Religious and Moral Society, formed in Salem in 1819. The forty or fifty members of the society were too numerous to consist merely of the wives and daughters of the Christian propertied elite, and must have included women of more limited means interested in belonging to a mutual benefit society that paid a sickness and disability benefit.[5] In exchange for weekly dues set at the reasonable rate of a penny a week, members were eligible for an extremely modest sickness and destitution benefit—the first time black women in New England on their own had tried to meet emergency needs. Members were required to take an oath of secrecy much like the oath the black Freemasons took; as a society dedicated to the principles of respectability women known to engage in "scandalous sin" could be expelled but also readmitted if they showed genuine repentance.[6] The naming of this organization reflected a subtle shift in racial messages: the term African was intended to signify racial pride in Africa and may have indicated acceptance of emigration to Africa. The "colored" in the name of this organization expressed no particular allegiance to Africa and seemed instead to suggest opposition to colonization plans.

After a few of the founding members of the Colored Female Society died, the society stopped meeting. Lawrence, retired from her teaching position, was still interested in encouraging black women's activism in Salem and was among the members of the first women's abolitionist society in the United States. The Women's Anti-Slavery Society, formed in Salem in

1832, supported the abolitionist newspaper *Liberator* in its opposition to the colonization movement. Sensing interest among black women in Salem, Lawrence re-formed the Colored Female Society in 1833, presumably with a younger membership. The majority of black opinion in New England had begun to turn against emigration because of the several unsuccessful expeditions of New England blacks to Sierra Leone and Liberia. The society endorsed Garrison's espousal of immediate abolition of slavery and his opposition to colonization but its main focus was confronting racism in the North. The Women's Anti-Slavery Society dedicated itself to promoting "the welfare of our colour" through local reform. The desire of the Society for "union and morality" and its constitution affirmed respectability as part of the strategy to secure equal rights and diminish racial hostility. The women also purchased books so that members could engage in "mutual improvement" in their reading skills.[7] Two years after their first meeting the society was folded into a largely white female anti-slavery society in Salem with more resources and Lawrence was elected its vice president.

Lawrence took the national stage at the third annual convention of abolitionist women in Philadelphia in 1838. Every attendee was a woman of courage since the previous year an angry white mob had burned down the hall where they had been meeting. She was the only black woman abolitionist to speak at the convention and among the few black women in attendance. Now elderly she was pleased that so many young women were drawn to the cause of abolitionism. Philadelphia's antislavery activist women considered a resolution calling for the convention to improve educational and employment opportunities for free blacks in the North and confront racial discrimination. The white women in attendance were especially eager to encourage other white women to teach in black Sunday schools. Lawrence seconded the resolution, addressing her audience as a religious woman and as a schoolteacher who believed educating black children was a necessity. She broadened the resolution by asking white women to "place yourselves, dear friends, in our stead." Appealing to the conscience of delegates, she told them, "We meet the monster prejudice everywhere.... We cannot elevate ourselves.... We want light; we ask it, and it is denied us. Why are we thus treated? Prejudice is the cause."[8]

On her return home Lawrence encountered precisely the monster prejudice she had just denounced. By the 1830s black women were experiencing widespread discrimination in public transportation—on stagecoaches, horse cars (where they were not allowed to sit inside), and on ships. On the steamboat from New York to Providence white ladies were allowed to sleep in cabins overnight, where they could keep warm, but black women were forced to sleep on the deck. A Quaker abolitionist from Lynn, also en route to Providence, had purchased ladies' cabin tickets for Lawrence and Julia

Williams, a young black schoolteacher and delegate to the convention from Boston. When it was discovered that black women were sleeping in the ladies' cabin, the passengers revolted and assembled for a mass meeting in the captain's quarters. Amidst screaming and shouting, they took a voice vote and decided to kick the women out of their cabin. Williams and Lawrence stood silently during the meeting but looked "down with pity on their degraded assailants."[9] The incident became a cause célèbre for abolitionists in New England, revealing the extent of white opposition to interracial gatherings and the problem of the color line in the North.

A generation younger than Lawrence, Maria Stewart was a woman leader who fused the emotional power of evangelical religion with the moral righteousness and certainty of Garrisonian abolitionism. Lawrence raised the race issue among white women, whereas Stewart challenged the gender barrier among free blacks. Stewart's personal friendship with the fiery Boston black abolitionist David Walker had influenced her militancy and philosophy of racial self-help. Like Wheatley and Prince Hall, Stewart believed in Ethiopianism, the prophetic redeeming power of African Christians. Born in freedom in Hartford, Connecticut, she was orphaned at an early age and placed in an indenture to a clergyman. She had learned to become a proficient writer by attending a Sunday school in Hartford. After moving to Boston she met a man twice her age with two grown daughters who made a good living as a "shipping agent" for sailors. She married, and three years later her husband died; her husband's persistent and possibly dishonest creditors had first crack at his estate, taking almost everything, with the widow's thirds not clearly laid out.[10] She seems to have been willing to consider the prospect of self-support from writing and selling religious tracts and possibly from lecture fees.

The Stewart's Boston neighbor, David Walker, was a used-clothing dealer who joined the vision of redeeming Ethiopia with his evangelical zeal, demanding equal rights and calling for the emancipation of slaves in the South. In his incendiary pamphlet, *Appeal to the Coloured Citizens of the World*, published in 1829, Walker asserted that the black man was physically stronger than the white man and a better fighter. He called upon enslaved men to engage in armed revolt against their masters if attempts at a nonviolent end to slavery failed. Soon thereafter Walker died; his body was found on Bridge Street in Boston in what at the time was seen as a highly suspicious circumstance. Lost in her grief for her husband and close friend Stewart experienced "an encounter with the divinity," and was called to testify to her faith. During her spiritual interrogation a voice from within asked, " 'Who shall go forward, and take off the reproach that is cast upon the people of color? Shall it be a woman—'And my heart made this reply—'if it is thy will, be it even so, Lord Jesus.' "[11] She had taken on the identity of "a war-rior" in "the cause of God and my brethren," just as Wheatley's David had picked up a slingshot to do battle on behalf of his people. The abolitionist generation, like the previous revolutionary one, were ready to die in the fight for freedom. Stewart vowed that she was willing to go to her grave "for the cause of God and my brethren." She took her manuscript to the abolitionist William Lloyd Garrison who published it immediately as a religious tract.[12]

As women moved into male territory, they confronted barriers they may not even have been aware of before. The black press, an entirely new outlet for black personal and political opinion, had more to say about gender conventions than Prince Hall or Lemuel Haynes; in fact, it was a publishing outlet for articles about personal conduct for men and women. Male authors of articles in black newspapers insisted on the limits of the private sphere, whereas black women activists wanted to expand the domain of women's activities in the name of defending the home. The whole way of thinking about public and private and the black woman's place in the home was a new one, since the ideal of the African lady had not explicitly delimited the lady's areas of activity, except to imply that education for herself and schooling for children was an appropriate female interest. An article in the first black newspaper in the United States, *The Freedom's Journal*, in 1829 stated the conventional view, opining that "women are not formed to great cares themselves, but to soften ours." Wives were expected to reclaim their husbands "from vice" and train up their children "to virtue."[13] "The black home," according to anonymous authors in another article in the newspaper, constituted a distinct and separate space where women "are confined within the narrow limits of domestic assiduity, and when they stray beyond them, they move out of their proper sphere, and consequently without grace."[14] The authors of these articles were repeating the standard rhetoric about gender roles in their day, doing so at the time when black women were actually taking a more active part in free black communities. For example, women were the majority of the people attending a pledge drive in New Haven to solicit subscribers for the *Freedom's Journal* and a plurality of members in a newly founded black temperance organization in Hartford.[15]

All of the talk about public and private, male and female, made some boundaries more visible. Women were not supposed to parade in public, definitely not at night, nor were they supposed to speak to "promiscuous assemblies" of men and women. Women in New York City tested the first barrier by marching in the evening with their banners and insignia of their societies; Maria Stewart of Boston ended up confronting the second barrier, challenging the bar to women speaking in public because she felt that she had been called by God to "speak her sentiments on the improvement of colored Americans." Her "Boston circle of friends" discouraged her from engaging in public lectures but William Lloyd Garrison persuaded her to do it, assuring her that she was engaged in a great and holy task. Testing the waters, Stewart spoke first to a black woman's organization, an acceptable venue for a woman, then branched out to address an anti-slavery society of men and women, and then an audience probably comprised of both sexes as well as including a significant number of black men held at the African Masonic Hall.[16]

In the 1740s Flora of Ipswich had shown that during religious revivals white people might listen to a black woman itinerant speaker. Among the dissenting sects in New England, such as the Free Will Baptists, a traveling black woman preacher received an attentive hearing precisely because of the "novel spectacle" she presented.[17] Stewart's speaking was perceived entirely differently; she read from a prepared text she had written herself, rather than preaching extemporaneously and she delivered her speeches at a podium or at a pulpit, taking on a role reserved for men, that of the orator. Already warned that she would meet hostility, she mentioned the issue in her first speech before the black women's literary society in Boston. She spoke to them about what they shared in common, the belief that a female literary society lay wholly within the sphere of woman. Trying to show the members of the society that she, too, valued enhancing traditional activities of women she emphasized the importance of women as prudent housekeepers and guardians of the morality of the home. (As was true for many women of her day, she applauded women's maternal role but was not herself a mother.) She also called on women to raise funds for a black vocational high school, and for expanded occupational opportunities to enable black girls to become schoolteachers, seamstresses, store clerks, or small business owners. Sensing hostility in her audience she offered the reassurance that "I am not your enemy, but a friend both to you and your child." She asked the women to listen to her views "however severe they may appear to be."[18]

Emboldened by her prophetic vision, Stewart prodded, cajoled, and challenged her audience. In front of the largely white abolitionists she decried white women business owners who said they would like to hire black women clerks but feared the opposition of their customers. Before a group of largely black men at the Masonic Hall she recalled the days when black men had truly been men, fighting for their freedom in the Revolution and defending their rights to equal citizenship. She drifted into dangerous territory, however, challenging black manhood, calling on black men to sign a petition to Congress to abolish the slavery in the District of Columbia and telling them that if they did not, they did not possess "the spirit and principles of a man." Given their concern with protecting their honor black men felt very vulnerable when they were attacked for not being manly enough. The fact that Stewart abandoned her career as a public speaker after this speech suggests her audience perceived an insult to their manhood.

In her fourth and farewell address Stewart had concluded that she enjoyed little support for her calling as a public lecturer and orator. Even though she recognized she was engaged in a losing cause, she persisted in the belief that it was important to refute the views of St. Paul who enjoined women to keep silent in the churches. A black woman—even a feminine, respectable Christian widow—had to defend her right to speak in public. Stewart was not the first woman to test the limits of the "sphere" to which women were confined. Three years before the English radical Frances Wright embarked on a lecture tour of many cities in the Midwest and East. Attacking the institution of marriage and the church she was widely denounced by the white press as a "female monster" and in the black press as "a disgrace to the fairer part of creation."[19]

Because her right to speak on behalf of the race was challenged, Stewart became more conscious of the restrictions facing women. She was the first black woman to show evidence of looking for female role models in the Bible—Deborah, Queen Esther, Mary Magdalene, and a woman in history, her personal favorite, a medieval woman who taught law to scholars "and joined the charms of accomplishments of a woman to all the knowledge of man."[20] Thanking her Boston friends who supported her, she urged those who did not to discover the true faith in Christ. Provoking her audiences and articulating a brighter future for Ethiopia, public disapproval had forced Stewart off the battlefield, abandoning "the short period" of her "Christian warfare." In their abolitionist involvement both she and Clarissa Lawrence politicized the question of black woman's citizenship and participation in public life. They had addressed two key questions, the expectations black women held for abolitionist white women and the place of black women in free black society. Well aware of the constraints and restrictions facing them daily, even as free women in the North, they felt compelled to speak unpopular truths.[21] Freedom and equality were not achieved during the lifetimes of these two women; black women continued to seek religious freedom, to acquire property, to unify their families, and to look for opportunities to educate themselves and their children. While black women have constantly pressed against the boundaries of acceptable behavior for women, those barriers have never completely disappeared, reminding us of the importance of equality as well as freedom, indeed, of recognizing the impoverished understanding of freedom when it does not also hold out the promise of equality.

NOTES

INTRODUCTION

1. For more on the political context for Sewall's tract, see Mark A. Peterson, "The Selling of Joseph: Bostonians, Antislavery, and the Protestant International, 1689–1733," *Massachusetts Historical Review* 4 (2002): 1–22; *Boston News-letter* (April 9, 1716); *Boston Gazette* (August 2, 1725).

2. "The Earliest Wills on Record and On the Files in the County of Suffolk, Massachusetts," *The New England Historical and Genealogical Register* 19 (October 1865): 308.

3. Testimony of Hagar Blackmore, April 15, 1669, Miscellaneous Collections, Massachusetts Historical Society, Boston.

4. Elizabeth Donnan, ed., *Documents Illustrative of the History of the Slave Trade to America*, vol. 3, *New England and the Middle Colonies* (Washington, D.C.: Carnegie Institution, 1932), 6–9.

5. There were quite a few variations in naming practice, however. Hagar Muntero, originally from Angola, kept her Portuguese surname although it seems likely that she acquired a new first name from a New England owner. *A Report of the Record Commissioners Containing Boston Births, Baptisms, Marriages, and Deaths, 1630–1699* (Boston: Rockwell and Churchill, 1883), 111. She was only one of several slaves who was described as "of Angola."

6. A mixed reading of how Shakespeare viewed a Moor can be found in Emily C. Bartels, "*Othello* and Africa: Postcolonialism Reconsidered," *William and Mary Quarterly* 54 (January 1997): 45–64; Thomas Newton, D.D., *Dissertations on the Prophecies* (London: J. and R. T. Tonson and S. Draper, 1754), 59.

7. Africans from West Central Africa were more than 90 percent of the total number of Africans shipped to the New World between 1601 and 1650. Joseph C. Miller, "Central Africa during the Era of the Slave Trade, c. 1490s–1850s," in *Central Africans and Cultural Transformations in the American Diaspora*, ed. Linda M. Heywood (New York:

Cambridge University Press, 2002), 67. The most important work on the Angolan origins of the early slaves is Linda Heywood and John K. Thornton, *Central Africans, Atlantic Creoles, and the Foundation of the Americas, 1585–1660* (Cambridge: Cambridge University Press, 2007).

8. David E. Eltis, "The Volume and Structure of the Transatlantic Slave Trade: A Reassessment," *William and Mary Quarterly* 60 (January 2001): 17–46; Emma Christopher, *Slave Ship Sailors and Their Captive Cargoes, 1730–1807* (Cambridge: Cambridge University Press, 2006), 153.

9. On the experience on board the ship see Marcus Rediker, *The Slave Ship: A Human History* (New York: Viking Adult, 2007); Jerome S. Handler, "The Middle Passage and the Material Culture of Captive Africans," *Slavery and Abolition* 30 (March 2009): 1–6.

10. Heywood and Thornton, *Central Africans*, 6; John Thornton, e-mail message to authors, October 11, 2007; Joseph C. Miller, *Way of Death: Merchant Capitalism and the Angolan Slave Trade, 1730–1830* (Madison: University of Wisconsin Press, 1988), 398, 403 n. 92.

11. James Horn and Philip D. Morgan, "Settlers and Slaves: European and African Migrations to Early Modern British America," in *The Creation of the British Atlantic World*, ed. Elizabeth Mancke and Carole Shammas (Baltimore: Johns Hopkins University Press, 2005), 26, 30.

12. On drunken Harvard students: Roger Thompson, *Cambridge Cameos: Stories of Life in Seventeenth-Century New England* (Boston: New England Genealogical Society, 2005), 117–18.

13. Depositions of Anna Angier, Barbara Corlet, Elizabeth Bridges, and Anna Stedman, Middlesex Folio Collection, 49–VIII, Massachusetts Archives. On a similar interrogation of an enslaved woman who accused a Lutheran pastor of fathering her child, see Graham Russell Hodges, "The Pastor and the Prostitute: Sexual Power among African Americans and Germans in Colonial New York," *Sex, Love, Race: Crossing Boundaries in North American History,* ed. Martha Hodes (New York: New York University Press, 1999), 60–71. Joanne Pope Melish also emphasizes the depersonalization and deprivation of kinship as defining features of slavery in *Disowning Slavery: Gradual Emancipation and "Race" in New England, 1780–1860* (Ithaca, N.Y.: Cornell University Press, 1998), 25.

14. Orlando Patterson, *Freedom: Freedom in the Making of Western Cultures* (London: I. B. Tauris and Company, 1991), 24–28; Joseph C. Miller, "Imbangala Lineage Slavery," *Slavery in Africa: Historical and Anthropological Perspectives,* ed. Suzanne Miers and Igor Kopytoff (Madison: University of Wisconsin Press, 1977), 24.

15. "Spear Family Record," *New England Historical and Genealogical Register* 18 (1864): 160; *Newport Mercury* (June 5, 1763); *Newport Mercury* (August 12, 1765); *Newport Mercury* (September 16, 1765); Deborah Gray White, *Arn't I a Woman? Female Slaves in the Plantation South* (New York: Norton, 1985), 79–84. For his appendix listing shipboard revolts by date and origin of the ship, see Eric Robert Taylor, *If We Must Die: Shipboard Insurrections in the Era of the Atlantic Trade* (Baton Rouge: Louisiana State University Press, 2006), 179–214. Documents about the voyage of the *Sally* and the

participation of the Brown Brothers in the slave trade can be found at "The Voyage of the Sally" www.stg.brown.edu/projects/sally/(August 1, 2008). For an example of slave suicide, see Shebnah Rich, *Truro-Cape Cod* (Boston: D. Lothrop, 1883), 251.

16. For Pegg's murder of her two children in Swansea, see Massachusetts Superior Court of Judicature, 1760–1762, 271–72, Massachusetts Archives and Suffolk County Files, 8102 and 82379, Massachusetts Archives, Boston. For doubts about the over-interpretation of Bakongo symbols, see Philip D. Morgan, "Archaeology and History in the Study of African-Americans," in *African Re-Genesis: Confronting Social Issues in the Diaspora,* ed. Jay B. Haviser and Kevin C. MacDonald (London: University College London Press, 2006), 53–61.

17. Many of the same conclusions are reached by Shirley J. Yee, *Black Women Abolitionists: A Study in Activism, 1828–1860* (Knoxville: University of Tennessee Press, 1992), 40–59, 155–57.

18. Gerda Lerner, *The Creation of Patriarchy* (New York: Oxford University Press, 1986), 239.

19. For the argument in favor of coverture, see Hendrik Hartog, *Man and Wife in America: A History* (Cambridge: Harvard University Press, 2002), 125.

20. Ibid., 39, 135.

21. Pauline Schloesser makes these unwarranted assumptions in *The Fair Sex: White Women and Racial Patriarchy in the Early American Republic* (New York: New York University Press, 2002). For the prohibition against an enslaved wife testifying against her husband in *Caesar v. Taylor* (1772), see Massachusetts Superior Court of Judicature, *Reports of Cases Argued and Adjudged in the Superior Court of Judicature of the Province of Boston* (Boston: Little, Brown, 1865), 30.

22. In so doing, they made clear that the rationale for the enslavement of Africans was not that they were heathens but that they were of African descent.

23. Another definition of fitness to be free is what Evelyn Brooks Higginbotham refers to as "the politics of respectability," which, she argued, "equated public behavior with individual self-respect and with the advancement of African Americans as a group." The politics of respectability did not originate in the late nineteenth century, which Higginbotham studied, but with the Christian conversion of slaves in the eighteenth century. Evelyn Brooks Higginbotham, *Righteous Discontent: The Women's Movement in the Black Baptist Church, 1880–1920* (Cambridge: Harvard University Press, 1993), 14. Kevin Gaines thinks the ideal of respectability widened class differences among blacks in *Uplifting the Race: Black Leadership, Politics, and Culture in the Twentieth Century* (Chapel Hill: University of North Carolina Press, 1996). For the application of the idea of respectability to free blacks in the North before the Civil War, see Patrick Rael, *Black Identity and Black Protest in the Antebellum North* (Chapel Hill: University of North Carolina Press, 2002), ch. 2 and Eddie S. Glaude, Jr., *Exodus: Religion, Race, and Nation in Early Nineteenth-Century Black America* (Chicago: University of Chicago Press, 2000), 118–25. By the 1830s Maria Stewart certainly thought that respectability required that "rising youth" abstain from gambling and dancing. No doubt such prohibitions had the effect of

castigating as disreputable a large swath of black lower-class cultural life. Shane White, "The Death of James Johnson," *American Quarterly* 51 (December 1999): 753–95.

24. New England law punished the rape of black women and punished black rapists severely. Black men were overrepresented in prosecutions and convictions for rape, punished by banishment, or hanging. On one occasion, white women took the law into their own hands in castrating a black man engaged in the act of raping a white woman. *Boston News-Letter* (February 24, 1718); Barbara S. Lindemann, "'To Ravish and Carnally Know'": Rape in Eighteenth Century Massachusetts," *Signs* 10 (Autumn 1984): 63–82; Richard Slotkin, "Narratives of Negro Crime in New England, 1675–1800," *American Quarterly* 25 (March 1973): 3–31; Cornelia Hughes Dayton, *Women Before the Bar: Gender, Law, and Society in Connecticut, 1639–1789* (Chapel Hill: University of North Carolina Press, 1995), 265–75; Sharon Block, *Rape and Sexual Power in Early America* (Chapel Hill: University of North Carolina Press, 2006), 171–72, 204–5; Daniel A. Cohen, "Social Injustice, Sexual Violence, Spiritual Transcendence: Constructions of Interracial Rape in Early American Crime Literature, 1767–1817," *William and Mary Quarterly* 56 (July 1999): 481–526; T. H. Breen, "Making History: The Force of Public Opinion and the Last Years of Slavery in Revolutionary Massachusetts," in *Through a Glass Darkly: Reflections on Personal Identity,* ed. Ronald Hoffman, Mechal Sobel, and Fredrika J. Teute (Chapel Hill: University of North Carolina, 1997), 67–95.

25. African American historiography spans the spectrum from those who insist on the cultural survival of African culture to those who believe that in the household slavery of New England little of African culture survived. The folklorist William Piersen took the strongest stance in favor of survivals. James and Lois Horton emphasized a new multiracial culture, white, Indian, and African. Robert E. Desrochers, Jr., argues that African Americans recognized many correspondences between West African and New England culture. Robert E. Desrochers, Jr., "'Not Fade Away': The Narrative of Venture Smith, an African American in the Early Republic," *Journal of American History* 84 (June 1997): 40–66; William D. Piersen, *Black Yankees: The development of an Afro-American subculture in eighteenth-century New England* (Amherst: University of Massachusetts Press, 1985); James Oliver Horton and Lois E. Horton, *In Hope of Liberty: Culture, Community, and Protest among Northern free blacks, 1700–1860* (New York: Oxford University Press, 1997).

26. On black male fugitives carrying their fiddle with them, see *Boston News-Letter* (July 2, 1761); *Boston News-Letter* (September 16, 1761); *Newport Mercury* (April 22, 1760); Sarah Ann Emery, *Reminiscences of a Nonagerian* (Newburyport: William H. Huse, 1879), 203. For more about black fiddlers, see Henry Stedman Nourse, *History of the Town of Harvard, Massachusetts, 1732–1893* (Harvard, Mass.: Warren Hapgood, 1894), 403; Kate Van Winkle Keller, *Dance and Its Music in America, 1528–1789* (Hicksdale, N.Y.: Pendragon Press, 2007), 359–60.

27. Graham Russell Hodges, *Slavery and Freedom in the Rural North: African Americans in Monmouth County, New Jersey, 1665–1865* (Madison, N.J.: Madison House, 1997), 55. Stephanie M. H. Camp argues that in the antebellum South enslaved women were

likely to be truants and that truancy should be considered a form of slave resistance. Although there are advertisements for fugitive slaves in colonial New England, the evidence about truancy in New England concerns young black men. Stephanie M. H. Camp, "'I Could Not Stay There': Enslaved Women, Truancy and the Geography of Everyday Forms of Resistance in the Antebellum Plantation South," *Slavery and Abolition* 23 (December 2002): 1–20.

28. Gloria L. Main, "Gender, Work, and Wages in Colonial New England," *William and Mary Quarterly* 51 (January 1994): 54; Charles R. Foy, "Seeking Freedom in the Atlantic World, 1713–1783," *Early American Studies: An Interdisciplinary Journal* 4 (Spring 2006): 46–77; Alexandra A. Chan, *Slavery in the Age of Reason: Archaeology at a New England Farm* (Knoxville: University of Tennessee Press, 2007), 220; Samuel Abbott Green, *An Historical Sketch of Groton, Mass., 1655–1890* (Groton, Mass.: Groton, 1894), 156.

29. Janet Duitsman Cornelius, *When I Can Read My Title Clear: Literacy, Slavery, and Religion in the Antebellum South* (Columbia: University of South Carolina Press, 1991); Ruth Wallis Herndon, "Research Note: Literacy among New England's Transient Poor, 1750–1800," *Journal of Social History* 29 (Summer 1996): 963–65.

30. Sharon V. Salinger, *Taverns and Drinking in Early America* (Baltimore: Johns Hopkins University Press, 2002), 235–36.

31. For a black man marrying a white woman in the mid-1760s see Michael Sokolow, *Charles Benson: Mariner of Color in the Age of Sail* (Amherst: University of Massachusetts Press, 2003), 10. For the marriage of an Indian/black man and a white woman in the 1760s, see "The Inhabitants of Medway versus the Inhabitants of Natick," *Reports of Cases argued and Determined in the Supreme Judicial Court*, vol. 11 (Boston: Little, Brown and Company, 1864), 74. Sometime between 1761 and 1773 Nathaniel Paul married a white woman from Exeter, New Hampshire. On their marriage, see Lois Brown, *Pauline Elizabeth Hopkins: Black Daughter of the Revolution* (Chapel Hill: University of North Carolina Press, 2008), 26. For a Connecticut white woman who indentured herself to her enslaved husband's master to purchase her husband's freedom at his master's death, see *Boston News-Letter* (October 26, 1759). A biracial free man in Connecticut also married a white woman in the early eighteenth century. See George Waller-Frye, "The Mulatto Adam Rogers and his White Wife Katherine Jones," *The American Genealogist* 53 (1977): 217–24.

32. But there was no standardized practice; in some cases, voting was done by proxy and in some instances masters chose the Governor. George S. Roberts, *Historic Towns of the Connecticut River Valley* (Schnectady, N.Y.: Robson and Adee, 1906), 218.

33. Shane White, "'It was a Proud Day': African Americans, Festivals, and Parades in the North, 1741–1834," *Journal of American History* 81 (June 1994): 48; Dorothy Sterling, ed., *Speak out Thunder Tones: Letters and Other Writings by Black Northerners, 1787–1865* (New York: Da Capo Press, 1998), 51; Samuel Adams Drake, *A Book of New England Legends and Folk Lore in Prose and Poetry* (Boston: Little, Brown, 1901), 300; William Chauncey Fowler, *Local Law in Massachusetts and Connecticut, Historically Considered* (Albany, N.Y.: Joe Munsell, 1872), 129.

34. Jane de Forest Shelton, "The New England Negro," *Harper's New Monthly Magazine* 88 (March 1844): 536–37; C. H. Webber and W. S. Nevins, *Old Naumkeag: An Historical Sketch of the City of Salem* (Salem, Mass.: A. A. Smith, 1877), 200; Roberts, *Historic*, 218.

35. The sources on Election Days are voluminous and corroborate each other. Thomas Bailey Aldrich, *An Old Town by the Sea* (Boston: The Riverside Press, 1893), 79; Frances Manwaring Caulkins, *History of Norwich, Connecticut* (Norwich, Conn.: Thomas Robinson, 1945), 330–31; *Publications of the Rhode Island Historical Society*, vol. 2, *1894* (Providence: Society by the Standard Printing, 1894), 140. On interpretations of Negro Election Days, see Joseph P. Reidy, "Negro Election Day and Black Community Life in New England: 1750–1860," *Marxist Perspectives* 1 (Fall 1978): 102–17; Melvin Wade, "Shining in Borrowed Plumage: Affirmation of Community in the Black Coronation Festivals of New England, c 1750–c 1850," *Western Folklore* 40 (July 1981): 211–31; Genevieve Fabre, "Performing Freedom: Negro Election Celebrations as Political and Intellectual Resistance in New England, 1740–1850," in *Celebrating Ethnicity and Nation: American Festive Culture from the Revolution to the Early 20th Century*, ed. Jurgen Heideking, Genevieve Fabre, and Kair Dresbach (New York: Berghahn Books, 2001), 91–123; White, "It was a Proud Day": 13–50.

36. Sarah Loring Bailey, *Historical Sketches of Andover* (Boston: Houghton, Mifflin, and Company, 1880), 43. The question is not simply how black people manipulated the category of race but how officials used race terms. "Negro" was not synonymous with slave for two reasons. The free black population was fairly large and Indians and white prisoners of war were not merely indentured servants but "slaves for life"; the word servant was vague and broad and might designate an indentured servant, a servant for life, or a slave in a system of hereditary slavery. Moreover, blacks could turn into whites not simply by passing as white but also a result of confused classification by a census taker. In point of fact, many official records, by no means confined to the census, did not consistently classify people by race. As is standard in the rules of race, a white mother could give birth to a black child. Equally interesting is that no one seemed to question a black mother claiming a "clear white" child as her own. For the most part, terms for race were mutually exclusive, but a phrase such as "molatto negro" indicates that was not always the case. Around the time of the American Revolution there was a tendency to classify Indians as well as "mixed race" people as "mustee", "people of color", or "black"; the term quadroon seems to have been confined to the South; one white Northerner preferred to designate someone as "yellow." Joanne Pope Melish argues that state control of Indian tribes and gradual emancipation of slaves in Rhode Island and Connecticut led to the emergence of white and black as the dominant racial categories, with other categories such as mulatto, Indian, and mustee becoming less common. The effect of the disappearance of the term Indian was to strengthen the belief among whites than Indians had disappeared and that it was no longer necessary to accord Indians special status. See Jack D. Forbes, *Africans and Native Americans: The Language of Race and the Evolution of Red-Black Peoples* (Urbana: University of Illinois Press, 1993); Melish, *Disowning Slavery*; Ruth Wallis

Herndon, "Racialization and Feminization of Poverty in Early America: Indian Women as 'the poor of the town' in Eighteenth-Century Rhode Island," in *Empire and Others: British Encounters with Indigenous Peoples*, ed. Martin Daunton and Rick Halpern (London: UCL Press, 1999), 186–205; Ruth Wallis Herndon and Ella Wilcox Sekatu, "The Right to a Name: The Narragansett People and Rhode Island Officials in the Revolutionary Era," *Ethnohistory* 44 (Summer 1997): 433–62; John Wood Sweet, *Bodies Politic: Negotiating Race in the American North, 1730–1830* (Baltimore: Johns Hopkins University Press, 2003), 252; Joanne Pope Melish, "Emancipation and the Embodiment of Race," *A Centre of Wonders: The Body in Early America,* ed. Janet Moore Lindman and Michele Lise Tarter (Ithaca, N.Y.: Cornell University Press, 2001), 223–36; Joanne Pope Melish, "'The Racial Vernacular': Contesting the Black/White Binary in Nineteenth-Century Rhode Island," in *Race, Nation, and Empire in American History*, ed. James T. Campbell, Matthew Pratt Guterl, and Robert G. Lee (Chapel Hill: University of North Carolina Press, 2007), 17, 39; Daniel R. Mandell, *Tribe, Race, History: Native Americans in Southern New England, 1789–1880* (Baltimore: Johns Hopkins University Press, 2008).

37. Thomas L. Doughton, "'Long Wide de Grande 'Folkes'": Slave Literacy and Participation in the World of Social Communication in Colonial New England," unpublished paper, American Antiquarian Society, June 2005.

38. Venture Smith, *A Narrative of the Life and Adventures of Venture, a Native of Africa: But Resident Above Sixty Years in the United States of America. Related by Himself* (New London: C. Holt, 1798); Philip Gould, "Free Carpenter, Venture Capitalist: Reading the Lives of the Early Black Atlantic," *American Literary History* 12 (Winter 2000): 659–84; Chandler B. Saint and George A. Krinsky, *Making Freedom: The Extraordinary Life of Venture Smith* (Middletown, Conn.: Wesleyan University, 2009).

39. New England whites narrated, in dialect, the story of the faithful servant who did not want her freedom or was anxious about who would take care of her in old age. For a few examples of this kind, see Hezekiah Butterworth, *The Patriot Schoolmaster* (New York: D. Appleton and Co, 1844), 1–6 and Nathaniel Bouton, *The History of Concord* (Concord, N.H.: Berning W. Sanborn, 1856), 253. For the general trope of the faithful slave see George Boulokos, *The Grateful Slave: The Emergence of Race in Eighteenth-Century British and American Culture* (Cambridge: Cambridge University Press, 2008).

40. Healers included African women as well as men such as Tapheny of Connecticut, who identified herself as Indian, but appears to have had a black father. General information can be found in William D. Piersen, "Black Arts and Black Magic: Yankee Accommodations to African Religion," and Peter Benes, "Fortunetellers, Wise Men, and Magical Healers in New England, 1644–1850," in *Wonders of the Invisible World: 1600–1900,* ed. Peter Benes and Jane Montague Benes (Boston: Boston University Scholarly Publications, 1995), 34–43, 127–48.

41. William Cooper Nell, *The Colored Patriots of the American Revolution, with Sketches of Several Distinguished Colored Persons* (Boston: Robert F. Wallcut, 1855).

42. Henry David Thoreau, *Walden: A Life in the Woods* (Boston: Ticknor and Fields, 1854), 116–17. For blacks squatting on Walden Pond, see Elise Lemire, *Black Walden:*

Slavery and Its Aftermath in Concord, Massachusetts (Philadelphia: University of Pennsylvania Press, 2009).

43. Margot Minardi, "The Inevitable Negro: Making Slavery History in Massachusetts, 1770–1863," PhD diss., Harvard University Press, 2007.

44. The women who fit in this category are Flora of Marblehead, Lucy Terry, Chloe Spear, Phillis Wheatley, Elizabeth Freeman, Duchess Quamino, and Mareer. Minardi discusses Spear, Wheatley, and Freeman; Lois Brown emphasizes the remembrance of Flora, Spear, and Terry in "Memorial Narratives of African Women in Antebellum New England," *Legacy* 20 (2003): 38–61; Gretchen Gerzina describes the way stories about Lucy Terry were passed down in *Mr. and Mrs. Prince: How an Extraordinary Eighteenth-Century Family Moved out of Slavery and into Legend* (New York: Amistad, 2008), 205–7. For the story of Mareer of Newport, see Elizabeth Buffum Chace, *Anti-Slavery Reminiscences* (Central Falls, R.I.: R. L. Freeman, 1891), 7–8.

45. The program inspired interest in tracing African ancestry, even though Haley admitted that his work was "historical fiction" and genealogists cast doubt on his claims that he had located the West African village of his earliest known African ancestor, Kunta Kinte, The debate about reparations for slavery led to major interest in retrieving documents about the slave trade. For example, archivists at several major New England collections have catalogued their holdings in detail. The Massachusetts Historical Society has digitized its major documents about slavery and emancipation at http://wwww.masshistory.org/endofslavery (December 1, 2006). For critiques of Haley's research, see Gary B. Mills and Elizabeth Shown Mills, "*Roots* and the New 'Faction': A Legitimate Tool for CLIO," *The Virginia Magazine of History and Biography* 89 (January 1981): 3–26; Gary B. Mills and Elizabeth Shown Mills, "The Genealogist's Assessment of Alex Haley's *Roots*," *National Genealogical Society Quarterly* 72 (March 1984): 35–49.

46. The first books to emerge from the renewal of interest were James M. Rose, *Tapestry, a Living History of the Black Family in Southeastern Connecticut* (New London: New London County Historical Society, 1979); Barbara W. Brown and James M. Rose, *Black Roots in Southeastern Connecticut 1650–1900* (Detroit: Gale, 1980); Joseph Carvalho, *Black Families in Hampden County, Massachusetts, 1650–1855* (Boston: New England Historical and Genealogical Society and Institute for Massachusetts Studies, 1984).

47. Charles L. Hill, "Slavery and Its Aftermath in Beverly, Massachusetts: Juno Larcom and Her Family," *Essex Institute Historical Collections* 116 (Spring 1980): 111–130. For a historian's defense of genealogy see Allegra Hogan, " 'Buzzeling' as Historical Method: In Praise of Genealogy," *Connecticut History* 40 (Fall 2001): 247–63.

48. Dana Ripley Bullen and Adelaide Bullen, "Black Lucy's Garden," *Bulletin of the Massachusetts Archeological Society* 6 (1945): 17–29; Vernon G. Baker, "Archeological Visibility of Afro-American Culture: An Example from Black Lucy's Garden, Andover, Massachusetts," in *Archeological Perspectives on Ethnicity in America,* ed. Robert L. Schuyler (Farmingdale, N.Y.: Baywood, 1980), 29–37; James Deetz, *In Small Things Forgotten: Archaeology of Early American Life* (Garden City, N.Y.: Anchor Press/Doubleday, 1977), 187–211; Alfred M. Bingham, "Squatter Settlements of Freed Slaves in New England,"

Connecticut Historical Society Bulletin 41 (July 1976), 65–80; Alexandra Chan, *Slavery in the Age of Reason: Archaeology at a New England Farm* (Knoxville: University of Tennessee Press, 2007); Ellen Marlatt, Kathleen Wheeler, and Shannon Provost, "Archaeological Excavations at the Portsmouth African Burial Ground," preliminary unpublished report (Portsmouth, Independent Archaeological Consulting, 2005); Janet Woodruff, Gerald F. Sawyer, and Warren R. Perry, "How Archaeology Exposes the Nature of African Captivity and Freedom in Eighteenth and Nineteenth Century Connecticut," *Connecticut History* 46 (Fall 2007): 155–83; Joel Lang, "Chapter One: The Plantation Next Door," *Hartford Courant* (September 29, 2002).

49. Penelope Overton, "No DNA Help in Slave Story," *Hartford Courant* (March 19, 2007). For the analysis of the bones of an African American man in Waterbury, Connecticut, see www.FortuneStory.org (July 1, 2008).

50. Juba, the slave of president Edward Holyoke, married Ciceely, one of the three slaves of Judah Monis, the Italian Jewish convert who was the Hebrew instructor at the College. *Vital Records of Cambridge, Massachusetts to the Year 1850* (Boston: Wright and Potter, 1915), 2:441–42.

51. Gerzina, *Mr. And Mrs. Prince*. For the family history of Agrippa Hull, a black Revolutionary War veteran who became a Stockbridge landowner, see Gary B. Nash and Graham Russell Gao Hodges, *Friends of Liberty: A Tale of Three Patriots, Two Revolutions, and the Betrayal that Divided a Nation: Thomas Jefferson, Thaddeus Koscuiszko, and Agrippa Hull* (New York: Basic Books, 2008). For the view of the Revolutionary War from the perspective of a slave boy in New England see Joyce Lee Malcolm, *Peter's War: A New England Slave Boy and the American Revolution* (New Haven: Yale University Press, 2008).

52. "Traces of the Trade: A Story from the Deep North," DVD, directed by Katrina Browne (Cambridge, Mass.: Ebb Pod Productions, 2008); "Testimonies of a Quiet New England Town: The Film," short film, directed by Matthew Troy (Hebron, Conn.: Patio Productions, 2008). The descendant of a Portsmouth slave owner wrote a historical novel about the family's slave. See Stephen B. Clarkson, *Patriot's Reward* (Portsmouth: Peter E. Randall Publications, 2007). The story of Arthur, an executed black rapist, became the basis for T. J. Anderson's opera, "Slip Knot," in 2003. It was based on Breen, "Making," 67–95. A color photograph of the Bush-Holley house in Greenwich, Connecticut, shows the recreation of the slave attic quarters above the kitchen. Bush-Holley Historic Site, www.hstg.org/content/view/111/395 (July 1, 2008).

Chapter 1

1. Usher Parsons, *The Life of Sir William Pepperell* (Boston: Little, Brown, and Company, 1855), 28. For a discussion of slave mortality in the West Indies see Kenneth F. Kiple, *The Caribbean Slave: A Biological History* (Cambridge: Cambridge University Press, 1984), 64–158; Wilkins Updike, *History of the Episcopal Church of Narragansett, Rhode Island* (New York: Henry M. Onderonk, 1847), 324.

2. Ira Berlin, *Many Thousands Gone: The First Two Centuries of Slavery in North America* (Cambridge: The Belknap Press of Harvard University, 1998), 8–9; Lorenzo Johnston Greene, *The Negro in Colonial New England* (New York: Columbia University Press, 1942), 339, 347; William D. Piersen, *Black Yankees: The Development of the Afro-American Sub-Culture in New England* (Amherst: University of Massachusetts Press, 1988).

3. Edward Channing, "The Narragansett Planters: A Study of Causes," *Johns Hopkins University Studies in History and Political Science*, ed. Herbert B. Adams, 4th ser., no. 3 (March 1886), n. 1, 10; Jackson Turner Main, *Society and Economy in Colonial Connecticut* (Princeton: Princeton University Press, 1985), 177; Peter Benes, "Slavery in Boston Households, 1647–1770," in *Slavery/Antislavery in New England*, ed. Peter Benes and Jane Montague Benes (Boston: Boston University Scholarly Publications, 2005), 25; Elaine Forman Crane, *A Dependent People: Newport, Rhode Island in the Revolutionary Era* (New York: Fordham University Press, 1985), 82.

4. Michael Gomez, *Exchanging Our Country Marks: The Transformation of African Identities in the Colonial and Antebellum South* (Chapel Hill: University of North Carolina Press, 1998), 27. It is not known whether white women owners manumitted their slaves by will more often than white men. In rural New Jersey there was no difference in the rate of manumission by gender. Graham Russell Hodges, *Root and Branch: African Americans in New York and East Jersey, 1613–1863* (Chapel Hill: University of North Carolina Press, 1999), 114.

5. Mary Negro's Deposition, Deposition of Besse, wife of Angola, Suffolk Files, no. 605, v. 5, 28, Massachusetts Archives, Boston. Thanks to Melinde Lutz Sanborn for supplying us with this document. Kate Van Winkle Keller, *Dance and Its Music in America, 1528–1789* (Hillsdale, N.Y.: Pendragon Press, 2007), 365.

6. Population estimates were entirely unreliable at this time for blacks as well as whites. Owners had an economic incentive for not reporting their slaves, since slave property was subject to taxation. The superstitious held that their slaves were more likely to die if they were counted. Some viewed the census, of whites or blacks, as an arbitrary imposition of British authority. The point of these figures is not so much that they are accurate estimates of the population but rather that consistent patterns emerge, even among imprecise measures. Ben Z. Rose, *Mother of Freedom: Mum Bett and the Roots of Abolition* (Waverly, Mass.: Treeline Press, 2009), 13.

7. Joanne Pope Melish, *Disowning Slavery: Gradual Emancipation and "Race" in New England, 1780–1860* (Ithaca, N.Y.: Cornell University Press, 1998), 19–21; Robert E. Desrochers, Jr., "Slave-for-Sale Advertisements and Slavery in Massachusetts, 1704–1781," *William and Mary Quarterly* 59 (July 2002): 623–64. Greg O'Malley points to the 1720s to the 1740s as the peak for importing slaves from the Caribbean in "Beyond the Middle Passage: Slave Migration from the Caribbean to North America, 1619–1807," *William and Mary Quarterly* 66 (January 2009): 1–47. For more information about Caribbean exports to New England, see Greg O'Malley, "Final Passages: The British Inter-Colonial Slave Trade, 1619–1807," PhD diss., Johns Hopkins University, 2007, table 2.7, 108. The greatest number of slaves in probated estates in Portsmouth, New Hampshire, were in the

1760s. Holly Mitchell, "The Power of Thirds': Widows and property in Portsmouth, New Hampshire, 1680–1830," PhD diss., Brandeis University, 2006, 139.

8. Daniel Cruson, *The Slaves of Central Fairfield County: The Journey from Slave to Freeman in Nineteenth-Century Connecticut* (Charleston, S.C.: Historical Press, 2007), 26.

9. Virginia Bever Platt, "'And Don't Forget the Guinea Voyage': The Slave Trade of Aaron Lopez of Newport," *William and Mary Quarterly* 32 (October 1975): 606; Leonard Price Stavisky, "Negro Craftsmanship in Early America," *American Historical Review* 54 (January 1949): 319–320; Quincy Thaxter, Journal, 1774–1778, Thaxter Family Papers, Massachusetts Historical Society, Boston; Letter of Abraham Pererira Mendes, November 8, 1767, and Letter of John Cohoone, Jr., to Ayrault, October 27, 1736, *Commerce of Rhode Island 1726–1800*, vol. 1, *Collections of the Massachusetts Historical Society* 9 (1914), 21, 46; Alexandra A. Chan, *Slavery in the Age of Reason: Archaeology at a New England Farm* (Knoxville: University of Tennessee Press, 2007), 73; Henry Barnard Worth, "Wills and Estates Part I, 1680 to 1778," *Nantucket Lands and Land Owners* 2 (1901), 305; John Saillant, *Black Puritan, Black Republican: The Life and Thought of Lemuel Haynes 1753–1833* (New York: Oxford University Press, 2003), 13; *Collections of the Worcester Society of Antiquity* 13 (1894), 262.

10. *Boston News-Letter* (January 25, 1706); Platt, "And Don't Forget," 607; Jane DeForest Shelton, "The New England Negro: A Remnant," *Harper's New Monthly Magazine* 88 (March 1894): 536; James Hammond Trumbull, *The Memorial History of Hartford County, Connecticut, 1633–1884* (Boston: Edward L. Osgood, 1886), 139; *Newport Mercury* (April 17, 1769); Joseph T. Buckingham, *Specimens of Newspaper Literature* (Boston: Redding and Company, 1852), 162; Pension File, Saunders, Phillis, Revolutionary War, *HeritageQuest:com*, series M 805, roll 851, image 41, File W18103 (August 13, 2008); Amos P. Cheney, *A Review of the First Fourteen Years of the Historical Natural History and Library Society of South Natick, Massachusetts* (South Natick, Mass.: Printed for the Society, 1884), 118; Harriet F. Woods, *Historical Sketches of Brookline, Mass.* (Boston: Robert S. Davis, 1874), 154; Waterbury Selectmen's Bill, 1749/1750, Waterbury's African Americans, http://www.fortunatestory.org/waterburyafrican americans/phyllis.asp (July 1, 2008).

11. Robert B. Dishman, "'Natives of Africa, Now Forcibly Detained': The Slave Petitioners of Revolutionary Portsmouth," *Historical New Hampshire* 61 (Spring 2007): 14.

12. For lady's maids, see Joanna Livingston to Robert Livingston, March 17, 1713, July 6, 1713, Robert Livingston, General Correspondence, Roll No. 3, Livingston Family Papers, Gilder Lehrman Collection 3107, Gilder Lehrman Library, New York, New York. Divorce case quoted in Cornelia Hughes Dayton, *Women before the Bar: Gender, Law, and Society in Connecticut, 1639–1789* (Chapel Hill: University of North Carolina, 1995), 147–48; Edward Warren, *The Life of John Warren, M.D.* (Boston: Noyes, Holmes and Company, 1874), 31; George Francis Dow, ed., *The Holyoke Diaries 1709–1856* (Salem, Mass.: The Essex Institute, 1911), 37; Rev. E. O. Jameson, *The History of Medway, Mass., 1713–1885* (Millis, Mass.: E. O. Jameson, 1886), 109; Kenneth P. Minkema, "Jonathan Edwards's Defense of Slavery," *Massachusetts Historical Review* 4 (2002): 39.

13. S. F. Smith, *History of Newton, Massachusetts* (Boston: The American Logotype Company, 1788), 228; *Bill of sale or indenture made by Eliphalet Adams of New London, Conn. to Joseph and Jonathan Trumble of Lebanon, Conn. Whereby he sells his mulatto girl Flora, a slave for Life,* May 12, 1738, Connecticut State Archives, Hartford. Flora was a common black name. Flora, enslaved in Milford, Connecticut, in 1796, whose silhouette adorns the cover of this book, was born about fifty years after this woman. On Salem see Daniel Vickers and Vince Walsh, "Young men and the Sea: the Sociology of Seafaring in Eighteenth-Century Salem, Massachusetts," *Social History* 24 (January 1999): 32; Gerald Mullin, *Flight and Rebellion: Slave Resistance in Eighteenth-Century Virginia* (New York: Oxford University Press, 1972), 34–38.

14. Philas the negro of Mr. Southmayd, Waterbury Selectmen's Bill, 1749–1750, Collection of the Mattatuck Museum, Waterbury, Conn.; Marla R. Miller, *The Needle's Eye: Women and Work in the Age of Revolution* (Amherst: University of Massachusetts Press, 2006), 102, 107–8; City Document No. 87, *A Report of the Record Commissioners of the City of Boston* (Boston: Rockwell and Churchill, 1886), 25; Bettye Hobbs Pruitt, ed., *The Massachusetts Tax Valuation List of 1771* (Boston: G. K. Hall and Company, 1978); David W. Conroy, *In Public Houses: Drink and the Revolution of Authority in Colonial Massachusetts* (Chapel Hill: University of North Carolina Press, 1995), 118, 119, 125.

15. Diana Paton, "Punishment, Crime, and the Bodies of Slaves in Eighteenth-Century Jamaica," *Journal of Social History* 34 (Summer 2001): 930.

16. Shelly A. M. Gavigan, "Petit Treason in Eighteenth Century England: Women's Inequality Before the Law," *Canadian Journal of Women and the Law* 3 (1989–90): 335–74. In 1734 Angelique, an enslaved woman in Montreal, was hanged and her body burned; an Angolan, she was tried and convicted of having burned down her mistress's roof in revenge for being sold. Afua Cooper, *The Hanging of Angelique: The Untold Story of Canadian Slavery and the Burning of Old Montreal* (Athens: University of Georgia Press, 2007). For the suggestions that Maria was burned alive without being hung first, see Robert C. Twombly and Robert H. Moore, "Black Puritans: The Negro in Seventeenth-Century Massachusetts," *William and Mary Quarterly* 24 (April 1967), 235, n. 22.

17. John Noble, "The Case of Maria in the Court of Assistants in 1681," *Publications of the Colonial Society of Massachusetts* 6 (1904): 323–26; Abner Cheney Goodell, Jr., "The Trial and Execution, for Petit Treason, of Mark and Phyllis, Slaves of Capt. John Codman, Who Murdered Their Master at Charlestown, Mass., in 1755; for which the Man was Hanged and Gibbeted, and the Woman was Burned to Death, Including, also, Some Account of other Punishments by Burning in Massachusetts," *Proceedings of the Massachusetts Historical Society* (1882): 122–49; *A few lines on Occasion of the untimely End of Mark and Phillis who were executed at Cambridge, September 18th for poysoning their master, Capt. John Codman of Charlestown* (Boston: no publisher, 1755); Mary Caroline Crawford, *Little Pilgrimages among Old New England Inns* (Boston: L. C. Page, 1907), 70. For a discussion of the significance of the displayed dead body as a weapon of master rule see Vincent Brown, "Spiritual Terror and Sacred Authority in Jamaican Slave Society," *Slavery and Abolition* 24 (April 2003): 24.

18. Inquest of Ginny, January 25, 1725/1726, Hartford County Superior Court Records, Inquests, 1711–1849, RG 3, Box 11, Archives, Connecticut State Library, Hartford, as quoted in Diane Cameron, "Circumstances of Their Lives: Enslaved and Free Women of Color: Wethersfield, Connecticut, 1648–1832," *Connecticut History* 44 (Fall 2005): 251.

19. Her master may have beaten her because she had become pregnant, killed her child, and then hid the body in a pile of ashes. *Rex v. Jenny Chapman*, Superior Court, Newport County, Rhode Island, March 1767, E: 324, Rhode Island Supreme Court Judicial Records Center, as quoted in John Wood Sweet, *Bodies Politic: Negotiating Race in the American North, 1730–1830* (Baltimore: Johns Hopkins University Press, 2003), 156; H. H. Price and Gerald E. Talbot, *Maine's Visible Black History: The First Chronicle of its People* (Portland, Maine: Tilbury House, 2006), 9.

20. Nicholas Lechmere, New London County Superior Court Record, Files, Box 12, File of 1751; Superior Court, New London County Dockets, 1713–1835, Box 35, September 1751, Connecticut State Library.

21. Paul J. Lindholt, ed., *John Josselyn, Colonial Traveler: A Critical Edition of Two Voyages to New England* (Hanover, N.H.: University of New England Press, 1988), 24; Wendy Anne Warren, "'The Cause of Her Grief': The Rape of a Slave in Early New England," *Journal of American History* 93 (March 2007): 1031–49.

22. For the advertisements touting the sale of a slave breeder, see *Boston Evening-Post* (August 9, 1736); *Boston Gazette* (June 5, 1738); *Boston Weekly News-Letter* (March 14, 1744); *New England Weekly Journal* (February 24, 1741); *Boston Evening-Post* (February 25, 1745); *Boston Evening-Post* (November 18, 1745); *Boston Evening Gazette* (December 24, 1764); *Boston News-Letter* (October 17, 1765). On separate cabins: Benes, "Slavery," 20.

23. *Boston Gazette* (May 7, 1745).

24. Middlesex County Court Records, April 13, 1686, File 123, as quoted in Roger Thompson, *Sex in Middlesex: Popular Mores in a Massachusetts County, 1649–1699* (Amherst: University of Massachusetts Press, 1986), 107–8.

25. Ibid. Robert Calef, *Salem Witchcraft* (Salem, Mass.: H. P. Ives and A. A. Smith, 1861), 448.

26. Ellen Marlatt, Kathleen Wheeler, and Shannon Provost, "Preliminary Report: Archaeological Excavations at the Portsmouth African Burial Ground (27-RK-384) Chestnut and Court Streets, Portsmouth (Rockingham County), New Hampshire, October 2003, Report submitted to the New Hampshire Division of Historical Resource, Concord, New Hampshire, by Independent Archaeological Consulting, LC, Portsmouth, New Hampshire.

27. Edna Greene Medford, The New York African Burial Ground History Final Report, Washington, D.C.: U.S. General Services (November, 2004). http://www.africanburialground.gov/FinalReport (August 1, 2007).

28. C. Wilcazak, R. Watkins, C. Null, and M. L. Blakey, "Skeletal Indicators of Work: Musculoskeletal Arthritic and Traumatic Effects," in *The African Burial Ground Project* (Washington, D.C.: General Services Administration, 2004), 403–47.

29. Kenneth F. Kiple and Virginia Himmelsteib King, *Another Dimension to the Black Diaspora: Diet, Disease and Racism* (New York: Cambridge University Press, 1981), 10–11, 79–95.

30. "A Short Account of the Life of Elizabeth Colson A Molatto Woman, who now must Dye for the Monstrous Sin of Murdering her Child," *New England Weekly Journal* (June 19, 1729).

31. John Jea, "The Life, History and Unparalleled Sufferings of John Jea, the African Preacher," in *Pioneers of the Black Atlantic: Five Slave Narratives from the Enlightenment, 1772–1815*, ed. Henry Louis Gates and William L. Andrews (Washington, D.C.: Civitas, 1998), 369; Karen J. Friedmann, "Victualling Colonial Boston," *Agricultural History* 47 (July 1973), 198.

32. Susan Klepp, "Seasoning and Society: Racial Differences in Mortality in Eighteenth-Century Philadelphia," *William and Mary Quarterly* 51 (July 1994): 473–506.

33. Maureen Richard, "Washing Household Linens and Linen Clothing in 1627 Plymouth," in *Women's Work in New England, 1620–1920*, ed. Peter Benes and Jane Benes (Boston: Boston University, 2003), 10–21; Jane C. Nylander, *Our Own Snug Fireside: Images of the New England Home, 1760–1860* (New Haven: Yale University, 1993), 117–18, 130. On laundry work in the late nineteenth century South see Tera Hunter, *To 'joy my Freedom: Black Women's Lives and Labor after the Civil War* (Cambridge: Harvard University Press, 1997), 56–65. On such work in antebellum New York City see Jane E. Dabel, *A Respectable Woman: The Public Roles of African American Women in 19th Century New York* (New York: New York University Press, 2008), 82–83.

34. Lorena S. Walsh, *From Calabar to Carter's Grove: The History of a Virginia Slave Community* (Charlottesville: University Press of Virginia, 1997), 100.

35. Abram English Brown, *Bedside Old Hearth-Stories* (Boston: Lee and Shepard Publishers, 1897); Will of Anne Bradstreet, *Historical Collections of the Essex Institute*, vol. 14 (1862), 186; George Chandler, *The Chandler Family* (Worcester: Press of C. Hamilton, 1883), 102; Benes, "Slavery," 20; Kevin M. Sweeney, "Mansion People: Kinship, Class, and Architecture in Western Massachusetts in the Mid Eighteenth Century," *Winterthur Portfolio* 19 (Winter 1984): 247.

36. Ruth Wallis Herndon, "'Who Died an Expence to This Town': Poor Relief in Eighteenth-Century Rhode Island," *Down and Out in Early America*, ed. Billy Gordon Smith (University Park: Pennsylvania State University Press, 2004), 135.

37. William D. Piersen, *Black Yankees: The Development of an Afro-American Subculture* (Amherst: University of Massachusetts Press, 1988), 19; Edward J. McManus, *Black Bondage in the North* (Syracuse, N.Y.: Syracuse University Press, 1973), 37–38; Lorenzo J. Greene, *The Negro in Colonial New England* (New York: Columbia University Press, 1942), 213–16; Elizabeth Hafkin Pleck, *Black Migration and Poverty in Boston, 1865–1900* (New York: Academic Press, 1979), 180.

38. *Calculations on American Population, with a table for estimating the annual increase of inhabitants in the British colonies: the manner of its construction explained: and its use illustrated* (Boston: John Boyle, 1775).

39. Jesse Chickering, *A Statistical View of the Population of Massachusetts, 1765 to 1840* (Boston: C. C. Little and J. Brown, 1846), 128.

40. *Report of the City Registrar, of Births, Marriages, and Deaths...Boston...1859*, Boston City Docs. No. 84 (Boston: Rockwell and Hill, 1860), 10–11.

41. Darlene Clark Hine, "Female Slave Resistance: The Economics of Sex," in *Black Women in American History*, ed. Darlene Clark Hine (Brooklyn: Carlson Publishing, 1990), 2:661.

42. Jennifer Morgan, *Laboring Women: Reproduction and Gender in New World Slavery* (Philadelphia: University of Pennsylvania Press, 2004), 114.

43. "A Short Account." The numbers look differently if viewed from the point of view of black infants. About a fifth of the murders of black infants in eighteenth century New England were committed by white mothers who presumably did not want to endure the stigma of giving birth to a biracial child. Randolph Roth, "Twin Evils? Slavery and Homicide in Early America," *The Problem of Evil: Slavery, Freedom, and the Ambiguities of American Reform*, ed. Steven Mintz and John Stauffer (Amherst, Mass.: University of Massachusetts Press, 2007), 77.

44. Four out of eight infanticide cases occurred between 1743 and 1767. Peter Hoffer and N. E. Hull claim that eleven African and African American women were accused of infanticide in colonial New England but do not provide a list of the cases. Peter C. Hoffer and N. E. H. Hull, *Murdering Mothers: Infanticide in England and New England 1558–1803* (New York: New York University Press, 1983), 47–48; Cornelia Hughes Dayton, *Women Before the Bar*, 210–13; Randolph H. Roth, "Child Murder in New England," *Social Science History* 25 (Spring 2001): 101–47; Kathleen M. Brown, "Murderous Uncleanness," in *A Centre of Wonders: The Body in Early America*, ed. Janet Moore Lindman and Michele Lise Tarter (Ithaca, N.Y.: Cornell University Press, 2001), 77–94.

45. Roth, "Child Murder," table 6, 117.

46. Warren R. Perry, Jean Howson, and Barbara A. Bianco, eds., *New York African Burial Ground Archaeology, Final Report* 3 (Washington, D.C.: U.S. General Services Administration, 2000), 104; Cheryl J. LaRoche, "Beads from the African Burial Ground, New York City: A Preliminary Assessment," *Journal of the Society of Bead Researchers* 6 (1994): 2–20.

47. Laurel Thatcher Ulrich, *Good Wives: Image and Reality in the Lives of Women in Northern New England, 1650–1750* (New York: Vintage, 1991), 138–44; Paula A. Treckel, "Breastfeeding and Maternal Sexuality in Colonial America," *Journal of Interdisciplinary History* 20 (Summer 1989): 25–51. For evidence that enslaved women in the antebellum South used cotton roots as a form of contraception, see Liese M. Perrin, "Resisting Reproduction: Reconsidering Slave Contraception in the Old South," *Journal of American Studies* 35 (August 2001): 255–74.

48. John Duffy, *Epidemics in Colonial America* (Baton Rouge: Louisiana State University Press, 1953); John B. Blake, *Public Health in the Town of Boston, 1630–1822* (Cambridge: Harvard University Press, 1993); Kathleen M. Brown, *Foul Bodies: Cleanliness in Early America* (New Haven: Yale University Press, 2009), 129.

49. Diane Miller Somerville, *Rape and Race in the Nineteenth-Century South* (Chapel Hill: University of North Carolina, 2004), 64–68. To be sure, a white servant or slave charging a man with rape was quite rare. It was also rare for a white woman to do so because of the master's status and the legal requirement that it took two witnesses to bring a legal complaint of rape. In fact, between 1660 and 1700 only one white servant in Massachusetts brought a charge of rape against her master. Mary Michelle Jarrett Morris, "Under Household Government: Sex and Family in Massachusetts, 1660–1700," PhD diss., Harvard University, 2005, 199. A white husband's attempt at "criminal commerce" with a "Negro wench" could also appear in his wife's divorce suit. See Leonard Woods Labaree, *The Public Records of the State of Connecticut* (Hartford, Conn.: Press of the Case, Lockwood and Brainard, 1894), 193.

50. M. Halsey Thomas, ed., *The Diary of Samuel Sewall, 1674–1729* (New York: Farrar, Straus, and Giroux, 1973), 2:853.

51. Case of James Studley, Plymouth, 1758, David Thomas Konig, ed., *Plymouth Court Records, 1686–1859* (Wilmington, Del.: Michael Glazier, 1978), 3:96, 97

52. "Newhall Indicted in Salem, Essex," Superior Court of Judicature Records, June–Nov. 1768, November 7, 1768, Suffolk County Files 113633, Massachusetts Archives; Henry M. Brooks, *Some Strange and Curious Punishments* (Boston: Ticknor, 1886), 5:49; Howard Kendall Sanderson, *Lynn in the Revolution* (Boston: W. H. Clarke, 1909), 370; *Vital Records of Lynn Massachusetts to the End of the Year 1849* (Salem, Mass.: Essex Institute, 1906), 2:154.

53. *Herald of Freedom* (April 22, 1791). New England law punished the rape of black women and punished black rapists severely. Black men were overrepresented in prosecutions and convictions for rape, punished by banishment or hanging. On one occasion, white women took the law into their own hands in castrating a black man engaged in the act of raping a white woman. *Boston News-Letter* (February 24, 1718); Barbara S. Lindemann, " 'To Ravish and Carnally Know": Rape in Eighteenth Century Massachusetts," *Signs* 10 (Autumn 1984): 63–82; Richard Slotkin, "Narratives of Negro Crime in New England, 1675–1800," *American Quarterly* 25 (March 1973): 3–31; Dayton, *Women Before the Bar*, 265–75; Sharon Block, *Rape and Sexual Power in Early America* (Chapel Hill: University of North Carolina Press, 2006), 171–72, 204–5; Daniel A. Cohen, "Social Injustice, Sexual Violence, Spiritual Transcendence: Constructions of Interracial Rape in Early American Crime Literature, 1767–1817," *William and Mary Quarterly* 56 (July 1999): 481–526; T. H. Breen, "Making History: The Force of Public Opinion and the Last Years of Slavery in Revolutionary Massachusetts," in *Through a Glass Darkly: Reflections on Personal Identity*, ed. Ronald Hoffman, Mechal Sobel, and Fredrika J. Teute (Chapel Hill: University of North Carolina Press, 1997), 67–95.

54. Thomas D. Morris, " 'Villeinage … as it existed in England, reflects but little light on our subject': The Problem of 'Sources' of Southern Slave Law," *American Journal of Legal History* 32 (1988): 115–16.

55. The city of London defined citizenship based on blood and did not allow for naturalization of the children of foreign immigrants. English citizenship law emphasized

birth in England as well as English descent. In the Abda case it was assumed that being born in the English colony of Connecticut constituted being born on English soil. Jacob Selwood, "'English-Born Reputed Strangers': Birth and Descent in Seventeenth-Century London," *Journal of British Studies* 44 (October 2005): 728–53. For Foucault's argument that blood was a symbol of one's standing in relationship to the king, see Michel Foucault, *The History of Sexuality*, trans. Robert Hurley (New York: Vintage Books, 1990), 133–50. Maria Elena Martinez discusses Spanish concepts of race in "'The Black Blood of New Spain': *Limpieza de Sangre,* Racial Violence, and Gendered Power in Early Colonial Mexico," *William and Mary Quarterly* 61 (July 2004): 479–520. For French views see Guillaume Aubert, "'The Blood of France': Race and Purity of Blood in the French Atlantic World," *William and Mary Quarterly* 61 (July 2004): 439–78. For the phrase "Guinea blackbirds," see Shebnah Rich, *Truro-Cape Cod* (Boston: D. Lothrop, 1884), 251.

56. F. C. Gray, "Remarks on the early laws of Massachusetts Bay; with the code adopted in 1641, and called the Body of Liberties, now first printed," in *Collections of the Massachusetts Historical Society* 8 (1843): 191–237.

57. Thomas D. Morris, *Southern Slavery and the Law, 1619–1860* (Chapel Hill: University of North Carolina Press, 1999), 42–46; Morris, "Villeinage," 95–137; Warren M. Billings, "The Cases of Fernando and Elizabeth Key: A Note on the Status of Blacks in Seventeenth Century Virginia," *William and Mary Quarterly* 30 (July 1973): 467–74. In Maryland the white mother of a black child and her biracial child were both enslaved. Other slave colonies were rather slow to follow Virginia's lead. South Carolina legislators adopted the principle of maternal inheritability of slavery after the Stono rebellion in 1740, and Georgia did likewise only during the revolutionary era.

58. Charles William Manwaring, *A Digest of the Early Connecticut Probate Records* (Hartford, Ct,: R. S. Peck and Co., 1904), 2:58; Hannah Duce, Negro slave of Thomas Richards, question of slavery of her child Abda, whom she claimed was son of John Gennings, a white man, 1702/1703, II, doc. 14, 21a, c RG 1, Early General Records, Miscellaneous Papers, Connecticut State Archives; Charles J. Hoadly, *The Public Records of the Colony of Connecticut, from May, 1775, to June 1776, inclusive* (Hartford, Ct: Case, Lockwood, and Brainard, 1890), 548.

59. Connecticut State Archives: Miscellaneous, 1662–1789, 1st ser. no. 2, 10–12; "Saltonstall's Argument, in Favor of Slavery," *Historical Magazine* 3 (Jan. 1784): 14–18; George H. Moore, *Notes on the History of Slavery in Massachusetts* (Boston: D. Appleton and Company, 1866), 24–25, 112.

60. Manwaring, *Digest*, 2: 58; Rosell Lewellyn Richardson, *Amos Richardson of Boston and Stonington* (New York: published by the author, 1906), 122.

61. Morris, "Villeinage," 95–137.

62. Cornelia Hughes Dayton, *Women Before the Bar*, 1–14; Mary Sarah Bilder, *The Transatlantic Constitution: Colonial Legal Culture and the Empire* (Cambridge: Harvard University Press, 2005).

CHAPTER 2

1. *Suffolk Deeds,* Liber 8 (Boston: Rockwell and Church, 1896), 298–99; Boyrereau Brinch and Benjamin F. Prentiss *The blind African Slave* (St. Albans: Harry Whitney, 1810), 161. For Richard Cheswell of Exeter, New Hampshire, see Erik R. Tuveson, " 'A People of Color': A Study of Race and Racial Identification in New Hampshire, 1750–1825," MA thesis, University of New Hampshire, 1995, n. p.

2. On a grant of town land, see J. H. Temple, *History of North Brookfield, Massachusetts* (Boston: North Brookfield, 1887), 180; Charles L. Hill, "Slavery and Its Aftermath in Beverly, Massachusetts: Juno Larcom and Her Family," *Essex Institute Historical Collections* 116 (Spring 1980): 117; Elizabeth Rauh Bethel, *The Roots of African-American Identity* (New York: St. Martin's, 1997), 37–38; George Thomas Little, *Genealogical and Family History of the State of Maine* (New York: Lewis Historical Publication, 1909), 1574; Charles J. Hoadly, *The Public Records of the Colony of Connecticut from August, 1689, to May, 1706* (Hartford, Conn.: Case, Lockwood and Brainard, 1868) v.4, 72; Silas R. Coburn, *History of Dracut Massachusetts* (Lowell, Mass.: Courier Citizen, 1922), 331; Henry Allen Hazen, *History of Billerica, Massachusetts* (Boston: A. Williams and Company, 1883), 215; Henry J. Cadbury, "Negro Membership in the Society of Friends," *Journal of Negro History* 21 (April 1936): 185; Grace and Sebastian Cane migrated to the free black area of the eastern shore of Virginia where they purchased land. April Lee Hatfield, *Atlantic Virginia: Intercolonial Relations in the Seventeenth Century* (Philadelphia: University of Pennsylvania Press, 2004), 166; Angola: *Suffolk Deeds,* Liber 2 (Boston: Rockwell and Churchill, 1883), 297; T. H. Breen and Stephen Innes, *"Myne Own Ground": Race and Freedom on Virginia's Eastern Shore, 1640–1676* (New York: Oxford University Press, 1980), 87–88.

3. William B. Weeden, *Early Rhode Island: A Social History of the People* (New York: The Grafton Press, 1910), 224. For the prenuptial agreement of Thomas and Katharine: *Suffolk Deeds,* Liber 10 (Boston: Municipal Printing Office, 1899), 295–96; William D. Johnston, "Slavery in Rhode Island, 1755–1776," *Publications of the Rhode Island Historical Society* 2 (July 1894): 141.

4. Charles William Manwaring, *A Digest of the Early Connecticut Probate Records* (Hartford, Conn.: R. S. Peck, 1904), 7:110; Bernard A. Drew, "Cuffee Negro in the Wilderness," *Berkshire Eagle* (October 9, 2004); Peter Benes, "Slavery in Boston Households, 1647–1770," *Slavery/Antislavery in New England,* ed. Peter Benes and Jane Montague Benes (Boston: Boston University Scholarly Publications, 2005), 20.

5. Edward Willoughby Probate, 1762, Hartford District, as quoted in Diane Cameron, "Circumstances of their Lives: Enslaved and Free Women of Color Wethersfield, Connecticut, 1648–1832," *Connecticut History* 44 (Fall 2005): 254.

6. Suffolk County, Massachusetts, Deeds, 7:43–44, 16:284, 17:104, 20:443, as quoted in Melinde Lutz Sanborn, "Angola and Elizabeth: An African Family in the Massachusetts Bay Colony," *New England Quarterly* 72 (March 1999): 121. Melinde Lutz Sanborn, e-mail message to authors, September 3, 2007.

7. Manwaring, *A Digest,* 1:488, 2:100, 6:574; Edwin H. Risely, *The Risely Family History* (New York: The Grafton Press, 1909), 42. For a much later example, see the will of Catherine Cornwell, February 8, 1752, Mary Hartford Papers, Jeremy Belknap Papers, Massachusetts Historical Society, Boston. For a free woman naming the executor of her estate in South Kingstown in 1738, see Christian McBurney, "The South Kingstown Planters: Country Gentry in Colonial Rhode Island," *Rhode Island History* 45 (May 1986): 90. In 1768 John Nichols, the executor of the estate of Sackee, a free black woman, successfully sued on her behalf. Two white men, Seth and Elisha Dunbar, owed debts to her estate. The will of Sackee is missing but it can be assumed that she needed an executor because she owned property. Emily Blanck, "Revolutionizing Slavery: The Legal Culture of Slavery in Revolutionary Massachusetts and South Carolina" (PhD diss., Emory University, 2003), 271.

8. James Russell Trumbull, *History of Northampton, Massachusetts* (Northampton, Mass.: Gazette Printing, 1902), 2:331.

9. James Oliver Horton, *Free People of Color: Inside the African American Community* (Washington, D.C.: Smithsonian Press, 1993), 108; Kathryn Grover and Janine V. Da Silva, "Historic Resource Study: Boston African American National Historic Site 31 December 2002 (Boston: unpublished paper, 2002), 31.

10. Other alternatives are that Robin and Lucy each inherited seventeen acres of land in New Hampshire and that they were both owned by Lydia Plant at her death. In one version they lived in a house of Plant's for four years before moving out on their own. The disparities in figures as to how much land they owned are great. But there is no dispute that Lucy inherited £202 at Robin's death. John J. Currier, *History of Newbury, Mass., 1635–1902* (Boston: Damrell and Upham, 1902), 255. For Robin's sale of land in New Hampshire in 1755 see Alden M. Rollins, *The Rollins Family in the New Hampshire Provincial Deeds, 1655–1771* (Bowie, Md.: Heritage Books, 1997), 20. For the record of her first and second marriages and of other slaves owned by Little, see *Vital Records of Newbury, Mass. To the End of the Year 1849* (Salem, Mass.: Essex Institute, 1911), 2:530.

11. *Newburyport Herald* (June 23, 1815); *Vital Records of Newbury,* 2: 530, 758.

12. Suzanne Lebsock, *The Free Women of Petersburg: Status and Culture in a Southern Town, 1784–1860* (New York: W. W. Norton, 1984), 103.

13. *Vital Records of Ipswich, Massachusetts to the End of the Year 1849* (Salem, Mass.: Essex Institute, 1910), 2:342. There is no information as to when Scipio bought the house but he did sell it at auction in 1788. *Essex Journal* (December 3, 1788).

14. He claimed he received only £12 from his wife's estate but provided no accounting of what had happened to the other £190. Cornelia Hughes Dayton, "'The Case Study as Web-Site?' Early Thoughts on the Case of Lucy Pernam or 'Black Luce,'" unpublished paper for the Microhistory Conference, October, 1999.

15. Elizabeth Pleck, *Domestic Tyranny: The Making of Social Policy Against Family Violence from Colonial Times to the Present* (New York: Oxford University Press, 1987), 17–33.

16. It was common for husbands in early modern England to claim that a wife's behavior justified his violence. Susan Dwyer Amussen, "'Being Stirred to Much Unquietness':

Violence and Domestic Violence in Early Modern England," *Journal of Women's History* 6 (1994): 73.

17. Pleck, *Domestic Tyranny*, 17–33.

18. *Boston Gazette* (May 12, 1760).

19. The record about Maria can be found in Henry Fritz-Gilbert Waters, *The New England Historic and Genealogical Register* (Boston: New England Historical Genealogical Society, 1874), 110; Sylvester Judd, *History of Hadley, Including the Early History of Hatfield, South Hadley, Amherst and Granby, Massachusetts* (Springfield, Mass.: H. R. Hunting, 1905), 261; John Noble, "The Case of Maria in the Court of Assistants in 1681," *Publication of the Colonial Society of Massachusetts* 6 (1904): 323–26; John Noble, ed., *Records of the Court of Assistants of the Colony of Massachusetts Bay, 1639–1692* (Boston: John Noble, 1904), 1:198–99; Lorenzo Johnston Greene, *The Negro in Colonial New England, 1620–1776* (New York: Columbia University Press, 1942), 161. In Haverhill a black woman set fire to the house of her owner. See Wingate Chase, *The History of Haverhill, Massachusetts from its First Settlement in 1640* (Haverhill, Mass.: privately published, 1861), 241.

20. Peter Charles Hoffer, *The Great New York Conspiracy of 1714: Slavery, Crime, and Colonial Law* (Lawrence: University Press of Kansas, 2003); T. J. Davis, *A Rumor of Revolt: The "Great Negro Plot" in Colonial New York* (New York: Free Press, 1985); Jill Lepore, *New York Burning: Liberty, Slavery, and Conspiracy in Eighteenth-Century Massachusetts* (New York: Knopf, 2005).

21. *Boston News-Letter* (July 23, 1741).

22. For the two African men who burned a man's windmill and cut the sails from his boat in 1677, see Jane Fletcher Fiske, *Gleanings from Newport Court Files, 1650–1783* (Boxford, Mass.: by author, 1998), 579–80. Fortune Negro was executed for setting fire to stores in Newport, Rhode Island in 1764. Henry Fritz-Gilbert Waters, *The New England Historic and Genealogical Register* (Boston: New England Historical Genealogical Society, 1874), 354; *Newport Gazette* (April 13, 1782). For additional examples, see John Wood Sweet, *Bodies Politic: Negotiating Race in the American North, 1730–1830* (Baltimore: Johns Hopkins University Press, 2003), 77; C. Bancroft Gillespie and George Munson Curtis, *An Historic Record and Pictorial Description of the Town of Meriden, Connecticut* (Meriden, Conn.: Journal Publishing, 1906), 248–49; *Boston News-Letter* (January 24, 1760). For a woman setting fire to a well-furnished house, see *The Connecticut Courant* (September 14, 1767).

23. Mrs. E. Vale Smith, *History of Newburyport, from the Earliest Settlement of the Country to the Present Time* (Newburyport, Mass.: Damrell and Moore, 1854), 56.

24. Kali N. Gross, *Colored Amazons: Crime, Violence, and Black Women in the City of Brotherly Love, 1880–1910* (Durham, N.C.: Duke University Press, 2006), 72–100. For the latest in the long line of historical writing about the impact of slavery on the psyche of slaves, see Alex Bontemps, *The Punished Self: Surviving Slavery in the Colonial South* (Ithaca, N.Y.: Cornell University Press, 2001).

25. Today psychiatrists characterize the typical woman arsonist as deeply depressed, often with a history of sexual abuse in childhood. Moreover, subjecting a child to repeated

whippings, along with bullying and belittling, raises the risk of fire setting. Arsonists often grow up in households in which they learn early on to distrust adults and dissemble. In adulthood women usually commit such acts after a major rejection or a loss, acting on impulse but motivated by a desire to settle a grudge. Dian L. Williams, *Understanding the Arsonist: From Assessment to Confession* (Tucson, Ariz: Lawyers and Judges Publishing Company, 2005).

26. Deposition of Ebenezer Knap, dated January 26, 1767, Pernam Divorce Case, Suffolk File, 129751, Massachusetts State Archives, Boston.

27. Knap's writ, as quoted in Dayton, "Case Study as Web Site?"

28. For the sequence of sales, see Divorce Libel of Lucy Purnam, November 19, 1766, Suffolk File 129751, Massachusetts State Archives. One common legal standard was that a wife had left "without sufficient excuse for leaving."

29. Testimony of Caleb Haskell, v. 793, April 1765, Suffolk File 12975.

30. Samuel Pyeatt Menefee, *Wives for Sale: An Ethnographic Study of British Popular Divorce* (New York: St. Martins, 1981); Clare A. Lyons, *Sex Among the Rabble: An Intimate History of Gender and Power in the Age of Revolution, Philadelphia, 1730–1830* (Chapel Hill: University of North Carolina Press, 2006), 16; Arthur Calhoun, *A Social History of the American Family* (Cleveland: Arthur H. Clark, 1917), 1:86.

31. Oliver P. Fuller, *The History of Warwick, Rhode Island* (Providence, R.I.: Angell, Burlingame, 1875), 189. For the full sequence of sales of Lucy Pernam, see Divorce Libel of Lucy Purnam, dated November 19, 1766, Suffolk File 129751, Massachusetts State Archives.

32. On their marriage record: Boston, Massachusetts, Marriages, 1700–1809. [database online] Provo, Utah: 2000; from Boston, Massachusetts, Registry Department, *Boston Marriages from 1752–1809* (Boston: Municipal Print, 1898), 2:1721; Kathryn Grover and Janine da Silva, "Historic Resource Study Boston African American National Historic Site," http://www.cr.nps.gov/history/online_books/boston/hrs,pdf (August 1, 2006), 199; e-mail from Cornelia Hughes Dayton, June 26, 2006; Robert Love, June 5, 1766, Diary, 1765–1766, Reel 6, Vol. 6, 6, Revolutionary Diaries at the Massachusetts Historical Society, 1635–1790, microfilm, Massachusetts Historical Society.

33. Elaine Forman Crane, *Ebb Tide in New England: Women, Seaports, and Social Change 1630–1800* (Boston: Northeastern University Press, 1998), 196.

34. Nancy F. Cott, "Eighteenth-Century Family and Social Life Revealed in Massachusetts Divorce Records," *Journal of Social History* 10 (1976): 43.

35. Physical cruelty was grounds for a separation, not a divorce. The court recognized and provided for a return of the property a wife brought to marriage. In this case, it is not clear whether the court deliberately chose not do so or whether the property had already been sold.

36. The odds of a woman securing alimony were best in Vermont and worst in Connecticut; the chances in Massachusetts fell in between. In six out of nine alimony awards in eighteenth-century Massachusetts a husband did not pay. Nancy F. Cott, "Divorce and the Changing Status of Women in Eighteenth-Century Massachusetts," *William and Mary Quarterly* 33 (October 1976): 611. For the difficulty of a wife securing alimony in

nineteenth-century Massachusetts, see Elizabeth Ann Clark, "The Inward Fire: A History of Cruelty in Marriage in the Northeastern United States, 1800–1860" (PhD diss., Harvard University, 2006), 239. For the jailing of a Tiverton, Rhode Island, man for failure to pay alimony in 1806, see Peter J. Coleman, *Debtors and Creditors in America: Insolvency, Imprisonment for Debt, and Bankruptcy 1607–1900* (Washington, D.C.: Beard Books, 1999), 89.

37. Petition of Lucy Pernam, by her attorney Benja: Kent, to Gov. Thomas Hutchinson and council, November 1771, Governor and his council, December 10, 1771, Massachusetts State Archives; Marcia Schmidt Blaine, "The Power of Petitions: Women and the New Hampshire Provincial Government," *Petitions in Social History*, ed. Lex Herman Van Voss (Cambridge: Cambridge University Press, 2002), 57–78.

38. Petition of Lucy Pernam, Massachusetts Archives.

39. *A Report of the Record Commissioners of the City of Boston containing the Selectmen's Minutes from 1769 through April 1775* (Boston: Rockwell and Churchill, 1893), 165; "A Journal Kept by John Leach, During His Confinement by the British," *The New England Historical and Genealogical Register* 19 (July 1865): 255.

40. *State v. Lucy Pernum*, wife of Scipio Pernum, June 1782 term, Suffolk File 132775, Massachusetts State Archives; Thomas Gage and James Bradford, *The History of Rowley* (Boston: Ferdinand Andrews, 1840), 27.

41. She was listed on the "descriptive list of the state's poor, 1795." Newburyport was claiming she was not entitled to consider the town as her town of settlement and that therefore the state, rather than the town, was responsible for her support. Cornelia Hughes Dayton raises the question of whether the woman in the records was Lucy's daughter. Dayton, "The Case Study as Web-Site?"

42. Cheryl Eggen, comp., *Essex County, Massachusetts Death Records to 1850: Newburyport* [database online] Provo, Utah: Ancestry.com, 2001; Original data: *Vital Records of Newburyport MA to the End of the year 1849* (Salem, Mass.: The Essex Institute, 1911).

43. *Newburyport Herald* (December 23, 1814); *Newburyport Herald* (June 23, 1815).

44. Lucy Terry, "Bars Fight," in J. G. Holland, *History of Western Massachusetts*, (Springfield, Mass.: S. Bowles and Co., 1855), 2:360.

45. David R. Proper, *Lucy Terry Prince: Singer of History* (Deerfield, Mass.: Pocumtuck Valley Memorial Association and Historic Deerfield, 1997), 25.

46. There was another version of the poem with an additional couplet. Bernard Katz, "A Second Version of Lucy Terry's Early Ballad," *Negro History Bulletin* 29 (1966): 183–84.

47. For the history of a Stockbridge black man, known to sell liquor to the Indians, and charged with irregularities in selling land to the Indians, see Drew, "Cuffee Negro."

48. George Sheldon, "Negro Slavery in Old Deerfield," *New England Magazine*, New Series 8 (1893): 59–60.

49. Proper, *Lucy Terry Prince*, 39–40.

50. Ibid., 39.

51. Ibid., 32. Gretchen Holbrook Gerzina, *Mr. and Mrs. Prince: How an Extraordinary Eighteenth-Century Family Moved out of Slavery and into Legend* (New York: Amistad,

2008), 164, 206–7 argues that "it seems plausible" that Lucy argued for the admission of her son to Williams College because she knew several of the trustees and valued education for her sons.

52. Gerzina, *Mr. and Mrs. Prince*, 66. Among 1075 blacks in New London County court records between 1701 and 1744, 87 percent had a first name and a surname. Bruce P. Stark, "Finding Aid," RG 3, New London County Court African Americans and People of Color Collection, http://www.cslib.org/archives/RG003_NLCC_AA.html (July 1, 2008).

53. Sheldon, "Negro Slavery," 52.

54. Proper, *Lucy Terry Prince*, 15.

55. Gerzina, *Mr. and Mrs. Prince*, 14; *Boston News-Letter* (July 24, 1704); *Boston News-Letter* (November 13, 1704).

56. Francis Parkman, *A Half-Century of Conflict* (Boston: Little, Brown, and Company, 1893), 2:274–77.

57. Gerzina, *Mr. and Mrs. Prince*, 25.

58. Ibid., 26.

59. Proper, *Lucy Terry Prince*, 15; Kenneth Minkema, "Jonathan Edwards' Defense of Slavery," *Massachusetts Historical Review* 4 (2002): 23–60; Kenneth Minkema, "Jonathan Edwards on Slavery and the Slave Trade," *William and Mary Quarterly* 54 (1997): 823–34; N. H. Eggleston, "A New England Village," *Harper's* 43 (June–November 1871), 823.

60. Gerzina, *Mr. and Mrs. Prince*, 50–51, 53.

61. For the store accounts of enslaved men and women in Lebanon, Connecticut, see William Williams, Account Book of Lebanon, CT, merchant, one volume, 1767–1773, Connecticut Historical Society, Hartford. There were eighteen slave, as well as free black customers of another merchant, Elijah Williams of Deerfield. His enslaved customers tended to purchase luxuries such as shoe buckles, gloves, snuff boxes, rum, cider, and buttons as well as clothes (stockings, globes, garters, handkerchiefs), whereas free blacks bought necessities for farming. Gerzina, *Mr. and Mrs. Prince*, 73, 89.

62. Elijah Williams, Account Book, v. 2, 1746–1756, Account Book Transcriptions, http://www.memorialhall.mass.edu/classroom/curriculum_6th/lessons6/acctbks.html (May 15, 2004).

63. Gerzina, *Mr. and Mrs. Prince*, 92–94.

64. Elijah Williams, Account Book; Elise Lemire, *Black Walden: Slavery and Its Aftermath in Concord, Massachusetts* (Philadelphia: University of Pennsylvania Press, 2009), 131.

65. Newbell Niles Puckett, *Black Names in America: Origins and Usage* (Boston: G. K. Hall, 1975), 54.

66. Herbert G. Gutman, *The Black Family in Slavery and Freedom, 1750–1925* (New York: Pantheon Books, 1976), 189–91.

67. Even at the time of the American Revolution Cesar was a common first name for black men—it was the most common name of black men who fought at Bunker Hill

and Battle Road in Lexington. George Quintal, Jr., *Patriots of Color 'a Peculiar Beauty and Merit': African Americans and Native Americans at Battle Road and Bunker Hill* (Boston: Boston National Historical Park, 2004), 18.

68. James Oliver Horton and Lois E. Horton, *In Hope of Liberty: Culture, Community and Protest among Northern Free Blacks, 1700–1860* (New York: Oxford University Press, 1997), 16–17.

69. Gerzina, *Mr. and Mrs. Prince*, 111–12.

70. Ibid., 126, 147, 149–50; Josiah Howard Temple, George Sheldon, and Mary F. Stratton, *A History of the Town of Northfield, Massachusetts, for 150 Years* (Albany, N.Y.: Joel Munsell, 1875), 282.

71. Vermont, *Records of the Governor and Council of the State of Vermont, ed. And pub. By Authority of the State of Vermont*, vol. 3, *1782–1792* (Montpelier, Vt.: J. and J. M. Poland, 1875), 66. The petition used the word "on the representation of Lucy Prince," a phrase rarely used in petitions to the Governor. If the petitioner was not present, the record usually stated that the petition was "read." E-mail from Anthony Gerzina to authors, February 16, 2008.

72. But there is always the question of whether Lucy presented the petition or the family's lawyer presented it on their behalf.

73. E-mail from Anthony Gerzina to authors, February 16, 2008.

74. Vermont, as quoted in Proper, *Lucy Terry Prince*, 28.

75. Gerzina, *Mr. and Mrs. Prince*, 162. For a white Revolutionary War captain who successfully stood up to his white neighbors who did not want blacks living nearby, see Judith L. Van Buskirk, "Claiming their Due: African Americans in Revolutionary War and its Aftermath," *War and Society in the American Revolution: Mobilization and Home Front*, ed. John Resch and Walter Sargent (DeKalb: Northern Illinois University, 2007), 142.

76. Glendyne R. Wergland, "Women, Men, Property, and Inheritance: Gendered Testamentary Customs in Western Massachusetts, 1800–1860" (PhD diss., University of Massachusetts, 2001), 207–8; Gerzina, *Mr. and Mrs. Prince*, 168.

77. There is no direct documentary evidence that she appeared before the Vermont Supreme Court because the court's records were destroyed in a fire. The name of the Princes did not appear in any lawyer's account books for the time. Given the absence of legal representation, she would have been forced to argue the case on her own behalf. E-mail to authors from Anthony Gerzina, February 16, 2008.

78. Gerzina, *Mr. and Mrs. Prince*, 185–87. Lucy and her son Festus were the legal administrators of Abijah's estate. Since Festus was traveling when many of the town meetings were held, Lucy would have had to represent the family. A town meeting entry also refers to a case as those of "Lucy Prince and others," which indicates that she was the person arguing the case. E-mail to authors from Anthony Gerzina, February 16, 2008.

79. Sheldon, "Negro Slavery in Old Deerfield," 57.

80. *Franklin Herald* (August 21, 1821).

81. *Vermont Gazette* (August 1, 1821).

82. *Memoir of Mrs. Chloe Spear, a Native of Africa, Who was Enslaved in Childhood, and Died in Boston, January 3, 1815 ... Aged 65 Years. By a Lady of Boston* (Boston: James Loring, 1832), 10, 15.

83. Albert L. Vail, *Mary Webb and the Mother Society* (Philadelphia: American Baptist Publication Society, 1914), 5–37, 70–72.

84. Ibid. The New York Public Library's edition of *Memoir of Mrs. Chloe Spear* includes below the title '"by a Lady of Boston': Mary Webb who died May 24, 1861 at Boston." Subsequent editions listed the lady of Boston as Rebecca Warren Brown but then added a page that said "attributed to Mary Webb, who died May 24, 1861, at Boston in the 93rd year of her age." Rebecca Warren Brown was the daughter of Boston patriot Joseph Warren and playwright Mercy Otis Warren and published her children's books with Loring. She was not a Baptist, however, but instead a lifelong member of the Arlington Street church. It appears likely that Loring or his printer in subsequent editions simply confused two women authors of children's books and mistakenly listed Brown's name on the author's page. There are many possible reasons why Webb did not challenge this mistake. One is that she had not claimed authorship in the first place since she had listed herself as a Lady of Boston rather than using her name. Arlington Street Church Records, BMS 4/9 (5), Andover-Harvard Theological Library, Harvard University, Cambridge, Mass.

85. Vail, *Mary Webb,* 5–37, 70–72; Helen Emery Falls, "Baptist Women in Missions Support in the Nineteenth Century," *Baptist History and Heritage* 12 (1977): 26–36.

86. *A Concise History of the Baldwin Place Baptist Church, Together with the Articles of Faith and Practice* (Boston: William. H. Hutchinson, 1854), 76; Anne M. Boylan, *Sunday School: The Formation of an American Institution 1790–1880* (New Haven: Yale University Press, 1990), 23.

87. *Youth's Companion* (May 23, 1832), 6.

88. *Liberator* (May 26, 1831); *Liberator* (April 28, 1832); "Descriptive Catalogue of Anti-Slavery Works, for Sale by Isaac Knapp," *Liberator* (November 10, 1837).

89. Christina Accomando, *"The Regulations of Robbers": Legal Fictions of Slavery and Resistance* (Columbus: Ohio State University Press, 2001), 36–38.

90. *Memoir of Mrs. Chloe Spear,* 9.

91. Many of the details of the family history are fleshed out in Beth Anne Bower, "African American Family History Resources at NEGHS," http://www.newenglandancestors.org/education/articles/researchspecialtopics/africaname/africanamerican_neghgs.asp (October 1, 2005). For the view that the *Memoir* is a narrative about death and mourning see Lois Brown, "Memorial Narratives of African Women in Antebellum New England," *Legacy* 20 (2003): 38–61. Margot Minardi first raised questions about the missing elements of motherhood and Cesar Spear's membership in African Lodge No. 1 in "A Rugged Maze: The Emancipation of Belinda and Chloe Spear" (senior honors thesis, Harvard University, 2000). See also Margot Lee Minardi, "The Inevitable Negro: Making Slavery History in Massachusetts, 1770–1863" (PhD diss., Harvard University, 2007).

92. John Bradford, Trading records, Boston and Jamaica, 1760–1783, Samuel Bradford papers, Massachusetts Historical Society, Boston.

93. Sidney Kaplan, *The Black Presence in the Era of the American Revolution 1770–1800* (Greenwich, Conn.: New York Graphic Society, 1973), 186–88; "Spear Family Record," *The New England Historical and Genealogical Register* 18 (1864): 158.

94. Suffolk Probate, 104:301; Suffolk County Registry of Deeds, 190:153. Certainly the city of Boston recognized him as the owner of the property when they billed him for repair of a drain in White Bread Alley, *Records Relating to the Early History of Boston* (Boston: Municipal Printing Office, 1904), 163.

95. Inhabitants and Estates of the Town of Boston, 1630–1800, Thwing Reference Code 34378.

96. Suffolk County Probate Records, 113:16, Massachusetts Archives.

97. [Thomas Baldwin], "Biography of Mrs. Chloe Spear," *The Massachusetts Baptist Missionary Magazine, 1803–1816* (March, 1815), 157; *Independent Chronicle* (January 5, 1815); *Boston Daily Advertiser* (January 6, 1815); *New-England Palladium* (January 6, 1815); *Boston Patriot* (January 7, 1815); *Repertory* (January 7, 1815); *Columbian Centinel* (January 7, 1815).

98. *Memoir of Mrs. Chloe Spear,* 52–58; Suffolk County Register of Deeds, 190–193, Inventory of Chloe Spear, Suffolk Probate 113:16. Cesar Spear died in 1806. Will of Cesar Spear, 1806, Suffolk Probate, 104:301, Massachusetts Archives.

99. Petition to the General Court of Massachusetts, January 4, 1787, the African Petition, as quoted in Sidney Kaplan and Emma Nogrady Kaplan ed., *The Black Presence in the Era of the American Revolution* (Amherst: University of Massachusetts Press, 1989), 207; Harold V. B. Corrhis, *Negro Masonry in the United States* (New York: H. Emerson, 1940), 11.

100. Henry Wilson Coil, Sr., and John MacDuffie Sherman, ed., *A Documentary Account of Prince Hall and Other Black Fraternal Orders* (St. Louis: The Missouri Lodge of Research, 1982), 27, 34, 117. For extensive social history about Prince Hall and the members of the lodge see Chernoh Momodu Sesay, Jr., "Freemasons of Color: Prince Hall, Revolutionary Black Boston, and the Origins of Black Freemasonry, 1770–1807" (PhD diss., Northwestern University, 2006).

101. *Memoir of Mrs. Chloe Spear,* 54–55.

102. Ibid., 70.

103. For more on the significance of clothing, see Shane White and Graham White, "Slave Clothing and African American Culture in the Eighteenth and Nineteenth Centuries," *Past and Present* 148 (August 1995): 149–86; Helen Bradley Foster, *"New Raiments of Self": African American Clothing in the Antebellum South* (New York: Oxford University Press, 1999); Sophie White, " 'Wearing three or four handkerchiefs around his collar, and elsewhere about him': Slaves' Constructions of Masculinity and Ethnicity in French Colonial New Orleans," *Gender and History* 15 (January, 2004): 528–49.

104. *Memoir of Mrs. Chloe Spear,* 57.

105. Ibid., 57–58.

106. Ibid., 58.

107. Ibid., 54.

108. Ibid., 72.

109. *Report of the Record Commissioners of the City of Boston* (Boston: Rockwell and Churchill, 1880). 133. On the female ritual of tea drinking see Rodris Roth, "Tea-Drinking in Eighteenth-Century America: Tea Etiquette and Equipage," *Material Life in America, 1600–1860* (Boston: Northeastern University Press, 1988), 61–91. On the tea table see Margaret M. Lovell, " 'Such Furniture as Will be Most Profitable': The Business of Cabinet-making in Eighteenth-Century Newport," *Winterthur Portfolio* 25 (1991): 359–60.

110. *The Ladies Repository* (1855), 115.

111. Toby L. Ditz, "Ownership and Obligation: Inheritance and Patriarchal Households in Connecticut, 1750–1820," *William and Mary Quarterly* 47 (1990): 257.

CHAPTER 3

1. Boyrereau Brinch and Benjamin F. Prentiss, *The Blind African Slave* (St. Albans, Vt.: Harry Whitney, 1810), 154; Nathaniel Bouton, *The History of Concord* (Concord, N.H.: Benning W. Sanborn, 1856), 253; Wilkins Updike, James MacSparran, and Daniel Goodwin, *A History of the Episcopal Church in Narragansett, Rhode Island* (Boston: Merrymount Press, 1907), 3:85–86; Guocon Yang, "From Slavery to Emancipation: The African Americans of Connecticut, 1650s–1820s," PhD diss., University of Connecticut, 1999, 274; William H. Robinson, ed., *The Proceedings of the Free African Union Society and the African Benevolent Society* (Providence: Urban League of Rhode Island, 1976), xi; Rita Roberts, "Patriotism and Political Criticism: The Evolution of Political Consciousness in the Mind of a Black Revolutionary Soldier," *Eighteenth Century Studies* 27 (1994): 572; John Saillant, *Black Puritan, Black Republican: The Life and Thought of Lemuel Haynes, 1753–1833* (New York: Oxford University Press, 2003), 13. James Sullivan to Dr. Jeremy Belknap, July 30, 1795, in "Letters and Documents Relating to Slavery in Massachusetts," *Massachusetts Historical Collections* (Cambridge: Wilson, 1877), 3:414; George G. Channing, *Early Recollections of Newport, R.I. from the year 1793 to 1811* (Newport, R.I.: A. J. Ward, C. E. Hammett, Jr., 1868), 48.

2. *Memoir of Mrs. Chloe Spear, a Native of Africa, Who was Enslaved in Childhood, and Died in Boston January 3, 1815 ... Aged 65 Years. By a Lady of Boston* (Boston: James Loring, 1832), 27–28.

3. Thomas S. Kidd, *The Great Awakening: The Roots of Evangelical Christianity in Colonial America* (New Haven: Yale University, 2007), xiv; Joshua Rotenberg, "Black-Jewish Relations in Eighteenth Century Newport," *The Rhode Island Jewish Historical Notes* 111 (1992): 117–71; Franklin Bowditch Dexter, ed., *The Literary Diary of Ezra Stiles*, (New York: Charles Scribner's Sons, 1901), 1:174.

4. "Petition of an African Slave, to the Legislature of Massachusetts," *The American Museum, or Repository of Ancient and Modern Fugitive Pieces, Prose and Poetical* (June 1787).

5. Emil Oberholser, *Delinquent Saints: Disciplinary Action in the Early Congregational Churches of Massachusetts* (New York: Columbia University Press, 1956), 125.

6. Elias Nason, "Public Worship in the Church at Hopkinton, (Mass.), in the Old Colonial Times," *The New England Historical and Genealogical Register* 20 (April 1866): 2; William B. Stevens, *History of Stoneham, Massachusetts* (Stoneham, Mass.: F. L. and W. E. Whittier, 1891), 138; James Oliver Horton and Lois E. Horton, *In Hope of Liberty: Culture, Community, and Protest Among Northern Free Blacks, 1700–1860* (New York: Oxford University Press, 1997), 130. For the story of the slave of Cotton Mather who chose not to convert, see Kathyrn S. Koo, "Strangers in the House of God: Cotton Mather, Onesimus, and an Experiment in Christian Slaveholding," *Proceedings of the American Antiquarian Society* 117, part 1 (2007): 143–75.

7. Henry Melville King, *Historical Catalogue of the Members of the First Baptist Church in Providence* (Providence, R.I.: Townsend, 1908).

8. John Winthrop, *The History of New England from 1650 to 1649*, rev. ed. (Boston: Little Brown, 1853), 2:31.

9. *Publications of the Colonial Society of Massachusetts* (Boston: Colonial Society of Massachusetts, 1961), 323.

10. Letter to Joseph Fish, ca. July 1766, Sarah Osborn, Letters, American Antiquarian Society, Worcester, Mass.; King, *Historical Catalogue*; George Levesque, "Inherent Reformers-Inherited Orthodoxy: Black Baptists in Boston, 1800–1873," *Journal of Negro History* 60 (October 1975): 495.

11. Folder 35, April 26, 1762, Box 6, North Church Papers, MS 036, Portsmouth Athenaeum, Portsmouth. Evangelical preachers found that blacks took "ecstatic" delight in singing the psalms and hymns of the English minister, Isaac Watts. Blacks who belonged to the North Church in Portsmouth even subscribed to the printing of a book of the hymns and psalms by Watts.

12. *Rules for the Society of Negroes, 1693* (Boston: B. Harris, 1693). For the punishment of Hagar for fornication, see MS Records of the North Stonington Church, December 1, 1746, Connecticut State Library, Hartford.

13. Kidd, *Great Awakening*, xvii–xviii.

14. Kenneth P. Minkema, "Jonathan Edwards's Defense of Slavery," *Massachusetts Historical Review* v. 4 (2002): 23–59. For a general review of the impact of the First Great Awakening on African Americans, see Kidd, *Great Awakening*, 213–33; Thomas Prince, "Some Account of the Late Revival of Religion in Boston" in *The Christian History Containing Accounts of the Revival and Propagation of Religion in Great Britain, America* (Boston: S. Kneeland and Green, 1774–1775) 2:395; Andrew Eliot, March 22, 1741, Diary in Ames' Almanac (1742), Pre-Revolutionary Diaries, Massachusetts Historical Society Series, no. 3, Massachusetts Historical Society, Boston; J. M. Bumsted, "Orthodoxy in Massachusetts: The Ecclesiastical History of Freetown, 1683–1776," *New England Quarterly* 43 (June 1970): 280.

15. Horton and Horton, *In Hope of Liberty*, 133.

16. Mechal Sobel, *Trabelin' On: The Slave Journey to an Afro-Baptist Faith* (Princeton: Princeton University Press, 1988), 98; Joanna Brooks, *American Lazarus: Religion and the*

Rise of African-American and Native American Literatures (New York: Oxford University Press, 2003), 21. Moreover, black men who were full members at (some) congregations had the right to vote on church matters, such as the dismissal of the pastor; black women did not have that right. Eric R. Seeman,"'Justice Must Take Plase': Three African Americans Speak of Religion in Eighteenth-Century New England," *William and Mary Quarterly* 56 (April 1999): 402.

17. Christopher M. Jedrey, *The World of John Cleaveland: Family and Community in Eighteenth-Century New England* (New York: W. W. Norton and Company, 1979), 65, 87–88, 117.

18. Kidd, *Great Awakening*, 213.

19. Folder I B, Box 1, Testimonials, John Cleaveland Papers, MSS 204, Phillips Library at the Peabody Essex Museum, Salem.

20. Arlin Ira Ginsburg, "Ipswich, Massachusetts During the American Revolution, 1763–1791" (PhD diss., University of California at Riverside, 1972), 47–48.

21. E. O. Jameson, *The Choates in America, 1643–1896* (Boston: Alfred Mudge and Son, 1896), 27.

22. Two Centuries of Church History, *Celebration of the Two Hundredth Anniversary of the Organization of the Congregational Church and Parish in Essex, Massachusetts* (Salem, Mass.: J. H. Choate, 1884), 209, 210.

23. Ibid., 203.

24. *Vital Records of Ipswich, Mass., to the End of the Year 1849* (Salem, Mass.: Ancestor Publishers, 1910), 2:471; George Thomas Little, *Genealogical and Family History of the State of Maine* (New York: Lewis Historical Publishing, 1909), 2:707–708; Loose sheet of temporary records, 1746, Folder 3, Box 1, John Cleaveland Papers, Jameson, *Choates*, 37.

25. See also Stephen Paschall Sharples, *Records of the Church of Christ at Cambridge in New England 1632–1830* (Boston: Eben Putnam, 1906), 172. For suspension of a black woman communicant for drunkenness, profanity, and disobedience, see *Plymouth Church Records, 1620–1859* (New York: New England Society of the City of New York, 1920–23), 2:332, 374; J. Rixley Ruffin, *A Paradise of Reason: William Bentley and Enlightenment of Christianity in the Early Republic* (New York: Oxford University Press, 2008), 84.

26. Flora's Conversion Narrative, Folder 13, Box 1, John Cleaveland Papers. For the discipline of Abigail Carr by the First Baptist Church of Providence, see John Wood Sweet, *Bodies Politic: Negotiating Race in the American North, 1730–1830* (Baltimore: Johns Hopkins University Press, 2003), 436.

27. Phillis' Conversion Narrative, Folder 1B, Box 1, John Cleveland Papers.

28. A white woman, Susanna Low, also repeated this passage for her conversion narrative. Folder I B, Testimonials, John Cleaveland Papers. Sweet mistakenly identified Low as black in Sweet, *Bodies Politic*, 124–25.

29. Folder 1 B, Testimonials, John Cleaveland Papers.

30. A white woman and a white man also chose the same passage. Ibid.

31. Mechal Sobel, *Teach Me Dreams: The Search for Self in the Revolutionary Era* (Princeton: Princeton University Press, 2000), 128–29.

32. Thomas Franklin Waters, *Ipswich in the Massachusetts Bay Colony* (Ipswich, Mass.: Ipswich Historical Society, 1912), 2:217; *Vital Records of Ipswich, Mass., to the End of the Year 1849* (Salem, Mass.: Ancestor Publishers, 1910), 2:470; Will of Francis Choate of Ipswich, December 22, 1777, Essex County Probate Records, vol. 352, Massachusetts State Archives, Boston.

33. Charles E. Hambrick-Stowe, "The Spiritual Pilgrimage of Sarah Osborn (1714–1796)," *Church History* 61 (December 1992): 408–21.

34. Charles E. Hambrick-Stowe, "All Things Were New and Astonishing: Edwardsean Piety, the New Divinity, and Race," in *Jonathan Edwards at Home and Abroad: Historical Memories, Cultural Movements, Global Horizons*, ed. David William Kling and Douglas A. Sweeney (Columbia: University of South Carolina Press, 2003), 136; Benjamin Carp, *Rebels Rising: Cities and the American Revolution* (New York: Oxford University Press, 2007), 138.

35. Sarah Osborn to the Rev. Joseph Fish, April 21, 1765, as quoted in Mary Beth Norton, "'My Resting Reaping Time': Sarah Osborn's Defense of Her 'Unfeminine' Activities, 1767," *Signs* 2 (1976): 519.

36. Norton, "My Resting," 524; Samuel Hopkins, *Memoirs of the Life of Mrs. Sarah Osborn* (Catskill, N.Y.: N. Elliott, 1814), 77.

37. Sarah Osborn to Reverend Joseph Fish, Feb. 28–March 7, 1767, in Norton, "My Resting," 524.

38. Kenneth P. Minkema and Harry S. Stout, "The Edwardsean Tradition and the Antislavery Debate, 1740-1865," *Journal of American History* v. 92 (June, 2005), 57; Hopkins, *Memoirs*, 77; Abigail Adams, Letter to John Adams, Sept. 22, 1774, Adams Family Papers, Massachusetts Historical Society.

39. Phillips Moulton, "John Woolman's Approach to Social Action: As Exemplified in Relation to Slavery," *Church History* 35 (December 1966): 403–5; Charles Eliot, ed., *The Journal of John Woolman* (New York: P. F. Collier, 1909), 251–52.

40. Joseph A. Conforti, *Samuel Hopkins and the New Divinity Movement: Calvinism, the Congregational Ministry, and Reform in New England Between the Great Awakenings* (Grand Rapids, Mich.: Christian University Press, 1981), 29; Jonathan D. Sassi, "'This whole country have their hands full of Blood this day': Transcription and Introduction of an Antislavery Sermon Manuscript Attributed to the Reverend Samuel Hopkins," *Proceedings of the American Antiquarian Society* 112, part 1 (2004): 49–51; John Ferguson, *Memoir of the Life and Character of Rev. Samuel Hopkins, D.D.* (Boston: Leonard W. Kimball, 1930), 87; *The Works of Joseph Bellamy, D.D., First Pastor of the Church in Bethlem, Conn.* (Boston: Doctrinal Tract and Book Society, 1853), 1:5.

41. Phillis Wheatley to Samuel Hopkins, February 9, 1774, in John C. Shields, ed., *The Collected Works of Phillis Wheatley* (New York: Oxford University Press, 1988), 175–76.

42. Minkema, "Jonathan Edwards' Defense of Slavery," 23–60; William Allen, *An Address, Delivered at Northampton, Massachusetts, on the evening of October 29, 1854* (Northampton,

Mass.: Hopkins, Bridgman and Company, 1855), 52. Joab Binney's admission to Edwards's church in Northampton can be found in Rev. Solomon Clark, *Historical Catalogue of the Northampton First Church, 1661–1891* (Northampton, Mass.: Gazette Printing Co., 1891), 57; Electa F. Jones, *Stockbridge, Past and Present* (Springfield, Mass.: S. Bowles, 1854), 238–39; Bettye Hobbs Pruitt, *Massachusetts Tax Valuation List of 1771* (Boston: G. K. Hall, 1978), 480; Emilie Piper, "The Family Life of Agrippa Hull," *Berkshire Genealogist* 22 (2001): 3–6. For Rose Binney's church membership, see *An Historical Sketch of the Congregational Church in Stockbridge* (Stockbridge, Mass.: Stockbridge First Congregational Church, 1874), 26. For Joab Binney's will (1784), see Berkshire County Probate 1211, as quoted in Glendyne R. Wergland, "Women, Men, Property, and Inheritance: Gendered Testamentary Customs in Western Massachusetts, 1800–1860," PhD diss., University of Massachusetts, 2001, 194. Their son Titus was owned by Timothy Edwards in 1771, but appears to have been manumitted by him and given land in Tioga, New York.

43. Rev. Stephen West, "Conversion of an African Woman," *The Theological Magazine, or Synopsis of Modern Religious Sentiment on a New Plan* (January–February 1797): 191–95.

44. West, "Conversion."

45. Bernard A. Drew, *If They Close the Door on You, Go Through the Window* (Great Barrington, Mass.: Attic Revivals Press, 2004), 15–16.

46. "On Messrs. Hussey and Coffin," *Newport Mercury* (December 21, 1767).

47. *Ignatius Sancho: Letters of the Late Ignatius Sancho, an African,* ed. Vincent Carretta (London: 1782; New York: Penguin Books, 1998), 112; *An Address to Miss Phillis Wheatley ... Composed by Jupiter Hammon* (Hartford, Conn.: no publisher, 1778).

48. Proposal of Phillis Wheatley, *Proceedings of the Massachusetts Historical Society* (September 1865), 461.

49. For more on Ethiopianism, see Wilson Jeremiah Moses, *Afrotopia: The Roots of African American Population History* (Cambridge: Cambridge University Press, 1998).

50. David Grimsted, "Anglo-American Racism and Phillis Wheatley's 'Sable Veil,' 'Lengthen'd Chain,' and 'Knitted Heart,'" in *Women in the Age of the American Revolution,* ed. Ronald Hoffman and Peter J. Albert (Charlottesville: University of Virginia Press, 1989), 370.

51. Margaretta Matilda Odell, *Memoir and Poems of Phillis Wheatley, a Native African and Slave, Dedicated to the Friends of the Africans* (Boston: George W. Light, 1834), 10.

52. Astrid Franke, "Phillis Wheatley, Melancholy Muse," *New England Quarterly* 77 (June 2004): 224–51.

53. Julian D. Mason, Jr., ed., *The Poems of Phillis Wheatley* (Chapel Hill: University of North Carolina Press, 1989), 53.

54. Sondra O'Neale, "A Slave's Subtle War: Phillis Wheatley's Use of Biblical Myth and Symbol," *Early American Literature* 21 (Fall 1986): 149.

55. Grimsted, "Anglo-American Racism," 357 n. 41.

56. Betsy Erkkila, "Phillis Wheatley and the Black American Revolution," in *A Mixed Race: Ethnicity in Early America,* ed. Frank Shuffleton (New York: Oxford University Press, 1993), 225–40.

57. Shields, ed., *Collected Works*, 246–47.

58. Ibid., 246.

59. John Montague Smith, *History of the Town of Sunderland* (Greenfield, Mass.: E. A. Hall, 1899), 162; Thomas Weston, *History of the Town of Middleboro, Massachusetts* (Boston: Houghton, Mifflin, 1906), 102.

60. Grimsted, "Anglo-American Racism," 384.

61. Phillis Wheatley, *An Elegiac Poem, on the Death of that Celebrated Divine and Eminent Servant of Jesus Christ, the Late Reverend and pious George Whitefield* (Boston: Ezekiel Russell, 1770); John F. Collin, *Political Affairs of the Country* (Hudson, N.Y.: M. Parker Williams, 1883), 3:16.

62. Antonio T. Bly, "Wheatley's To the University of Cambridge, in New-England," *Explicator* 55 (Summer 1997): 205–8.

63. Margot Minardi, "The Poet and the Petitioner: Two Black Women in Harvard's Early History," in *Yards and Gates: Gender in Harvard and Radcliffe History*, ed. Laurel Thatcher Ulrich (New York: Palgrave Macmillan, 2004), 53–68.

64. Grimsted, "Anglo-American Racism."

65. On possible negotiations for manumission between Phillis Wheatley and her owner, see Vincent Carretta, "Phillis Wheatley, the Mansfield Decision of 1772, and the Choice of Identity" in *Early America Re-Explored: New Readings in Colonial, Early National, and Antebellum Culture*, ed. Vincent Carretta and Philip Gould (Lexington: University Press of Kentucky, 1999), 175–89. For Wheatley's visit to London, see Mukhtar Ali Isani, "Notes: Phillis Wheatley in London: An Unpublished Letter to David Wooster," *American Literature* 51 (May 1979): 255–60.

66. Letter of Samson Occom to Susannah Wheatley, Sept. 21, 1773, in the *Collected Writings of Samson Occom, Mohegan Leadership and Literature in Eighteenth-Century Native America*, ed. Joanna Brooks (New York: Oxford University Press, 2006), 197.

67. Henry Louis Gates, Jr., *The Trials of Phillis Wheatley* (New York: Basic Books, 2003), 14–15.

68. *The Connecticut Gazette* (March 11, 1774).

69. Mukhtar Ali Isani, "The Contemporaneous Reception of Phillis Wheatley: Newspaper and Magazine Notices during the Years of Fame, 1765–1774," *Journal of Negro History* 85 (September 2000): 271.

70. On Wheatley's evangelical community see James A. Rawley, "The World of Phillis Wheatley," *New England Quarterly* 50 (December 1977): 666–777 and Samuel J. Rogal, "Phillis Wheatley's Methodist Connection," *Black American Literary Forum* 21 (1987): 85–97; Mukhtar Ali Isani, "The Methodist Connection: New Variants of Some of Phillis Wheatley's Poems," *Early American Literature* 22 (Fall 1987): 108–13.

71. Julian D. Mason, Jr., *The Poems of Phillis Wheatley* (Chapel Hill: University of North Carolina Press, 1966), 197; Lynne Withey, *Urban Growth in Colonial Rhode Island: Newport and Providence in the Eighteenth Century* (Albany: State University of New York Press, 1984), 81–83.

72. Phillis Wheatley to John Thornton, October 30, 1774, in *Phillis Wheatley and Her Writings*, ed. William H. Robinson (New York: Garland Press, 1984), 341; Rev. R. W. Wallace, *Sermons on Congregationalism in Newport* (Newport, R.I.: Daily News, 1896), 41.

73. Franklin Bowditch Dexter, ed., *Literary Diary*, 2:377.

74. Wheatley to Obour Tanner, February 14, 1776, http://www.npr.org/templates/story/story.php?stsoryID=5021077 (July 1, 2007).

75. "Newport Gardner (1746–1826)," *The Black Perspective in Music* 4 (July 1976): 205.

76. Minkema and Stout, "Edwardsean Tradition," 55.

CHAPTER 4

1. George Sheldon, "Negro Slavery in Old Deerfield," *New England Magazine* 8 (March 1893): 53.

2. For different types of marriage, with varying roles and responsibilities for spouses, see Alma Gottlieb, *Under the Kapok Tree: Identity and Difference in Beng Thought* (Bloomington: Indiana University Press, 1992), 73; Laura Bohannan, "Dahomean Marriage: A Reevaluation," *Africa* 19 (1949): 273–80; Christine Oppong, "From Love to Institution: Indications of Change in Akan Marriage," *Journal of Family History* 5 (Summer 1980): 197–209; Anne Hilton, "Family and Kinship among the Kongo South of the Zaire River from the Sixteenth to the Nineteenth Centuries," *Journal of African History* 24 (1983): 189–206. For ready access to divorce in West Africa, see John S. Mbiti, *Love and Marriage in Africa* (London: Longman, 1973), 81–82, 189–201. For the argument that age was a more significant category than gender in precolonial West Africa see Oyeronke Oyewumi, *The Invention of Women: Making an African Sense of Western Gender Discourses* (Minneapolis: University of Minnesota, 1997).

3. Sarah Anna Emery, *Reminiscences of a Nonagerian* (Newburyport, Mass.: William. H. Huse, 1879), 203.

4. An example is John C. MacLean, A *Rich Harvest: The History, Buildings, and People of Lincoln, Massachusetts* (Lincoln, Mass.: Lincoln Historical Society, 1987), 217.

5. Charles Warren Brewster, *Rambles about Portsmouth* (Portsmouth, N.H.: Lewis W. Brewster, 1873), 159.

6. Alexandra Chan, *Slavery in the Age of Reason: Archaeology at a New England Farm* (Knoxville: University of Tennessee Press, 2007).

7. Christian Barnes, Letter Book, Library of Congress Manuscript Division, as quoted in Mary Beth Norton, *Liberty's Daughters: The Revolutionary Experience of American Women, 1750–1800* (Boston: Little, Brown, and Company, 1980), 67; Samuel Roads, Jr., *The History and Traditions of Marblehead* (Boston: Houghton, Osgood and Company, 1881), 78.

8. Queries respecting slavery in Massachusetts with answers, Jeremy Belknap, April 1795, Jeremy Belknap Papers, Massachusetts Historical Society, Boston; Nian-Sheng Huang, "Franklin's Father Josiah: Life of a Colonial Boston Tallow Chandler, 1657–1745," *Transactions of the American Philosophical Society,* new ser., 90 (2000): 63.

9. *Boston News-Letter* (September 23, 1706). The first New England newspaper appeared two years before; George B. Kirsch, *Jeremy Belknap* (New York: Arno Press, 1982), 190.

10. Petition for freedom to Massachusetts Governor Thomas Gage, His Majesty's Council, and the House of Representations, May 25, 1774, Jeremy Belknap Papers, Massachusetts Historical Society. When an African mother died on board the slave ship, her infant was nursed by another woman and was usually given away rather than sold for a purchase price. Thomas Franklin Waters, *Ipswich in the Massachusetts Bay Colony* (Ipswich, Mass.: Ipswich Historical Society, 1917), 2:214; Nathaniel Bouton, *The History of Concord* (Concord, N.H.: Bening W. Sanborn, 1856), 253; Martha E. Sewall Curtis, *Ye Old Meeting House* (Boston: Anchor Linotype, 1909), 61; Joyce Lee Malcolm, *Peter's War: A New England Slave Boy and the American Revolution* (New Haven: Yale University Press, 2008), 6–7.

11. John Greenleaf Whittier, *Old Portraits and Modern Sketches* (Boston: Ticknor, Read, and Felds, 1850), 158; Bouton, *History*, 253; "Bill of Sale of a Negro Servant in Boston, 1724," *The New England Historical and Genealogical Register* (1864), 18:78; James Otis Lyford, *History of the Town of Canterbury, New Hampshire, 1727–1912* (Concord, N.H.: Rumford Press, 1912), 143; Charles William Manwaring, *A Digest of the Early Connecticut Probate Records* (Hartford, Conn.: R. S. Peck, 1904), 1:569; Alonzo Lewis, *The History of Lynn* (Boston: J. H. Eastburn, 1829), 181. Indian wives indentured themselves to their husband's master to gain a husband's freedom. Beverly, Mass., *Vital Records of Beverly, Mass., to the end of the Year 1849* (Topsfield, Mass.: Topsfield Historical Society, 1907), 2:361.

12. Venture Smith, *A Narrative of the Life and Adventures of Venture, A Native of Africa, But Resident Above Sixty Years in the United States of America, Related by Himself* (New London: Printed by C. Holt, 1798); Robert E. Desrochers, Jr., "'Not Fade Away': The Narrative of Venture Smith, an African in the Early Republic," *Journal of American History* 84 (June 1997): 40–66.

13. Smith, *Narrative*.

14. Rev. A. P. Martin, *History of the Town of Winchendon* (Worcester County, Mass.) (Winchendon, Mass.: published by the author, 1868), 277–79; *Massachusetts Soldiers and Sailors of the Revolutionary War* (Boston: Wright and Potter, 1902), 9:916, 931–32.

15. Ruth Wallis Herndon, *Unwelcome Americans: Living on the Margin in Early New England* (Philadelphia: University of Pennsylvania Press, 2001), 87–91; J. E. A. Smith, *The History of Pittsfield, Massachusetts from the Year 1734 to the Year 1800* (Boston: Lee and Shepard, 1869), 137; Boyrereau Brinch and Benjamin F. Prentiss, *The blind African Slave* (St. Albans, Vt.: Harry Whitney, 1810), 36–37.

16. John Wood Sweet, *Bodies Politic: Negotiating Race in the American North, 1730–1830* (Baltimore: Johns Hopkins University Press, 2003), 256; Massachusetts, General Court, House of Representatives, *Committee on the Admission into Massachusetts of free Negroes and mulattoes* (Boston: True and Green, 1822), 18.

17. Billy G. Smith, "Black Women Who Stole Themselves in Early America," *Inequality in Early America*, ed. Carla Gardina Pestana and Sharon V. Salinger (Hanover, N.H.: University Press of New England, 1999), 134–59. For a fugitive headed for her mother's place, see *Newport Mercury* (October 8, 1770).

18. Barbara W. Brown and James M. Rose, *Black Roots in Southeastern Connecticut, 1650–1900* (New London, Conn.: New London County Historical Society, 2001), 526. For a similar example, of a mother running away with her three-year-old child, see Brown and Rose, *Black Roots,* 500.

19. Christian Barnes Letterbook, in Norton, *Liberty's Daughters,* 66.

20. Case of James and Mary Newell, March 13, 1689, in *Plymouth Colony Records,* ed. C. H. Simmons, Jr. (Camden, N.J.: Picton Press, 1966), 1:200; James M. Rose and Barbara W. Brown, *Tapestry: A Living History of the Black Family in Southeastern Connecticut* (New London, Conn.: New London County Historical Society, 1997). Initially the Puritans sought to punish fornication, regardless of who committed it. As they relaxed their religious standards, economic considerations became uppermost, and it seemed foolhardy to make masters pay for the sexual indiscretions of their slaves. Still, every once in awhile, a charge of fornication was brought against a black woman, free or enslaved, who had a long-term relationship with a black man in the town. Someone may have been trying to punish an enslaved woman or was shocked by the immorality of sex and pregnancy outside of marriage. Roger Thompson, *Sex in Middlesex: Popular Mores in Massachusetts County, 1649–1699* (Amherst: University of Massachusetts Press, 1986), 108–9; Lorenzo Johnston Greene, *The Negro in Colonial New England, 1620–1776* (New York: Columbia University Press, 1942), 202–7. Only two African women were prosecuted for fornication in Worcester, Suffolk, and Middlesex Counties from 1740 to 1780. Kelly Alisa Ryan, "Regulating Passion: Sexual Behavior and Citizenship in Massachusetts, 1740–1820" (PhD diss., University of Maryland, 2006), 53.

21. John Lathrop, *Massachusetts Reports 127: Cases Argued and Determined in the Supreme Judicial Court of Massachusetts* (Boston: Little, Brown, 1880), 467–68.

22. Rev. James MacSparran, *Letter Book and Abstract of Out Services, 1743–1751* (Boston: Merrymount Press, 1899), 15; Wilkins Updike, *A History of the Episcopal Church in Narragansett Rhode Island* (Boston: Merrymount Press, 1907), 133, 239, 254. For a more extended discussion of Rev. MacSparran, see Joanne Pope Melish, *Disowning Slavery: Gradual Emancipation and "Race" in New England, 1780–1860* (Ithaca, N.Y.: Cornell University Press, 1998), 12.

23. *Laws of Massachusetts,* ch. 10 (1705), 528.

24. For legal marriages among slaves in Boston prior to 1705 see *A Volume of Records, Relating to the Early History of Boston, Containing Boston Marriages from 1752 to 1809* (Boston: Municipal Printing Office, 1903), VI–VII; Melinde Lutz Sanborn, *Third*

Supplement to Torrey's New England Marriages prior to 1700 (Baltimore: Genealogical Publishing Company, 2003); *A Report of the Record Commissioners Containing Boston Births, Baptisms, Marriages, and Deaths, 1638–1699* (Boston; Rockwell and Churchill, 1883), 48; *A Report of the Record Commissioners of the City of Boston, 1700 to 1751* (Boston: Municipal Printing Office, 1898), 5, 13, 20; "Diary of Samuel Sewall, 1674–1729," *Massachusetts Historical Society, Collections* 6 (1859), 22.

25. Marriages between men designated as "Negro" and women not designated by race were frequently recorded before 1705. One reason to think these were interracial marriages is that there were no women who were listed as "Negro" who married a husband without a racial designation. Robert J. Cottrol, *The Afro-Yankees: Providence's Black Community in the Antebellum Era* (Westport, Conn.: Greenwood, 1981), 21–22; Lorenzo J. Greene, *The Negro in Colonial New England* (New York: Columbia University, 1942), 202. On the marriage of James Newell and Mary White, see Samuel Deane, *History of Scituate, Massachusetts: From its First Settlement to 1831* (Boston: James Loring, 1831), 314.

26. Bernard A. Drew, "Cuffee Negro in the Wilderness," *Berkshire Eagle* (October 9, 2004); Bernard A. Drew and Emilie Piper, "Cuffee and Nana Negro: Pioneer Blacks in Berkshire County," and "Stockbridge," *African American Heritage in the Upper Housatonic Valley,* ed. David Levinson (Great Barrington, Mass.: Berkshire Publishing, 2006), 23, 184; Bernard A. Drew, *If They Close the Door on You, Go in the Window* (Great Barrington, Mass.: Attic Revivals Press, 2004), 12, 13; Edward A. Collier, *A History of Old Kinderhook* (Boston: Knickerbocker Press, 1914), 100. For DuBois' telling of the family history, see W. E. B. DuBois, *Dusk of Dawn: An Early Essay Toward an Autobiography of a Race Concept* (New York: Harcourt, Brace, and World, 1940), iii.

27. William Lamson Warren, "Lewis Lyron of Milford, Connecticut, 1650–1738," typescript, one column, MS 88316, Connecticut Historical Society, Hartford; *York Deeds,* Book 2, Fol. 37 (Bethel, Me.: Maine Genealogical Society, 1903), 38.

28. George Elliott Howard, *A History of Matrimonial Institutions, chiefly in England and the United States* (Chicago: University of Chicago Press, 1904), 2:223.

29. Boston and Hagar, March 1741, Petitions to the Governor and Council, Divorce and Separation, Massachusetts Archives 9, 248–50; *New England Historical and Genealogical Register* 34 (January 1880), 96.

30. Rose and Brown, *Tapestry,* 13, 24; George Champlin Mason, *Reminiscences of Old Newport* (Newport, R.I.: Charles E. Hammett, 1884), 106; Massachusetts Daughters of the American Revolution, *Catalogue of a Loan Collection of Ancient and Historic Articles* (Boston: Commonwealth of Massachusetts, 1897), 105; Mary H. Northend, *Historic Homes of New England* (Boston: Little, Brown, 1914), 214; Christian Barnes Letterbook, in Norton, *Liberty's Daughters,* 66.

31. Francis M. Thompson, *History of Greenfield, Shire Town of Franklin County, Massachusetts* (Greenfield, Mass.: Town of Greenfield, 1929), 3:1002.

32. George H. Moore, "Slave Marriages in Massachusetts," *Historical Magazine* 5 (1869): 135–37.

33. *Historical Magazine and Notes and Queries Concerning the Antiquities* (February 1869): 137. For another example of such conditional vows, see Testimony of the Reverend John Graham, February 7, 1784, *Exeter v. Hanchett*, Suffolk County Files 158594, Massachusetts State Archives.

34. Petet Benes, "Slavery in Boston Households, 1647–1770," in *Slavery/Antislavery in New England*, ed. Peter Benes and Jane Montague Benes (Boston: Boston University Scholarly Publications, 2005), 26.

35. Fortunatus [Sharper] to Col. [James] Otis, undated correspondence, Otis Family Papers, Massachusetts Historical Society, as quoted in Kirsten Denise Sword, "Wayward Wives, Runaway Slaves and the Limits of Patriarchal Authority in Early America," PhD diss., Harvard University, 2002, 215.

36. Sword, "Wayward Wives," 215.

37. Melinde Lutz Sanborn, "Venus and Peter Hanson, An Early African Divorce in Nottingham, New Hampshire," *The New Hampshire Genealogical Record* 22 (2005): 112–14; *Collections of the Dover, N.H. Historical Society*, vol. 1 (Dover, N.H.: Scales and Quimby, 1894), 165, 166, 167.

38. There is also the question as to whether a Connecticut jury had actually declared her an indentured servant who had two years more time to serve. Exeter's suit may have been timed to coincide with the end of his wife's two-year term of service. Sword, "Wayward Wives," 229. For more on this case, see Emily Blanck, "Seventeen Eighty-Three: The Turning Point in the Law of Slavery and Freedom in Massachusetts," *New England Quarterly* 75 (March 2002): 38–42; John Hooker, *Some Reminiscences of a Long Life* (Hartford, Conn.: Belknap and Warfield, 1899), 31.

39. Deposition of the Rev. John Graham, *Exeter v. Hanchett* (1783).

40. Hooker, *Some Reminiscences*, 31–33; Pension File W 181803, Saunders, Phillis, Revolutionary War, *HeritageQuest.com*, series M 805, roll 851, image 41 (August 13, 2008).

41. [E. Russell] *The Appendix. Or some Observations of the expediency of the Petition of the Africans, living in Boston, etc., lately presented to the General Assembly of this Province. To which is annexed, the petition referred to Likewise, thoughts on slavery with a useful extract from the Massachusetts Spy, of January 28, 1773, by way of an Address to the Members of the Assembly. By a Lover of Constitutional Liberty* (Boston: Ezekiel Russell, 1773). For an analysis of four petitions by enslaved men in Massachusetts, see Thomas J. Davis, "Emancipation Rhetoric, Natural Rights, and Revolutionary New England: A Note on Four Black Petitions in Massachusetts, 1773–1777," *New England Quarterly* 62 (June 1989): 248–63.

42. "Petition of a Grate Number of Blackes," January 13, 1777, Massachusetts Historical Society.

43. Lynne E. Withey, "Household Structure in Urban and Rural Areas: The Case of Rhode Island, 1774–1800," *Journal of Family History* 3 (Spring 1978): 37; Joanne Pope Melish, *Disowning Slavery: Gradual Emancipation and "Race" in New England, 1780–1860* (Ithaca, N.Y.: Cornell University Press, 1998), 129–30.

44. Sheldon S. Cohen, "'To Parts of the World Unknown: The Circumstances of Divorce in Connecticut, 1750–1797," *Canadian Review of American Studies* 11 (Winter 1980): 288–89.

45. Because the advertisements rarely mentioned race, historians have not paid attention to the disproportionate number of black women running away from their husbands. The names of black husbands Leavitt, Brown and Rose, Sword, and Grover identified formed the initial sample. We searched advertisements for posted wives in New England newspapers from 1780 to 1800 in newspapers available through the Early American Newspapers online database. The definition of a black man included a man who identified himself as a black man or who had a first name used exclusively by blacks (Quam, Congo, Archelaus, Jupiter, Neptune, etc.). Sarah Leavitt, "'She Hath Left My Bed and Board': Runaway Wives in Rhode Island, 1790–1810," *Rhode Island History* 58 (August 2000): 90–104; Kathryn Grover, *The Fugitive's Gibraltar: Escaping Slaves and Abolitionism in New Bedford, Massachusetts* (Amherst: University of Massachusetts Press, 2001), 295; Brown and Rose, *Black Roots*, 9; Rose and Brown, *Tapestry*, 25; Sword, "Wayward Wives," 231. For newspapers only the first advertisement of a posting by a husband is indicated here. *Independent Chronicle* (January 18, 1781); *Boston Evening Post* (October 15, 1783); *Connecticut Courant* (December 20, 1783); *United States Chronicle* (August 19, 1784); *Independent Chronicle* (March 24, 1785); *Boston Gazette* (May 30, 1785); *New Hampshire Mercury* (September 13, 1786); *Western Star* (November 28, 1796); *Independent Chronicle* (December 13, 1787); *Massachusetts Centinel* (October 17, 1789); *Western Star* (June 5, 1792); *New Hampshire Spy* (July 4, 1792); *Western Star* (October 29, 1793); *Connecticut Courant* (September 22, 1794); *Vermont Gazette* (December 5, 1794); *United States Chronicle* (February 4, 1796); *Western Star* (May 24, 1796); *Western Star* (November 28, 1796); *Independent Chronicle* (August 9, 1798); *Salem Gazette* (April 3, 1798); *United States Chronicle* (September 5, 1799); *United States Chronicle* (October 3, 1799); *Independent Chronicle* (March 24, 1800); *Boston Constitutional Telegraph* (September 17, 1800). For first names used exclusively by black men in New England, see George Quintal, *Patriots of Color: 'A Peculiar Beauty and Merit'*, (Boston: Boston National Historical Park, 2007).

46. Randolph Roth points out that the Indian spousal murder rate was higher than that for blacks in "Twin Evils? Slavery and Homicide in Early America," *The Problem of Evil: Slavery, Freedom, and the Ambiguities of American Reform*, ed. Steven Mintz and John Stauffer (Amherst: University of Massachusetts Press, 2007), 81; Linda K. Kerber, *Women of the Republic: Intellect and Ideology in Revolutionary America* (Chapel Hill: University of North Carolina Press, 1980), 163.

47. *Salem Gazette* (April 3, 1798).

48. Brinch and Prentiss, *The Blind African Slave*, 17.

49. Toby Ditz, "Shipwrecked; or, Masculinity Imperiled: Mercantile Representations of Failed and the Gendered Self in Eighteenth Century Philadelphia," *Journal of American History* 81 (June 1994): 65.

50. Margaretta Matilda Odell, *Memoir and Poems of Phillis Wheatley, a Native African and a Slave* (Boston: George W. Light, 1834), 20; Boston Taking Books, 1784, Rare Book

Room, Boston Public Library, Boston; Robert A. Feer, "Imprisonment for Debt in Massachusetts before 1800," *Mississippi Valley Historical Review* 48 (Sept. 1961): 252–69; Sword, "Wayward Wives," 97; Peter J. Coleman, "The Insolvent Debtor in Rhode Island, 1745–1828," *William and Mary Quarterly* 22 (July 1965): 413–34; Bruce H. Mann, *Republic of Debtors: Bankruptcy in the Age of American Independence* (Cambridge: Harvard University Press, 2003), 85–86; Cato Vernon to William Vernon, August 24, 1793, Vernon Papers, Newport Historical Society, as quoted in Louis P. Masur, "Slavery in Eighteenth-Century Rhode Island: Evidence from the Census of 1774," *Slavery and Abolition* 6 (September 1985): 147–48.

51. Sword, "Wayward Wives," 47– 66.

52. *United States Chronicle* (September 5, 1799).

53. *Newport Mercury* (September 9, 1765); William J. Brown, *The Life of William J. Brown of Providence, R.I.* (Providence, R.I.: Angell & Co., 1883), 10; Daniel T. Huntoon, *History of the Town of Canton, Norfolk County, Massachusetts* (Cambridge: J. Wilson & Son, 1893), 32.

54. On the war record of Pomp Magus, see Elbridge Henry Goss, *The History of Melrose County of Middlesex, Massachusetts* (Melrose, Mass.: City of Melrose, 1902), 215–16; Pension Record, Pomp Magus, S 13851, March 18, 1818, Revolutionary War Pension and County Land Warrant Application Files, 1800–1900, M-804, roll 1615, National Archives, Washington, D.C. For Archelaus Temple: Joyce M. Tice, Tri-Counties Genealogy and History, http://www.rootsweb.com/~srgp/jmtindex.htm (August 1, 2007); Prince Hull and Salem Poor: Quintal, *Patriots of Color*, 135–36, 174–75.

55. Irene Siege, "Freed Slave's Story Uncovered by Owner's Descendant," *Boston Globe* (February 21, 2007); David Allen Lambert, "Salem Poor (1743/1744–1802): A Forgotten Hero of Bunker Hill Rediscovered," *New England Ancestors* 8 (Fall 2007): 40–42; Quintal, *Patriots of Color*, 170–73; Petition of Jonathan Brewer and others, December 5, 1775, Massachusetts State Archives, Boston, 180/241.

56. *Vermont Gazette* (December 5, 1794).

57. *Independent Chronicle* (March 21, 1785); *Western Star* (June 1, 1792); *Western Star* (June 5, 1792); *Boston Constitutional Telegraph* (September 17, 1800). On the average length of service of a black soldier in the Continental Army, see Judith L. Van Buskirk, "Claiming their Due: African Americans in the Revolution and its Aftermath," *War and Society in the American Revolution: Mobilization and Home Front*, ed. John Resch and Walter Sargent (DeKalb, Ill.: Northern Illinois University, 2007), 138.

58. Henry Wilson Coil, Jr., and John McDuffie Sherman, ed., *A Documentary Account of Prince Hall and Other Black Fraternal Orders* (St. Louis: The Missouri Lodge of Research, 1982), 27; George A. Levesque, *Black Boston: African American Life and, Culture in Urban America, 1750–1860* (New York: Garland Publishing, 1994), 294–95; *Massachusetts Mercury* (September 16, 1800).

59. *Independent Chronicle* (January 18, 1781); *Independent Chronicle* (January 25, 1781); *Independent Chronicle* (February 1, 1781).

60. *Documentary Account of Prince Hall,* ed. Coil and Sherman, 5, 7; Warren F. Schwartz, Keith Baxter, and David Ryan, "The Duel: Can These Gentlemen be Acting Efficiently," *Journal of Legal Studies* 13 (June 1984): 321. On dueling on Boston Common, Mary Furwell Ayer, *Early Days on Boston Common* (Boston: privately printed, 1910), 7; Mark Antony de Wolfe Howe, *Boston Common* (Cambridge: Riverside Press, 1910), 24; Edwin Monroe Bacon, *Historic Pilgrimages in New England* (New York: Silver Burdett and Company, 1898), 239. For dueling between enslaved men in Boston, see *Boston Weekly Newsletter* (March 11, 1742); *Boston Evening Post* (March 22, 1742). For the honor code among Southern gentlemen, see Bertram Wyatt-Brown, *Honor and Violence in the Old South* (New York: Oxford University Press, 1986), 140-53; Ariela J. Gross, *Double Character: Slavery and Mastery in the Antebellum Southern Courtroom* (Princeton: Princeton University Press, 2000), 47-71.

61. Leslie A. Schwalm, *A Hard Fight for We: Women's Transition from Slavery to Freedom in South Carolina* (Urbana: University of Illinois Press, 1997), 272-73; Roger Ransom and Richard Sutch, *One Kind of Freedom: The Economic Consequences of Emancipation* (New York: Cambridge University Press, 1997), 44-55.

62. Quintal, *Patriots of Color,* 135-36; Pension File S 36596, Hull, Prince, Revolutionary War, *HeritageQuest.com,* series M 805, roll 453, image 693 (August 13, 2008).

63. *Hartford Courant* (January 6, 1784); *American Mercury* (March 14, 1791); *American Mercury* (March 21, 1791).

64. Ibid.

65. Mary Beth Sievens, *Stray Wives: Marital Conflict in Early National New England* (New York: New York University Press, 2005).

66. Jacqueline Barbara Carr, *After the Siege: A Social History of Boston, 1775-1800* (Boston: Northeastern University Press, 2005), 135.

67. Nantucket Court Records, 2, 87, 89, 1799, as quoted in Isabel Kaldenbach's Inventory of Black Nantucketers, http://www.nha.org/library/NantucketBlacksdatabase2.htm (October 1, 2007). There were only two spousal murders committed by blacks before 1800, both axe murders committed by free black husbands. Cloyes, a free black man in Stamford, Connecticut, took an axe to the head of his wife in 1675. Daniel Allen Hearn, *Legal Executions in New England: A Comprehensive Reference, 1623-1960* (Jefferson, N.C: McFarland, 1999), 48. Joseph Nanno murdered his wife Nanny with an axe in Boston in 1721. See Cotton Mather, *Tremenda: The Dreadful Sound with which the Wicked are to be Thunderstruck* (Boston: B. Green, 1721). His trial and execution is discussed in Mark S. Weiner, *Black Trials: Citizenship from the Beginnings of Slavery to the End of Caste* (New York: Knopf, 2004), ch. 1. On the death of an enslaved husband who beat his wife severely, tried to set fire to the house where she was living, and then committed suicide see *The Massachusetts Gazette* (March 9, 1772).

68. Sword, "Wayward Wives," 140.

69. *Vermont Gazette* (April 5, 1802); *Vermont Gazette* (April 12, 1802); *Vermont Gazette* (April, 19, 1802). Details about the couple's marriage and information about Samuel Cesar's parents can be found in Franklin A. Dorman, *Twenty Families of Color in*

Massachusetts, 1742–1998 (Boston: The New England Historic and Genealogical Society, 1998), 60.

70. *Providence Phoenix* (October 26, 1805). On the patriarchal assumptions of the black church in Philadelphia, see James Oliver Horton and Lois E. Horton, *In Hope of Liberty: Culture, Community and Protest among Northern Free Blacks, 1700–1860* (New York: Oxford University Press, 1997), 148.

CHAPTER 5

1. Graham Russell Hodges, *Root and Branch: African Americans in New York and East Jersey, 1613–1863* (Chapel Hill: University of North Carolina Press, 1999), 129–30.

2. Ibid. For Virginia see Warren M. Billings, "The Cases of Fernando and Elizabeth Key: A Note on the Status of Blacks in Seventeenth-Century Virginia," *William and Mary Quarterly* 30 (July 1973): 467–74.

3. Kate was listed as free but still a servant of the former owner at her marriage in 1772. *Vital Records of Andover, Massachusetts, to the End of the Year 1849* (Topsfield, Mass.: Topsfield Historical Society, 1912), 11:358; L. Kinvin Wroth and Hiller B. Zobel, *Legal Papers of John Adams* (Cambridge: Harvard University Press, 1965), 2:49. Lawrence William Towner suggests an additional freedom suit by Penelope in Middlesex County in 1691 but other sources have not verified it. He cited Manuscript Middlesex Sessions, I, 171, 1705, in Lawrence William Towner, *A Good Master Well Served: Masters and Servants in Colonial Massachusetts, 1620–1750* (New York: Garland, 1998), 172. More importantly, a broader definition of a freedom suit would include any legal action by a free or enslaved woman trying to become free or maintain her freedom—or testifying on behalf of black man suing to become free. By this broader definition one could also include the suits and petitions of free women seeking not to be re-enslaved, petitions to state legislatures to claim freedom, damage suits against former masters, and testifying on behalf of the plaintiff in a black man's freedom suit. Sons also brought lawsuits on the grounds that their mother was free.

4. Joan Jackson's suit is mentioned in *Stone v. Livingston*, 1717, New London County Court, Court Trial Records 10:142; New London County Court, County Court Files, Box 12, Folder 12, Connecticut State Archives, Hartford; Sarah Chauqum: *Sarah v. Edward Robinson*, Court of Common Pleas, South Kingstown, January 1733–34, Record A: 121; *Edward Robinson v. Sarah Chauqum*, Court of General Sessions of the Peace, Kings County, Jan. 1733/34, Bond for Appeal; Rhode Island Supreme Court Judicial Records Center, Pawtucket, Edward Robinson, Petition to the General Assembly of Rhode Island, Petitions, 2:14, Rhode Island State Archives, Providence; *Sarah v. Edward Robinson*, Superior Court, Newport Court, September 1734, Record B: 481 and Files, Rhode Island Judicial Records Center, as quoted in John Wood Sweet, *Bodies Politic: Negotiating Race in the American North, 1750–1830* (Baltimore: Johns Hopkins University Press, 2003), 67–68; *Elisha Webb v. Daniel Wentworth*, 1739, Provincial Court Records, No. 26121, in

Robert B. Dishman, "Breaking the Bonds: The Role of New Hampshire's Courts in Freeing Those Wrongly Enslaved, 1640s–1740s," *Historical New Hampshire* 59 (Fall 2005):
86–90; *Phebe Nong v. Vincent Torr and Wife Lois*, Feb. 1, 1750, Provincial Court Records,
New Hampshire, No. 22, 138, in Dishman, "Breaking the Bonds," 84–86; *Slew v. Whipple*,
1765–66, Massachusetts Supreme Judicial Court, No. 131426, with transcript reprinted
in George H. Moore, *Notes on the History of Slavery in Massachusetts* (New York: D.
Appleton, 1866), 113–14; Esther: *John Randall v. Matthew Robinson*, Superior Court,
King's County, Rhode Island, Oct. 1772, Record B: 342–53; *John Randall v. Matthew
Robinson*, Superior Court, Kings County, October 1774, Record B: 414–15 and Files,
Rhode Island Judicial Record Center; John Randall Petition to the Rhode Island Gen-
eral Assembly, February 1770, Rhode Island Superior Court; John Randall Petition to
the Rhode Island General Assembly, August 1773, Petitions 15:50, Rhode Island State
Archives; John Randall, Petition to the Rhode Island General Assembly, June 1774,
Rhode Island State Archives, as cited in Sweet, *Bodies Politic*, 443; *Margaret (Peg) v. Wil-
liam Muzzey*, 1770, Massachusetts Supreme Judicial Court Case No. 147830, in Mas-
sachusetts Superior Court of Judicature, *Reports of Cases Argued and Adjudged in the
Superior Court of Judicature of the Province of Boston* (Boston: Little, Brown, 1865), 30;
Kate v. Moody Bridges, Newbury, Massachusetts Court Records, as cited in Worth and
Zobel, *The Legal Papers of John Adams* 2:53–54; *Susan Warmsley v. Jeffrey Watson*, Superior Court, Newport, Sept. 1772, Record F: 33–34 and Files, *Susan Warmsley v. Jeffrey
Watson*, Court of Common Pleas, Newport, May 1772, Declaration 184; *Susan Warms-
ley v. Samuel Rose*, Court of Common Pleas, South Kingstown, Dec. 1771, Files, Rhode
Island Judicial Records Center, as cited in Sweet, *Bodies Politic*, 228–39; *Hill v. Meech*,
1773, New London County African Americans Collection 275, Box 3, File 1, November
1, 1773, Connecticut State Library, Hartford; *Juno v. David Larcom* (1774), Salem Court
Records, as cited by Charles E. Hill in "Slavery and Its Aftermath in Beverly, Massachu-
setts: Juno Larcom and Her Family," *Essex Institute Historical Recollections* 116 (April
1980): 120; *Salem and Rose Orne v. Elisha Haskett Derby*, Suffolk Files Collection, Case
No. 12575, July 16, 1777, Massachusetts State Archives, Boston; *Chloe Hale v. Nathaniel
Hale* (1782), Newbury Court Records, as cited in Hill, "Slavery and Its Aftermath," 120;
Brom & Bett vs. J. Ashley Esq., Court Records, Berkshire County Court Courthouse,
Great Barrington, Mass., Inferior Court of Common Pleas, Berkshire County, Great Bar-
rington, Massachusetts, 1781, v. 41, no. 1, 28, May 1781, 55; *Brom & Bett vs. John Ashley*,
1783, Massachusetts Supreme Judicial Court Case No. 9966.

    5. In 1785 Jane Coggeshall petitioned the Rhode Island legislature to confirm her
freedom because she was concerned that her former master's family was planning to
re-enslave her. John Russell Bartlett, ed., *Records of the State of Rhode Island and Providence Plantations in New England* (Providence, R.I.: Providence Press, 1865), 10:143.
The General Assembly of Rhode Island in 1783 voted to free Amy Allen because she
claimed to be white, an abandoned white child raised by an enslaved mother. Bartlett, ed.,
Records, 10:70–71. Moses Brown handled the petition for freedom to the Rhode Island
General Assembly of an unnamed enslaved woman and her child in 1786. Moses Brown

to [unknown], May 29, 1786, Rhode Island Historical Society, as quoted in John Wood Sweet, "Bodies Politic: Colonialism, Race and the Emergence of the American North Rhode Island, 1739–1830," PhD diss., Princeton University, 1995, 368. For the joint petition of Cesar and Lowis Peters see Leonard Woods Labaree, *The Public Records of the State of Connecticut from May, 1785 through January, 1789* (Hartford, Conn.: published by the state, 1945), 531. Moses Brown also petitioned the town of Providence to set free Tom, his wife, and four children in 1774 and after that worked with his brother to prevent the re-enslavement of the family to a purported owner in the West Indies. Charles Rappleye, *Sons of Providence: The Brown Brothers, the Slave Trade, and the American Revolution* (New York: Simon and Schuster, 2006), 143–44. A free black husband also took his wife's owner to court when the owner reneged on an agreement to manumit the man's wife. Elaine Forman Crane, *Ebb Tide in New England: Women, Seaports, and Social Change, 1630–1800* (Boston: Northeastern University Press, 1998), 146.

6. Dishman, "Breaking the Bonds," 79–91.

7. The Connecticut suit was *Hill v. Meech* (1773). Vermont and Maine were not separate legal jurisdictions at this time; Vermont's judicial system became independent from the New Hampshire judicial system only during the Revolutionary War, and Maine remained part of Massachusetts until 1820.

8. Emily Blanck, "The Legal Emancipations of Leander and Caesar: Manumission and the Law in Revolutionary South Carolina and Massachusetts," *Slavery and Abolition* 28 (August 2007): 235–54.

9. Sweet, *Bodies Politic*, 238; Dominic DeBrincat, "Discolored Justice: Blacks in New London County Court, 1710–1750," *Connecticut History* 44 (Fall 2005): 187; William E. Nelson, "The Reform of Common Law Pleading in Massachusetts, 1760–1830: Adjudication as a Prelude to Legislation," *University of Pennsylvania Law Review* 122 (November 1973): 97–110.

10. Edward Everett Hale, *Memoirs of a Hundred Years* (New York: Macmillan, 1902), 9; John J. Waters, Jr., *The Otis Family, in Provincial and Revolutionary Massachusetts* (Chapel Hill: University of North Carolina Press, 1968), 133.

11. Moore, *Notes on the History of Slavery*, 117; Willis P. Hazard, *Recollections of Olden Times* (Newport, R.I.: Sanborn, 1879), 23; *Newport Mercury* (May 4, 1792). On Kent: *The Boston News-Letter* (September 15, 1768); *Boston News-Letter* (October 5, 1769); *Proceedings of the Massachusetts Historical Society* 16 (1902): 116–17. There is no lawyer identified for Joan Jackson's freedom suit. The lawyer for John Jackson and John Rogers, Jr., in New London was James Rogers, Jr., the nephew of John Rogers, Jr. William Parker of Portsmouth, described as the leading lawyer of the province, had been practicing law for eighteen years when he took the case of Phebe Torr. Matthew Livermore was the attorney general of New Hampshire when he sued on behalf of Elisha Webb. Benjamin Kent, Lucy Pernam's divorce lawyer, handled the freedom suits of Jenny Slew and Rose and Salem Orne. Thomas Robinson of Newport was the lawyer for Mary Warmsley. Theodore Sedgwick and Tapping Reeve were the attorneys for Elizabeth Freeman. The attorneys for the other enslaved women plaintiffs are not known.

12. Emory Washburn, *Sketches of the Judicial History of Massachusetts from 1630 to the Revolution in 1775* (Boston: Charles C. Little and James Brown, 1840), 202, 232; *The Journal and Letters of Samuel Curwen an American in England from 1775 to 1784* (Boston: Little, Brown, 1842), 500; Sweet, "Bodies Politic," 280, 348–50; Thomas Robinson to Moses Brown, Newport, June 14, 1776, Moses Brown Papers, Rhode Island Historical Society, as quoted in Sweet, "Bodies Politic," 365; Hazard, *Recollections*, 20.

13. The first freedom suit, that of an enslaved couple in Massachusetts, never actually went to trial. The Reverend Samuel Sewall noted in his diary in June of 1700 that while he was reading the Bible "in came Bro Belknap to shew me a Petition he intended to present to the Genl Court" for "the freeing of a Negro and his wife, who were unjustly held in Bondage." M. Halsey Thomas, ed., *The Diary of Samuel Sewall* (Boston, 1700; New York: Farrar, Straus, and Giroux, 1973), 2:118. Brother Belknap may have been working with the couple to bring their case to court.

14. However, their son Adam remained the trusted servant of Joshua Hempstead of New London, never trying to run away or seek his freedom in the courts. William Richard Cutter, *Historic Homes and Places and Genealogical and Personal Memoirs Relating to the Families of Middlesex County, Massachusetts* (New York: Lewis Publishing Company, 1908), 2:1159; *James Rogers, Junr. v. Samuel Beebe*, June 1710, Box 1, Folder 2; January 31, 1711; Testimony of John Jackson and John Rogers, May 30, 1711, Box 5, Folder 9; *Samuel Beebe v. John Rogers and John Jackson*, June 1711, Box 1, Folder 3; November 8, 1717, Box 12, To the Sheriff of County of New London to his depute the constable of Norwich, January 5, 1718, Box 14, Folder 19; [no date] To the Sheriff of County of New London or his deputy, Box 34, Folder 8; June 1719, Box 14, Folder 19; November, 1726, Box 24, Folder 16; March 2, 1729, Box 24, Folder 9; [no date] Box 24, Folder 16, July 14, 1735, Box 44, Folder 4, In Court in Saybrook, August 12, 1741, Box 34, Folder 2; [no date], Box 45, Folder 12, RG 3, New London, County Court Collections, Connecticut State Library.

15. M. Louise Greene, *The Development of Religious Liberty in Connecticut* (Boston: Houghton, Mifflin and Company, 1905), 157, 160–64, 187, 204–6, 371; Frances Manwaring Caulkins, *History of New London, Connecticut: From the First Survey of the Coast in 1612, to 1860* (New London: H. D. Utley, 1895), 211; Robert G. Gardner, *Baptists of Early America: A Statistical History, 1639–1790* (Atlanta: Georgia Baptist Historical Society, 1983), 49.

16. New London Superior Court Files, September 1716–September 1717, Box 2, Petition by Hagar Wright, August 21, 1716, Connecticut State Archives, Connecticut State Library; Charles J. Hoadly, *The Public Records of the Colony of Connecticut* (Hartford, Conn.: Case, Lockwood and Brainard, 1890), 582–83.

17. George Waller-Frye, *Adam and Katherine Rogers of New London, Ct: James and Katherine Merritt of Killingworth, Ct.* (Storrs, Conn.: Spring Hill Press, 1977); New London County Court Files, 1691–1855, Sept. 1701, Box 1, Connecticut State Archives; Disposition of Widow Abigail Camp, *Jackson v. Stone*, Suffolk Files, v. 110, 11708, 71–74, Massachusetts Archives.

18. New London County Court Records, April 1708–November, 1711, Box 156, Connecticut State Archives.

19. She may have given birth in New London rather than on the island.

20. Testimony of John Jackson and John Rogers, May 30, 1711, Record Group 003, New London County Court Records, Files, Box 5, Folder 9, Connecticut State Archives. On the choice of a bench trial, see Allegra di Bonaventura, "This Little World: Family and Slavery in Old New England, 1678–1764," PhD diss., Yale University, 2008; New London County Court Files, Sept. 1698, Box 1, Folder 7; New London County Court Trials, vol. 7, September 1698, New London County Court Files, Connecticut State Library.

21. John R. Bolles and Anna B. Williams, *The Rogerenes; some hitherto unpublished annals belonging to the colonial history* (Boston: Dunhope Press, 1904), 223, 225.

22. It was known in Massachusetts that she was married and had a husband in Connecticut. William Barry, *A History of Framingham, Massachusetts* (Boston: James Munroe, 1847), 402.

23. R.G. 3, November 8, 1717, New London County Court, Box 12, Folder 7, Connecticut State Archives.

24. New London County Court Records, November 1715–November, 1716, Box 159, Connecticut State Archives.

25. There is no record of the legal argument in this case.

26. On kidnapping: William Willis Hayward, *The History of Hancock, New Hampshire, 1764–1889* (Lowell, Mass.: Vox Populi Press, 1889), 958. Her owner in New London Edward Robinson argued that he had been defrauded when he had purchased Sarah since she was actually a free person as determined by the Newport Superior Court. Robinson won his suit and received damages from Sarah's first owner for the cost of her lost services and his expenses incurred in pursuing her to Rhode Island. *Robinson v. Richards* (1734), New London Court Trials 18; New London County Court Files, Box 14, Folder 6 and Box 43, Folder 13, as cited in DeBrincat, "Discolored Justice," 193. Sons of Indian mothers and African fathers also sued for freedom on the basis that their mother was born free.

27. Robert D. Dishman, "'Natives of Africa, Now Forcibly Detained': The Slave Petitioners of Revolutionary Portsmouth," *Historical New Hampshire* 61 (Spring 2007): 6–28.

28. *Elisha Webb v. Daniel Wentworth*, Provincial Court Records No. 26121, as quoted in Dishman, "Breaking the Bonds," 88–90.

29. Perhaps Elisha did become a poor but respectable member of the Portsmouth free black community, but not before being defined as a sexual sinner. The year after she was free, she was brought before the quarter sessions court for having "a bastard child born of her body," probably fathered by Cesar. It is unclear how she pleaded or whether she was convicted of bastardy. The crime was punishable by a whipping of no more than ten stripes, or a fine. Thereafter she and Cesar lived their remaining years in Portsmouth and had six more children. It is not possible to learn from New Hampshire records whether she was legally married. The other women's freedom suit, that of Phebe Nong in 1750,

involved a master ignoring a valid indenture agreement and treating Nong as his slave. She sued in court, claiming she had been manumitted and was indentured. She won in a trial by jury and was awarded court costs. Her owner appealed to the Superior Court, which ordered a second jury trial. The jury confirmed the inferior court's decision to free Nong and award her court costs. *Nong v. Vincent Torr*, 1750, in Dishman, "Breaking the Bonds," 84–86.

30. Moore, *Notes on the History of Slavery*, 121; Theodore Parsons and Eliphalet Pearson, *A Forensic Dispute on the Legality of Enslaving the African* (Boston: Boyle for Leverette, 1773); on James Warren's slaveholdings, see *Proceedings of the Massachusetts Historical Society*, 1st ser., vol. 13 (1876): 101. For the role of "public opinion" in antislavery, see T. H. Breen, "Making History: The Force of Public Opinion and the Last Years of Slavery in Revolutionary Massachusetts," *Through a Glass Darkly: Reflections on Personal Identity*, ed. Ronald Hoffman, Mechal Sobel, and Fredrika J. Teute (Chapel Hill: University of North Carolina Press, 1997), 67–95.

31. Wroth and Zobel, *Legal Papers of John Adams* 2:54.

32. Legal status as a free person is one of the ways that Cheryl I. Harris thinks that whiteness was defined as a "property right." For her definitions of the property right of whiteness, see Cheryl I. Harris, "Whiteness as Property," *Harvard Law Review* 106 (June 1993): 1710–28.

33. Benjamin Kent may have argued that Jenny Slew was a spinster since her two marriages may not have been legally valid. But the legal notes of John Adams are unclear as to Kent's argument. Wroth and Zobel, *Legal Papers of John Adams*, 2:53.

34. Moore, *Notes on the History of Slavery*, 121.

35. On Oliver's slave owning, see Thomas Weston, *History of The Town of Middleboro, Massachusetts* (Boston: Houghton Mifflin, 1906), 104, 105. There was one exception to the prevailing sentiment in favor of slaves seeking their freedom in Massachusetts courts. Two years after Jenny Slew's successful freedom suit the Massachusetts Superior Court ruled against Amos Newport who sued for his freedom. Newport may have lost because he was elderly, purchased forty years before, and likely to become a public charge if he was freed. In a Cambridge court Margaret in *Margaret v. Muzzy* (1768) made the standard claim in a freedom suit, that she had been illegally imprisoned. Her attorney claimed that she was a free woman who had been kidnapped and later enslaved. John Adams, also a Son of Liberty who believed in the gradual emancipation of slavery, defended William Muzzy. The jury sided with Margaret; her owner appealed but the original verdict was upheld. She won her freedom but did not seek damages from Muzzy. Wroth and Zobel, *Legal Papers of John Adams*, 2:54.

36. Hill, "Slavery and Its Aftermath," 123; *Essex Institute of Historical Collections* 58 (1922), 139; "A List of Deaths in Beverly, Made by Robert Hale," *Historical Collections of the Essex Institute* 99 (1963), 94–95.

37. Hill, "Slavery and Its Aftermath," 121.

38. Mary Larcom Dow, *Old Days at Beverly Farms* (Beverly, Mass: North Shore Printing, 1921), 32; Beverly First Church Records, *Essex Institute Historical Collections* 36

(1900), 317; *Vital Records of Beverly, Massachusetts to the End of the Year 1849* (Topsfield, Mass.: Topsfield Historical Society, 1907), 2:361.

39. Beverly Historical Society Document 8300, *Juno v. David Larcom of Beverly*, 1774, as cited in Hill, "Slavery and Its Aftermath," 121; *Vital Records of Beverly*, 1:399–400.

40. Miss Sedgwick, "Slavery in New England," *Bentley's Miscellany* 34 (1853): 417–24. The younger sister was named Lizzie. Because it is unlikely that two sisters were both named Elizabeth, some have claimed that the younger Elizabeth was actually Freeman's daughter, Little Bett. For a biography of Freeman see Ben Z. Rose, *Mother of Freedom: Mum Bett and the Roots of Abolition* (Waverly, Mass.: Treeline Press, 2009).

41. One possibility is that Brom became a coachman for the Sedgwicks after he was emancipated. Drew, *If They Close the Door*, 43–44.

42. For his undergraduate days see *Life and Letters of Catharine M. Sedgwick* ed. Mary E. Dewey (New York: Harper and Brothers, 1871), 20 and Timothy Kenslea, *The Sedgwicks in Love: Courtship, Engagement, and Marriage in the Early Republic* (Boston: Northeastern University Press, 2006), 5.

43. John Fellows to Theodore Sedgwick, July 1, 1777, Sedgwick Family Papers, Massachusetts Historical Society, Boston; Electa F. Jones, *Stockbridge, Past and Present* (Springfield, Mass.: S. Bowles, 1854), 241; Drew, *If They Close the Door*, 30.

44. Bettye Hobbs Pruitt, ed., *The Massachusetts Tax Valuation List of 1771* (Boston: G. K. Hall, 1978).

45. Arthur Zilversmit, "Quok Walker, Mumbet, and the Abolition of Slavery in Massachusetts," *William and Mary Quarterly* 25 (Oct. 1968), 620; William O'Brien, "Did The Jennison Case Outlaw Slavery in Massachusetts," *William and Mary Quarterly* 17 (April 1960): 219–41; John D. Cushing, "The Cushing Court and the Abolition of Slavery in Massachusetts: More Notes on the 'Quock Walker Case,'" *American Journal of Legal History* 5 (April 1961): 118–44; Robert M. Spector, "The Quock Walker Cases (1781–1783)—Slavery, Its Abolition, and Negro Citizenship in Early Massachusetts," *Journal of Negro History* 53 (October 1968): 12–32; Harry Downs, "Unlikely Abolitionist: William Cushing and the Struggle against Slavery," *Journal of Supreme Court History* 29 (June 2004): 123–35. For an alternate reading of *Brom and Bett v. Ashley,* see Elaine MacEacheren, "Emancipation of Slaves in Massachusetts: A Reexamination 1770–1790," *Journal of Negro History* 55 (October 1970): 289–306; Drew, *If They Close the Door*, 36–40. A description of the Ashley house can be found in Arthur C. Chase, *The Ashleys: A Pioneer Berkshire Family* (Beverly, Mass.: Trustees of Reservations, 1982). For the record of the case in the Inferior Court of Common Pleas in 1781, see James M. Rosenthal, "Free Soil in Berkshire County, 1781," *New England Quarterly* 10 (March 1937): 781–85.

46. Theodore Sedgwick, *The Practicality of the Abolition of Slavery: A Lecture Delivered at the Lyceum in Stockbridge, Massachusetts, February 1831* (New York: J. Seymour, 1831), 13–18. The lecture was excerpted in *The Anti-Slavery Record* 2 (1836): 4–5.

47. Zilversmit, "Quok Walker"; O'Brien, "Did the Jennison"; Cushing, "Cushing Court"; Spector, "Quock Walker"; Downs, "Unlikely Abolitionist"; MacEacheren, "Emancipation."

48. *Brom & Bett v. J. Ashley Esq.*, Court Records, Berkshire County Courthouse. The fact that Brom's name was first probably reflected the assumption of the lawyers that a man had higher standing than a woman and therefore deserved first place. The court record suggests that at the time both Ashley slaves did not have surnames. Bernard A. Drew and Emilie Piper, "Mum Bett (Elizabeth Freeman), Antislavery Pioneer," *African American Heritage in the Upper Housatonic Valley*, ed. David Levinson (Great Barrington, Mass.: Berkshire, 2006), 23.

49. Catharine Maria Sedgwick, "Recollections of Childhood," Dewey, *Recollections*, 29, 53. For Lucy Lancaster of Newbuyport, another woman servant who nursed her ailing and insane master, see Fred E. Keay, "A Yankee Lord," *New England Magazine* 21 (February 1897): 734–43; Samuel Adams Drake, *New England Legends and Folklore* (Boston: Little, Brown, 1910), 300; Kevin N. Sweeney, "Mansion People: Kinship, Class, and Architecture in Western Massachusetts in the Mid Eighteenth Century," *Winterthur Portfolio* 19 (Winter 1984): 247.

50. Kenslea, *Sedgwicks in Love*, 57.

51. Drew, *If They Close the Door*, 33. Ben Z. Rose suggests that Humphrey was Elizabeth Freeman's common-law husband. He does not explain why Freeman would have been willing to buy out her "husband's" share six years later. Rose, *Mother*, 99.

52. Electa F. Jones, *Stockbridge, Past and Present: Or Records of an Old Mission Station (1854)* (Springfield, Mass.: Samuel Bowles, 1864), 243.

53. Drew, "Stockbridge," in *African American Heritage*, 184; Elizabeth Freeman, Stockbridge Assessor's Valuation List for 1829, Berkshire County Probate, 12008, in Glendyne R. Wergland, "Women, Men, Property, and Inheritance: Gendered Testamentary Customs in Western Massachusetts, 1800–1860," PhD diss., University of Massachusetts, Amherst, 2001, 192; Berkshire County Deed Books, Pittsfield Registry of Deeds, 46:98, 392–93 in Gary B. Nash and Graham Russell Gao Hodges, *Friends of Liberty: A Tale of Three Patriots, Two Revolutions, and the Betrayal that Divided a Nation: Thomas Jefferson, Thaddeus Koscuszko, and Agrippa Hull* (New York: Basic Books, 2008), 199.

54. For another version of her exchange see *Federal Writer's Project of the U.S. Works Progress Administration for Massachusetts, The Berkshire Hills* (New York: Funk and Wagnalls, 1939), 111. For her minister's support of the Massachusetts government, see Richard E. Welch, Jr., *Theodore Sedgwick, Federalist: A Political Portrait* (Middletown, Conn.: Wesleyan University, 1965), 49; Joanna Brooks, *American Lazarus: Religion and the Rise of African-American and Native American Literatures* (New York: Oxford University Press, 2003), 136–37. For an interpretation of the rebellion as a tax revolt against the state government, see Leonard I. Richards, *Shays' Rebellion: The American Revolution's Final Battle* (Philadelphia: University of Pennsylvania Press, 2002).

55. Jack Larkin, "The Faces of Change: Images of Self and Society in New England, 1790–1850," in *Meet Your Neighbors: New England Portraits, Painters, and Society, 1790–1850*, ed. Caroline F. Sloat (Amherst: University of Massachusetts Press, 1992), 9–22; Laurel Thatcher Ulrich, *The Age of Homespun: Objects and Stories in the Creation of an American Myth* (New York: Knopf, 2001), 237, 246–47; The First, Second, and Last Scene

of Morality, embroidered picture by Prudence Punderson, Preston, Conn., 1780, Connecticut Historical Society, Hartford.

56. Marla R. Miller, e-mail message to Elizabeth Pleck, October 19, 2005.

57. Linda France Stine, Melanie A. Cabak, and Mark D. Grover, "Blue Beads as African-American Cultural Symbols," *Historical Archaeology* 30 (1996), 65.

58. On the necklace, see Robert C. Winthrop, *Addresses and Speeches on Various Occasions, from 1878 to 1886* (Boston: Little, Brown, 1886), 478.

59. Dewey, ed., *Recollections*, 42; Mark Hopkins, *Early Letters of Mark Hopkins, and Others from His Brother and Their Mother, A Picture of Life in New England from 1770 to 1857* (New York: John Day, 1929), 196.

60. The Last Will and Testament of Elizabeth Freeman, Sheffield Family History Center, Sheffield, 1829; Glendyne R. Wergland, "Women, Men, Property, and Inheritance: Gendered Testamentary Customs in Western Massachusetts, 1800-1860," Ph.D. diss.: University of Massachusetts, Amherst, 2001, 202; Dewey, *Life and Letters*, 21; Newport Probate Records, 1, 219, 1784, as cited in Akeia A. F. Benard, "The Free African American Cultural Landscape: Newport, Rhode Island, 1774-1826," PhD diss., University of Connecticut, 2008, 198.

61. Sidney Kaplan and Emma Nogrady Kaplan, ed., *The Black Presence in the Era of the American Revolution* (Amherst: University of Massachusetts Press, 1989), 247.

62. Allen Walker Read, "The Speech of Negroes in Colonial America," *Journal of Negro History* 24 (July 1939): 247-58.

63. On Lemuel Haynes: Ruth Bogin, " 'Liberty Further Extended': A 1776 Antislavery Manuscript by Lemuel Haynes," *William and Mary Quarterly* 40 (January 1983): 85-105; Mary Kelley, ed., *The Power of Her Sympathy: The Autobiography and Journals of Catharine Maria Sedgwick* (Boston: Massachusetts Historical Society, 1993), 125-26. Cloe Tibbitt told men in East Greenwich, Rhode Island, helping her gain manumission that "it seemed like Death to her to go back to her masters again." John Reynolds to Moses Brown, May 22, 1790, Rhode Island Historical Society, as quoted in Sweet, *Bodies Politic*, 254.

64. Joanne Pope Melish thinks instead that Sedgwick's statement implied that other blacks, who were not as "saintly" as Elizabeth Freeman, might not be truly equal in Joanne Pope Melish, *Disowning Slavery: Gradual Emancipation and "Race" in New England, 1780-1860* (Ithaca, N.Y.: Cornell University Press, 1998), 183-84.

65. Sedgwick, *Practicality*, 18. Moses Brown, for example, believed that black people were intellectually inferior to whites. Brown was the leading abolitionist in Rhode Island, the sponsor of its gradual emancipation act, and had freed all of his own slaves. See Mark Thompson, *Moses Brown: Reluctant Reformer* (Chapel Hill: University of North Carolina Press, 1962), 186-89.

66. Harriet Martineau, *Retrospect of Western Travel* (New York: Harper and Brothers, 1838), 1:242-249.

67. Dewey, *Recollections*, 41.

68. Miss Sedgwick, "Slavery in New England," *Bentley's Miscellany* 34 (1853), 417-44. Black history in New England was based on both oral tradition and written sources.

William Cooper Nell's version of the story of Elizabeth Freeman was derived from the published version of the Sedgwick lecture. William C. Nell, *The Colored Patriots of the American Revolution, with sketches of Several Distinguished Colored Persons* (Boston: Robert F. Wallcut, 1855). W. E. B. DuBois asserted that Mumbet was the second wife of his great-grandfather and wrote to several relatives asking them if that was true. In fact, his cousin Lucinda told him that his great-grandfather's second wife was named Betsey Humphrey. W. E. B. DuBois, *Darkwater: Voices from within the Veil* (New York: Harcourt, Brace, 1920), 173. Douglas R. Egerton repeated DuBois' claim in *Death or Liberty: African Americans and Revolutionary America* (New York: Oxford University Press, 2009), 170.

69. *Berkshire Journal* (January 21, 1830).

Chapter 6

1. John Wood Sweet, *Bodies Politic: Negotiating Race in the American North, 1730–1830* (Baltimore: Johns Hopkins University Press, 2003), 436; Theophilus Parsons, *Memoir of Theophilus Parsons* (Boston: Ticknor and Fields, 1859), 176.

2. Kaplan and Emma Nogrady Kaplan ed., *The Black Presence in the Era of the American Revolution, 1770–1800*, Sidney (Amherst: University of Massachusetts Press, 1989), 17. For Phillis Wheatley's redefinition of her poetry as revolutionary verse, see Frank Shuffleton, "On Her Own Footing: Phillis Wheatley in Freedom," *Genius in Bondage: Literature of the Early Black Atlantic*, ed. Vincent Carretta and Philip Gould (Louisville, Ky.: University Press of Kentucky, 2001), 175–89; Charles L. Hill, "Slavery and Its Aftermath in Beverly, Massachusetts: Juno Larcom and Her Family," *Essex Institute Historical Collections* 116 (April 1980): 119, 122; *Newburyport Herald* (June 23, 1815); David O. White, *Connecticut's Black Soldiers, 1775–1783* (Chester, Conn.: Pequot Press, 1973), 20.

3. Harry Alonzo Cushing, *The Writings of Samuel Adams* (New York: G. P. Putnam's Sons, 1907), 3:218.

4. *Records of Governor and Council* (Montpelier, Vt: no publisher, 1878), 1:93.

5. Michael A. Bellesiles, *Revolutionary Outlaws: Ethan Allen and the Struggle for Independence on the Early American Frontier* (Charlottesville: University of Virginia Press, 1993), 234–35.

6. William James Morgan, ed., *Naval Documents of the American Revolution* (Washington, D.C.: Department of the Navy, 1980), 9:930–31. However, enslaved women were also taken on board American privateers and not freed. Glenn A. Knoblock, *"Strong and Brave Fellows": New Hampshire's Black Soldiers and Sailors of the American Revolution, 1775–1784* (Jefferson, N.C.: McFarland Publishing, 2003), 116.

7. Rhode Island General Assembly, Report to Congress concerning Negroes Carried off by the British in 1779, vol. 14, 61, Rhode Island Historical Society, Providence; *The Black Loyalist Directory: African Americans in Exile after the American Revolution*, ed. Graham Russell Hodges (New York: Garland Publications, 1996), 217–23; Graham Russell Hodges, *Root and Branch: African Americans in New York*

and East New Jersey, 1613–1863 (Chapel Hill: University of North Carolina Press, 1999), 155.

8. Edward Alfred Jones, *Loyalists of Massachusetts: Their Memorials, Petitions and Claims* (London: The Saint Catherine Press, 1930), 239; Cassandra Pybus, *Black Founders: The Unknown Story of Australia's First Black Settlers* (Sydney: University of New South Wales Press, 2006), 191; "Newton Prince, London pensioner," October 26, 2006, http://Boston1775:blogspot.com/2006_10_01_archive.html (October 1, 2008).

9. *Records of the State of Rhode Island, October, 1785* (Providence, R.I.: Providence Press Company, 1865), 143–44.

10. Holly Mayer, *Belonging to the Army: Camp Followers and Community during the American Revolution* (Columbia: University of South Carolina Press, 1999), 219.

11. George Washington Papers at the Library of Congress, 1741–1799: Series 5, Financial Papers, Margaret Thomas to Caleb Gibbs, April 4, 1778, Revolutionary War Accounts, Vouchers and Receipted Accounts, http://memory.loc.gov/ammem/gwhtm/gwhome.html (April 1, 2007); Worthington Chauncey Ford, *The Writings of George Washington: 1782–1785* (New York: G. P. Putnam's, 1891), 10:397–98.

12. Katherine Ray Greene, Warwick, Rhode Island, 1776, MSS. 9000-1, Rhode Island Historical Society.

13. *Berkshire Eagle* (April 24, 2005).

14. Leonard Woods Labaree, *The Public Records of the State of Connecticut from May, 1785, through January, 1789* (Hartford, Conn.: published by the state, 1945), 531–32; *Caesar Peters v. John Mann and Nathaniel Mann*, December 1789, Box 3, Folder 39, RG 3, New London County Court African Americans and People of Color Collection, Connecticut State Library, Hartford. Peters put a high price tag on being kidnapped, suing for £2000 damages and appealing the case to Superior Court where his damage suit was dismissed.

15. Journal of Sarah Winslow Demin, 1775, *The American Monthly Magazine* 69 (July, 1894): 69. Abigail's legal owner petitioned the Rhode Island General Assembly for permission to sell her but it was not clear if the permission was granted. John Wood Sweet, *Bodies Politic*, 247–48; *Memoir of Mrs. Chloe Spear, A Native of Africa, Who was enslaved in Childhood, and died in Boston, January 3, 1815 . . . Aged 65 Years* (Boston: James Loring, 1832), 34.

16. K. E. Conlin, "Dinah and the Slave Question in Vermont," *Vermont Quarterly* 21 (October 1953): 289–92. The state's Bill of Rights stipulated gradual emancipation, thereby raising the question of the intent of the authors of the state's constitution. For a general history of the end of slavery in the North, see Arthur Zilversmit, *The First Emancipation: The Abolition of Slavery in the North* (Chicago: University of Chicago Press, 1967).

17. It has been wrongly claimed that a "slave auction" occurred in Cambridge in 1793. Instead, the estate of a former owner whose slave had been freed offered land instead of the guarantee of a yearly annuity to his former slave. *Watson v. Cambridge*, 15 Mass. 287 (1818); Lucius R. Paige, *History of Cambridge, Mass., 1630–1877* (Boston: H. O Houghton, 1877), 681.

18. In Rhode Island Moses Brown attached a provision for gradual emancipation to legislation providing for the public funding of the education of the children of slave mothers; the provision disappeared in subsequent legislation. On gradual emancipation in Connecticut, see David Menschel, "Abolition without Deliverance: The Law of Connecticut Slavery1784–1848," *Yale Law Journal* 111 (2001): 187–91.

19. For the real-estate holdings of Phillis, a free black woman in Killingly, Connecticut, in 1775, see Charles J. Hoadly, *The Public Records of the Colony of Connecticut from May, 1775 to June, 1776, v. 15* (Hartford, Conn.: Case, Lockwood, and Bainard Company, 1890), 66; Hazel Blossom owned property in Pittsfield in 1790. Frances Jones-Snead, "Pittsfield," *African American Heritage in the Upper Housatonic Valley* (Great Barrington, Mass.: Berkshire Publishing Company, 2006), 166; Newport Probate Records, 2: 353, as quoted in Akeia A. F. Benard, "The Free African American Cultural Landscape: Newport, Rhode Island, 1774–1826," Ph.D. diss., University of Connecticut, 2008, 185.

20. Benard, 33; Edmond Frank Peters and Eleanor Bradley Peters, *Peters of New England: A Genealogy, and Family History* (New York: The Knickerbocker Press, 1903), 260–61; Elizabeth Buffum Chace, *Anti-Slavery Reminiscences* (Central Falls, R.I.: R. L. Freeman, 1891), 7; "Notes and Queries," *The Newport Historical Magazine* (July 1882): 261.

21. Mark J. Sammons and Valerie Cunningham, *Black Portsmouth: Three Centuries of African-American Heritage* (Durham: University of New Hampshire Press, 2004), 105–6; Erik R. Tuveson, "'A People of Color': A Study of Race and Racial Identification in New Hampshire, 1750–1825," MA thesis, University of New Hampshire, 1995, no page.

22. Kaplan and Kaplan, *The Black Presence*, 261–63; Edmund Wheeler, *The History of Newport, New Hampshire: From 1766 to 1878* (Concord, N.H.: Republican Press Association, 1879), 9; E. Merrill Beach, *From Valley Forge to Freedom: A Story of a Black Patriot* (Chester, Conn.: Pequot Press, 1975), 41; Knoblock, *Strong*, 249; Elise Lemire, *Black Walden: Slavery and Its Aftermath in Concord, Massachusetts* (Philadelphia: University of Pennsylvania Press, 2009), 131–132.

23. Reverend Samuel Hopkins, *The System of Doctrines, Contained in Divine Revelation, Explained and Defended* (Boston: Isaiah Thomas and Ebenezer T. Andrews, 1793), xi; John White Chadwick, *William Ellery Channing: Minister of Religion* (Boston: Houghton and Mifflin, 1903), 22; Pam Mathias Peterson, *Marblehead Myths, Legends and Lore* (Charleston, S.C.: History Press, 2007), 30.

24. Sweet, *Bodies Politic*, 336; *Report of the Record Commissioners, Selectman's Minutes, 1787–1798* (Boston: Rockwell and Churchill, 1894), 27:82, 83; Benjamin L Carp, *Rebels Rising: Cities and the American Revolution* (New York: Oxford University Press, 2007), 39; Ralph E. Luker, "'Under Our Own Vine and Fig Tree': From African Unionism to Black Denominationalism in Newport, Rhode Island, 1760–1876," *Slavery and Abolition* 12 (September 1991): 29; Abram English Brown, *Faneuil Hall and Faneuil Hall Market* (Boston: Lee and Shepard, 1900), 135; *A Report of the Record Commissioners of the City of Boston Containing the Records of Boston Selectmen, 1787 through 1798* (Boston: Rockwell and Churchill, 1896), 27:189; Silence Will, "Waterbury's African Americans," http://www.fortunatestory.org/Waterburyafricanamericans/silencewill.asp (July 1, 2008).

25. *Massachusetts Mercury* (September 29, 1797); Ruth Wallis Herndon, "The Domestic Cost of Seafaring: Town Leaders and Seamen's Families in Eighteenth Century Rhode Island," in *Iron Men, Wood Women: Gender and Seafaring in the Atlantic World, 1700–1920,* ed. Margaret Creighton and Lisa Norling (Baltimore: Johns Hopkins University Press, 1996), 55–60.

26. Ezra Stiles, *The Literary Diary of Ezra Stiles* (New York: Scribner's Sons, 1901), 3:51.

27. Letter of Abigail Adams, Jan–Feb. 1784, *The Book of Abigail and John: Selected Letters of the Adams Family, 1762–1784,* ed. L. H. Butterfield, Marc Friedlander, and Mary-Jo Kline (Boston: Northeastern University Press, 2002), 375; Eric Nellis and Anne Decke Cecere, *The Eighteenth-Century Records of the Boston Overseers of the Poor* (Boston: The Colonial Society of Massachusetts, 2007), 80; Gary B. Nash and Graham Russell Hodges, *Friends of Liberty: A Tale of Three Patriots, Two Revolutions, and the Betrayal That Divided a Nation: Thomas Jefferson, Thaddeus Koscuisko, and Agrippa Hull* (New York: Basic Books, 2008), 13; Nathaniel Boutin, *The History of Concord* (Concord, Mass.: Bening W. Sanborn, 1856), 252; Ruth Wallis Herndon and Ella Wilcox Sekatau, "Pauper Apprenticeship in Narragansett County: A Different Name for Slavery in Early New England," *Slavery/AntiSlavery in New England,* ed. Peter Benes and Jane Montague Benes (Boston: Boston University Scholarly Publications, 2005), 56–70.

28. *Vital Records of Salem, Mass. To the end of year 1849* (Salem, Mass.: Essex Institute, 1916); Hill, "Slavery and Its Aftermath," 123; Judith L. Van Buskirk, "Claiming their Due: African Americans in the Revolutionary War and its Aftermath," *War and Society in the American Revolution: Mobilization and Home Front,* ed. John Resch and Walter Sargent (DeKalb: Northern Illinois University, 2007), 140; Len Watson, "The History of the Cross Street African Episcopal Zion Church," MS., as quoted in Kathleen Housley, "'Yours for the Oppressed': The Life of Jehiel C. Beman," *Journal of Negro History* 77 (Winter 1992): 27.

29. Mary Hartford Papers in Jeremy Belknap Papers, Massachusetts Historical Society, Boston.

30. Inhabitants and Estates of the Town of Boston, 1630–1900, Thwing Reference Code 40127; Daniel Cruson, *The Slaves of Central Fairfield County: The Journey from Slave to Freeman in Nineteenth-Century Connecticut* (Charleston, S.C.: History Press, 2007), 50.

31. *List of Persons Whose Names Have Been Changed in Massachusetts 1780–1892* (Boston: Wright and Potter, 1893), 62.

32. Between 1770 and 1790 the pace of manumission quickened: more than 40 percent of probated wills mentioning slaves provided for their unconditional manumission. It is not known whether manumission rates were higher among women than men, but there is no reason to think that was so. Peter Benes, "Slavery in Boston Households, 1647–1770," *Slavery/Antislavery,* 25; Elaine MacEachern, "Emancipation of Slavery in Massachusetts: A Reexamination, 1770–1790," *Journal of Negro History* 55 (October 1970): 296.

33. *Berkshire Chronicle* (July 14, 1788); *Berkshire Chronicle* (February 20, 1798); *Albany Centinel* (June 29, 1798); *Connecticut Courant and Weekly Intelligencer* (March 9, 1779); "Pioneer Colored People of Berkshire," *The Berkshire Hills* 1 (September 1900): no page; Graham Russell Hodges and Alan Brown, *Pretends to Be Free: Runaway Slave Advertisements from Colonial and Revolutionary New York and New Jersey* (New York: Garland, 1994), 64; *Salem Gazette* (January 16, 1783).

34. *Granite Freeman* (May 22, 1846); *The Liberator* (January 1, 1847). Evelyn B. Gerson spent ten years researching the story of Ona Judge for her master's thesis. Evelyn B. Gerson, "A Thirst for Compleat Freedom: Why Fugitive Slave Ona Judge Staines Never Returned to her Master," MA thesis, Harvard University, 2000; William Wiencek's *An Imperfect God: George Washington, His Slaves, and the Creation of America* (New York: Farrar, Straus, and Giroux, 2003) devotes a chapter to Ona Judge's struggle for freedom. Fritz Hirschfeld published some of the major documents about her life and Washington's efforts to recapture her in *George Washington and Slavery: A Documentary Portrayal* (Columbia: University of Missouri Press, 1997), 112–17; Robert B. Dishman, "Ona Maria Judge Takes French Leave to Live Free in New Hampshire," *Historical New Hampshire* 62 (Spring 2008): 41–65.

35. Jacqueline Barbara Carr, *After the Siege: A Social History of Boston 1775–1800* (Boston: Northeastern University Press, 2000), 101; "Warnings to Negroes in Salem in 1790," *Essex Institute Historical Collections* 44 (1908): 93–94; George H. Moore, *Notes on the History of Slavery* (New York: D. Appleton and Company, 1866), 23; John F. Collin, *History of the Country, having Particular Reference to the Tariff, Slavery and State Sovereignty* 4 (Hudson, N.H.: M. Parker Williams, 1884), 7; "Notice to Blacks," *Massachusetts Mercury* (September 16, 1800). Authorities took seriously the claim of a black man, one of the few remaining slaves in Massachusetts, who told them that local blacks were planning to kill white people; Chernon Momodu Sesay, Jr., "Freemasons of Color: Revolutionary Black Boston and the Origins of Freemasonry, 1770–1807," PhD diss., Northwestern University, 2006, 120.

36. Kunal M. Parker, "Making Blacks Foreigners: The Legal Construction of Former Slaves in Post-Revolutionary Massachusetts," *Utah Law Review* 75 (2001): 99, 107.

37. Nellis and Cecere, *Eighteenth-Century Records*, 60–62; Ruth Wallis Herndon, "'Who Died an Expence to this Town': Poor Relief in Eighteenth Century Rhode Island," in *Down and Out in Early America*, ed. Billy G. Smith (University Park, Pa.: Pennsylvania State University Press, 2004), 147; Selectmen's Minutes, 1789, *A Report of the Record Commissioner of the City of Boston* (Boston: Rockwell and Churchill, 1896), 79.

38. Parker, "Making Blacks Foreigners," 84–88.

39. Ibid., 117.

40. Warning out persisted into the early nineteenth century in Massachusetts but the rules of town residence on which it was based were eliminated. Nellis and Cecere, *Eighteenth-Century Records*, 97–98. On warning out and settlement laws see Josiah Henry Benton, *Warning Out in New England* (Boston: W. B. Clarke, 1911); Margaret Greech, *Three Centuries of Poor Law Administration: A Study of Legislation in Rhode Island* (Chicago: University of Chicago Press, 1936).

41. "Warnings to Negroes in Salem," 93; Warning Out Book 1791–1793, Records of the Overseers of the Poor, Massachusetts Historical Society; Bernard A. Drew, *If They Close the Door on You, Go in the Window* (Great Barrington: Attic Revivals Press, 2004), 11; Allan Kulikoff, "The Progress of Inequality in Revolutionary Boston," *William and Mary Quarterly* 28 (July 1971): 399–401; J. M. Opal, *Beyond the Farm: National Ambitions in Rural New England* (Philadelphia: University of Pennsylvania Press, 2008), 47.

42. Lynne Withey, *Urban Growth in Colonial Rhode Island: Newport and Providence in the Eighteenth Century* (Albany: State University of New York Press, 1984), table D-5, 134.

43. Ruth Wallis Herndon, *Unwelcome Americans: Living on the Margin in Early New England* (Philadelphia: University of Pennsylvania Press, 2001), 20.

44. Ibid.

45. Ibid., 206.

46. Ibid., 50.

47. Order for the removal of Roseannah Brown, June 8, 1797; Indenture of Susannah Brown, October 2, 1797, Exeter Town Records, 1740–1869, Box 8, Folders 2 and 6, MSS. 197, Rhode Island Historical Society.

48. Herndon, *Unwelcome Americans*, 85.

49. Ibid., 57–60.

50. Providence Town Papers, Warrant, July 23, 1782, Series 1, Vol. 6, No. 2754, MS. 214, Rhode Island Historical Society.

51. Dr. John Eliot to Dr. Jeremy Belknap, n.d., in "Letters and Documents Regarding Slavery," ed. Charles Deane, orig. printed in *Massachusetts Historical Society Collections* 3 (Cambridge: Wilson, 1877), 383. There were major crackdowns against brothels in Boston in this period, but largely ones operated by white women; the one black person prosecuted for running a lewd and disorderly house in Boston was a man. Anti-brothel riots in Providence may have helped pave the way for legislation in the state barring interracial marriage in 1798 and slapping a stiff penalty of $200 against anyone who solemnized such a marriage. Kelly Alisa Ryan, "Regulating Passion: Sexual Behavior and Citizenship in Massachusetts, 1740–1820," PhD diss., University of Maryland, 2006, 304; *An Act to Prevent Clandestine Marriages, sec. 5, The Public Laws of the state of Rhode Island . . . January, 1798* (Providence: no publisher, 1798), 483, 611.

Chapter 7

1. Pension File, Saunders, Phillis, Revolutionary War, *HeritageQuest.com*, series: M 805, roll 851, image 41, File W 18103 (August 13, 2008).

2. Rev. James Hill Fitts, *History of Newfields, New Hampshire, 1638–1911* (Concord, N.H.: Rumford Press, 1912), 103; Glenn A. Knoblock, *"Strong and Brave Fellows": New*

Hampshire's Black Soldiers and Sailors of the American Revolution, 1775–1784 (Jefferson, N.C.: McFarland and Company, 2003), 41; Nellie Palmer George, "Mansion House of Wentworth Cheswill," *The Granite Monthly* 142, no. 7 (July 1916): 203–8.

3. Joanna Brooks, "The Early American Public Sphere and the Emergence of a Black Print Counterpublic," *William and Mary Quarterly* 62 (January 2005): 67–92; Joanna Brooks, *American Lazarus: Religion and the Rise of African-American and Native American Literatures* (New York: Oxford University Press, 2003), 136–38; Nathaniel Bouton, *The History of Concord* (Concord, N.H.: Bening W. Sanborn, 1856), 739; Eldridge Henry Goss, *The History of Melrose, County of Middlesex, Mass.* (Melrose, Mass.: City of Melrose, 1902), 215; Richard S. Newman, *Freedom's Prophet: Bishop Richard Allen, the AME Church, and the Black Founding Fathers* (New York: New York University Press, 2008), 102.

4. *Genius of Universal Emancipation* (January 1832), 212; William Cooper Nell, *The Colored Patriots of the American Revolution* (Boston: J. B. Yerrinton and Son, 1855), 65; *The Imperial Magazine, or Compendium of Religious, Moral, and Philosophical Knowledge* (1832), 152.

5. Roy Finkenbine argues that those who sued for their freedom and won court damages from their owners were receiving a form of compensation from their owners, but in fact, any winner in a court case that was appealed received such damages. Owners were paying damages not because the plaintiff had been a slave but because they lost a case upon appeal. See his "Belinda's Petition: Reparations for Slavery in Revolutionary Massachusetts," *William and Mary Quarterly* 64 (January 2007): 95–104.

6. Letter of Timothy Pickering, Sr., June 4, 1777, *Proceedings of the Massachusetts Historical Society* 53 (1920): 221.

7. James Swan, *A Disuasion to Great-Britain, 1772*, reprinted in *Am I Not a Man and a Brother: The Antislavery Crusade of Revolutionary America 1688–1788*, ed. Roger Bruns (New York: Chelsea Brothers, 1977), 200–15; Samuel Francis Batchelder, *Notes on Colonel Henry Vassal (1721–1769), his wife Penelope Royall, his house at Cambridge, and his slaves Tony & Darby* (Cambridge: Cambridge Historical Society, 1917), 69; "A Brief History of the White and Black Vassals," *Longfellow House Bulletin* 7 (June 2003): 3–4; *Acts and Laws of the Commonwealth of Massachusetts* (Boston: Wright and Potter, 1890), 262. When Anthony Vassal died in 1810, his wife Cuba tried to receive his pension, but was told it did not cover her. A member of the Massachusetts House of Representatives presented a petition on her behalf and she received her husband's pension during her lifetime. *The Cambridge of 1776* (Cambridge: Lockwood, Brooks, and Company, 1875), 100; "Darby Vassal," *The Liberator* (November 22, 1861). The John Vassal house remains, now called the Longfellow house. Anthony and Cuba moved out of their cabin in 1787 and purchased a home in Cambridge on the corner of Massachusetts Avenue and Shepard Street.

8. Robert E. Desrochers, Jr., "Slave-for-Sale Advertisements and Slavery in Massachusetts, 1704–1781," *William and Mary Quarterly* 59 (July 2002): 623–64.

9. On the Surinam plantation of Elizabeth Royall, see Henry Fritz-Gilbert Waters, *New England Historical and Genealogical Register 1896* vol. 50 (Boston: New England

Historical and Genealogical Register, 1896), 538; *Boston Evening Post* (March 22, 1762); Edwin M. Bacon, *Walks and Rides in the Country Round About Boston* (Cambridge, Mass.: Riverside, 1897), 90. *Isaac Royall and His Family*, Robert Feke, 1741, is in the Harvard Law Art Collection. The Museum of Fine Arts in Boston owns *Mary and Elizabeth Royall, c. 1758*, and *Isaac Royall, 1769*, both painted by John Singleton Copley.

10. James Oliver Horton, *Free People of Color: Inside the African American Community* (Washington, D.C.: Smithsonian Press, 1993), 108; "The Belcher Papers," *Collections of the Massachusetts Historical Society* 6 (1893), 7.

11. James Kirby Martin, "A Model for the Coming American Revolution: The Birth and Death of the Wentworth Oligarchy in New Hampshire, 1741–1766," *Journal of Social History* 4 (Autumn 1970), 50; Anne Rowe Cunningham, ed., *Letters and Diary of John Rowe* (Boston: W. B. Clarke, 1903), 44; *New London Gazette* (November 30, 1775).

12. *The Manuscripts of the Earl of Dartmouth* (London: Eyre and Spottiswoode, 1895), 2:273; Henry Welder Foote, *Annals of King's Chapel* (Boston: Little, Brown, & Co., 1896), 2:311; *Massachusetts Spy* (July 17, 1770); *Boston Post-Boy* (May 31, 1773); *Vital Records of Medford Mass. To the end of the Year 1849* (Boston: New England Historic Genealogical Society, 1907), 1:466; Mary H. Northend, *Historic Homes of New England* (Boston: Little, Brown & Co., 1914), 228. For an enslaved woman who committed suicide when her master died, see *Collections of the Dover, N.H. Historical Society*, Dover: Scales and Quimby, 1894, 1:193.

13. David Maas, "The Massachusetts Loyalists and the Problem of Amnesty, 1775–1790," *Loyalists and Community in North America*, ed. Robert M. Calhoon, Timothy M. Barnes, and George A. Rawlyk (Westport, Conn.: Greenwood Press, 1994), 65–74; Colin Nicolson and Stuart Scott, "A 'great national calamity': Sir William Pepperell and Isaac Royall, reluctant Loyalists," *Historical Journal of Massachusetts* 28 (Summer 2000): 117–41.

14. Will and Codicils of Isaac Royall, item 6th, May 26, 1778, Harvard Law School Library, Cambridge.

15. The record of her children's baptism is the first time Belinda's name appears in Royall's records. *Vital Records*, 173. Her son could have died or been sold. In his will Royall gave "my Negro Joseph" to his son-in-law. Since he owned several slaves named Joseph, it is unclear whether this Joseph was Belinda's son.

16. Belinda, "Petition of an African slave, to the legislature of Massachusetts," *The American Museum, or, Repository of Ancient and Modern* Fugitive Pieces, *Prose and Practical* 1 (June 1787): 538–40; Samuel A. Drake, "Hobgoblin Hall," *Appleton's Journal of Literature, Science and Art* 10 (August 9, 1873): 161; ed., Sidney Kaplan and Emma Nogrady Kaplan, *The Black Presence in the Era of the American Revolution,* (Amherst: University of Massachusetts Press, 1989), 243.

17. For the sentimental portrayal of Africa, see Mukhtar Ali Isani, " 'Far from Gambia's Golden Shore': The Black in Late Eighteenth-Century American Imaginative Literature," *William and Mary Quarterly* 36 (July 1979): 353–72. The only area in West Africa with heavily forested mountains is in the Volta region, now part of Ghana.

18. Jerome S. Handler, "Survivors of the Middle Passage: Life Histories of Enslaved Africans in British America," *Slavery and Abolition* 23 (April 2002): 36.

19. Belinda, "Petition of an African slave."

20. *The Union Magazine, and Imperial Register* (1801), 154.

21. *Massachusetts Spy* (May 29, 1783); *Salem Gazette* (May 29, 1783); *Impartial Herald* (July 12, 1784); *Western Star* (August 5, 1784); *Newport Mercury* (May 31, 1783); *Pennsylvania Evening Post* (June 11, 1783); *New Jersey Gazette* (June 18, 1783).

22. "The Complaint of Belinda, an African," *The Weekly Miscellany* 2, no. 35 (September 1, 1783): 207–8; Finkenbine, "Belinda's Petition," 1–17.

23. "Colonial Era African Americans Who Lived at or May Have Visited the Royall House, the Royall House and Slave Quarters," http://royallhouse.org/slaves.php (July 1, 2008).

24. Charles E. Hall, *Portrait of an Abolitionist: A Biography of George Luther Stearns, 1809–1867* (Westport, Conn.: Greenwood, 1996), 4; David Brainard Hall, The *Halls of New England: Genealogical and Biographical* (Albany, N.Y.: Munsell's, 1883), 334; Bettye Hobbs Pruitt, ed., *The Massachusetts Tax Valuation List of 1771* (Boston: G. K. Hall and Company, 1978).

25. Belinda, "Petition of an African slave," 538–40.

26. *The Union Magazine*, 154.

27. Receipt dated August 21, 1786, in David Stoddard Family Greenough Papers, Massachusetts Historical Society, as quoted in Margot Lee Minardi, "A Rugged Maze: The Emancipation of Belinda and Chloe Spear," BA honors thesis, Harvard University, 2000, 35–36.

28. "Petition of Belinda an African, to the Honourable Senate and House of Representatives in General Court Assembled, February 14, 1783," Revolution Resolves, 239: 11–14, Massachusetts Archives, 1787; *Acts and Resolves of Massachusetts, 1786–1787* (Boston, 1893), 816; "Petition of Belinda, an African, to the Honorable Senate and the Honorable House of Representatives of the Commonwealth of Massachusetts in General Court Assembled," March 5, 1790, in House Unpassed Legislation, docket no. 3304, Massachusetts Archives; "Committee Report on Belinda, an African," 1790, docket no. 3314, Massachusetts State Archives, Boston. Roy E. Finkenbine uncovered the 1790 petition in the Massachusetts State Archives. Finkenbine, "Belinda's Petition," 1–17.

29. *Genius of Universal Emancipation* (May 30, 1832), 12; William Cooper Nell, *Colored Patriots of the American Revolution* (Boston: J. B. Yerrinton and Son, 1855), 65; *The Imperial Magazine* (1832), 152. For the reading of Belinda's petition by the DAR in 1904, see *The Medford Historical Register* 7 (1904): 68.

30. Daniel T. V. Huntoon, *History of the Town of Canton* (Cambridge, Mass.: John Wilson, 1893), 503–4.

31. Harry E. Davis, "Documents Relating to Negro Masonry in America," *Journal of Negro History* 21 (October 1936): 426; David O. White, *Connecticut's Black Soldiers 1775–1783* (Chester, Conn.: Pequot Press, 1973), 54. Noticeably absent were any black organizations in Connecticut or the emergence of a singular black leader there. On Newport:

William H. Robinson, ed., *The Proceedings of the Free African Union Society and the African Benevolent Society Newport Rhode Island 1780–1824* (Providence: Urban League of Rhode Island, 1976), 84.

32. Michael A. Gomez, *Exchanging Our Country Marks: The Transformation of African Identities in the Colonial and Antebellum South* (Chapel Hill: University of North Carolina Press, 1998), 101; Melville J. Herskovits, *The Myth of the Negro Past* (New York: Harper, 1941), 161–67.

33. J. R. Pole, *Political Representation in England and the Origins of the American Republic* (New York: St. Martin's Press, 1966), 273.

34. For a general history of the African Union see Ralph E. Luker, " 'Under Our Own Vine and Fig Tree': From African Unionism to Black Denominationalism in Newport, Rhode Island, 1760–1876," *Slavery and Abolition* 12 (1991): 23–48. Elsa Barkley Brown argues that in the immediate aftermath of the Civil War black women in the South thought of the franchise as a community rather than individual right. They appeared at political rallies and made sure that black men showed up at the polls; they even punished those men who voted Democratic. One eyewitness observed a black woman place her husband's vote in the ballot box. By contrast, in New England black women considered collective political protest as a man's domain. Elsa Barkley Brown, "Negotiating and Transforming the Public Sphere: African American Political Life in the Transition from Slavery to Freedom," *Public Culture* 7 (Fall 1994): 107–46.

35. Akeia A. F. Benard, "The Free African American Cultural Landscape: Newport, RI, 1774–1826," PhD diss., University of Connecticut, 2008, 181; Robinson, *Proceedings,* 23–24.

36. James C. Garman, "Viewing the Color Line Through the Material Culture of Death," *Historical Anthropology* 28 (1994): 74–93; Franklin Bowditch Dexter, *The Literary Diary of Ezra Stiles, D.D., L.L.D* (New York: Scribner's, 1901), 1:52.

37. Robinson, *Proceedings,* 81, 83, 94, 97. For black women's role in the North, see Jane E. Dabel, *A Respectable Woman: The Public Roles of African American Women in 19th-Century New York* (New York: New York University Press, 2008).

38. Wilkins Updike, *Memoirs of the Rhode-Island Bar* (Boston: Thomas H. Webb and Co., 1842), 100. Although Mrs. Phillis Bradstreet died in the almshouse, her obituary, published in eleven New England newspapers, claimed that she was "once a Princess in Africa." *Newburyport Herald* (January 13, 1815); *Reporter* (February 1, 1815); *Poulson's American Daily Advertiser* (January 12, 1817); *Columbia Centinel* (January 11, 1815); *The Repertory* (January 12, 1815); *Salem Gazette* (January 13, 1815); *Boston Yankee* (January 13, 1815); *Essex Register* (January 14, 1815); *Portsmouth Oracle* (January 14, 1815); *New England Palladium* (January 17, 1815); *New Hampshire Gazette* (January 17, 1815).

39. George C. Channing, *Early Recollections of Newport, R.I., from the Year 1783 to 1811* (Newport: A. J. Ward, 1868), 170–71; Theresa Guzman Stokes, "Duchess Quamino: The Pastry Queen of Rhode Island," *East Bay Newspapers* (February 22, 2005).

40. Robinson, *Proceedings,* 93.

41. Charles T. Brooks, *William Ellery Channing: A Centennial Memory* (Boston: Roberts Brothers, 1880), 56–57. So close was she to the Channings that the doctor who treated her in her final illness referred to her as Duchess Channing. Accounts, 1804, Senter Papers, Pawtucket, MS 165, Rhode Island Historical Society, Providence.

42. Mary Beth Norton, *Founding Mothers and Fathers: Gendered Power and the Forming of American Society* (New York: Knopf, 1996), 139–40.

43. Ann and Dickran Tashijan, "The Afro-American Section of Newport, Rhode Island's Common Burying Ground," in *Cemeteries and Gravemarkers: Voices of American Culture,* ed. Richard E. Meyer (Logan: Utah State University Press, 1992), 195; Garman, "Viewing the Color Line," 21–31; Cesar Lyndon, Journal, Dec. 17, 1765, January 2, 1765, June 27, 1766, Rhode Island Historical Society, Providence.

44. Robinson, *Proceedings,* 137.

45. Ibid., xvi–xiv.

46. Norton, *Founding Mothers and Fathers,* 253.

47. Letter of Phillis Wheatley to John Thornton, October 30, 1774, as quoted in John Shields, ed., *The Collected Works of Phillis Wheatley* (New York: Oxford University Press, 1985), 184.

48. House Unpassed Legislation, SC1, Ser. 230, 1798, 430, Petition of Africans to Enable Them to Return to Africa, Massachusetts State Archives.

49. For black correspondence regarding emigration that emphasized the importance of young women available to live in a black settlement in Sierra Leone, see Dorothy Sterling, ed., *Speak Out in Thunder Tones: Letters and Other Writings by Black Northerners 1787–1865* (New York: DaCapo Press, 1998), 7–12. For the failure of an exploratory effort by Rhode Island free blacks to buy land from the British in Sierra Leone, see George E. Brooks, Jr., "The Providence African Society's Sierra Leone Emigration Scheme, 1794–1795: Prologue to the African Colonization Movement," *The International Journal of African Historical Studies* 7 (1974): 183–202. For more on black emigrationists in New England, see Floyd J. Miller, *The Search for a Black Nationality: Black Emigration and Colonization 1787–1863* (Urbana: University of Illinois Press, 1975), 3–20; James T. Campbell, *Middle Passages: African American Journeys to Africa* (New York: Penguin, 2006), 1–13; W. Bryan Rommel-Ruiz, "Colonizing the Black Atlantic: The African Colonization Movements in Postwar Rhode Island and Nova Scotia," *Slavery and Abolition* 27 (December 2006): 349–65; W. Bryan Rommel-Ruiz, *Between African and Colored: The Black Atlantic and African Americans in Rhode Island and Nova Scotia, 1750–1850* (Philadelphia: University of Pennsylvania Press, 2008).

50. In the North the first black women's organization was the Female Benevolent Society of St. Thomas, founded in Philadelphia in 1793. It consisted of members from a newly formed black church, St. Thomas Episcopal Church in Philadelphia, the first black church in the North. Most of the women who belonged to this church were laundresses and one was a huckster. This mutual benefit society grew out of women's economic need and their sense of financial responsibility for themselves. Within St. Thomas Episcopal itself, the women's organization preceded by two years the founding of a similar men's

organization. Bruce Dorsey, *Reforming Men and Women: Gender in the Antebellum City* (Ithaca, N.Y.: Cornell University Press, 2002), 12.

51. *The Farmer's Cabinet* (February 26, 1846).

52. John Lord, *Beacon Lights of History* 8 (New York: Fords, Howard, and Hulbert, 1896), 19; Mark J. Sammons and Valerie Cunningham, *Black Portsmouth: Three Centuries of African-American Heritage* (Lebanon, N.H.: University Press of New England, 2004), 91–94.

53. Charles W. Brewster, *Rambles about Portsmouth: Sketches of Persons, Localities, and Incidents of Two Centuries* (Portsmouth, N.H.: Lewis W. Brewster, 1878), 155.

54. The other version of their family history was that they were cousins.

55. Valerie Cunningham, "'That the name of slave may not more be heard': The New Hampshire Petition for Freedom, 1779," *Slavery/Antislavery in New England*, ed. Peter Benes and Jane Benes (Boston: Boston University, 2005), 71–81; H. H. Price and Gerald E. Talbot, *Maine's Visible Black History* (Portland, Maine: Tilbury House, 2006), 10; Knoblock, "Strong," 184.

56. Brewster, *Rambles*, 177.

57. Sammons and Cunningham, *Black Portsmouth*, 93; *The Oracle of the Day* (November 23, 1796); Blaine Whipple, *History and Genealogy of "Elder" John Whipple of Ipswich, Massachusetts* (Victoria, B.C.: Trafford Publishing, 2006), 146–47.

58. *Portsmouth Journal of Literature and Politics* (May 30, 1829); "North Church Records," *The New Hampshire Genealogical Record* (January 1908–October 1903), 5:13, 15, 16, 74, 77, 79. On widows remarrying, see Knoblock, "Strong," 79, 186, 255, 276.

59. Valerie Cunningham, "New Hampshire Forgot: African Americans in a Community by the Sea," *Harriet Wilson's New England: Race, Writing, and Region*, ed. JerryAnne Boggis, Eve Allegra Raimon, and Barbara W. White (Durham: University of New Hampshire Press, 2007), 97–105.

60. Brewster, *Rambles*, 28; "Pioneer Colored People of Berkshire," *The Berkshire Hills* 1 (September 1900): no page; Sammons and Cunningham, *Black Portsmouth*, 106; Ethel Stanwood Bolton and Eva Johnston Coe, *American Samplers* (Boston: The Massachusetts Society of the Colonial Dames of America, 1921), 36.

61. Holly Bentley Mitchell, "'The Power of Thirds': Widows and Property in Portsmouth, New Hampshire, 1680–1830," PhD diss., Brandeis University, 2007, 242. On "sable ladies," see *Boston Post-Boy* (April 9, 1744).

Epilogue

1. Hiram Barrus, *History of the Town of Goshen, Hampshire County, Massachusetts* (Boston: published by the author, 1881), 116; Gary B. Nash and Graham Russell Gao Hodges, *Friends of Liberty: A Tale of Three Patriots, Two Revolutions, and the Betrayal that Divided a Nation* (New York: Basic Books, 2008), 198; Silas R. Coburn, *History of Dracut, Massachusetts* (Lowell, Mass.: Courier-Citizen, 1922), 331.

2. For the rose garden of Toah of Sheffield see Bernard A. Drew, *If They Close the Door on You, Go in the Window* (Great Barrington, Mass.: Attic Revivals Press, 2004), 46.

3. *Liberator* (March 25, 1808).

4. *List of Persons Whose Names Have Been Changed in Massachusetts 1780–1892* (Boston: Wright and Potter, 1893), 62.

5. Joseph Warren Chapman, *Vital Records of Marblehead, Massachusetts, to the End of the Year 1849* (Salem, Mass.: Essex Institute, 1904), 2:471; Rebecca R. Noel, "Salem as the Nation's Schoolhouse," in *Salem: Place, Myth, and Memory,* ed. Dame Anthony Morrison and Nancy Lisignan Schultz (Boston: Northeastern University Press, 2004), 145.

6. For Salem, Dorothy Sterling, ed., *We Are Your Sisters: Black Women in the 19th Century* (New York: W. W. Norton, 1984), 107–9. Historians have confused a white women's organization in Newport called the Female Benevolent Society with the African Female Benevolent Society, an auxiliary of the African Benevolent Society. In turn the ABS was a successor to the African Union established in 1780. William H. Robinson, ed., *The Proceedings of the Free African Union Society and the African Benevolent Society Newport, Rhode Island 1780–1824* (Providence: Urban League of Rhode Island, 1976), 158, 162, 163; African Benevolent Society, October 10, 1808, Papers of the American Slave Trade, Series B: Selections from the Newport Historical Society, Part 1; Microfilm Reel 39; *Liberator* (February 16, 1833). For the existence of the white women's organization, see Newport Female Benevolent Society, *The Newport Female Evangelical Miscellany* (Newport, R.I.: Newport Female Benevolent Society, 1805).

7. Sterling, ed., *We Are Your Sisters,* 107–9.

8. *Proceedings of the Third Anti-Slavery Convention of American Women held in Philadelphia, May 1st, 2nd and 3d, 1839* (Philadelphia: Merrihew and Thompson, 1839), 8.

9. Deborah Gold Hansen, *Strained Sisterhood: Gender and Class in the Boston Female Anti-Slavery Society* (Amherst: University of Massachusetts Press, 1993), 14; *Liberator* (May 17, 1839); "Scene on Board of a Steam-Boat," *Liberator* (May 24, 1839); *Liberator* (May 31, 1839); *The Liberator* (April 5, 1834).

10. Julie Roy Jeffrey, *The Great Silent Army of Abolitionism: Ordinary Women in the Antislavery Movement* (Chapel Hill: University of North Carolina Press, 1998), 44–45.

11. Maria W. Stewart, A Lecture given at Franklin Hall, Boston, September 21, 1832, in *Early Negro Writing 1760–1837,* ed. Dorothy Porter (Washington, D.C.: Black Classic Press, 1995), 136; Randall J. Burkett, "Elizabeth Mars Johnson Thomson (1807–1864): A Research Note," *This Far by Faith: Readings in African-American Women's Religious Biography,* ed. Judith Weisenfeld (New York: Routledge, 1996), 189–202.

12. Excepts from her religious tract were published in *The Liberator* (January 31, 1831); Angela Vietto, *Women and Authorship in Revolutionary America* (Burlington, Vt.: Ashgate Publishing, 2005), 53–76.

13. *Freedom's Journal* (February 14, 1829).

14. "Woman—the modest virgin, the prudent wife, or the careful matron," *Freedom's Journal* (February 14, 1829).

15. Jacqueline Bacon, *Freedom's Journal: The First African American Newspaper* (Latham, Md.: Lexington Books, 2007), 140.

16. Letter of William C. Nell, in *Maria W. Stewart, America's First Black Woman Political Writer: Essays and Speeches*, ed. Marilyn Richardson (Bloomington: Indiana University Press, 1987), 90; Bacon, *Freedom's Journal*, 141.

17. John W. Lewis, ed., *The Life, Labors, and Travels of Elder Charles Bowles, of the Free Will Baptist Denomination* (Watertown, Mass.: Ingalls and Stowell's, 1852), 31.

18. Maria Stewart, "An Address Delivered Before the Afric-American Female Intelligence Society of America," *Maria W. Stewart*, 50–55.

19. *Freedom's Journal* (December 12, 1828). For more free black criticism of Frances Wright, see Shirley J. Yee, *Black Women Abolitionists: A Study in Activism, 1828–1860* (Knoxville: University of Tennessee Press, 1992), 115.

20. Maria Stewart, "Mrs. Stewart's Farewell Address to Her Friends in the City of Boston," in *Maria W. Stewart*, 70.

21. Maria Stewart, "Mrs. Stewart's Farewell," in *Maria W. Stewart*, 65–74.

INDEX

Abolitionists, 22, 71, 73, 109, 137, 135, 142

  Edwards, Richard, 48

  Garrison, William Lloyd, 193–194

  juvenile literature of, 73–75

  memory and, 64, 146–148, 186–187

  Pickering, Timothy, 168

  Strong, Caleb, 116

  Thoreau, Henry David, 22

  Thornton, John, 181

  Walker, David, 192. *See also* other individual abolitionists

Africa

  Angola, 7, 37, 52, 53, 197–198, 208

  artifacts from, 24

  Bakongo symbols, 22, 40, 199

  colonization and, 181

  Edenic view of, 74

  emigration to, 40, 75, 142, 256

  marriage in, 229

  memories of, 9, 173

  secret societies in, 177

  survivals from, 24, 200. *See also* slave trade

African Burial Ground, (New York, N.Y), 39–40

African Female Benevolent Society, Newport, R.I., 189–190, 258

African Lodge (Boston, Ma.), 121, 122, 166, 176

African Society (Boston, Ma.), 122

African Union (Newport, R.I.), 178

Andover, Ma., 24, 114

Arnold, Ann, 33

Barbados. *See* West Indies

Belinda the African, 167–176, 253

Benevolent societies. *See* individual societies

Berlin, Ira, 29

Bernoon, Emanuel, 52

Bernoon, Mary, 52

Bett, Mum. *See* Elizabeth Freeman

Beverly, Ma., 138

Binah, 130

Binney, Joab, 227

Binney, Rose, 92–93, 161, 227

Blackmore, Hagar, 6–9

Boston, Ma., 31, 32, 37, 42, 44, 51, 52–53, 57–58, 60, 74, 84, 92–93, 111–113, 118–122, 222, 281

  taverns, 25. *See also* Revolutionary War

Bowler, Margaret Fairchild, 162–163

Bristol, R.I., 65

Brown, Moses, 238, 239, 243, 245, 248

Brown University, 24

Cambridge, Ma., 153, 168. *See* Revolutionary War

Cheswell, Wentworth, 166

Christianity, 225

  baptism, 65, 122, 131, 138, 253

  Baptists, 74, 76, 83–84, 131, 156, 194

  Catholicism, 81

Naming, 37, 150, 197, 219
  emancipation and, 157–158
  free blacks and, 68–69
  masters and, 65, 68
  widows and, 158
Negro, Joanna, 38, 43
New Haven, Ct., 118
New London, Ct., 134–135
New York, N.Y., 30–40, 193
Newbury, Ma., 56, 218
Newport, R.I., 31, 90–91, 100, 144, 156, 198
  Common Burial Ground, 178, 180
Newspapers, 230, 234
  Black, 193
  fugitive slave advertisements, 107, 110
  fugitive wife advertisements, 118, 120
  slave sale advertisements, 38
Northampton, Ma., 53, 92
Northfield, Ma., 66

Occom, Samson, 99–100
Osborn, Sarah, 84, 89–91, 93

Paton, Diana, 36
Patriarchy, 10–11, 61, 62, 125
  gender division of labor and, 76–77, 78
  master's role, 10, 29
  petit treason and, 36
  town, 150. See also coverture, wife abuse
Pease, Violet, 152
Pernam, Lucy, 54–61, 215
Peters, Cesar, 153–154
Peters, John, 119
Peters, Lowis, 153–154
Petitioning, 17, 220
Philadelphia, Pa, 40, 158, 175
Phillis (Cambridge, Ma.), 36
Portsmouth, N. H., 31, 39, 105, 135, 155,
    158–159, 205, 206–207, 224
Prince, Lucy Terry, 23, 62–71
  Bars Fight, 62, 219
Prince, Phillis, 152

Prince, Sally Larnard, 121
Providence, R.I., 83, 84, 118, 124, 125,
    162–163, 251

Quakers, 82, 91, 93, 115, 130, 131,135,
    136, 155, 173, 174
Quamino, Duchess, 91, 101, 179, 256
Quamino, John, 179

Race
  concept of blood, 212–213
  determination of, 46–49, 137, 138
  stereotypes, 13, 14
  terms for, 190, 202. See also identity
Rape, 38, 44–45, 173–175
  black men as rapists, 42, 45, 200, 212
Religious Revivals
  Great Awakening, 66, 85–87
  Seacoast Revival, 89–90
Reparations for slavery, 168
Revolutionary War, 121, 139, 140, 246
  Battle of Ticonderoga, 151
  Cambridge and, 153
  New London, 154
  Newport, 151–152, 162
  sailors in, 151
  siege of Boston, 150–152
  slave emancipation during, 91
  slave sales during, 36, 138–139
  Valley Forge, 153
Robinson, Matthew, 129, 130–131, 135
Robinson, Thomas, 130
Rogerenes, 131–132
Rogers, John, J., 132–134
Rowley, Mass., 60
Runaways. See slave resistance
Royall, Isaac, Jr., 125, 157–172, 174

Salem, Ma., 31, 160, 190–191
Saltonstall, Gurdon, 48, 133–134
Sedgwick Catharine, 146, 147–158
Sedgwick, Theodore, 139, 239